D0839111

John Fekete

Moral Panic: Biopolitics Rising

Second edition, revised (January 1995)

Robert Davies Publishing
MONTREAL-TORONTO

This book may be ordered in Canada from
General Distribution Services
☎1-800-387-0141 / 1-800-387-0172 FAX 1-416-445-5967.
In the U.S.A., toll-free 1-800-805-1083.
Or from the publisher: 1-800-481-2440,
or 514-481-2440, FAX (514)481-9973.

Canadian Cataloguing in Publication Data

Fekete, John

Moral Panic : Biopolitics Rising
(Food for thought)
Includes bibliographical references and index.

ISBN 1-895854-09-1

1. Biopolitics. 2. Political correctness. I. Title.
II. Series : Food for thought (Westmount, Quebec).

JA79.F44 1994   320'.01'9   C94-941565-0

JA
79
,F45
1995

The publisher takes this opportunity to thank the
Canada Council and the Ministère de la Culture du Québec
for their continuing support.

Cover illustration: *Western Star* (1985, acrylic polymer
emulsion on masonite, 73,8 x 73,8 cm.)by Alex Colville
(Musée d'Art contemporain de Montréal, Lavalin Collection)

For Feri Fehér (1933-1994)
and
Victoriana

Two sources of inspiration

Contents

Preface and Acknowledgements

There are always too many threads in the braid of a book's origin to say with assurance what motives gave rise to it, or what hopes govern its release to a public. Part of it is a perception of the times; and part of it is a perception of the self. In our own moment, both of these are under stress. Autobiography is no more certain than historiography or sociography. Biopolitics and moral panic affect us both personally and through our associations. My family's life, and my own, have been touched by some of the most disturbing and cruel forces of biopolitics in this century. I yield the moral high ground to nobody in claiming the right to address it. As it happens, I can say that this book has not been difficult to write. But I can also attest that it has been very difficult to become ready to write it. Affinities with the 1960s, and a life-long connection intellectually and practically with social movements, have proved both preparation and barrier. In the end, it is one's values and not one's habits that must prevail. My hopes for the women and men I love, and for the others I write for, including my young students, have kept me on course during the periods of reevaluation. If I feel the calling, once again, to challenge the dominant cultural discourses in my milieu, it is with a sense of both timely obligation and privilege that I answer to it.

What cultural theory calls the "postmodern" refers to a splitting in our culture: we live otherwise, in ways that we lose the ability to describe with assurance. At the same time, everyone wants to tell a story, but not in the usual ways that have served for over a century: not according to the powerful overarching frames of reference of modern scientific progress, enlightened political utopia, class history, or sublimation and unconscious repression. Who we

11

are is defined in part by how we tell our stories, individually and collectively. This book, in a deliberate way, is at odds with the sexual politics of storytelling at the end of the century. It would like to resist the easy regression of public accounts to a biopolitical frame of reference, to the dark mythologies of race and gender, to skin colour and sex organs as regulators of perception, and to all-embracing explanatory fictions like "patriarchy." This is the underside of our century, and the *fin de siècle* experimentation with recycling this mental debris in a benign formulation is more risky than we have acknowledged.

My voice, in the past, has been upbeat, devoted to the utopian prospects made possible by the radical will. I have come to believe that the radical (utopian) will and the radical (atopian) will-to-openness set up between them the indeterminate energies that can keep us creative in the actual world and tolerant of its differences. This book, I hope, tells a very strong story. In fact, it tells a lot of stories. I should emphasize that the stories are Canadian, although their implications are in many ways international. Most discussions of the issues I deal with draw overwhelmingly on American examples. That is hardly necessary. It is a dubious pleasure to disclose that in the domain of biopolitics, and especially biopolitical policy, Canada yields second place to none, and these stories can serve as cautionary tales for others. The stories related here, and the story-telling, may sound critical. They may even be critical of the radical will. But we have to know that, left to their own devices, utopian practices can go over the top and diminish the life they hope to improve. The impact of the utopian will can be as negative as its absence.

It is a deep paradox of our scope for change that uncertainty must be taken into account. If we cannot be sure of the future, then the present must not be treated with contempt. My intention remains upbeat, and also decidedly open-ended. I resist the degradation of the past, in the name of the present, and in the name of the unfulfilled hopes of the past. I resist the degradation of the present, in the name of the future, and in the name also of the complex density of our being. I resist the effort to change the historical world in rhetorical time. I defend the most precious achievements of human rights struggles in Western modernity: the fundamental freedoms (including freedom of expression, attitude, and opinion), and due process. I believe these are primary substances and enabling frameworks of equality as well.

I talk about biopolitics in this book, under conditions of moral panic. These phenomena loom large in our times, and impose themselves on the attention, and on more and more of our expectations, partly because they have been embraced by our major social institutions (governments, the legal system, the schools), and partly because they have been promoted by social movements. One of the central arguments in this book is that there is not only one issue before us: the reforming agendas of the "equity" movements and institutions. Equally at issue is the actual nature of the movements and institutions that say they are fighting against racism, sexism, and the like. Both what they preach, and what they practice.

This issue has to be raised, and raised from a perspective (like the one in this book) that loathes bigotry and injustice and detests discrimination and damage to individuals. Sometimes, as the wonderful man to whom this book is dedicated said: it is the duty of intellectuals to be rude to the movements. Those times, of course, would be the ones where the proposed incivility was in defence of civilization, and would be addressed to the movements whenever they veered from the service of freedom and life.

It should be said that the issues that arise in biopolitics are not non-issues. There are problems of sex-oppression, not to mention race-oppression, even if they do not add up in the way they are biopolitically presented. Indeed, it is a major argument of the book that biopolitics get in the way of the kinds of civil solidarity that could address these issues as pressing social issues, worthy of consideration in the light of the richest and best factors of human culture, without patronizing or diminishing any of the interlocutors. Without doubt, there are imbalances of power and wealth in our public institutions and also in the private sphere. These are not, however simple matters of possession and dispossession, and the imbalances cut across one another in multi-dimensional ways that embrace the twists of history and vary with situations and with interpretive frameworks.

Indeed, the portmanteau formula of "race-class-gender" is often a mantra used to ward off intimations of complexity. Research built around preprogrammed scripts will often discredit its findings, and actually damage its own ostensible agenda. This book does not deny the existence of social problems. It does show, however, why we should be very sceptical of the snake-oil remedies that are peddled to the well-intentioned gulls. I believe that women, in particular, are not helped by the indiscriminate scare campaigns that are designed to paralyze them, ghettoize them, distort their perspectives, patronize them, and rob them of their potentials in the present and future—in sexuality, relationships, civic life, education, work, and play.

Biofeminism has much to answer for, for hijacking the discourse of women's "liberation," diminishing and redirecting the concept of liberation to aim at "equity," and deforming and abusing the goals and practices of equity to assault all the libertarian principles that could provide meaning and moral value to it. As the most prominent form of biopolitics in our society at present, biofeminism is in the foreground of attention in this book. One of the contentions of the book, in fact, is that feminists whose methods and practices are at variance with biofeminism, and whose aims and politics are damaged by biofeminism, should advertise their differences from it.

Hannah Arendt and Agnes Heller form part of a tradition of anti-authoritarian thinking about issues of sexual politics, ethics, and history, which I acknowledge with intellectual gratitude. Ferenc Fehér, one of the world's great literary and political philosophers, whose untimely death cut short a legacy of work of the first order, stepped, like Heller, into the forefront of a new scrutiny of biopolitics in our day. My thinking about biopolitics, especially leading up to the memorable Biopolitics Workshop in Vienna in May 1994, organized loosely around Fehér and Heller's text, was encouraged and stimulated by his own example and by his collaborative energies. In a world without mentors, he was an unofficial mentor and friend. His spirit will continue to motivate and animate, but I must say, I will miss his presence.

There are too many intellectual debts to recount in a short prefatory note. In complicated ways, the cultural-theoretical engagements of my friend, now also passed away, Raymond Williams, not least his enduring commitments to a "long revolution," and the memory of my anti-authoritarian friend, also prematurely dead, Rudy Dutschke, have had a memorable influence, perhaps precisely because they are no longer here to exchange doubts and differences. Of others, the most important without doubt was Michel Foucault, now also recently deceased. Foucault's body of work on sexuality and the history of the supervision and disciplining of the body was a large and compelling meditation on biopolitics that left behind both a towering monument in our culture and also dynamically dispersed effects that continue to ramify. He was a discourse generator, and although he did not always say so, the discourse he generated had its centre of gravity in biopolitics.

Of those who remain, I want to mention first my good friends Misu Vajda and Sándor Radnoti, once of the Budapest School of philosophers, who have had their own experiences with political rectitude and craziness. They have survived it with their own brands of courage, sanity, and good humour. For more than twenty years now, conversations with them about one thing or another, always on a congenial wave-length, have continued to stimulate my thinking. I would like to express admiration for Jean Baudrillard, whose motifs of info-panic and seduction have percolated though my head and writings since I first began to read them back in 1969, in connection with some work on Marshall McLuhan. His work makes a huge contribution to the domain of biopolitics, though he never uses the term. Talking over the years with McLuhan's student, my good friend Donald Theall, has also helped me to consolidate a long trail of anti-censorship commitments. I am grateful to Donald, and also Joan Theall, who have provided unfailing encouragement.

I want to mention Arthur Kroker's work on panic and postmodernism, which is unmistakeably on the horizon of Canadian cultural theory. Although my intellectual strategies are not exactly the same as his, and there are no entries on either moral panic or biopolitics in his *Panic Encyclopedia* collection, I want to acknowledge his achievement, and the value of our exchanges. Two other traditions that have had an impact on my work need mention here as well, although their effects are hard to describe or measure. I have been reading and teaching feminist texts for more than twenty years, and cannot imagine *not* engaging with this imposing material, in one way or another. More recently, the debate over education and the universities, in the U.S. in particular, has generated a whole subculture of texts, from Alan Bloom to Dinesh D'Souza, Jonathan Rausch, David Bromwich, and a host of others, including Canada's Peter Emberley and Waller Newell. All of these texts, along with all the texts produced in the "political correctness" debates over the past five years, make it clear that we are in a period of very lively reflections on the university.

I must turn to people close to home, whose involvement with the larger domain of the material in this book has been of real help. During last year, the campaign for freedom of expression in Ontario universities was an indescribable source of energy and inspiration. Without naming them all, I would like to thank the 90 professors and librarians of Trent University, men and women, who signed my petition on Freedom of Inquiry and Expression, and took a moral and political stand together, through public meeting after public meeting. Naturally, I want to single out for acknowledgment the colleagues in my own department of Cultural Studies, who got the initiative off the ground. I owe thanks as well to the Executive members of the McMaster University faculty association and the Concordia University faculty association, who publicly supported these efforts. I am grateful also to the anonymous Association of Abominable Agitators in Windsor who sent their scroll of greetings, apostolic benedictions, and support for our offensiveness at just the right moment in February 1994 to lift my spirits. Nicholas Rowe, at Carleton, was a terrific ally, and I hope our paths will cross again. David Warrick, at Humber College, has never stopped being a dynamo of information and energy, engaged in the same causes, tirelessly, against all the odds.

Shelley Hornstein, Jody Berland, Len Findlay, Ioan Davies, and Marty Kreiswirth invited me last year to give talks on material related to this book at conferences or speaking events that they organized. I want to express my appreciation for their interest in my work, and for allowing me the opportunity to sharpen the arguments. I am grateful also to the Social Sciences and Humanities Research Council for a grant that provided material support for this project.

It is also true to say that this book might never have taken shape had it not been for the initiative, steady encouragement, and easy friendship of my publisher, Bob Davies. The warm stimulus of friends is difficult to describe, but anybody who has completed a large project knows how indispensable it is. I want to record the regular exchanges about the book in its development with Susan Wheeler, my dear long-time friend. For their reliable and unfailing support and collaboration over the past year, and for their willingness to read the manuscript, I want to thank Ivan and Eva Varga, Graham Cogley, Michael Neumann, Andy Wernick, and Ian McLachlan. Graham's detailed precision, comprehensive scope, and good humour have been particular gifts that I feel privileged to have received. I want to acknowledge my indebtedness as well to Christine Ury and Charles Levin, and to Wodek Szemberg. I cannot count the many lengthy conversations, sometimes pointed and sometimes rambling, but always exciting, that I have had with Charles and Wodek about the subject matter of this book. I cannot measure their contribution, and I am grateful for their friendship.

This is the place to thank Mary Ritter, my research assistant from May to September, for the wonderful work that she did. She was intelligent and tireless in her work, she shared with me the excitement of seeing the book develop and grow, and she organized a support network for this work. I want to acknowledge her outstanding contribution to this book. As always, my debt and gratitude to Stephen and Lily Fekete, my parents, is considerable. Over the years, from their remarkable lives, they have given me a perspective on many of the matters I write about. My mother, who is an excellent reader, has read every word, more than once, and has helped me to feel good about it.

Finally, Victoria de Zwaan. My feelings threaten to overflow the bounds of privacy and propriety. Her intelligence, her sanity, and her zest for living have found their way into every aspect of this book. Her generosity of spirit, and time, have moved me again and again. Without her editing, the book would have taken far longer, and been far longer, than it needed. Without her, there would be no book, no life.

Peterborough, October 1994

I
Biopolitics and Moral Panic

*"All her life she had looked for a group
of people she could hold hands with
and dance with in a ring. First she
looked for them in the Methodist
Church (her father was a religious fa-
natic), then in the communist party,
then among the Trotskyites, then in the
anti-abortion movement (A child has a
right to life!), then in the pro-abortion
movement (A woman has a right to her
body!); she looked for them among the
Marxists, the psychoanalysts, and the
structuralists; she looked for them in
Lenin, Zen Buddhism, Mao-Tse-tung,
yogis, the nouveau roman, Brechtian
theater, the theater of panic; and finally
she hoped she could at least become one
with her students, which meant she always forced them to think and say exactly what she thought and said, and
together they formed a single body and a
single soul, a single ring and a single
dance." (Milan Kundera, Book of
Laughter and Forgetting 63)*

This book is about biopolitics and moral panic. It is written out of the deep conviction that biopolitics falls far short of politics, and that moral panic falls far short of morality. Politics has historically begun where biological factors and the demands of the body give way to the common concerns of a cultural community, a body politic. Morality is called to the scene exactly when biological needs and ties no longer directly dominate the whole scope of human decision and interaction, and where politics opens up a plurality of avenues, so that individuals have to negotiate conflicts of value. The complicated relations between the family, the economic and social institutions, and the political state have evolved through the *cultural* demarcation of specific boundaries around a variety of distinct domains in which both the bodily and the spiritual manifestations of human life can interact.

But *biopolitics* is anti-politics; a regression *from* politics to a new primitivism which promotes self-identification through groups defined by categories like race or sex. Biopolitics has no time for humankind; nor does it care about individuals. In fact, even its concern for individual members of its own ingroup depends on the extent to which they behave and express themselves in accordance with the stipulated essence of the group, with the features by which the group is *identifiable,* with *collective* identity. The concern is to promote the group, and to advance the group's cause *against* its enemies.

Panic is a product of imaginative intensity, an amplified sense of a collapse of boundaries or a loss of confidence in the logic, reasonableness, or rationality of particular structures that provide life-support for distinct activities. Financial panics, like the 1929 stock market crash, are occasioned by a nightmare vision of rapid changes in the economic or financial structure. Psychological panics arise from terrifying disturbances in the perceptual order. Moral panics, often about sex on the surface, also appear to be related to fearful imaging of shifting or collapsing

22

boundaries in the meanings, values, codes, and institutions that make up our cultural world.[1]

State of Panic

I was impressed by the following statement in *Changing the Landscape: Achieving Equality - Ending Violence* (hereafter CL), the Final Report of the Canadian Panel on Violence Against Women (hereafter CanPan): "The tentative responses of the international community to the systematic rapes of women in Bosnia-Hercegovina were constant reminders to us that tolerance of violence against women knows no geographic boudaries *[sic]*" (xiv). Here is an extreme example of *biopolitics*. Obsessively self-dramatizing, fixated in gender-thinking, and bristling with hostility, the CanPan opportunistically pirates the terrible ordeal of an entire people to service its political agenda.

Of course, the quotation is self-cancelling: it displays such a lack of due proportion that it instantly caricatures itself. The CanPan report evokes the image of the cartoon feminist, on the bridge of the *Titanic,* shouting out her narcissistic SOS: "Help, help, innocent *women* are going to drown!" What matters to the cartoon is what is missing in the picture. Aren't there others on this doomed boat? The "violence against women-of-the-world" link-up is a cheap contact high. Not because the rape of the Bosnian women is not one of the great expressions of human evil in this century. It is. But here the link is designed to inflate Canadian feminism at the expense of the humanity of Bosnian men, and the human tragedy of the Bosnian community, including the Bosnian women whose fate is not isolated from the rest of their world. This is the price of extreme adversarial thinking. Its insight is also its blindness, which indicts itself finally for its inhumane callousness in spite of its limited caring. The moral imagination is, one hopes, indivisible; but biopolitics shrinks its dimensions instead of expanding its scope.

The promotion of a particular group identity, the exaggeration of particular differences from others, is much more than opportunistic. It is not simply seeking advantage. It has another aspect. If the comment were only a tactical ploy to improve the fate of those particular Canadian women whose suffering from violence is a dark reality to be alleviated, then the Bosnian link would be merely exploitation. What makes us uneasy about the comment, however, is the quality of *excess* that testifies to the nervous energy of *panic*. In the vision of the CanPan's co-chairs, Canadian women are in bondage, bound by inequality and violence and gagged by fear, trapped in *"lives few in the world would choose to lead"* (xiv, italics added). What an intensely concentrated point of view! It does not invite assent or dissent so much as collusion. None of us can buy into this "message" without abandoning ourselves to the vapours of a shared and relentless anxiety.

Panic helps nobody. It is a barrier. It blocks the way to reasonable action. We know that Canadians live lives that many envy and emulate; we are a privileged and fortunate people.[2] We also know what planet we're on, and that we don't get out of bed each morning in Paradise; indeed we know and endlessly discuss the catalogue of ills that beset us. We feel, as well, the obligation to address the sufferings of those who are less fortunate than others. To the extent that we are deficient in compassion, we have to prod ourselves; and for this we need precisely the kind of many-voiced, pluralistic public discourse that biopolitical panic would make impossible. For this panic appears and appeals to us as a *moral* panic. It is not about pluralism but about *virtue*. It is not about doing the right thing, but doing the righteous thing. It is not about public policy, but about setting affairs in order. It is about cleansing, rectification. It is about holy war. What it is about, according to the CanPan, is "the war against women."

I will look at the final report of the $10 million CanPan, *Changing the Landscape*, in much greater detail in chapters four, five, and six. It is a scandalous document, and it does great disservice to those of the female population who suffer in Canada, as well as to suffering men, and to the general

24

well-being of all Canadian adults and children. Those of us who are surprised to find the Canadian government supporting, financing, and issuing a document that accuses Canadian society and Canadian institutions of abuse of power and hatred of women (xiii) will have to take stock of the extent to which organized biopolitical advocacy is becoming official policy in the Canadian government. This is the case both federally and provincially, in terms of assigned ministerial responsibility, committees of government, high-budget government agencies like the Ontario Women's Directorate, statutory administrative agencies like all the provincial human-rights commissions, and public funding for local advocacy group activities and programs, including challenges to existing legislation. As a result, biopolitics is fast becoming deeply integrated into the central practices of public policy and administration.

The Federal Contractors Program, for example, uses the muscle of federal government financing to require contracting agencies and institutions to comply with its program of employing four biologically defined groups in representative numbers. These groups are women, aboriginals, visible minorities, and people with disabilities. The Ontario government's new Employment Equity Act (Bill 79), effective September 1, 1994, requires *all* 17,000 employers in Ontario to conduct a workforce review of their employment policies regarding hiring, retention, treatment, and promotion of these same four designated groups, so they can prepare and implement an employment equity plan, with lists of barriers to be eliminated and numerical goals. The fact that *within* each of these target groups individual persons have vastly different capabilities and opportunities—for example, that different women, by virtue of social and cultural, rather than biological, factors, already have widely divergent life options and dispositions—is effectively irrelevant to the preferential schematization of bio-equity policy.

Education policies, especially as they intersect with issues of social equality and justice, are also being rapidly biopoliticized. To give only two examples (see chapter VII for details): as of 1994, the Ontario government is encouraging the voluntary race identification of students applying to universities and colleges, with ultimate objectives that are not clear. The official Applications Service proposes to develop statistical profiles of applicant groups on the basis of the applicants' ancestral origins, not citizenship or nationality, coded on an Educational Equity Questionnaire on the basis of seven available categories: North American Aboriginal, African, East Asian, European, Latin American, South Asian, South East Asian, West Asian and Arab, and Other. African, by the way, includes West Indians and black Americans and Canadians, while European includes White Africans.

Meanwhile, the Ministry of Education and Training in Ontario has issued an even more ominous directive for the school system which may well have the effect of institutionalizing racism in the schools. The directive called "Antiracism and Ethnocultural Equity in School Boards" is to be implemented by September 1995, and its measures go far beyond preaching sensitivity, tolerance, and equality. They extend into classroom lessons, student testing, teacher hiring and training, and the like, and will likely stereotype and ghettoize minority students. Furthermore, school boards will be required to "collect data relating to the race and ethnicity of students" ("Marked for failure").

Biopolitical sex bias is speedily transforming the law. The Canadian judiciary and legislators have sharply shifted legal procedures to favour complaints from women. Canada, according to a minister responsible for the status of women, has "become recognized as a leader in the world community on this issue" (Collins 4). First, the legal definition of sexual consent has shifted the entire onus of responsibility for securing consent to men, and leaves women—those who may drink in a bar, for example, and will therefore be considered incapable of giving consent—without any responsibility for their actions and, moreover, with a "morning after" chance to bring charges against their consensual lovers of the night before. Second, the inadmissibility of past sexual activity in sexual assault cases, which makes sense in cases of stranger assault, makes impossible any contextualizing defence by an intimate partner that would place an action within the framework of a sequence of events or a whole relationship. Third, changes that have eliminated the requirement to have evidence corroborated make any apparently credible woman's testimony unimpeachable in a criminal proceeding, even when it is only her word against his. Charges laid by prosecutors on the basis of uncorroborated complaints reaching back twenty years are now flooding the courts and creating a whole new class of male victims. It is only a short step from this kind of legal provision to the Supreme Court decision in the case of Donald Butler (see chapter VII), where the court found it easy to redefine "harm to society" in biological terms, as "harm to women."

This expansion of the agenda of biopolitics is paradoxical and self-defeating. In the very process of making claim to them, it destroys the social and cultural payoffs that are expected to legitimate and reward its strategies. Culture and society decay wherever biology rules. Whites against blacks; men against women. Politics gets reduced to power; that aspect of politics, which concerns the common management of what different citizens have *in common*, leaks out of the picture. The biopolitical protagonist experiences alarm, imagines herself at war, and strikes out at her undeclared enemies. In this respect, the culture of biopolitics is the culture of panic, precipitated and supported by a liquidation of cultural boundaries, which are increasingly replaced by rigid and obsessive biological demarcations.

Biofeminism, comprising mutations of the emergent feminism which, in the late 1960s and early 1970s, shared with the new left and the youth counter-culture a moment and a hint of a new enlightenment, is a case in point. It is built on hostility and anxiety, the dual stigmata of biopolitical panic, and its attention is divided between its discourse of aggression toward its adversary, the fiction of a biologically defined group, "men," and the discourse of fear in the face of threats to its safety and security, the panic fiction of "violence against women."

Note, for example, the corruption of boundaries and distinctions in the universe of Catherine MacKinnon, professor of law at Harvard University. She writes: "the similarity between the patterns, rhythms, roles, and emotions, not to mention acts, which make up rape (and battery) on the one hand and intercourse on the other ... makes it difficult to sustain the customary distinctions between pathology and normalcy, . . . violence and sex" (*Toward* 146). When MacKinnon collapses the two categories of intercourse (normal) and rape (pathological), the male lover and the rapist are revealed as one and the same. Sex and violence are rendered identical. This kind of logic encourages not only panic, but also its corollary of aggression. The scapegoating and witch hunts endemic to panic are all too frequently the main clues to its power. Biopolitics and moral panic dovetail, then, as natural allies, aggressive and virulent.

An enduring attraction to a mirage of (pseudo)scientific certainty is a compelling outcome of the marriage of biopolitics and panic uncertainty. Statistics emerge as the exact symbol and operational instrument of this union, especially survey data where input can guarantee output. Statistics can fulfil all the functions of simulating objective truth, legitimating the continual reproduction of some essential bio-identity against all personal, idiosyncratic, or dialogical sources of knowledge, and permitting any amount of selection and spin of information. The hostile polarizations on which biopolitics thrive are thus subsidized by the promotional imagery of statistical science.

Statistical methods cannot tell us the truth in the old ways of science before Einstein, relativism, and quantum indeterminacy. Nothing can. But they make a virtue out of necessity. They offer up *probability* as a model of truth, in the hope of constructing provisional order and stability on the shifting strands of permanent, intolerable uncertainty. Indeed, as a *model*, statistics can be valued as much for its patterning capacity, its qualities of meaning, its ability to deliver the spin that we desire, as for its actual connection with the way things are. It is not clear at all how much these ever-expanding data-handling technologies are in touch with the real world. Indeed, it is not clear that what statistics do for us in *making* our world picture can any longer be sorted out from how we imagine the *match* between our picture and the real world. In truth, statistics play an ever-increasing role as the screens on which we project our desires and anxieties, so that we may exchange them and shape them into a livable psychic order.

State of War: State of Mind

The 1990s open with the language and images of war. The American TV war in the Gulf, with its false reports from the front and its demonized ethnicities, turns out to be merely a temporary distraction from the permanent biopolitical panic scenario of the decade: the "war against women." Astonishingly, in a Canadian political community whose most divisive trauma in recent memory has been the declaration of the "War Measures Act" in the conflict known as the FLQ Crisis of 1970, Pat Marshall, biopolitical warrior extraordinaire, asks the Status of Women Sub-Committee of the House of Commons for a "war budget" and boasts to reporters about her role in the "federally financed revolution" (Lees 102).[3]

At the same time, in the U.S., Susan Faludi was publishing her monumentally successful satire on everybody who did not agree with her, *Backlash: the Undeclared War Against American Women* (1991), and Marilyn French also piped in with *The War Against Women* (1992). For wars, of course, you need enemies, and, in the style of demonization set by the Gulf War experiment, "men" were to be cast in the role of both the Great Satan and the blood-thirsty, irrational dictator. Moreover, this was to be recycled as a drawing room drama, in what came to be called "domestic violence" or "family violence," where the psychotic stranger of our greatest fears turned out to be the great betrayer of trust whom we had known all along. American women were setting out to replay the holocaust in the domestic version that was closer to home: "the enemy within."

Unique to Canada was how rapidly the government fell—at least, fell into its role in the scenario. Brian Mulroney, prime minister, the alpha male politician, was widely photographed waving his white ribbon, surrounded by Cabinet colleagues similarly decked out, emulated around the country by ever-correct good-guys like Bob Rae, premier of Ontario, all of whom thus indicated their willingness to surrender the beast within. My faculty union sent me and all other (male?) faculty at my university a white ribbon, with sober urgings to share in expressing our collective guilt. Of course, the expiation had to have an official scapegoat who could serve as the object of universal hatred and whose very memory could be blackened by all our collective sins. This was to be the mass murderer, Marc Lépine.

December 6, 1989, when this obscure figure went supernova in public and made international headlines, has become unofficially commemorated in Canada as a day to reflect on the demon. Lépine's own personal story has by now completely disappeared into the myth of male evil. Marc Lépine, crazed with hostility, walked into a classroom at the École Polytechnique in Montreal with a gun and slaughtered 14 female students. We all felt—with various asymmetries—the terror and the pity and the tragic necessity that every so often shatter the veneer of our remarkably successful systems of sublimation and control. But the panic that followed the mourning transformed individual deaths into biopolitical symbols.

The 14 young female students became the essence of woman-victim; Lépine, the essence of male-predator. "Beasts in suits and ties," Craig McInnis's article for the *Globe and Mail*, summarizes the lesson learned: "Never before has Canadian society had more insight into the nature of the beast and the certainty of its gender." One year earlier, in contrast, Laurie Dann, a Chicago woman, shot five elementary-school boys, poisoned food at two fraternities, burned down the Young Men's Jewish Council, burned two other boys in their basement, shot her own son, and justified her murder of an 8-year old boy by claiming that he was a rapist. This story did *not* garner international headlines; nor did it come to symbolize a bloody and fundamental biological divide between women and men.[4] In the aftermath of a single, male psychotic's twisted internal narratives and outward violence, we continue to be robbed of the common humanity of a dark moment, which now survives only under glaring illumination as a sectarian cliché, and therefore a dangerous fraud about the nature of violence in the world.

Yes, it is true, some men do commit acts of unjustifiable, horrible violence against women. It is also the case that some women too manifest terrible violence. The numbers may not match. More deeply, for our common fate, we need to know that the will and the power to violate, to transgress, are part of our evolutionary success, just as they are part of our potential doom. Without this will, in a utopia of utter pacification, we would be diminished beneath human dignity. We need to know this, and we need to meditate on its wrenching paradox. It belongs to this knowledge as well that women are diminished if we imagine them devoid of these forceful capabilities, for good and ill—indeed if we imagine women to have a net deficit of any of the capabilities that belong to the species of humankind.

In the end, the Lépine myth—which rests on the myth of the continuum of male violence—fails from both directions. All the white ribbons in the world cannot turn him into a sacrificial (Christ) figure who can absorb all the masculine sins in a ritual of substitute atonement. Nor can he do service for women as a symbol of the evil (Devil) whose poison can be seen to run in all men's veins, coloured by a dye that makes itself visible to anyone equipped with the theory that "patriarchal violence" is omnipresent, malign, and genetically coded into male testosterone.

The truth is that our social norms do *not* promote interpersonal violence. On the contrary, we make every desperate and hopeful effort to shore up our institutions and symbolic persuasions against it; and we consider it a failure both in our system and in ourselves as individuals when interpersonal violence happens, *especially* to women. The biopolitical attitude, however, lacks both a psychology and an ethics: it is not about persons but groups and, moreover, groups that are imagined to be in essential conflict. When social norms are seen to be transgressed, biopolitics (*faute de mieux*) promotes panic, and *vice versa.*

Even more significantly, the continuum theory (see detailed analysis in chapter X), and the collapse of the theoretical boundary between what is normal and what is pathological, spreads panic to those areas of common life where the social norms hold together. Everything appears polluted. Of course, this is panic projection, but it introduces panic responses into the whole culture: paralysis or lashing out; trampling, scapegoating, witch-hunting, or lynch-mobbing. We can learn to spot these in our daily lives, and in the changes being pressed on our institutions.

The Perception of Public Opinion

The shaping of perception is a shaping of reality, and panic shapes an anxiety-ridden world of meanings and values. After a university class, a male acquaintance offers to walk a female student to her car in the parking lot. Once there, she offers him a lift to his home, which is on her way. Both offers are accepted with apparent appreciation. No unpleasant incident occurs, of any kind. What stays in my mind is the conclusion to the anonymous letter in the student newspaper, where the girl relates her story. She denounces her classmate for his insensitivity in setting up a situation where she had to be alone with him!

I also cannot forget a young woman in a TV moment, during the demonstration that a group of female students held in front of the courthouse in Kingston when a Queen's University student was acquitted of date rape. She looked into the camera with tears in her eyes as she said, with deep sincerity, "There is so much violence against women, and it's just getting worse and worse all the time." Her life-chances, though she seemed well-dressed, well-groomed, well-educated, and gifted with a privileged life, appeared to her to be enclosed in a tightening circle of fear. It was not by way of her own experience that she rejected the legal findings of due process by judge and jury; it was by way of her identity as a member of a defined group, whose substance it was to encounter a certain reality. Hers was one face of moral panic. Her perceptions had been shaped by others, and now her perceptions, broadcast electronically to an indeterminate audience, were in turn going to shape those of countless other young women.

Anxiety information today travels at electronic speeds—what Marshall McLuhan once called the speed of angels—and creates instantaneous communication and community. A community of electronic panic: our special gift to the millennium. Contagion, assisted by our new media, is as much a feature of contemporary panic as delusion. It is clearly possible to live this panic mythically and in depth, as McLuhan also said; indeed, it is nearly impossible not to, given the speed with which it spreads out its patterned net. What people come to share is less and less based on exchange of immediately personal stories, and more and more on mythic participation in a common fate captured in numbers. This is the legacy of polling and numbers research.

Numbers combine with particular stories, like those I mentioned above, to tell us that we live in a society in which we are constantly vulnerable to random and traumatic violence. "The drive-by shooting of a British man in Ottawa, the shotgun slaying of a young woman in a trendy

Toronto cafe and, most recently, the killing of a Toronto cop and the disappearance and suspected slaying of a teenaged Edmonton girl have added to the perception that crime is out of control" (Blackwell, "Canadians fear rising tide of violent crime"). The occasional surfacing of genuine evil, like the Bernardo-Homolka couple, compounds our sense of vulnerability. The kinds of crimes that terrify us are the extraordinary, "out-of-the-blue" incidents. These become the screens on which we project our non-specific anxieties, and they are turned into a daily diet of statistics that terrify us by confirming what we think we know. The fear is amplified a thousand times by situation violence dramatized in the entertainment media, which is generally formulaic and predictable, but whose very familiarity links it falsely to our panic about falling victim to the random violence against which we are helpless. The deliberate *making* of panic relies on this false sense of continuum, this failure to distinguish between the symbolic repetition (of which there is a great deal) and the actual random singularities (which are mercifully rare). The move that *biopolitics* makes is to polarize the population and valorize only the fear of selected groups, biologically demarcated. That is, it cashes in on women's fear, and transforms it into a political identity; it simultaneously denies to men (even though they continue to be the main victims of all but sexual violence) any share of the generalized anxiety, and instead points the finger, to invoke guilt among men about violence against women.

It is clearly this violence-against-women scare that has stampeded the integration of biopolitics into the Canadian elite structures of politics, law, education, business, and even the arts. The casual sneer at "political correctness" is a monumental error of inattention: in Canada at least, this is not just a cultural style but a transformation, and there is nothing marginal about it. It does not have to do with the disadvantaged in our society, but with the powerful, the newly powerful, and the nearly powerful. In fact, political correctness is itself a misnomer because what is now going on at the levels of institutional reform is not political but moral administration, not correct or even sane, but deluded and panicked, and especially not laughable but sinister. The only aspect of correctness that characterizes this transformation is correctness in the sense of *being* correct—the old rightist sense of corporate decorum, and the old leftist sense of orthodoxy.

Orthodoxy, decorum, and correctness today are all on the side of a script that pits men against women, the strong against the weak, the oppressor against the oppressed. This is a theatre of supremacy and submission, and of groups who share nothing but their antagonism. Biofeminist patriarchy theory, abducting the last third of this century, is exactly as divisive, exactly as false, and exactly as seductive as theories of racial supremacy and class supremacy had been in the first and second thirds of this century. Every malign force in history has perhaps had its grain of truth, as well as its appeal to fantasies of both resentment and utopian hope for a better life. But the seduction is always in the partiality of the perspective and the appeal.

Inflationary Victimization: The Numbers Racket

The panic about violence against women certainly has its grain of truth, but the panic itself is sustainable only by fixating on a small *part* of the picture. Panic is a specialist, and modern, "expert" scholarship is its handmaiden. The "perception of public opinion" is built out of studies that "show." Scholarship offers both the data and the legitimation of public emotion. Nowadays, where social issues are concerned, this is most likely to be social science scholarship, and almost inevitably quantitative scholarship. If the media decide what people talk about, what issues move public opinion, it is the concepts and numbers thrown up in journalistic and academic scholarship that people see with, that public opinion perceives *with*, like a pair of corrective glasses. Thus: one half of all Canadian women have experienced ...; 60% were the targets of ...; one in

35

four Canadian women will be ...; four out of five female undergraduates recently surveyed at Canadian universities said that ...; 29% reported ...[5] We learn to think of numbers as facts, and to treat them as revelations. We come to them like voyeurs, for the cheap thrill of overseeing the experiences of others; like applicants for membership in a statistical community that includes us and tells us who we are. Some of us are dragged there, to learn our fate. Others march in, as we have seen, like warriors.

The main, and most emotionally compelling, source of proof offered for the patriarchy theory, for the subordination of women, is the alleged violence against women, the instant proof of hostile power. As we shall see (in chapters III, V. VI), ironically, the reverse is the case: the *fact* of violence against women *depends on* the theory of patriarchal hierarchy and subordination. The paradox here is that heated emotional conclusions about male rage and female victimization are always demonstrated with the cold calculation of the numbers developed in psychological and sociological—chiefly survey—research.

Humanists and cultural sociologists who have reflected on the nature of meanings and values have learned that what lie behind the cold numbers, concealed by the legitimating jargon of specialized expertise, are the warm emotions, desires, needs—the *investments*—of the researchers and the research community that supports them. When they do research, they want payoffs on their investments. When we buy into their results, their data, we subsidize their investments. We all become one large investment community, a kind of mutual fund. But we need to be very careful, because the bonds and securities we procure may not be the ones that we need. And it may all crash, with much damage to the small investor, and large-scale reorganization of the cultural economy.

I will look at some of the violence figures and how these come to promote the fear about violence. But I want to conclude this chapter with some comments on the responsibilities of scholarship, especially scholarship that expects

36

to have a significant impact on how we see and live in the world or, more institutionally, how public policies are to be set, how public funds are to be spent, and how public perceptions are to be shaped.

Culture of "Violence" Research

Survey research of the kind that I examine in this book is very costly. There are huge material, hardware, and labour needs, as well as some statistical expertise. The recent "Violence Against Women Survey" (1993), for example, a random-sample telephone survey conducted by Statistics Canada, cost around $2 million; the CanPan itself, involving hearings in addition to the organization of data, cost $10 million. In order to do their work, academics working in these fields often contract with government for their research. The two researchers for the Women's Safety Project were paid some $50,000 by the CanPan for a mere summary of their findings; Walter DeKeseredy and Katharine Kelly's 1993 campus-abuse survey was financed by Health and Welfare Canada's Family Violence Prevention Division. Katharine Kelly admits, "It is virtually impossible to understand the complexities of human interactions using survey instruments" (Kelly 81). Yet interviews on a national scale cost too much. Given a choice between smaller-scale interviews, which might help to understand interactive problems, but risk being "dismissed as not reflecting the Canadian reality," and a survey that can "put a problem on the map" (Kelly 82), the survey is the instrument of choice.

Research in the family violence field, as in most other fields, is highly competitive, and the results are potentially short-lived. The researchers have to keep on their toes, then, to stay in the active files of funding sources. Perhaps even more important than the number of publications are the numbers *in* the publications. The political economy of this research is not only "production-driven" (see Arthurs Committee Report), but also "inflation-driven." The high numbers on rape or attempted rape in U.S.

37

studies (e.g. the 1 in 4 figure of Mary Koss, 1987, and the 1 in 3 figure of Diana Russell, 1982) attract much attention; the low number studies of respectable researchers do not (e.g. the 1 in 17 figure of Linda George et al., 1990, or the 1 in 50 figure of Margaret Gordon and Stephanie Riger, 1981). Dean Kilpatrick got low-end results in 1983 (1 in 20), in 1987 changed methods to follow Koss and Russell, and got 1 in 4. This landed him a $1 million grant for further study, which has retained the high-end methods and settled on a result of 1 in 8 (1992).[6]

I mention U. S. studies here, because that is where the source materials come from for Canadian research, in terms of both research design and numerical horizons of significance, notwithstanding possible differences in the two societies. But the point is that the field of violence research shows a constant escalation in numbers and expansion in definitions. In academic research, once a paradigm is set, the road to success within it lies in consolidating the paradigm by expanding its scope of application or amplifying the significance of its results. It is virtually predetermined—programmed into the design and the presentation—that one violence research project will repeat the pattern set by another. What society hears, it will hear again and again. The only other way, which brings greater success when the time is right, but which is far too risky for most academics to attempt, is the radical dislocation of the ruling model, or the innovation of a new paradigm.

In my estimation, the field is getting ready for this now. Numbers have reached pretty well the saturation point, carried by the momentum, not of the object under study, but of the research community's interface with social desire, as that is translated into the protocols of research itself. The sensationalistic numbers released by the Can-Pan—98% of Canadian women are sexually violated—suggest that a reversal is imminent. Some U.S. studies now inadvertently put the figures over 100%.[7] McLuhan calls this the "reversal of the overheated medium"; and indeed, these results were greeted with more scepticism than admiration, even by those who had previously welcomed each new escalation in claims of violence against women. Soon, success in this area will come from redefining the problem, and renumbering the evidence, inside some new conceptual framework.

I would describe this as the pathology of an "outcome-driven research culture," as well as what the Arthurs Committee reported as "production-driven" research. In both cases, the stress falls on satisfying clients who stipulate, however indirectly, the results they want. As in the modern detective story, the whole of contemporary design culture, including research, works from the effect back to the cause, from the desired outcome back to the design that will yield that outcome. McLuhan, Buckminster Fuller, and other visionaries thirty years ago stressed this as an achievement of modern capability. But it clearly has its pathological dimensions as well. As long as funds come from corporate and government clients, and as long as research councils, such as the Social Science and Humanities Research Council of Canada, explicitly and increasingly encourage a turn to socially significant research that is addressed to the public, rather than esoterically communicated, it is unrealistic to expect much change.

And yet, when the assumptions and needs of a given historical moment are brushed against a larger history, they often turn out to be narrow and misdirected. It is a mistake to take at face value the research developed to suit a moment's fancy—as has happened in the galloping survey research in the violence against women field. If the lure of "self-aggrandizement" was strong for engineers (Arthurs 9), the seductions of "good causes" may be just as hard to resist in the social sciences. I do not think for a moment that differences in interpretation or judgment should be evaluated as instances of possible research misconduct. Researchers will often select results that support their hypotheses, and it is true that the master thinkers in the Western intellectual tradition have followed that course (Savage 8).

Nonetheless, in contemporary culture, where the research impact on public policy, the expenditure of public funds, and the interactions of the groups and individuals who make up the public can be direct, immediate, and powerful, the large-scale misdirection of what one might call externally seduced research calls for some attention. Since I am not friendly to disciplinary measures, especially for what is a cultural or social problem rather than a problem of individual misconduct, I favour a modification of the research culture in the direction of greater verifiability or falsifiability, or simply more access to *bona fide* contestability.

I mean that we should not take socially powerful research at face value. There should be greater public access to the research data. Policy formulation should be built on due scrutiny of pertinent research. Government agencies conducting research should be required to provide for input into the design. There should be fuller disclosure of the impact of design elements on results, and full access to the raw data. More than anything else, I would call on academics and journalists to treat the research results in the social sciences with intelligent scepticism on the basis of some understanding of the biases of the research culture. The more the results suggest policy moves that would curtail or infringe the liberal-democratic cultural framework that makes research possible in the first place, the more scepticism may be warranted.

If our tableau of possibilities includes mythology, fraud, and panic as prominent strategies of data management, we have then still some room to scrutinize our options. My own commitment is to *stop the panic*. The best competition for biopolitics is a *better* politics that can renew the public domains of policy formulation, do more justice to social issues, and more service for ostensibly marginal groups than can be expected from an acute division of society into friend and enemy. There may be, indeed, a social revolution in progress—recomposing the labour force, shifting gender roles, redefining the arrangements of domestic life, reshaping the public order, and transfiguring the cultural and ethnic mix in Canadian society. Many of the issues raised in biopolitical form may be relevant to social change, provided they are pursued as social and political debates, rather than as moral orthodoxies.

In the following chapters, I will be looking critically at the statistics of moral panic that tend to pre-empt dialogue, including the Statistics Canada study of *Violence Against Women*, and the Carleton study of campus dating relationships. I will consider the mythologies that support the demands for policy making engendered by biopolitical moral panic. Some public documents, like the CanPan's *Changing the Landscape*, will be examined in detail, in chapters four through six, not only to combat its poison, but also to call for much increased public scrutiny of the quality of policy-making research. In chapter seven, I will consider the fallout from the violence panic upon the normal activities of the general population, first by looking at the emerging notion of *zero tolerance* in policy making, particularly in connection with the biopolitical issues of harassment, discrimination, and equity in education. Then, in chapters eight and nine, I will go on to describe some cases of biopolitical panic in action in the universities. I review more than a dozen cases, some in considerable detail, of the abuse of professors by their own institutions. Some of this information, concerned with currently ongoing cases, relies on unpublished documents, and is presented to the public view for the first time. Finally, in chapter ten, I will provide an anatomy of the false logic of panic thinking, with examples that illuminate biopolitical strategies.

II
Data Rape: The Clinical Virus

*"...in the central painting of a triptych,
titled 'Bordando el Manto Terrestre,'
were a number of frail girls with heart-
shaped faces, huge eyes, spun-gold hair,
prisoners in the top room of a circular
tower, embroidering a kind of tapestry
which spilled out the slit windows and
into a void, seeking hopelessly to fill the
void; for all the other buildings and
creatures, all the waves, ships, and
forests of the earth were contained in
this tapestry, and the tapestry was the
world." (Thomas Pynchon, The Crying
of Lot 49 10)*

The Prevalence of Violence Data

I live in Peterborough, the "gateway" to the southern Ontario lake district of the Kawarthas. The city of 70,000 has a British base, and ethnic immigration from some 60 different cultures. It has traditional working-class factories, service industries, family businesses, schools, hospitals, and a small liberal-arts and science university. The city is conscious of its environment, proud of its technological marvel, the lift-lock on the river, and pleased with its little lake in the centre of town, though it could be less polluted. Unemployment is high, and the banks and financial institutions have occupied much of the prime real estate vacated in the downtown area by closures during the recession of recent years. Peterborough is an active sporting and fitness city, has a thriving arts, theatre, and music community, and recycles as much as anybody. Mulroney took away our train, but the city remains sufficiently average to be a favourite for test-marketing new products. Margaret Laurence, the late novelist and chancellor of Trent University, called Peterborough the perfect-sized community.

Peterborough has its share of violence, though it does not feel like a violent place to live; and, of course, the city has the currently predictable biopolitical ferment, including street banners promoting rape-awareness week, wife-assault prevention month, Take-Back-the-Night marches, and the like. In the student milieu, there are consciousness-raising events, and very active student media perpetually experimenting with the interfaces between resentments, virtuous projects, career prospects, and the current fashion for anger and anxiety. This is a conformist period, and none of this is out of the ordinary. Still, I found myself surprised at the information in a leaflet about sexual assault being locally distributed through the provincial courthouse, the police station, the public library, and a variety of convenience stores. It is published by the Sexual Violence Support and Information Centre of the Kawarthas, which distributes it widely enough to service five counties. The leaflet consists of procedures to follow, a list of services offered (counselling, referral, library, self-defence training, speakers' bureau, etc.), an appeal for support, single-paragraph personal testimonies of violation, and a section of information called "Some Things You Should Know About Sexual Assault ..." which contains one statistic: "47% of all women will be raped in their lifetimes." One out of two. One of your two sisters. Your mother or your aunt. Fifteen thousand of the 30,000 women in Peterborough. Five million Canadians. A staggering prospect. For good measure, the idea that all women are obviously gravely at risk is reinforced by the only other "finding" in the leaflet, that the risk never stops, because assaults happen "from the age of six months to 90 years."

This continuum of risk that is feared as the common condition of all women from birth to death is a half truth. The risk of assault is strongly correlated with age. The Uniform Crime Reporting Survey (UCR), conducted by Statistics Canada's Canadian Centre for Justice Statistics, tells us that nearly two thirds of reported sexual-assault victims are under 18 at the time of the assault. Young women, 18-24, are three times as much at risk as the national average, suffering 40% of the total number of assaults in a given year, and the risk drops off sharply for older women (see *Juristat* 14.7, 5, 7). In fact, for the 3 million Canadian women over the age of 54 (28% of the female population), there is no statistical risk of sexual assault at all. Of course, the age correlation does not do away with the possibilities of individual pain or the apparent social problem of a high level of violence, but the information, and its indications of how sexual activity and vulnerability are grouped, should make rational discussion possible, in a way that the folklore of a universal continuum of women's holocaust does not.

But now I turn back to the 47% "prevalence" figure, purporting to show what proportion of the female population is affected over a lifetime. Sociologists study both "incidence" of assaults, usually over a 12-month period, and "prevalence" of assaults, over a lifetime, or some other lengthy time period (in the campus survey, since leaving high school; or since the age of 16, in the StatsCan VAW survey—see below, in chapters II and III). The study of lifetime rates, like so much of this violence against women research, has exploded only in the 1980s. They can be 5 to 10 times higher than the annual incidence rates (dealing, after all, with a survey period of up to 50 years or more), and they therefore make good copy.

The prevalence approach is often combined, moreover, with definitions of assault that refer to some or all of the following: rape, sexual attack, unwanted touching, shoving, swearing, verbal criticism. Accordingly, summary characterization softens from rape to assault and abuse, and for a while the public swallows it all, as though it were listening to an alien anthropologist trying to describe what goes on among men and women. But you can't fool everybody forever. It may suit radical impulses to provide inflammatory descriptions of contemporary cultural forms, but the cost of diverting attention and resources in this way from the real hard cases that deserve it is too high. Besides, the panic thrust thereby on a generation of young women is too cruel to be supported for much longer.

If the data seem unreliable, then the whole problem will become attenuated, diminished, or gone altogether— or reformulated through a different set of models that make data intelligible. As we move into this discussion, we cannot avoid getting into questions of reliability, generalizability, applicability, validity, and significance, because *data do not speak for themselves.* They are always invited, encouraged, coaxed, teased, seduced, and coerced into speech.

Prevalence research must be called to account for its methodology. What existential meaning can be attached to a report that *once,* in an entire lifetime, someone that a woman knew touched her knee without her invitation; or that someone, who might have been another teen, *once* stole a kiss at a party; or that *once*, in her twenties, a pickup date got out of control, and she had to go through with a sex act, perhaps on the second, third, or fourth time of the night, against her direct will or consent? How, over a lifetime, do these possibly once-in-a-lifetime events stack up among other things we remember: the love of one's life, the birth of a child, the soup kitchen, being fired, the drudgery of repetitive acts, the excitement of an achievement, some unpleasantness at work, with the babysitter, with mother or sister, the death of a parent, a lover, or a child? How does a single act of what is called sexual assault weigh in the balance of a lifetime of sorrow and pleasure and all the dilemmas and serendipities of life?

No prevalence survey ever done gives us any indication of these matters of interpretation, personal narrative, and cultural style. What they all count on, in the fashion of the panic rush that drives this research, is cashing in on the fears and traumas attached to violent stranger rape. The research paradigms keep expanding as though every act of normal interaction over the entire culture were bound to have the same significance that we accord to the knife-point alleyway violation. After all, say Walter DeKeseredy and Katharine Kelly, two Carleton sociology professors recently famous for their sensational revelation that 81% of college and university women are physically, psychologically, and sexually victimized, "Many women state that psychological mistreatment hurts them more than acts of physical violence" ("Woman Abuse" 30).

But which psychological acts are compared with which physical acts? Do they mean that it is worse to be insulted or sworn at than to be raped at knife point? Or that a long, drawn-out scene of humiliation before your family and friends might be more memorable than a one-time push in a bar? DeKeseredy and Kelly say 86% of college and university women have been psychologically abused ("Incidence" 153) at least once since they left high school, but they make no distinction between insults, swearing, or spiteful words. Nor do they have any way to measure the weight of this event in the scale of what else goes on in a lifetime. Much of the survey research, with its revelations of violence, assault, and abuse, is like this, mixing apples and oranges with wild abandon. It will have to be the public, the media, and the saner academics as well, one hopes, who blow the whistle on this and say, enough.

Clinical Fallacy

I am still wondering about the 47% figure for rape, which is so obviously implausible. What can explain its selection as the one statistic worthy of publication? I think it was what Murray Straus, the leading researcher in the U.S. on family violence (the current euphemism for the violence against women panic), called the *clinical fallacy*. An extremely high figure, like one in two women raped in a lifetime, could well seem emotionally right to concerned workers in a rape crisis centre, who see the real casualties at the base of all the statistical abuse. Indeed, much of the emotional scaffolding for the violence scare has been assembled from responses to the stories, figures, and casualty reports coming out of the shelters for battered women, the rape crisis centres, the hospital emergency rooms, the police and court reports, and finally from the scholarship that has grown up around these social, legal, and medical life supports. One can call this the clinical sample in the population, and there is no doubt that social policy and social resources need to be directed to finding and applying the appropriate remedial interventions. Our sympathies, energies, and anger are properly and deeply engaged by the need on display in this cluster of hard cases.

At the same time, the individuals in this clinical sample, and the chronic and severe violence they have endured, must not be confused with the interactional frictions and different cultural styles of the general population. The conflict tactics employed at large can be studied and evaluated, and they can be criticized from some reforming standpoint if so desired; but the line between a representative sample and the clinical sample must not be blurred or washed away. The invention of a continuum along which there is unrelieved suffering—that is, the generalization from the clinical sample to the whole population—is disastrous and unwarranted. It is unwarranted, because the patterns in the clinical population are different from those in the general population; thus the name, clinical fallacy (Straus, "Physical Assaults" 77). It is disastrous because it stretches credibility to view all male-female interaction on the model of the experiences concentrated in shelter and criminal battery. The resulting scepticism risks rebounding on the extreme cases and, by resisting the pathologization of general behaviour, simultaneously trivializing or downgrading the pathology of the severely damaged. This is what Straus identifies as the *representative sample fallacy*: extrapolation from the general population to the clinical sample.

It is likely that well-intentioned distress at the denials flowing out of the representative sample fallacy accounts for abused women, social agencies, advocates, and researchers adopting the opposite, clinical fallacy: the overstatement of the case for a minority group through a desperate strategy to implicate the majority. After all, if everyone is at the same risk, then surely everyone must pay attention. This strategy can work only for a very short time, however, until the novelty of half-truths, false analogies, and partial identifications wears off. The fallacy will produce a strategy that fails as soon as there is a realization that the general population and the clinical sample have divergent histories and prospects and less in common than was imagined; and, correspondingly, that the line between normal and pathological cannot be based on an essential biopolitical construction that produces a strictly gender-based division between pathology and norm.

Travelling Statistics and Panic Transmission

So, I can understand the emotional attraction of the 47% rape figure for the Sexual Violence Support and Information Centre of the Kawarthas. But how did such a figure ever find its way into a southern Ontario publication issued and distributed in 1994? For a start, unlike the U.S., neither the Canadian police nor the Canadian Centre for Justice Statistics has published any figures on rape since rape disappeared from the Criminal Code in 1983, to be replaced by three levels of sexual assault, none of which corresponds to rape.[1]

We[2] called the Sexual Violence Support and Information Centre twice for information about the leaflet. Eventually, Rose Marble phoned back to say that it is a revision of one which she "picked up" while she was travelling in the U.S. She suggested that Andrea Smith at the Quetzel Centre in Chicago might be able to provide a copy of the original. So, we left a message for her. Isabel Kang phoned back with the information that Andy Smith, who wrote the leaflet, got the statistic about rape from, of all places, Catharine MacKinnon's book, *Feminism Unmodified* (1987). MacKinnon's index, we discovered, lists five references to rape rates, and each of the pages gives the same information: "44% of women have been victims of rape or attempted rape at least once in their lives" (23). She is careful each time she mentions the 44% figure to include attempted rape as part of the statistic. She cites a 1978 study by Diana E.H. Russell and Nancy Howell, in which 930 women were interviewed in San Francisco, "The Prevalence of Rape in the United States Revisited" (1983).

Russell says that the probability of rape is 26%, and for rape combined with attempted rape, 46%. Our leaflet's 47% rape figure misquotes MacKinnon's 44%, drops the reference to attempted rape, and therefore virtually doubles the rape figure. Russell herself has enough scruple to note that her data may be biased because of the "imperfect random household sample." She also allows that, although it seems unlikely to her, "our remarkably high prevalence rate raises the question of whether some respondents fabricated experiences" (694). She concludes that her risk analysis is valid only "for females in San

Francisco" (691). Peterborough and the Kawarthas farming and tourist area are surely no San Francisco.[3]

This is just one example of sheer panic transmission. I do not wish to blame the publishers of this leaflet in particular; but the story shows one aspect of an emotionally overdetermined research climate that permits the casual and careless adaptation of its results into the wider social help milieu and the perception of public opinion. Travelling statistics make up one important feature of data rape, and of the decontextualization on which panic feeds and grows.

Three Major Surveys

In Canada, three major surveys hit the public in the banner year of 1993, each claiming to be the first of its kind. Taken together, they lend support to Canada's claim, and to our unfortunate fate, of having "become recognized as a leader in the world community on this issue" (Collins 1993).

On February 8, 1993, DeKeseredy and Kelly released to the press the first national study of "woman abuse in Canadian university and college dating relationships" (hereafter WADR). I have already mentioned that their astounding figure of female victimization at the level of 81% combined sexual, physical, and psychological "abuse," based on a random sample survey of 1,835 women and 1,307 men. Then, on July 29, 1993, the final report of the Canadian Panel on Violence Against Women (CanPan), was hailed at a news conference by Mary Collins, then federal Minister responsible for the status of women, as "the world's first comprehensive national study on violence against women." The CanPan (see chapter VI) claims a global sexual violation rate of 98% of all Canadian women (based on a figure offered by two women calling themselves the Women's Safety Project—hereafter, WSP), and offers an action program of 427 Orwellian recommendations on the basis of a selection from personal testimonies, a literature review, and a salad of dressed-up data.

On November 18, 1993, assuming the mantle of "the first national survey of its kind anywhere in the world," Canada's reputable heavyweight, Statistics Canada, weighed in with its own national telephone survey of a random sample of 12,300 women over the age of 18 on "Violence Against Women" (hereafter SCVAW). The SCVAW claim is that 51% of Canadian women have suffered from male violence since the age of 16, and that 39% have been sexually assaulted, 5% in any given year, 16-20 times more than get reported to the police (see *Juristat*, 14.7, 1, 7). Each survey, reported in hundreds of articles, helps to build the panic. Each is also, in one respect or several, fatally flawed. Each, in spite of itself, by sheer overreaching, may well strengthen the possibilities for eventually returning to a more rational discussion of very sensitive issues.

I want to comment on these studies, or at least on some of the significant problems with them, problems that run deep in this whole area of research. I also want to suggest that sharp, critical scrutiny of the results, combined with pronounced caution in using them, is well warranted on the part of policy makers, in particular, but equally the public, the media, and the academic community. The press have respect for Statistics Canada, which is unwarranted in this case, but they have voiced scepticism of the two other reports. Not enough, however. Surveys which claim, on the basis of a probability sample, to tell us representative truths about the whole of Canadian society cannot expect to get a free ride. And yet that is exactly what reports from underground, purporting to represent the submerged continent of the experiences of silenced or oppressed sections of the population, tend to get in the current climate of a social recomposition masked by an ethos of guilt.

Surveys: Reliability and Validity

Survey research, as professionals well know, is a risky enterprise, especially when it means to draw conclusions about

25 million Canadians from information gathered about a few thousand at most. Although it is a given of survey research that it must control for bias, this is always imperfectly implemented and something of an illusion, because the bias to be controlled is always delimited by stipulated definition, and the stipulation itself rests on unrecognized biases of different sorts. Researchers have to be concerned with the reliability of their data, in terms of both the integrity of the data quality and the degree to which the results can be properly generalized beyond the immediate population surveyed. To make up an extreme example, interviews with the ten local members of the Deliberate Liars Club would likely provide unreliable information, because they would lie. Since this is not a representative sample of the Canadian population, if eight of them lied that they were vegetarians, it would be improper generalization to conclude that 80% of Canadians are vegetarians.

Likewise, however much truthful information may be provided by self-selected respondents about themselves, and the profile of others exactly like themselves, the self-selection (e.g. volunteering information, in response to a generalized invitation) limits severely the reliability of generalization. In any volunteer sampling, whether the criteria for eligibility call for grievances, achievements, or preferences, those who select themselves *in* cannot be assumed to have the same characteristics as those who are left *out* or are selected *out*. For example, the CanPan's call for submissions on violence against women, combined with hearings often held in physical locations associated with feminist activities, may elicit stories that tell a terrible truth, but it won't be the truth of many of those who do not volunteer information, much less the truth of all Canadian women.

The same point applies to designated group sampling. A survey of thousands of customers at McDonald's around the country would not give us reliable information about the eating habits of all Canadians, since it would miss out those who forgo the pleasures of fast foods. Likewise, a survey of the public spending beliefs of the audience at a hockey game would hardly be a reliable policy indicator for a decision over building an ice rink or an arts centre. In the same way, surveys of battered women in shelters may provide valuable and anguishing information about battered women and battery, and guidance for policies to assist the afflicted population, but they are not likely to produce results characteristic of the experiences or needs of the public as a whole. For reliable generalization, the sample has to be *representative*, both as to its initial construction, and also as to the results.

But reliability is difficult to nail down. In addition to randomness and response rates, surveys are plagued by the likelihood that they are somehow barred from the full picture, or an accurate picture, by underreporting, over-reporting, and false reporting. The various consistency tests rarely control for all these variables. Claims of reliability are as much a matter of turning a blind eye as having a solid product. Survey research is not even close to solving the problem of its evidence, and its data are uncontrollably corrupted by respondents who misunderstand the questions, have faulty memories, unconsciously or semi-consciously censor the information and provide half-truths, or answer carelessly, mischievously, or deceitfully.

The problem is compounded by the possibility of a kind of collusion between interviewees and interviewers, on the analogy of a psychoanalytic transference syndrome. This is a risk, when interviewers elicit material by offering comfort and solidarity, and virtually unavoidable when feminist interviewers, indeed any "committed" interviewers, conduct interviews ranging from 45 minutes to 25 hours, as in the WSP (CL A3). Moreover, whenever researchers make the unwarranted assumption that some group of people, for example women, always tell the truth—which has become something of a canon in much bad feminist research—a vitiating naivety is built into the claims about reliability. Even a casual survey of criminal accusations that turn out to be false shows that women do often lie about sexual assault, and do so for personal advantage or some other instrumental reason, which is pretty well why anybody lies.

False Charges

From recent issues of my local newspaper: A 10-year-old girl accuses a 16-year-old boy to police who are visiting her home on unrelated charges. He is booked for sexual assault and sexual interference. Later, charges are dropped, once the girl admits that she lied about the incident ("Lied to police"). A 31-year-old, mentally disabled, Windsor man spends 11 months in jail, awaiting trial without bail for molesting his young daughter. A social worker had noticed the girl's inflamed vagina and called a doctor. The doctor diagnoses a herpes or yeast infection, resulting from the mentally disabled mother's lack of hygiene skills. The mother then accuses her husband of assaulting the child regularly for two years. A year after the arrest, a week before trial, the mother reduces the two-year accusation to a single act of intercourse with the girl the day before the doctor examined her. Finally, just before her testimony in court, the mother admits that the stories she had told the police never happened ("Falsely accused man spent 11 months in jail" 1994).

The story of a 46-year-old Trent University employee who claims to have been kidnapped from work and sexually assaulted by a man wearing a balaclava causes fear on campus. Students who have not heard any reports of actual rapes, but who are trained by an atmosphere of sexual panic to expect sexual assaults everywhere, finally have justification. Three months later, the woman pleads guilty to making a false report and causing a public mischief (Marchen, "'Rape' victim guilty of hoax"). She had simply passed out while drinking on the job, and made up a story to explain why she was late getting home. She receives probation, and medical leave from work. Instead of being relieved, students express anxiety that now women won't be believed. Sue Hamer, the Walk Home Program Coordinator, is quoted in *Arthur*, the student newspaper: "The false reporting rate for sexual assault is the same as for any other crime," that is, "really rare" (Bowen, "Public Mischief Charges Laid in Abduction: Confusion and Concern Pervade Campus").

But it is *not* really rare, and it is *not* the same as for any other crime. According to Statistics Canada's UCR figures, 14% of sexual assault complaints are determined by the police to have been *not* committed or attempted, as compared to 8% for ordinary assault (*Juristat*, 14.7, 10). False claims of lesser offences, like thefts, tend to be even lower. Beyond this, of course, there are no statistics on how many cases that go through to the courts are found to be based on false accusations. The figures therefore can range from 14% to 100% in principle—though it would defy credibility to put the figure toward the higher end in practice.

As for rape, where we have to turn to U.S. records, a recent report by well-known U.S. sociologist Eugene Kanin states that 40% of rape charges investigated by city police and half of those investigated by (female) campus officials turned out to be false, according to a demanding test of falsehood: a recantation by the accuser, backed by other evidence (*Archives of Sexual Behaviour*, February 1994). Meanwhile, a U.S. Air Force investigation by Dr. Charles P. McDowell of 556 cases of alleged rape found that 27% of the women admitted that they had lied (Farrell 322). Three independent investigators then reviewed the other cases, developed 25 criteria for assessing evidence, and unanimously found 60% of the original accusations to be false.[4] According to various sources, including the Air Force study, which had the benefit of 75 false accusers volunteering their motivations, women lie most frequently for spite, revenge, compensation for guilt, or shame, and to account for pregnancy or to conceal an affair. This makes up two thirds of false accusations. The rest have to do with testing someone's love, avoiding personal responsibility, extortion, or some kind of mental/emotional disorder (Farrell 325).

I think it is fair to say that if some women are prepared to make false complaints when the risks of being found out are relatively high, through examination by police and crown attorneys, and cross-examination by defendants, then we cannot necessarily take at face value the grievances anonymously reported in surveys. The reconstruction of personal narratives in such a way that the burdens of personal responsibility are transferred to another person; remembering the past in such a way that moral ambiguities are resolved in the protagonist's favour; settling scores in a mental drama by purifying accounts with poetic licence. These are all temptations that cannot be dismissed out of hand. They are especially strong in a culture where women's sexuality has been in rapid transition from the stigmatization of the fifties (good girls don't) to the celebration of the pill, free love, and the zipless fuck (Erica Jong) of the sixties, to the more recent, puritanical, protection of women, considered as sexual victims in the wake of the post-1960s biofeminist backlash against heterosexual pleasure.

It is a sinister coalition which joins up the biofeminist hostility to men and the traditionalist alarm about sexual women, through a picture of women as sexual victims by definition: "The question is what comes first, men's need to get laid or women's dignity" (A. Dworkin 40). Once a panic atmosphere comes to reward accusers with moral honours and sometimes celebrity status and financial power (as with Anita Hill), and once major financial incentives are made available for successful claimants (like the $7.1 million in damages against the San Francisco law firm Baker & McKenzie that a jury awarded to a female secretary in September 1994 as compensation for a senior partner's physical harassment, including unwanted touching of her breast) (Murray, "Backlash"), [5] the spill-over copycat effect will also come to leave its mark on survey respondents. Some will call it "consciousness-raising," but it is just another many-layered twist in the story of data rape.

No Corroboration

I do not mean to suggest for a moment that female reporting is necessarily less reliable than male reporting. In matters of sexuality, where cultural training for a symbiotic interaction assigns different roles and perceptions, two interpretations of events may well go right past each other. One of the most interesting aspects of couples research, a small corner of the family-violence research industry, is that the research actually collects two viewpoints on the same event. Two small studies, one of 103 couples (Szinovacz 1983), and one of 65 couples attending a marital therapy clinic (Jouriles and O'Leary 1985), found that husbands and wives do not tell the same story. Their accounts of events do not match; their agreements hardly exceed chance expectation. On the question of whether either partner has administered or received a beating, as Dobash, Dobash, Wilson, and Daly highlight in a literature review, "Although there were respondents of both sexes who claimed to have administered beatings and respondents of both sexes who claimed to have been on the receiving end, there was not a single couple in which one party claimed to have administered and the other to have received such a beating" ("The Myth of Sexual Symmetry in Marital Violence" 77).

In short, there is very low level of agreement about who did what and what is what, i.e. a low level of interspousal reliability. Dobash et al. use this as a criticism of the reliability of a particular survey instrument, the Conflict Tactics Scales (CTS), and the results it yields. They want to argue toward discrediting the instrument and its use in *two-sex* surveys, where both men and women are interviewed (though generally only one or the other in any one couple) and the results show a sexual symmetry in marital violence. Dobash et al., who are pioneers of "patriarchy" analysis in violence research, find the result, that women commit violence as frequently as men do, politically un-palatable. Their intent is to discredit *part* of the findings that the CTS yields again and again, namely the finding of female-perpetrated violence, especially female-initiated violence (see next chapter for more on this). More gener-ally, however, the finding about couple mismatch raises questions about the corroboration of evidence, and about interobserver reliability, which points the finger at all the survey research in the violence field. A more repre-sentative random sample couple survey, with in-depth interviews, surely lies ahead.

After all, individuals are asked to self-report on their experiences and behaviour: have they been victims of violence or did they dish it out? These are data about grievances and confessions. But, in virtually all of the research, the individual reports are aggregated at face value. There may be some statistical testing for consistency and to isolate extremes of unreliability, but there is no effective strategy of corroboration, cross-examination, or critical inquiry into the status of evidence. And yet, as we see from the manipulative way in which the results of these surveys are made to enter the public awareness, increas-ingly the whole sex-group of men stands under indict-ment, if not summary conviction. The researchers act like court reporters, minuting the accusations and confes-sions, and announcing the inevitable judgments.

Indeed, many of the surveys—including the reputable SCVAW—use criminal-code type definitions in order to gather what amounts to crime data largely unreported to the police. But there is no effective trial! No testing of the evidence. No evidence of intimate relationships and cir-cumstances. No proof of malign intent. No due-process determination of whether the real victim is the accuser or the (falsely) accused. Sometimes, as in the single-sex sur-veys like the Statistics Canada interviews with thousands of women, there is no defence side at all—only a reverberant *j'accuse.* But the panic climate makes the "*j'accuse*" sound like a verdict; more a judgment than a complaint. Guilty if charged. The safety of "women" has no time for the presumption of innocence, as Pat Marshall argued before the House of Commons Sub-committee on the Status of Women in 1991, and before that at a Justice Department conference (Lees 102).

The issue of reliability intersects here, as at many points, with the question of *validity*. This latter question has to do with the research methods. Do they meet the purposes of the inquiry; do they produce a true picture, relative to some criteria that they have to meet? Design of the questionnaire, organization of the data, the selections that are shaped into a presentation of the data, and even the kind of dissemination of the results have a role to play in supporting (or undermining) the validity claims of a research project. In my view, the entire research industry on violence against women suffers from both a reliability crisis and a validity crisis. Researchers sharply disagree on even the most basic assessments, which should serve as a warning against public enthusiasm for the big numbers.

On the value of the WADR campus survey, for example, David Hay concludes that DeKeseredy and Kelly "have made a valuable contribution to our knowledge base" and commends them for a good survey, if not a perfect one (63). By contrast, two University of Toronto sociologists disagree. Bonnie Fox argues that DeKeseredy and Kelly have not shown what they claim, extensive and serious abuse in campus dating, and their high percentages are, in addition, "politically irresponsible" fear-mongering, which hurts women and undercuts public awareness (323). Rosemary Gartner says that "fundamental flaws in the work limit its potential contribution" (314) and that their national survey is not just benignly inaccurate but "distracting and detracting" from the search for knowledge and prevention of violence (318).

Fault Lines

In my estimation, there are at least four fault lines that run through all the results at the present time, and that could destroy the credibility of the violence sub-discipline, whether or not there is a shift in the prevailing winds of biopolitical preference. I will give examples of the first two in the balance of this chapter, and the other two in the next chapter.

(1) *Bias from category errors*: this involves all the mixing of apples and oranges in survey research designed to show that different heterosexual interactions are all variant fruits of the same poisonous tree.

(2) *Ends-justify-means politics*: this involves motivated distortions of design and presentation, in the apparent belief that a good cause gets better if women's victimization can be inflated.

(3) *Myth of objectivity in standard questionnaires*: this involves the mistaken belief that the questionnaires developed by Koss (Sexual Experience Survey) and Straus (the Conflict Tactics Scales) for the study of marital conflict and family violence yield objective knowledge.

(4) *Bias from the myth of patriarchy*: this is a response to the dilemmas of underdetermination, and proposes to make sense of the behavioural raw materials by organizing them into a schematic and, in many cases, axiomatic pattern of male dominance and female subordination as a global explanatory principle.

It was the apples-and-oranges mistake that got the WADR into immediate trouble. The press voiced scepticism of composite figures like 81% "abuse." The public proved reluctant to lump accusations of flirting into the same category as threats with a knife or gun, especially since only 9 students (.5%) claimed the more extreme experience during the past year, compared with the 614 (37.2%) figure given for abuse. In effect, the 6.6% (1 in 15) women who reported having been raped since high school, or the 2% (1 in 50) who were raped in the past year, were combined with (and thus overshadowed by) figures about girls persuaded to kiss or make out (31.8%). The researchers called it all "abuse," and concluded that more than a quarter of campus women were sexually abused last year. This figure includes those succumbing to verbal pressures as well as those participating in sexual activity while drunk or high. They also claim that nearly a quarter were physically abused last year: their definition here includes pushing, shoving, grabbing, and throwing something. Finally, they reported that, in the last year, nearly 80% were psychologically abused, many by such things as put-downs, insults, and swearing.

The claim pressed by the researchers is that "very serious forms of abuse are quite common in campus dating" ("Incidence" 155), supporting Elizabeth Stanko's contention "that Canadian female students' lives rest upon a continuum of violence" (138). As it turns out, however, DeKeseredy and Kelly view their data differently. Kelly regards psychological abuse as something that is part of a "continuum of control" that can *lead* to physical and sexual abuse ("The Politics of Data" 83); DeKeseredy views it as itself a form of abuse. When we talked with him by phone (May 17, 1994), he said that he and Kelly had "had a falling out" over this issue. In fact, they wrote separate responses to their critics. Kelly writes that she did not want to release the psychological data until everything had been analyzed: "Unfortunately, the data were released without my consent, against our express agreement, and in a form that, in my view, distorted the value of the research" ("The Politics of Data" 83).

One central criticism of the WADR study is dead on, deep, and fertile, irrespective of the researchers' nuances about the exact nature of the continuum and desirable media strategies. Both Gartner and Fox make it. Even though the researchers acknowledge that the questions they ask about incidents or events ignore the meaning of the acts to the persons themselves and ignore their place in the particular relationship, the researchers themselves ignore the implications of this limitation. They assert that all the various acts they catalogue *are* actually *abusive*, without waiting upon the motives and interpretations and contexts of the interacting actors that are needed to establish "abuse" (Gartner 315).

They claim that they are documenting cases of "intentional assault on a female by a male dating partner" ("Incidence" 146); but they have no analysis of *intentions*. For example there are probably quite *different* intentions behind a stolen kiss, flirting, and violent rape, unless we "*assume* that all men aim primarily to use or abuse women" (Fox 323). By the same token, DeKeseredy and Kelly cannot establish the continuum between verbal pressure and force. Since there are so many more incidents of verbal pressure and spiteful comments than physical violence, the data allow the interpretation that some men will not, in fact, move to force (323). No universality, and no slippery slope.

The wide application of this criticism pivots on the principle of subjectivity. To know the human meaning of an event, we need recourse to interpretation. Numbers do not tell their own story. Interpretive studies, however, tend to reduce the numbers by restricting the scope of the study and by introducing subtle distinctions. DeKeseredy, who wants to make policy to change the campuses, notes that you have to have big numbers if you want to make an impression on policy makers ("Response" 79). How do you get these numbers? You design an interview instrument that breaks experience into discrete incidents. This permits the researcher to manipulate the data, because the living subjects of the incidents are not asked for their interpretations, or, in fact, even for accounts of the relationship context.

Fears, Phobias, and Threats

Just in this way, Statistics Canada's "Violence Against Women" survey inflates figures to show that women are very anxious about their safety. The effect of this is to validate women in being anxious, and, moreover, to alert women that they should be anxious. When StatsCan concludes that "the threat of violence is considered so real that fully 60% of women in Canada who walk alone in their area after dark feel worried in doing so" (*Daily* 3), what responsibility is it required or willing to accept for the "threat" that women "consider" real in numbers that are implied to be significantly large: "fully" 60%? After all, how *actually* real is the violence? On the face of it, the fear appears to have a lot to do with the fact that Statistics Canada is making up the numbers and making up the interpretations that give the numbers meaning. The ends are expected to justify the means.

StatsCan interviewers ask a leading question, bonding with the interviewee, woman to woman, and signalling what is the rational position that they—an "us"—can share. The (telephone) interviewer starts the "Fear of Violence" section of the interview by reading the following from the questionnaire: "I would like to start by asking you some questions about your personal safety. Most of us worry, from time to time, about the threat that violence poses to our personal safety. I am going to ask you about some everyday situations, and I would like you to tell me how you feel in each of them. First, when walking alone in your area after dark, do you feel: Very worried? Somewhat worried? Not at all worried about your personal safety"? With a lead like that, how can you say "not at all worried about your personal safety?" Don't you live in the real world?

So then we get the results in the StatsCan *Daily*, November 18, 1993, manipulating the figures for panic presentation. In the highlights that get reprinted everywhere, we read: "Six-in-ten Canadian women who walk alone in their own area after dark feel 'very' or 'somewhat' worried in doing so." Inside the *Daily*, there is a headline in bold print: "Six-in-ten women fearful in their own areas" (8). "Very" or "somewhat worried" has become simply "fearful." The text, part of a summary list of fear, then says: "60% of women who walk alone after dark in their area were worried about their personal safety while doing so" (8). All distinctions are now simply rolled into a single feeling: "worried."

But are 60% of Canadian women worried walking alone in their areas after dark? No, not even given the leading questions. If we consult the shelf table (19A) for the actual frequency distributions, we find, to begin with, that only 41% of women, not 60%, fall into the two categories "very" and "somewhat worried." Twenty-seven percent are not worried at all, which is a pretty hefty group. But then it turns that there is another group, 33% or one third of women, who are never in the situation at all. So this group gets dropped out of the numbers, and we move over to shelf table 19B. The 41% of all women who said they were very worried or somewhat worried is now recalculated as a percentage out of those women only who do walk alone after dark, and that's how we get the higher figure of 60%.

But that's not all. After all, two categories of responses are rolled into one: "very worried" and "somewhat worried" are joined together in the 60% "worried" or 6-in-10 fearful women. But when we separate them again, we see that we could announce the survey results with equal or greater accuracy by saying: **6% of Canadian women are very worried when walking alone in their areas after dark.** Only 6%! This 6% is the same figure, it turns out, as the 6% of women who are very worried "when home alone in the evening" (Shelf Table 19A).

Home alone; out alone: no difference. Maybe only 6% of neighbourhoods are unsafe? Or, maybe 6% of women are just very nervous, and it has nothing to do with the objective safety conditions of their neighbourhoods? According to the National Institute of Mental Health in the U.S., 12.6% of the American population suffers from anxiety disorders, including panic disorders and phobias: irrational, involuntary terrors, like fear of heights, crowds, driving, plumbing, spiders, elevators (Rae 219). Maybe even *irrational* fear of *men*? Could it be that some or all of the 6% who are afraid in their homes or neighbourhoods are responding to their inner voices and not the sounds from the environment? Maybe the panic about violence against women won't help them at all.

In the same vein, the WADR campus survey could have noted that most of the sexual stuff on campuses was about sex play, alcohol, drugs, and verbal persuasion and, more importantly, that the incidence of violent force in this large and sexually active population was on a small scale. Or they might have contextualized their sensational "abuse" figures with the striking figures they published elsewhere which show that, of their sample, respondents overwhelmingly disagreed with and disapproved of what they call "patriarchal beliefs" supportive of men controlling and/or slapping women—at the 90%+ level, consistently to a host of questions. What an enlightened generation of young people!

Similarly, the StatsCan-sponsored Wilson and Daly piece on "Spousal Homicide" (1994) gives an inflammatory and misleading picture of the risks of women. Wilson and Daly belong, with Dobash and Dobash and DeKeseredy and Kelly, to the radical, patriarchy-theory wedge in family studies. They argue that violence against women is the inevitable concomitant of the subordination of women; it is the way that the supremacy of men is maintained. Virtually all aspects of women's lives are seen as manifestations of or responses to male control along a continuum of violence. So they write: "3.2 women have been killed by their husbands for each man killed by his wife." They could have said that this is age-related, and in some fair measure a problem of teen marriages. If teens are subtracted, their own graph shows a ratio more like 2 women for each man.

They offer another fear figure as well, along the current party line for frightening women about the men they know. They say that "a married woman was nine times more likely to get killed by her spouse as by a stranger" (1). It is easy to read this misleading formulation as proposing that women are better off taking their chances with strangers than with their intimate partners. But all it says, really, is that married women were at little risk of being killed by strangers. If we look at the figures (which takes some work, because they offer mostly graphs), 13 wives *per million* are killed by husbands, which therefore means that only 1.5 wives per million will be killed by strangers. As we all know, one in a million is the figure we all learn to use for virtually no chance, or pure chance: luck, good or bad. These numbers are so small that you cannot possibly hang a socially significant pathology on them. The authors therefore try to scare people with statistical abuse, twisting the descriptive representations until they pay off in fear— women's fear, and women's hatred of men.

What the figures actually show is that, out of some 11 million Canadian women, including 5.8 million women who count as spouses, 76 women (wives) per year are killed by their spouses (0.0013%), and 9 wives per year are killed by strangers. That's a total of 85 wives. Some more wives may be killed by non-spouses and non-strangers, i.e., acquaintances. I have not seen figures on this, and so I cannot calculate the total homicide/"femicide" risk for wives. However, altogether 200 women are killed in Canada per year, approximating a total risk for women of about 18 per million (0.0018%). The non-wife deaths may number 115 or fewer, depending on the number of additional wives killed by non-spousal intimates or acquaintances. But it looks like the risk for non-wives, who make up less than half the female population, is about the same or marginally higher than the spousal killing rate for wives: very, very low. For the sake of comparison, the female-to-male spousal killing rate is 4 per million, or about 24 men per year (0.0004%), though the overall homicide risk for men is twice as high as for women, with 400 men killed per year (0.0036%), some of whom may be additional spousal victims of contract killings. More men die than women, but the overall numbers are so low for both sexes that, much as we would like to eliminate all killing, it is not reasonable to describe Canada as a dangerous society on the basis of homicide figures.

Let me offer one more point of comparison, since spousal killing looms so large nowadays in the panic propaganda. It should help us to recover a sense of proportion, and to remember to ask, "Compared to what?" whenever we hear the sounds and numbers of advocacy statistics. In comparison to the 76 Canadian women killed in a given year by their husbands, the mortality tables assembled by Statistic Canada (1986), show that: three times as many women (229) are killed by influenza; three times as many women (206) are killed by bronchitis; the same number of women (79) are killed by obesity; almost four times as many women (279) are killed by Parkinson's disease; the same number of women (73) die by accidental drowning; and twice as many in fires (187) or by suffocation (146); twice as many women (145) fall to their deaths from one level to another; nearly the same number (57) die by falling on the same level; and more than ten times as many (865) die from other falls. More women's lives end in medical misadventure (106) and accidental poisoning (122). Indeed, Canadian women's risk of killing themselves deliberately, by suicide (820: includes guns—101; hanging—154; gas—80; drugs—300), is more than ten times as high as the risk of a wife being killed by a spouse, and more than four times as high as any Canadian woman being killed, period.

For a sense of proportion, it is also helpful to remember that Canadian men are at higher risk of violent death in every category but one (spousal killing, where after the age of 20, half as many men as women are killed). Nearly three times as many men as women are killed in vehicle accidents (3,225), twice as many in accidental poisonings (258), more than three times as many by suicide (2,850), and twice as many by homicide (400). A meaningless but interesting comparison (Viemeister 16, 226): there are about as many Americans struck dead each year by lightning (180) as the total number of Canadian women killed (200) by spouses, male and female acquaintances, and strangers.

The Ontario Women's Directorate's *Sexual Assault: Dispelling the Myths* pamphlet follows a related strategy for alarming women. It says: "Myth: The best way for a woman to protect herself from sexual assault is to avoid being alone at night in dark, deserted places, such as alleys or parking lots. Fact: Most sexual assaults (60%) occur in a private home and the largest percentage of these (38%) occur in the victim's home. The idea that most sexual assaults fit the 'stranger-in-a-dark-alley' stereotype can lead to a false sense of security" (1994, 2).

In truth, this is in part good news, and should be promoted to women in that light, with recommendations of due precaution. Women should be relieved to be freed from the burdens of fear about the knife-point rape in the alley or the abandoned parking lot. Instead, the image is conjured up only to infect the home with the sense that some intimate, currently above suspicion, is capable of suddenly becoming the equivalent of a knife-wielding monster. We know that 96-98% of sexual assaults do not involve weapons or any harm to the body, beyond the act itself. Indeed, 96-98% of what are called sexual assaults in any given year probably do not involve either forced intercourse or forced oral, anal, or other sex acts. (In the WADR national campus survey, where women were free to report their victimization on an anonymous question-naire, in the age group most sexually active and at highest risk of sexual miscommunication, especially with acquain-tances, less than 2% reported intercourse because of force or threat of force, and less than 4% reported an attempt at forced intercourse in the past 12 months.)

The exact numbers are difficult to compute, since the Canadian police no longer keep separate track of rape. The change in the Criminal Code in 1983, which lumped every imaginable sex-related offence under the single category of "sexual assault," makes it impossible to esti-mate the hard-core items. Many women would be relieved to hear that they need not worry about getting knifed or even hurt; and that their abrasions in life, such as they are, will come from people they associate with. An acquain-tance relationship that goes over the top, and a society in which this happens, are still closer to the orbit of what is understandable and predictable, and perhaps prevent-able, than perpetual risk from strangers. The Ontario

Women's Directorate should be helping to allay or diminish unnecessarily amplified anxieties.

Instead, in what is the most pernicious misuse of manipulated information, it promotes panic. Of course women would prefer to experience the occasional unwanted touching—some time in their lives—in the home, from acquaintances, than to suffer aggravated violence from strangers, away from home. This is actually a kinder and gentler image of a society than one in which the psychotic stranger roams the streets and danger is everywhere, and it is the latter we fear when we fear an increase in violence in our society. It can only assist the formulation of intelligent policy to deal with assault if we do not needlessly twist the available facts beyond recognition.

III
Statistical Abuse:
Surveying the Continuum

"The greatest magician ... would be the one who would cast over himself a spell so complete that he would take his own phantasmagorias as autonomous appearances. Would this not be our case? I conjecture that this is so. We (the undivided divinity operating within us) have dreamt the world. We have dreamt it as firm, mysterious, visible, ubiquitous in space and durable in time; but in its architecture we have allowed tenuous and eternal crevices of unreason which tell us it is false. (Jorge Luis Borges, "Avatars of the Tortoise" 208)

The Continuum of Behavioural Objectivism

I gave examples of category errors and imposed teleogies in the previous chapter. Now, I want to turn to the examples of bias from objectivism and ideology. Effect-inspired data management, as we saw, has proven to be a contagious instrument of biopolitical panic. A strategy of behavioural objectivism can produce equally impressive results. Specifically, it turns out that the numbers look more alarming if research subjects check off micro-actions from a list of event-descriptions, rather than describe their interpretation of their own experience. The discovery came about innocently, but soon caught on. Murray Straus and Richard Gelles, in the U.S., developed micro-action scales for use in their innovative family violence studies and employed them in two famous representative-sample National Family Violence Surveys, in 1975 and again in 1985 (2,143 and 6,002 married or cohabiting couples, respectively). This set of scales make up the Conflict Tactics Scales instrument (CTS). Use of the CTS has become standard in the violence field, sometimes with minor modifications. The Woman Abuse in Dating Relationships (WADR) survey uses it, as does the Statistics Canada *Violence Against Women* survey, and other major Canadian studies, including Brinkerhoff and Lupri (1988), Kennedy and Dutton (1989), Lupri (1990), and Sommer (1994). The CTS is considered to be "reliable and valid" (DeKeseredy and Kelly, "Incidents" 148), even by those who criticize it for the information it *fails* to produce (contexts, purposes, meanings, injurious consequences).

The CTS is a quantitative instrument, designed to measure how couples settle their differences and conflicts. It presents the interviewees with a choice of 18 micro-"acts," 10 non-violent and 8 violent, including "minor," "severe," and "very severe" violence. The idea is to measure the use of tactics of "reasoning," "verbal aggression," and "physical aggression," ranging from "discussed the issue calmly," to "sulked and/or refused to talk about it," "did or said something to spite the other one," and a list of physical

71

acts (in order of escalating possibility of injury), like grabbing, slapping, hitting, beating up, and knifing (Straus and Gelles 1979).

The Sexual Experiences Survey (SES) was developed by Mary Koss and colleagues, and made famous in a *Ms.* magazine-sponsored study (1987) of sexual aggression and victimization in a national sample of higher-education students. Like the CTS, the SES contains a list of acts, 10 of them, in ascending order of sexual coercion and force, from being talked into a kiss to forced intercourse and other sex acts. The CTS assumes a continuum of conflict tactics in a relationship; similarly, the SES assumes a continuum of sexual aggression and victimization.

One important difference in the assumptions governing these two scales is worth noting and remembering. The CTS was developed out of the explicit assumption that conflict is normal in societies and families, both of which might collapse without the dynamics of conflicting interests, but that some tactics in managing conflicts could be injurious (Straus and Gelles 1979). The SES, by contrast, evolved from Koss's rejection of earlier "typological" studies of subjects who were clearly classified as rapists, victims, or control subjects, in favour of a "dimensional" continuum, and was designed to produce a figuration of rape as an extreme behaviour "on a continuum with normal male behaviour within the culture" (Koss and Oros 455).

The SES continuum took on its character from the act of rape: all its "acts" signify, to some extent, sexual aggression and victimization. "Normal male behaviour" becomes here simply a milder form of rape. With the help of *Ms.* magazine, Koss's sensationalistic and misleading results came to promote the panic of a "rape culture." Unfortunately, in the seven years since the Koss survey, the understanding of the CTS within the violence survey milieu has shifted in the direction of Koss's innovation, i.e. defining all male behaviour as abuse.

This increasing characterization of reported incidents of conflict as instances of abuse raises ethical questions with respect to the treatment of respondents. The CTS questions are introduced to interviewees in an ascending order, from the mildest non-violent tactic to the most severe violence, in order to draw them in and elicit a full range of disclosures from the self-reports. In the Canadian WADR survey, moreover, the introductory frame indicates to its male subjects that their responses will be treated as normal, or at least will not all be treated with disapprobation in the presentation of the data: "We are particularly interested in learning more about your dating relationships. No matter how well a dating couple gets along, there are times when they disagree, get annoyed with the other person, or just have spats or fights because they're in a bad mood or tired or for some other reason. They also use many different ways to settle their differences. Below is a list of some things that you might have done to your girlfriends and/or dating partners in these situations" (DeKeseredy and Kelly, "Woman Abuse" 31).

In the last sentence, Straus's even-handed "things that you and your partner might have done when you had a dispute" has become "things that *you* might have done *to*." Apart from this nuance, as Kelly admits, "terms such as "abuse" or "violence" do not appear in these questionnaires" ("Politics" 82). Was it clear to the 1,307 men who provided information that *every* interaction they reported would be considered an act on the continuum of "woman abuse," defined as "intentional physical, sexual, or psychological assault on a female by a male dating partner" (DeKeseredy and Kelly "Woman Abuse" 29; "Incidence" 146)? Did the 1,835 women respondents know? Surely they should all have been clearly advised of researcher bias before they were drawn into the machinery of statistical abuse?

Methodological Violence

Why this casual duplicity toward subjects? The answer is, in part, that researchers in the 1980s learned that if they asked women explicitly whether they had been assaulted or abused, they would get a much lower number than if they simply inquired about the list of "acts." In fact, in cases where women were asked *both* "objective" questions about the incidence of some actions, and *also* their own interpretations of those actions, the women disagreed with the researcher's characterization.

Fully half of those whom Diana Russell classified as raped or attempted raped in her San Francisco survey did not think that they had had rape experiences. When Mary Koss developed her 1 in 4 figure for rape among college women, 73% of those who were classified by the researcher as rape victims said that they did not think that they had been raped, and 42% of them reported having consensual sex again with the same men. It is important to note that although both these studies are now widely disputed (see analyses by Neil Gilbert and by Katherine Dunn), the 1-in-4 figure continues to terrify women in Canada as well as in the U.S.

After these formative studies in the early to mid-80s, researchers who wanted high numbers simply stopped asking women what they thought of the events they reported, thereby substituting their own judgments for those of their subjects. It is sexual assault if the *researcher* decides it is, not if the participant-reporter says so. Violence research surveys are now routinely based on a deliberate methodological mistrust of their sample population. In the face of what they consider to be denial of abuse and coercion, researchers choose to downgrade their subjects' own descriptions and conceptualizations of what is happening in their interactions. This serves to justify to themselves a research design which some scrupulous, reputable feminist scholars consider unacceptably disrespectful of the respondent (Gartner 1993; Hoff Sommers 1994).

In my view, it is not simply the substitution of researcher interpretation for the subject's interpretation that matters here. It is not just a question of disrespect, but even more significantly, what it is that is disrespected and discounted. It is precisely the interviewee's *lack of alarm!* The women who described an incident to Koss as "miscommunication," for example, rather than rape (as Koss misrepresented it), were apparently choosing a low level of alarm from the registers of concern and emotion available to them. For biopolitical advocates, this is, naturally, simply a symptom of oppression: after all, writes Katherine Kelly, "it is only by questioning what goes unchallenged, that which is normalized, that we can begin to alter the way in which woman abuse is viewed" ("Politics" 83). Panic agendas are thus enabled by the research designs and rationalizations themselves: raising awareness (a principle of research science) is made equivalent to raising alarm (a principle of panic).

Sexual Symmetry; Ideological Assymetry

Methodological objectivity, or the underdetermination (desubjectivation) of the instrument and its results, produces high numbers and can serve the biopolitical campaign, for a while. But an irony has already appeared on the scene, and violence research is experiencing some disarray. It is all very well to leave the surveys free of built-in subject interpretations, all the better to introduce researcher interpretations at the presentation stage, *provided that* the data are clean and useable. As it happens, however, the underdetermined instruments also register data that are unacceptable to the advocacy machine.

When this happens, underdetermination is challenged by the overdetermination claims of theorists promoting a radical feminist line. Data need context, they say, and their preference would be to build it right in, even if it means jettisoning the behavioural objectivism of the CTS and comparable instruments of research: "The presumed gain in objectivity achieved by asking research subjects to report only 'acts' ... is illusory" (Dobash et al. 82). For holistic analysis, the argument goes, we need Theory, and the job of Theory, apparently, is to explain away inconvenient data, and especially data which, in the absence of Theory, might lead us to overlook the Big Picture (which is violence against women by men, in a patriarchal system that victimizes women in every way).

What got Dobash et al. so spooked that they are prepared to jettison behavioural objectivism? *Extensive evidence of female violence.* It's like a snake in paradise; it spoils everything. Nobody had to confront it as long as all the evidence about family violence came from feminist activism and social service, criminal justice, and medical emergency reports. The visible clinical picture is largely about women attacked by men. Battered women are the ones who speak. The general population profile, however, shows a different image: a relative symmetry between male-to-female and female-to-male violence in intimate partnerships, at every level of severity,[1] and including equivalence in initiating violence[2] without violent provocation.[3] These were the findings of the two National Family Violence Surveys conducted by Straus and Gelles that I mentioned in the previous chapter. These were the first representative, random-sample studies that interviewed *both* sexes about acts they perpetrated on others as well as those perpetrated against them. These findings of sexual symmetry have been confirmed by equivalent results from every one of more than 30 two-sex random sample surveys (Straus, "Physical Assaults" 70).[4]

Dobash et al. are much admired by advocates like Michele Landsberg, because of their relentless railing against "the myth of sexual symmetry in marital violence," a myth which, she says, could only be promoted by "misogynists, seeking to minimize and deny the harm that too many women suffer at men's hands" ("The Male Myth"). Landsberg enjoys their attack on the CTS. CTS results may look objective, she says, but they are far from it. CTS-generated data about female-perpetrated violence should be dismissed because the CTS does not ask about the context, meaning, intention, and consequence of the acts, all of which would show that if and when women do violence, which is rarely, it is justified, "in defence of self or children." Landsberg seems unaware of the irony of Dobash et al.'s attack on the validity of micro-"act" surveys for lacking context. After all, it was that technical decontextualization which put the violence scare on the map on a national and international scale in the first place, and which continues to keep it there in large, Canadian, feminist surveys like the recent SCVAW and the WADR.

Canadian national data on family violence tend to corroborate trends established for the United States (Brinkerhoff and Lupri 1988, Kennedy and Dutton 1989, and Lupri 1989). All reveal high rates of wife-to-husband violence. What is noteworthy about the moral panic in Canada is how readily uniformity of appropriate public attitude is reached or affected, and how often research that shatters the tyranny of biopolitical consensus dies at the design stage, or sits unpublished in somebody's desk drawer. Straus notes that a survey conducted for the Kentucky Commission of Women (Schulman 1979), as was later disclosed by Hornung et al., showed that 38% of attacks in violent couples were attacks initiated by women. These data on female-perpetrated assaults were intentionally suppressed. Straus suggests that this brings out a "troublesome question of scientific ethics" ("Physical Assaults" 70), and so it does. But the problem is not unique to Kentucky.

In Canada, Eugen Lupri, in Alberta, has conducted a random national survey on conjugal violence, based on 652 women and 471 men. Although he has not published his results in English, his study fully confirms Straus's work, and all the other random two-sex surveys showing symmetry of violence up and down the severity scale. Lupri used the self-report approach to gather offender information, and found that in every category (hitting, kicking, beating up, threatening, or violating with a weapon), women reported that they perpetrated more incidents of violence against their partners than the men did against the women. Before and since, Lupri has published work on male perpetrators; but the report on female perpetrators has so far been withheld. Lupri was kind enough to send us his paper when we called to ask for it. I cannot quote from it directly without his consent—he is unhappy with the use of his data by others. It is fair to say, however, that, in his unpublished paper, Lupri presents his data briefly, and then ties himself into a pretzel for the bulk of the paper, trying to explain away his own findings.

Lupri's story is not untypical in today's strange world of "family violence" research. Many of the male feminists in this field, such as Straus, DeKeseredy, and Russell Dobash—an early pioneer of patriarchy analysis in family studies—are deeply embarrassed by their own findings of sexual symmetry in violence perpetration. Perhaps the editor of *Social Trends*, a StatsCan publication which featured only the male violence data collected by Lupri, in spite of announcing it would reveal the female-perpetrated violence material, accounts for this most succinctly: "Current [political correctness] suggests you do not talk about that sort of thing" (quoted by David Lees in *Toronto Life* 99). So, there are some data, but they are not forthcoming.

Lupri is not the only one holding out in Canada. We gather that Kennedy and Dutton may have some unpublished work on female-perpetrated violence. And so do DeKeseredy and Kelly! Kelly writes that "the [WADR] study was designed for a specific purpose: to survey women's experiences with abuse" ("Politics" 83). It would appear from all that they have published, as well as from the way they show their questions and analyze their data, that they asked women for self-reports only of victimization and men for self-reports only of perpetration. The presentation of the results in several scholarly articles and to the media leaves a distinct impression of women as victims in intentionally assaultive relationships.

Yet there is an ambiguously worded passage in the report on the results that leads one to wonder what other data they have. They say that violent women act in self-defence, and that the CTS fails to show this because it lacks questions to contextualize the violence. They say that "in response to the above criticisms [of the CTS], also included in our version of the CTS were three questions asking male and female participants to explain why they engaged in dating violence since they left high school" ("Incidence" 147-48). It is hard to imagine that this modification of the CTS could be designed only to get information on male-to-female assaults. It seems to be about perpetration of violence by both sexes. The three questions are actually about self-defence, retaliation, and preemptive first strike: all designed, one would think, to provide justifying context for female perpetration.

Even if the questions were only asked of the men, any affirmative self-justifying answers indicating male self-defence or retaliation would simultaneously have to indicate female-perpetrated violence. So, *where are the data?* In the article, they promise "subsequent articles" (156) on a variety of contextual items, with not a hint about female violence. It is not until Kelly's reply to her critics in 1994 that we get a clear clue that they are sitting on crucial data for understanding dating relationships. Kelly writes: "The survey contains data on women's use of violence that is of considerable importance" ("Politics" 84). *Where are these data?* "In time, many of these things will be done," she writes. Not even a definite commitment.

We called DeKeseredy and Kelly in May 1994 to ask about this. Both confirmed independently that indeed they have data on female-perpetrated violence that they have not released. We asked if we could look at what they have. They said no. The Carleton survey data are not being released to any other scholar, except Dan Saunders of the University of Michigan, perhaps the leading self-defence theorist, and Martin Schwartz, another sceptic about female violence. DeKeseredy said that he, Saunders, and Schwartz would publish more on this in January 1995. There is some doubt about this, however. Kelly and DeKeseredy have fallen out over the release of data. She is working on something else. She says he is moving on to child abuse, and is no longer interested in the female-perpetrated violence data.

Even if there is a future publication, will it have the same sensational exposure as the female-victimization numbers? More to the point, if they applied the CTS to both sexes, they are likely to have discovered the same symmetry in their results as has every other researcher. Maybe they can explain away half of it, maybe not. But these are people who say over and over again that the operational data yielded by the CTS must be contextualized by motives, meanings, and consequences. The level of female-perpetrated violence was available to them, as to any other two-sex survey. How could they fail to recognize that, in a relationship study, the first, most direct, and most indispensable context for the level of male-to-female abuse would have to be the level of female-to-male abuse? I cannot accept that a future publication, which is in any case not certain, would be a satisfactory remedy for the panic they created, with their maximally sensationalized presentation of partial data. This kind of misleading research strategy must be called to account, with a degree of critical edge that so far neither the academy, nor the media, nor the public, nor the funding agencies and policy makers have been properly demanding.

Statistics Canada

Statistics Canada, in my view, is an even worse offender against basic scientific integrity and fairness. The "Violence Against Women" survey uses standard CTS questions to measure spousal violence. This is no surprise. What is scandalous is that this study, which purports to provide pioneering national information about relationship interaction in Canada, is a *single-sex survey*. In my view, the decision to ask only women about acts of violence perpetrated against them is highly partisan.

The inflammatory figure, which is this survey's claim to fame, is that 51% of Canadian women have experienced at least one incident of violence since the age of 16. But

Statistics Canada did nothing to discover the meaning of the *micro-acts* it induced women to report. By defining it as a strict male-to-female victimization survey, based only on complaints, they gave up any serious interest in the nature of interactions. They made no effort to discover if men and women might have different perceptions of the questions they asked. They made no effort to verify the accuracy of memory recall (back to the age of 16). Many of the questions, as is characteristic of CTS and SES type measures, "include poorly conceived categories of violence (combining threatened, attempted and actual violence) that are not mutually exclusive" (Dobash and Dobash, "Social Science" 450). For example, the question from which estimates were derived on sexual attack by non-spouses: "It is important to hear from women themselves if we are to understand the very serious problem of male violence against women ... Has a [male stranger, date or boyfriend, other man known to you] ever forced you or attempted to force you into any sexual activity by threatening you, holding you down or hurting you in some way? [Yes or No]" (SCVAW Questionnaire, *Daily* 3).

Similarly, the question that was one of the two main staples for generating the survey's physical-assault data is a yes/no question: "Now, I'm going to ask you some questions about physical attacks you may have had since the age of 16. By this I mean any use of force such as being hit, slapped, kicked, or grabbed to being beaten, knifed, or shot. Has a (male stranger, date or boyfriend, other man known to you) ever physically attacked you?" Later, in the marital-violence section, this question is simply broken into the usual CTS range, from pushing, grabbing and shoving to being knifed or shot. One real problem that has impact on the findings has been noted by critics of the CTS: items like "pushed, grabbed, or shoved," and items in even longer composite lists, include a large number of different behaviours inside each concept, as well as in the interplay among them, and therefore may lend themselves to divergent reporting (Szinovacz 643; Brinkerhoff and Lupri, "Interspousal Violence" 416). These questions yield high numbers which get even higher when this yield is combined with the estimates derived from the softer questions on unwanted touching, or threats of harm.

The planning document for the survey provides interesting background. For the period 1991-95, the federal government has allocated $136 million for the Family Violence Initiative. Six federal departments are committed. National Health and Welfare, which financed DeKeseredy and Kelly's Carleton study, is described as "the lead ministry in this Initiative." Health and Welfare, in turn, had requested the Canadian Centre for Justice Statistics to come up with a $3.2 million project. They in turn proposed a national wife-assault survey (among other smaller projects), eventually broadened to include violence against women by non-spouses as well, to take place in 1993. The objective was to get a big victimization study, and to talk to women about fear.

The contexts that were to be provided for the CTS included only the ones from the battery agenda, including medical consequences, and use of social or legal services. The questionnaire was developed in consultation with government, police, academics (advocacy experts like Wilson, Daly, and no doubt DeKeseredy and Kelly), and the network of people entangled in the violence against women institution: "Victims/survivors of violence, and front-line service providers (transition house workers, sexual assault crisis centres, ethno-cultural and refugee serving groups, and provincial and national associations)." There was endless consultation with feminists who were considered prime "stake-holders" in the issue. In short, this whole project was developed during the height of the post-Lepine "war-against-women" panic, and in a way that guaranteed that the survey would belong to the clinical population of violence victims and to its biofeminist advocates.[5]

In other words, the reputation of Canada's number-one number cruncher, the gold standard of the truths about Canadian life, is hostage in all this to the tyranny of pain, grievance, fear, and resentment. Still, it boggles the mind that Statistics Canada would have opted for the inferior, biopolitical option, the panic option of going through the motions of a fake survey. The one-sex survey of Canadian women is a completely uncorroborated, worthless waste of money and public trust.

This is a copycat survey, following up on the transformation of Canadian sex laws on consent and sexual assault. The change from rape laws to sexual-assault laws has meant that casual fondling gets thrown in with shattering transgression, with the result that although the statistics in the sex crime category get much bigger, they tell us much less about what is going on. "[Pressing] ahead with legislative changes which give greater recognition to victims' rights" (Collins 1993), the government has also created a new definition of consent, and removed the evidentiary requirement of corroboration from the sexual-assault law. Statistical science now puts itself at the service of this fictional Canadian woman, whose uncorroborated testimony about all the unwanted incidents in her life raises her to a level of mythic participation in a sacrificial ritual beyond her depth, where her chances at real equality are sacrificed to the creation of Woman-as-Victim.

Statistics Canada, which claims to be able to tell us about the invisible undercurrents and undergrowths of mass society, can equally lull us with stories of a fantastic and fantasized character. The actual woman loses her humanity, which belongs in an interactive manifold, and becomes instead an angel, an innocent, without mass or extension, a creature of air, simply registering on her body the turbulences of the climate. She floats entirely on winds that blow from elsewhere. She *does* nothing. She feels, and she fears. And she feels and fears in a kind of brutalized Ken and Barbie world, simple-minded and desexualized, but entrapped in an interviewing surround-sound of male malignancy and sexual intrusion.

Q. #B10: "Have you ever received unwanted attention from a MALE STRANGER? (e.g. blowing kisses)?" Q. #B14: "Have you ever been followed by a man in a way that frightened you? Q. #B19: "Has a man you knew ever made you feel uncomfortable by making inappropriate comments about your body or sex life?" Q. #B21: "Has a man you knew ever leaned over you unnecessarily?" Q. #C14: "Can you tell me how many men have done this to you?" Q. #C20: "Can you tell me how many men have done this to you? Q.#C25: "Since the age of 16, has ANY OTHER MAN YOU KNOW ever touched you against your will in a SEXUAL way (such as unwanted touching, grabbing, kissing or fondling?" Q.#C26, #C39, #C45, #D10, #D17: "Can you tell me how many men have done this to you?????

What business is it of the government's to collect information on blowing kisses, inappropriate comments, feeling uncomfortable, or unnecessary leaning? What authority do Canadians really want to give to the government to define these things, qualitatively and quantitatively, for us? Why mix this in with violence; I mean violence of the kind that most Canadians more or less understand by violence when they worry about "increasing violence"?

What can justify telling Canadians *in this context* the following misleading information: "For one-in-three (34%) victims of wife assault, the abuse or threats of abuse were so serious that they feared for their lives. While this percentage was higher in the case of past marriages (45%), it is important to note that 13% of women reporting violence in a current marriage had at some point felt their lives were in danger (130,000 or 2% of all currently married women)" (SCVAW, *Daily* 5)?

First of all, Statistics Canada is misreporting its own data: the figures here refer to perpetrators, not to victims. It is not that 34% of *women* fear for their lives; nor that 45% of *women* feared for their lives in a past marriage. It is that

34% of those *partners* who were complained about made the women fear for their lives, including 45% of the allegedly violent *partners* in past marriages. This makes a difference because Statistics Canada is double-counting in its tables (see footnote to Shelf Table 8): "Women who have experienced violence in both a current and a previous partnership are counted as two partnerships." This is a very curious rendering of prevalence data: if the issue is what percentage of ever-married women have ever feared for their lives from their partner(s), at some time in their lives, it does not matter how many partners have frightened them. One woman, one life. What we get is perpetrator data, presented as though it were victim data, though we are never told how many partners these ever-married women had altogether. We learn only how many partners they complained about.

This is a technical point, but it is this kind of manipulation that severely distorts the presentation of data. What is more significant, however, is how little purpose these data have, apart from validating and promoting fear. What the tables show is that about a million current, male, marital partners (1 in 6) stand accused of some form of abuse; of those, 13% are accused of being the cause of mortal fear (affecting 2.6% of some 6 million currently married Canadian women). The 34% prevalence figure accuses nearly a million men (944,000 past and present partners) of having been the cause of fear. We are not informed what percentage these scary partners make up of the total of past and present partners, and we do not know how many women have complained of such fear. From the tables, it seems that, if all previous partnerships are counted as only one partnership, then at least 807,000 women (8%, or 1 in 12 of all Canadian women; 9%, or 1 in 11 of ever-married women; 14%, or 1 in 7 currently married women) have feared at one time or another in their marital lives that their very lives were in danger from their spouses. This, in a country where the rate of spousal homicide/"uxoricide" is *13 per one million couples*, that is, *a total of 76 women in a year* (*Juristat* 14.8, 2-3)! The finding of statistical fear ("More than one-in-ten women who reported violence in a current marriage have at some point felt their lives were in danger," *Daily* 1) belongs to the psychopathology of everyday life. What does it have to do with "violence against women"?

This is a relationship survey. But Statistics Canada did not ask any men any questions at all. And Statistics Canada did not ask any woman to report on her own acts of violence toward a man in a relationship. This is then also a victimization survey: violence against women. But Statistics Canada did not ask any woman whether her mother has ever hit her? Whether her sister has said unkind things about her body? Whether her daughter pushed and shoved her around in her older years? Whether her lesbian lover humiliated her, threatened her, or beat her? Whether a female superior has taken advantage of her sexually?

It has to be said that Statistics Canada has sold itself to the dark powers of demonization. It has traded in science for voodoo. It has produced an inequitable and unjustifiable report. It has been captured by a faction. What good is it to us now that the reputation of Statistics Canada is known far and wide? Already *Cosmopolitan* magazine reports, in the middle of another O. J. Simpson story, "Still Going On Out There: Women Beaten Senseless by Men," that the crime wave against women is real, and not a paranoid delusion. How do we know? The Canadian government's information-gathering agency, Statistics Canada, has conducted "the most comprehensive study of violence against women ever undertaken [and] the results were worse than expected" (229). Panic feeds science, which in turn again feeds panic. Statistics Canada has entered a vicious circle.

There is no excuse for this *one-sex* survey. On the other hand, the fact that biopolitical feminism has been able to get the upper hand in an institution like StatsCan does indicate that the many findings of reciprocal female violence in relationships have not yet entered into the popular consciousness, or at least, have been excised from the official culture and our public institutions. Even the renowned Murray Straus, who fancies himself a feminist, has recently shed tears over the sad truth: "It is painful to have to recognize the high rate of domestic assaults by women. Moreover, the statistics are likely to be used by misogynists and apologists for male violence" ("Physical Assaults" 79). This, from a man who has been documenting male-perpetrated violence for twenty years, with nary a tear-drop for the perpetrators, and who has himself put the findings on female offenders on the research map.

Self-defence and Double Standards

In truth, the chauvinist double standards, designed for the "protection of women" in an earlier era, are possibly more firmly entrenched among feminist men than they ever were among the Victorian ancestors. In a maudlin mood, Straus laments: "The problem is similar to that noted by Barbara Hart (1986) in the introduction to a book on lesbian battering: '[It] is painful. It challenges our dream of a lesbian utopia. It contradicts our belief in the inherent non-violence of women. And the disclosure of violence by lesbians ... may enhance the arsenal of homophobes'" ("Physical Assaults" 79). This kind of juvenilia—the *inherent non-violence of women,* really!—runs through the sanctimonious underpinnings of a cultural affectation whose baggage of proverbial good intentions is busily paving our roads to that notorious hot spot of our darker imagination.

Straus, it is intriguing to note, when faced with the denials of the dominant biofeminist advocates, affects not quite believing his own data. In fact, he has come up with a bizarre, and ultimately rather dispiriting, formula: A man insults a woman. An indignant woman "slaps the cad." The man retaliates. A minor assault by a woman incites a severe assault. Hence it is important to accept that women do perpetrate minor violence, because they have to be trained out of it for their own good ("Physical Assaults" 79).

This is a neo-protectionist effort to split the difference with the self-defence lobby. It does no good. Furthermore, it turns into pure caricature: the objective "acts" in the CTS type surveys, writes Michele Landsberg, "equate a wife's playful slap of her husband's hand as he reaches to take a bite of her dessert with a husband's tooth-loosening assault intended to punish, humiliate and terrorize." This is, of course, totally false to the data found in dozens of surveys, Canadian as well as American, which show that women in relationships with men commit comparatively as many or more acts of physical violence as men do, at every level of severity. It is not a case of friendly slap against vicious beating. It is slap for slap, beating for beating, knifing and shooting for knifing and shooting, on the evidence of women's own *self*-reports.

Why is it so difficult to imagine that women are people too, and people who get fully entangled in life with all they've got? When they are under stress, when they drink, when they are jealous, when they reach for strategies witnessed in their own parents' relationships, when they abuse their power, their frustration, or their greed, just like men, but with motivations and tactics specific to their different conditioning, *some* women do enact patterns of violence. We have to believe that women are capable of equal wrongs if we want to make sure that women enjoy equal rights. I think most ordinary people know this, and all men and women in conflictual relationships know it. They also know that the public culture is lying about the innocence of women, and about the unique culpability of men, as well as committing barbaric acts of callousness toward men who are victimized and men who are being falsely persecuted.

Anyway, what about self-defence? Well, unfortunately, neither Brinkerhoff and Lupri's Calgary study (1988), nor Statistics Canada's *Violence Against Women Survey* (1993), not to mention the thoroughly unscientific and unfair

CanPan (1993), asked any questions about self-defence. The authors of the Carleton study (1993), DeKeseredy and Kelly, have not shared their self-defence data with other researchers or the public; and I know of no similar studies in the U.S. The only random, representative Canadian study which produces data on self-defence is Reena Sommer's 1994 Winnipeg study, *Male and Female Perpetrated Partner Abuse: Testing a Diathesis-Stress Model.*

Sommer looked at the behaviour of 899 randomly selected men and women (447 men and 452 women), through interviews and questionnaire self-reports. Later, she reinterviewed 737 of her sample (368 men and 369 women). She found that marital discord was remarkably symmetrical, contrary to the panic notion that dominates current biofeminism about the pervasiveness of male physical abuse of helpless women. Unfortunately, but not altogether surprisingly, her results have not produced the same headlines as the three other national Canadian studies of 1993 that inflated the scare figures, although she is perhaps beginning to get the exposure that is her due (see Verburg, "The Other Half"). Back in 1992, as the CanPan toured the country, gathering some women's tales of woe, a CP wire story about the results from the first wave of Sommer's study ("39 per cent of women in survey admit they abuse spouse") was mentioned only once, on page 18 of the *Toronto Star.*

In her questionnaire, Sommer asks the respondent the following: "In these episodes, were your actions in self-defence?" and "How many times were your actions in self-defence?" for each of 6 conflict strategies named in the CTS. She summarizes her results as follows: "The issue of self defence in perpetrated partner abuse [abuse *of* partner] has been discussed by feminist writers who have long argued that when a woman hits a man, it is usually in self defence (Pleck et al. 1978; Walker 1979). The findings of this study stand in the face of this argument. This study has found that only approximately 10% of women and 15% of men perpetrated partner abuse in self defence. In other words, for almost 90% of women and 85% of men, the perpetration of partner abuse was influenced by other factors. According to these findings, self defence is not a common motivation for the perpetration of partner abuse for males and females in the general population" (169).

Sommer's data also cast light on another controversy: "The issue of a spouse or partner requiring medical attention following a partner abuse incident has not been widely researched in general population research. This study provides the first insights into yet another dimension of this serious social problem for Canadians. It was reported that approximately 21% of males' and 14% of females' partners required medical attention as a result of a partner abuse incident. This represents approximately 3% of the total subsample of married, cohabiting and remarried males and females. This percentage is greater than that reported by Straus and Gelles 1990 based on the finding from their national survey (.4% of male and 3% of females needed to see a doctor following a violent incident). Moreover, while Straus and Gelles 1990 found that significantly more females required medical attention, the results of this study failed to find such a sex difference" (169).[6]

Straus's concessions to the patriarchy scenario, in which everything women do wrong is inconsequential, and explained by male domination and female vulnerability and fear, is simply an explanation of Theory, not borne out by the data. In any case, "slapping the cad" does not land a woman in the hospital. The very definition of a "cad" is his pettiness; the cad does not do felony assault. However, women, Canadian women, violent women, some women, do.

Violent Women

In Peterborough, 23-year-old Tracy Kyle violates her probation and threatens to kill two men with a butcher knife when they say they will call the police if she does not return a long-overdue video to the video store ("Video threat").

In Toronto, 37-year-old Susan Yeung gets seven years for manslaughter after strangling her lover with a thin rope from a pair of sweat pants in a fit of rage, having first drugged him with sleeping pills. She has a black belt in tae kwon-do. They had been childhood sweethearts, and he was leaving her, after a tumultuous relationship of four years. He acted badly; she acted worse. It was a volatile relationship to the end. After she killed him, she took sleeping pills, then tried to hang herself twice, and then slashed her own throat. Twenty hours later, she phoned an emergency number and confessed. There was a premenstrual syndrome and depression defence ("Woman gets seven years").

Women kill and attempt to kill: acquaintances, lovers, husbands. They also terrorize and brutalize others, sometimes other women, who are less powerful. Jane Gudrun Alexanderson lives in Scarborough. One day she takes on a roommate in her apartment, Charlene Ormston, 32, mildly disabled mentally. Alexanderson rapidly turns Ormston into a house slave. When Ormston misses a dirty spot while scrubbing the kitchen floor, Alexanderson chokes her until she blacks out. Alexanderson breaks four of the other woman's ribs, smashes her face with a glass, dislocates her shoulder, and knees her in the groin. One day, Ormston makes a chocolate cake for Alexanderson's young son; she gets a wooden spoon shoved down her throat until she gags. Alexanderson burns the other woman with cigarettes, beats her back and neck, and bends her fingers back until they break. She threatens Ormston's life if she ever tells. When arrested, Alexanderson pleads guilty. Ormston says she was scared to move out, and feared Alexanderson would not return her identification papers ("Woman guilty of enslaving roommate").

Women also castrate, literally. November 1993, the same month Statistics Canada released its survey on violence against women, we watched celebrity castrator Lorena Bobbitt on trial for cutting off her husband's penis. Lorena and John Wayne Bobbitt were a couple of working-class American kids, 24 and 26, types from the start, and the media loved them, so the story grew. But Lorena was not the first, or the last. A year earlier, September 1992, in Los Angeles, Aurelia Macias, 35, cuts off her sleeping husband's testicles with a pair of scissors. Husband James withholds the information from the police. He says only that he has cuts to his genitals, and she is charged with spousal battery. A year later, by the time prosecutors obtain complete medical records showing the castration, Lorena is in the news, and Aurelia and James Macias are jointly asking the judge to lift a restraining order against her so the couple may spend Thanksgiving and Christmas with their three children. A little later, in Manila, a seamstress called Gina Espina, 21, cuts off her husband's penis with a pair of scissors. She says "there is a limit to everything. The last straw for me was to catch him philandering with another female worker at the dress shop." She throws it on the floor of the motel where they had checked in to discuss their marital problems ("Snipped penis").

Exotic stories from foreign lands? In August 1993, a Toronto woman attacks her husband's penis with scissors ("Penis attack"). Another Canadian-angle story around this same time is about Laura Oppermann, charged with felony spousal assault and assault with a deadly weapon, "to wit acrylic fingernails." In November of 1993 (Bobbitt time; SCVAW time), she is living with a Hamilton native, Edward Cryer, in California. They argue about money. She grabs him from behind, and slashes his scrotum open with her razor-sharp false fingernails. Edward, whose left testicle was "hanging down on my leg and the cops and paramedics were throwing up," offers to stand bail for her, and wants to forgive and forget ("Woman's nails slash open scrotum").

Claims of abuse, jealousy, money conflicts: an assortment of motives. The biggest Canadian story of attempted castration preceded all of the others: Cynthia Johnson, 38, of Etobicoke, a woman spurned. A teacher, and the mother of a 14-year-old boy, she was having an affair in November of 1989 with Randy Atkins, a 51-year-old married man, an employee of her school board. His wife got pregnant, and he was planning to stop seeing Johnson. He visits her house, they have sex, and then she invites him to take a bath with her and turns out the lights. She stimulates him in the dark, and then attacks him with a knife she had prepared, cuts him and nearly severs his penis. She is convicted of attempted murder by a jury, which neither buys her self-defence plea nor believes her story that he raped her and forced her to have oral sex at knifepoint. She gets two years less a day. Does not show up in court for sentencing, and has to be pursued by police. Forfeiting $10,000 bail, she is thought to have fled to her native Barbados.

In this case, the story does not end there. The trial was in July 1991, eighteen months after Marc Lépine, and in the midst of the Status of Women war fever. Cynthia Johnson became a hero for a "Comunity Coalition" of 18 groups: eleven rape-crisis centres, and the southern Ontario branch of the National Action Committee on the Status of Women, the Toronto chapter of the Congress of Black Women, the Canadian Association of Sexual Assault Centres, the Black Women's Support Network, Wen-do Women's Self-Defence, Women's Health in Women's Hands, and the Women Prisoners' Survival Network. Why? Because she had been through "an agonizing experience." Mariruth Morton, of the Toronto Rape Crisis Centre, said that her conviction "sets a very dangerous precedent for women in Ontario." The coalition made plans to use Johnson as a "poster woman" in a campaign against the legal system, where she was to be portrayed as a victim of the system's bias against women ("Woman who knifed lover to be used in sexism ads"). According to the coalition, "Canada's justice system is not responsive enough to issues of violence against women" (Depradine, "Women's groups" 1).

There are all kinds of Canadian women in all kinds of circumstances who do things that are not very nice. Nearly half of 1,600 Ontario nurses surveyed said that they witnessed some form of physical or verbal abuse of (mostly female) patients by other nurses. Woman-on-woman abuse—the offender self-report replaced by the snitch report. Woman-to-men death threat: Gloria Amblin, 32, threatens to bash in the heads of several men in Young's Point ("Woman with bat charged for threats"). Evil consort: Karla Homolka, 23, convicted of manslaughter in the deaths of two teen-aged girls. Very little is as yet known in Canada about the details of the trial leading up to her conviction in July 1993, because of a gag order on the Canadian media ("Homolka blackouts contravene regulations, CRTC says").

Small-fry life abuser Darlene Topping, 21, of Buckingham, has ex-boyfriend Roger Nadon, 33, arrested on a charge of attempted murder. She accuses him of cutting her with a razor. She keeps him in jail for two weeks before admitting that she has lied. Her lawyer says she made up the story to try for a reconciliation with another boyfriend ("Service work"). Child-killer: Ingrid Matheson, 36, of suburban Etobicoke, is accused of first-degree murder. Police find her two sons, William, aged 2, and Jonathan, aged 4, in separate beds in a Brampton motel, apparently suffocated with bags and beaten with a blunt object. She is pulled from a burning car ("Mom to be charged with killing sons"). We will not know more details until the trial. Her husband, meanwhile, is in prison, on a drugs and violence charge.

Sandra Thomas of the University of Tennessee has done an in-depth study of women's anger and written a book about her findings called *Women and Anger*. She studied 565 healthy women, aged 25 to 66. Women recalled their anger in everyday situations: when their teenager was surly, the boss was yelling, the spouse committed a pet peeve, or the traffic was bad. They let off a lot of steam, "but typically at their husbands, instead of the person who really angered them" ("Hell hath no fury").

Half-truths Only, Please

I don't know how representative the Thomas survey was, but it brings us back to the point about context. It is commonplace now to criticize operationalized measures in surveys, such as the CTS, for lacking information on context, including motives, sequencing, and consequences. Feminists like Dobash and Dobash, DeKeseredy, Saunders, and others make this argument to explain away the high levels of inter-spousal female-to-male physical and verbal aggression to which women admit, on all surveys where they are given the opportunity. The argument is of course circular and begs the question. Random surveys were established to gather data on the rate of family violence. The results are found to violate feminist prejudices about the innocence of women. Instead of letting the data reform the prejudices, these prejudices are permitted to stand as the measure of the validity of the research.

The argument is that a slap is not the same slap when committed by men and by women. Even murder is not the same: men are culpable, regardless of their circumstances, but women have the battery syndrome defence, and a range of other self-defence strategies. In consequence, when the researchers want to invalidate the results of the CTS, including the women's own reports, they want to invalidate only one half of the data. The male offences are self-evidently violence against women; the female offences are to be construed as self-defence or retaliation, and if not a direct response to an immediate incident of male violence, then a response to the violence against women endemic to the relationship, and, failing any proof of that, then a response to the violence against women endemic to the whole society and all institutions.

In short, when they call for context, or for Theory, Dobash et al. already have the context fully scripted.

"Violence against wives ... is often persistent and severe, occurs in the context of continuous intimidation and coercion, and is inextricably linked to attempts to dominate and control women" ("Myth" 71). Women are victims of the *system*, and accountable for nothing. Anything they may do in response is either a manifestation of their vulnerability or an example of fighting back.

This is automated sociology without ethics and without psychology. It is described as a challenge to the "system," but it gets expressed in the form of relentless hostility to men, and lots of detailed busy legal work, erecting special status for women, special case defences, and double standard measures in every corner of policy and interpretation. The argument on behalf of the need for context is clearly useful, but biopolitical feminism, having pre-divided the world into patriarchy and its victims, is peddling a tired and predictable foreknowledge of every possible contextualization, because it is always the same contextualization. Context has become another code word for the cluster of meanings associated with biopolitical moral panic. Context, as a code word keyed to patriarchy theory, is a formula for haif-truths. In the war formula, men can do nothing right, and women can do no wrong. The half-truth of the feminist context argument is that it will keep sharply focussed whatever ostensible grievances can be assigned to women.

Indeed, the biofeminist context is even less than a half-truth, because it has little time for the grievances of women who suffer from other women, or children who are abused by their mothers, or elders who are mistreated by female caregivers. These are large categories of female misconduct. The violence of women against other vulnerables who may be female is not part of the violence-against-women script; nor is the fate of men who suffer from other men. All male victims, like male perpetrators, are considered genetically guilty. This is the biopolitical version of original sin. Yet all these men who are hurt in their jobs, in the streets, in the prisons, and in the wars, are women's husbands, women's sons, women's brothers and fathers, women's doctors, teachers, lawyers, builders, grocers, firemen, policemen, colleagues, co-workers, students, clients, lovers, and friends. To perceive all of these intricate relationships only in the discourse of men against women, of men's power over women, of men's damage to women, and to ignore how much women are implicated in their male associates' pain, is narcissistic and callous beyond measure.

The symbiotic mutual-aggression pact of marriage is not the whole story about marriage in any case. Brinker-hoff and Lupri report that "although violence is negatively correlated with marital satisfaction, significantly large proportions of highly satisfied couples report conjugal violence. Such evidence lends support to the dialectic notion that love and affection exist simultaneously with conflict and violence" ("Interspousal violence" 407). One aspect of this deeper insight is that the picture of the world that rests on concepts of sheer victimization and demonization will not serve. The active, creative, responsive, and transgressive energies and orientations of both women and men, in a manifold of interactive framings, call out for redescription, retheorization, and revaluation.

Outside marriage too, and increasingly, not only love and affection, but sexual desire, intellectual curiosity, cultural commitments, institutional roles, new work relationships, and the universal utopian search for adventure and delight, all bond individuals together in a complex variety of dimensions that are not properly coded by the sharp divisions of sex-thinking, or race-thinking, or any other half-truth or fractional truth. Biopolitical truth is always granular: a little grain of truth, that must be taken with a big grain of salt. And caution. Because biopolitics will lash out at anything and anybody that is not seen to be 100% with the essential(ist) script. Biopolitics is in a permanent state of panic.

IV
Seeing Through the Cracks: CanPan and the Biofeminist Lens

"People are always shouting they want to create a better future. It's not true. The future is an apathetic void of no interest to anyone. The past is full of life, eager to irritate us, provoke and insult us, tempt us to destroy or repaint it. The only reason people want to be masters of the future is to change the past. They are fighting for access to the laboratories where photographs are retouched and biographies and histories re-written." (Milan Kundera, Book of Laughter and Forgetting 22)

CanPan as the New Benchmark

Changing the Landscape, the Final Report of the Canadian Panel on Violence Against Women (1993) is the quintessential example of biopolitical moral panic in survey research. Not worth touching, intellectually speaking, the CanPan report cannot be ignored for three reasons. First, there is already in progress a well-financed follow-up program which nobody quite knows how to stop, and which has dangerous public policy implications. Second, the report is instructive as the encyclopedic version of everything that is wrong with contemporary biofeminism. Third, it spells out in astonishing detail the biopolitical vision of a properly administered society.

In welcoming the report, the then minister responsible for the status of women, Mary Collins, listed with approval the top three grievances cited by women's groups over the years: "That violence against women in Canada is pervasive; that it is tolerated; and that violence is the most deplorable symptom of women's inequality" ("Minister Collins Calls Panel's Report 'Historic'"). These favoured myths constitute not the scientific conclusions of the Report, but rather its very premises; and they account for a number of the misleading strategies employed by the CanPan. Violence against women is singled out as deserving of more concern than the far greater volume of violence against male victims in our society. The picture of violence in our society is falsified by the colouring *out* of violence perpetrated *by* women against other women, men, children, and the elderly, in favour of a picture, in stark black and white, in which men damage women. The most serious problem, perhaps, is in the massive exaggeration of traumatic violence in the day-to-day lives of Canadian women; and we have to talk about *traumatic* force if we are to have any measure of the types of violent human experiences that merit concern. We should not sell Canadian adults and children on the lie that we are a dangerous society, and that fear or anger, much less calculating, government-sponsored repression, should circumscribe our prospects and experiences.

The consistent, and consistently ugly, falsification of complex human realities when observed through a biopolitical lens will not sustain attention for long. The report describes its focus as a deliberately "feminist lens" (CL, 3), subsuming thereby all feminism into its paranoid version of biofeminist panic. What this means is a way of thinking that considers violence against women to be built systematically into the social structure of Canadian society. All of our institutions stand indicted, and every individual man is held personally accountable and punishable, while women, as an oppressed group, are to be absolved, both individually and collectively, from any moral responsibility for anything they do. The race-thinking of the Nazis, and the class-thinking of the Stalinists and Maoists, earlier in this century, both stigmatized and set about morally (and to an inconceivable extent, physically) to annihilate the race scapegoat (the racially "inferior") and the class scapegoat (the class "alien"). The biofeminist lens of the panel and its government sponsors would drag us into a third episode of aggravated, collective insanity.

The work in the report is actually stunningly bad and does not stand much scrutiny. But the first reason I mention above for attending to it imposes relentlessly: 105 pages in the 439-page report are devoted to an "Action Program." The tide may turn against it before it gets off the ground. But it has the weight of government behind it, and once it gets rolling, it might just keep on snowballing. Let us not kid ourselves that an egregious report will necessarily fade away. The recent change of government is only a ripple on the surface of the biopolitical tide rolling in. Part of the panel's pioneering mandate was to collect information. But part of it, the Minister said, was "to produce a report containing recommendations for governments at all levels, the non-governmental sector, business, labour and other institutions, to end the violence. The Panel was to report back ... with a national action plan for the federal government, with time frames" (Collins 3).

The minister got what she and the women's groups had wanted. She claimed that the report establishes "a new benchmark in the history of women in Canada" (Collins 1). In a more sinister vein, the press release stressed that the dramatic changes envisioned in the nearly 500 recommendations of the report would "touch us all." The plan was for Status of Women Canada to begin work immediately on a "Framework for Gender Equality and Safety" to ensure that all the government's policies, programs, and legislation promote women's equality and safety, as proposed by the panel. Collins also planned to discuss the report and its recommendations with her provincial and territorial colleagues, and with representatives from the eight sectors of society mentioned in the panel's report, to work out their participation in the short- and long-term solutions that are needed to eliminate violence against women ("News Release" 1).

We do ourselves—I mean women and men in the 1990s—a great favour, and we pass on a great gift of love to future generations, if we say no to the twisted poisons of the Canadian Panel. We have to try to put a stop to its programmatic drive today if we are to live with ourselves tomorrow.

Media Pan the CanPan: Fatally Flawed

The panel was launched August 15, 1991, with nine panelists, all front-line workers connected with the clinical side of female battery, through either social or legal services.[1] Its work, which took two years, cost $10 million.[2] It held hearings in 139 communities over five months, received 4,000 submissions, and produced a map of Canada, called "A Landscape of Voices," in August 1992. It was adorned with a sampling of horror stories ("I was 18 months old when my father and two grandfathers started abusing me"; "I was married to Satan at the age of 7, and was raped after the ceremony"—see Vienneau, "Map charts landscape of horror"). There was also, besides an interim report in August 1992, a collection of testimonies called *Collecting the Voices: A Scrapbook*; a half-hour video-tape, *Without Fear*, the final report, *Changing the Landscape*; an executive summary; and a Community Action Kit. Status of Women Canada, which inherited the aftermath of the CanPan once the panel dissolved into thin air, is currently collecting responses to this last item.

The CanPan attracted an immense outpouring of press attention during its travels and travails. Much of it was favourable and expository during early data gathering (e.g. "Churches admit failings on violence"; "Sex offenders want help inmates tell violence panel"; "Women's prison teaches violence, federal panel told"; "Women urge panel to seek changes to the legal system"). In the second half of 1992, however, the media coverage was distracted from the contents of the hearings by the unfolding power struggle between the panel and the feminist groups criticizing it for being too white, too middle class and, more-over, too distanced from feminist groups (e.g. "Women threaten to boycott violence hearings"; "NAC delegates issue ultimatum"; "Fifth group turns back on panel"; "Feuding in the family"; "Infighting mars task force on violence").

The theme raised at this time, on behalf of organizations like the National Action Committee on the Status of Women (NAC), the DisAbled Women's Network of Canada (DAWN), the Congress of Black Women, the Canadian Association of Sexual Assault Centres, and the National Organization of Immigrant and Visible Minority Women was that the panel was not representative (of them). Furthermore, it was wasting its time gathering horror stories when the government should be moving to action. In other words, the male-perpetrated holocaust in women's lives was to be taken for granted, and the war crimes tribunals and social re-engineering should get going as soon as possible.

These same criticisms were raised again on publication of the panel's final report in July 1993, not only by feminist groups, but also by Liberal critics of the Tory government. Both groups wanted to stress that the Tories would not have the will to implement the recommendations. The release of the final report was attacked for its timing, in mid-summer, just before the federal elections of fall 1993, in which Kim Campbell and the Tories were virtually wiped out of Canadian politics. According to Liberal MP Mary Clancy, a member of the Parliamentary Status of Women Subcommittee that had recommended in 1991, in its *War Against Women* report, that the panel should be established: the report "isn't worth the powder to blow it to hell." Her party, including Liberal leader (now prime minister) Jean Chrétien, shares her view, she said; and "she would move swiftly to implement many of the panel's recommendations if her party wins the federal election" ("Violence against women report ignored"). In short, the advocacy group criticism means only that the advocates are demanding ever more will and muscle to implement a program.[3]

The opposite concern also surfaced in the press early (DiManno, "Issue of violence hijacked by those with wider aims"), but found little public echo at the time. As Laframboise ("Men also get stuck in a rut") and DiManno ("Let's get real on sex-assault") were to repeat again after the report's release, the panel's work suffers from two systematic and unacceptable distortions, which vitiate whatever value there might have been in its efforts. The first fatal flaw is that the panel's work is totalitarian. It uses violence "as a metaphor for everything these women and their 'men of good will' don't like about our society," including advertising, pornography, competitive sports, linguistic expressions, the books we read, the movies we watch, the education we get, the jokes we laugh at (see DiManno, "Issues of violence hijacked", and "Let's get real"). As a result, the "feminist lens" requires massive social engineering under the direct control of biofeminists in every institution from the churches and schools to the businesses and prisons, as well as frivolous and dishonest definitions of physical, sexual, psychological, financial, and spiritual violence against women. And it requires scapegoats.

This is the second fatal flaw in the panel's work. The panel considers violence against women "more obscene than violence against men" (DiManno, "Let's get real"). And yet men are the overwhelming victims not only of violence in Canada, but also of homelessness, suicide, and incarceration.[4] Those who fear violence most, as Statistics Canada discovered in 1988, are women and the elderly; but those who experience it most are young and male (Boyce, "Male victims ignored"). Pat Marshall, co-chair, makes much of studies that show that "women's fear is treble that of men." Rosie DiManno draws precisely the right conclusion: "Yes, we have done a good job of scaring the bejeezus out of girls and women" ("Hijacked" 1992).

The general press reaction to the final report was mixed, with a good portion fairly sceptical. There was Pat Marshall, saying that the report does not contain one "naive or unrealistic recommendation" (Vienneau, "Abuse of women at crisis level, panel says"). Other news items, citing excerpts from the alarming statistics, and from the 500 recommendations, often demonstrated that these excerpts were actually self-caricaturing. Men should promise not to be violent, give up their need for power and control, and practice cooperation instead of competition. Consumers should read books by women of all races. The police should collect DNA evidence from all people *accused* of sex offences to help identify offenders. Nobody should ever laugh at sexist or racist jokes (Vienneau, "Abuse" 1993). There were the boosters, like the *Toronto Star* editorial, which pre-emptively predicted a "backlash of resentment and hostility" from those who are not prepared to believe that "we have a national disease on our hands" ("National shame: violence to women"). There were ideological fans, who appreciated the panel for showing how "racism, sexism, classism, homophobia, discrimination were all interrelated" and how "even non-violent men derive many social and economic benefits from the violence perpetrated against women by other men" (Parkes, "Report on violence makes sense out of jigsaw puzzle"). Later, there were some who tried to use the Statistics Canada *Violence Against Women* study, released three months thereafter, as a confirmation of the panic approach (Burrt, "Nielsen should open his eyes"; Riley, "Numbers don't lie, and neither do victims").

Still, the numbers looked to many as though they *were* lying, and the report was considered not only "misanthropic" (DiManno, "Let's get real"), but also wildly overreaching in its proposals for changing attitudes and behaviour in every sector of society (Fischer, "Violence Against Women: By asking for everything, women may gain little"). Many stories highlighted the sensational conclusions that 98% of Toronto women have suffered sexual violation; that two out of three women have been sexually assaulted; and that 51% of women over the age of 16, and 24% of girls under the age of 16, have been victims of rape or attempted rape (Boyle, "Report on Violence: 98% of Metro women suffer sexual violation, panel says"). These figures simply did not ring true, and the panel lost sensible moderates. For example, "National Affairs" columnist Carol Goar wrote: "Pat Marshall, co-chair of the panel said the study merely proved how blind Canadians are to the violence around them. But even her most sympathetic listeners had trouble believing a message that contradicted what their eyes, their ears and their friends were telling them. Their doubts were warranted ... [The panel] damaged its own credibility, let down the women who appeared before it and squandered a historic opportunity" ("Panel on Violence Against Women lost numbers game").

The panel, of course, loved the big numbers. The bigger the better. It is an intriguing feature of the psychopathology of the violence panic that its advocates and promoters delight in presenting ever-higher numbers as evidence of the ever-greater victimization of women. There is no relief from good news; no good news in no news. Only the very worst appeals to the morbid imagination of biofeminist advocacy. This syndrome runs through the distorted work of both the panel and its sources. In the case of the 98% figure, for example, the panel went out of its way to insist that "this finding, in particular, clearly supports our assertion that violence against women affects virtually all women's lives" (CL 10).

The panel's most basic working assumption, quite overtly spelled out in the report, is that a man always has power over a woman, in intimate, sexual, and social matters. Men exercise their power over women, with the help of violence, "in any social context where contact between women and men occurs" (CL 25). They assert (contrary to all reputable evidence) that family violence is "overwhelmingly violence against women" by men (7) and that there is even more violence against women outside families. In fact, seen through the biofeminist lens, "violence against women is socially structured" (6). Girls don't grow up to be abusers (39), and if they occasionally do, it is the result of patriarchal conditions; meanwhile, all men, violent or not, benefit from the system of woman abuse (6).

What are the consequences of this notion that patriarchy abuses women? A biopolitical double standard. To quote the report, "individual and social factors" cannot be allowed to serve as excuses for men, each of whom "must take personal responsibility for his violence" (39). At the same time, "we flatly reject any analyses that place any degree of responsibility for violence on the women themselves no matter what their actions, appearance, demeanour or behaviour" (4). This extraordinary principle saturates the report, giving it a crazy intensity and consistency. Original sin has been transferred to a long patriarchal chain stretching from the first father to the pathetic but ubiquitous contemporary fiction known only as the "male abuser." The world of humanity is seen as radically fallen, but the fall is now biologically rent into male sinners and female sinned-against. Period.

Getting with the Program: Testimony Abuse

Some of the media, across the country from the Maritimes to Victoria, were sceptical of the CanPan analysis, of its many incoherent, uneducated, and ill-considered recommendations, and of the numbers that were meant to justify an action program (see Strauss, Fraser, Byfield, Ney, Boyce, Goar, Laframboise, DiManno). It turns out that they were not sceptical enough. I will offer below some highlights from my own encounter with the shoddy work of the panel, whose findings crumble in the face of close critical scrutiny.

The final report combines its arguments with a barrage of statistics and a sampling of witnessing. It is sprinkled with anonymous quotations in purple ink, which provide a sampling of testimony from women who told their stories. The emotional fallout from these individual cases of atrocities is generalized to the whole female population through the extrapolation of abuse statistics: every woman is at risk. The stories of women who form part of a clinical population—women who are in psychiatric institutions, women's prisons, battery shelters, or work centres for the developmentally disabled, and women who are clients of rape-crisis centres, legal services, or medical facilities—are expanded to and identified with the lives and prospects of all women in the Canadian population as a whole.

This false reasoning, identified earlier as the "clinical fallacy," conceals the fact that the profiles of badly damaged, often chronic, cases, are not the same as the profiles of the majority of the population. The large numbers in statistics allegedly applying to the whole population are never collected with the same definitions that describe the stories of the wounded, who appeal to us from the depths of their savage mistreatment. The lacerated clinical population is, of course, deserving of support and compassion. But those who exploit their stories to suit the agendas of biopolitics are doing them a disservice and risk turning public sympathy to public allergy.

The culprit here, as elsewhere, is the biofeminist *continuum* theory, which holds that biology is destiny and that all women share not the "human condition" but, on the contrary, a "woman condition" (CL 59). All acts alleged to be against women—from flirting to aggravated, mutilating rape, from verbal disagreement to physical torture—are considered the same act: "violence against women." Statistics are used falsely to spread the worst experiences to all Canadian women. The atrocity stories are used to taint the general condition of Canadian women with the feel of dramatic horror. The result of this linking all women into one essential woman, and of seeing all social and sexual acts as one essential act of patriarchal male violence against women, is the dividing of women and men from each other, essentially and irremediably. This is a falsehood about women, about men, and about Canadian society; and the only option it leaves open is Pat Marshall's "federally financed revolution."

The panel has issued a 25-minute video called "Without Fear," executive produced by Breakthrough Films and Television, written by Rachel Low and directed by Aerlyn Weissman. Not since the notorious *Not a Love Story*, created in 1981 by Bonnie Klein for the National Film Board's Studio D, has there been such a manipulative film peddled for general consumption as a public service. The only apparent purpose of "Without Fear" is the creation of fear, in the tradition of classic propaganda movies like the anti-marijuana *Reefer Madness*. Unlike the earlier model, however, this movie combines dramatizations with the testimony of six female victims, and a lot of scare statistics.

The six women who are exploited in this movie as symbols of woman abuse were introduced to the panel during its consultation tours. Their stories disclose that their husbands attempted to murder them by drowning, savage beatings, shooting in the face; they were raped in childhood, and continually violated in adulthood. The stories are appalling; the women are likeable "survivors." One of them, Karen Jean Braun, was a feminist activist before her episode of spousal abuse, and she has resurfaced as an activist against violence. She is one of the panel's *stars*: she stands out in the video; her story is sprinkled throughout the final report; and her account is printed in full and at length as the lead evidence in the panel's selection of testimonies, *Collecting the Voices: A Scrapbook.*

These six stories are intercut in the video with dramatizations—for example, the popular but completely unfounded sports violence scenario, where sports fans, enraged by their team's loss, beat their wives.[5] The dramatizations and testimonies are further intercut with statistics which, according to the *Facilitator's Guide,* are "used throughout these sequences to underline the reality of this violence in Canada" (6). Viewers are to be frightened by false statistics popular in the biofeminist lexicon, such as: "One in two women has been the victim of rape or attempted rape" (see discussion in chapter VI of the way the Women's Safety Project got this figure); "55% of Canadian women say they fear walking home alone at night on their streets" (see discussion in chapter II of the misleading process through which Statistics Canada arrives at a number like this); "62% of reported assaults against women take place in the home" (see chapter II, on the subject of the Ontario Women's Directorate; assault here is chiefly "touching").

In segment 14, the video quotes from Linda MacLeod, well known for her exaggerated speculations on the scope of battered women in Canada (around a million): "The death of one woman is a tragedy. The death of one hundred becomes a statistic" (*Guide* 19). And the video tells us, quite soberly, that two women are murdered by their husbands every week. That's a hundred a year, but they don't mention that far more women die from bronchitis or influenza. Segment 17 ends the video on this note: "We got to do something to stop this. Whatever it takes." Viewers are referred to the National Action Plan, which "calls upon you, your community and your governments ..." (*Guide* 27).

The panel expects this video to be used for discussion by students, unions, professionals, government departments, women's organizations, teachers, associations, corporations, non-governmental organizations, and community and volunteer organizations. It recommends, furthermore, that its *Facilitator's Guide* should be included in school and university curricula "in all disciplines from social work to engineering" (*Guide* 3). It is available from the National Film Board, it has been screened on television, and it is evidently part of a wide national campaign that is far more imposing than a scholarly article or even a single survey that flashes into the public perception briefly, and then moves on to the data banks to await occasional retrieval.

The final report itself displays a similarly manipulated montage of materials. In the case of a tendentious public report on the basis of which policy recommendations are to be considered by government authorities, it is of the utmost importance that the document be open to public scrutiny, and that its findings be clear, convincing, and verifiable. Instead, the report throws around numbers and witness transcriptions in a higgledy-piggledy fashion that has the effect of overwhelming the reader with the virtual truth of both probability (statistics) and authenticity (personal testimony). Unless this information reveals itself to scrutiny as reliable and valid, its virtual truth remains a pseudo-truth, subordinated to potentially fake argument. In this case, the reader has no easy time following up on anything.

I got interested first in the testimonies. The report says that the italicized purple print scattered throughout the text transcribes the "voices of women" who spoke to the panel. "Their words—unadorned, unedited—tell the story more effectively than volumes of explanation, exhortation and interpretation" (CL 3). This leads one to wonder what *"the* story" can be, and how it can be established that self-selected, volunteer reports are valid beyond the individuals whose personal stories they are. But a prior question is where, indeed, are these stories to be found. After all, the panel gives only short paragraphs, out of context and out of sequence: fragments of stories. At least they are "unadorned, unedited." To a technical mind, chopping stories into pieces is already editing them, but reading the assurance more generously, one supposes the panel means something like verbatim, unchanged, just as the women spoke them and wrote them.

I wondered how many women: did each passage represent a different woman, or were some voices represented by more than one of these fragments? (I was not looking for individual identities, of course, but only for some way to match fragments of witnessing with whole persons.) My research assistant and I tried to find out about this, but the panel had disbanded, and the panelists were unavailable. We faxed Pat Marshall twice, to set up a time when we could talk to her by phone, but we never received a response. After some digging, the trail led to Status of Women Canada.

The office of Sheila Finestone, Liberal minister responsible for the status of women, referred us to Cathy McRae, Chief of Public Environment Analysis in StatsCan's Communications Directorate. McRae was on holiday, but we were able to reach her on her return and she was as helpful as she could be. Nobody else had ever asked for an attribution list, and, in fact, she was unable to find one. What she sent us instead was the twice 66-page book of samples (in English and French) that the CanPan had put out in December 1992 (her sense of a date; the publication itself is undated): *Collecting the Voices: A Scrapbook.* The *Scrapbook* says that it contains the voices of women "in their original form" (1). But there is a wide latitude in the interpretation of this: there are handwritten notes submitted to the panel; notes taken by members of the panel and secretariat, "reflecting various approaches by various notetakers," letters "reproduced in their original form," except for identifiers, and three lengthy written submissions, "in somewhat edited versions" (2). The horror is indisputable, but the CanPan does not make things easy for anyone who wants to understand the materials rather than just gag on them. One does not know what one is dealing with here, any more than in the report.

Many of the quotations in the section labelled "Transcribing the Voices," under the heading "Naming the Violence," are acontextual. One has no idea if all the quotations are from different women or just one. Often these are very brief: "I will always be afraid that nobody will believe me"; "My parents still don't know and I can't tell them"; "I'm from a small community. I have been harassed by a doctor since I was 15, I'm 23 now. Since then, five more of his victims have come to light. I was raped twice, at 16 and 18. I'm scared of all forms of control over me" (43). This last story shows up in the CanPan report, in italicized purple print, at the head of a section on "Sexual Abuse Involving Breach of Trust," followed by this: "The panel's hearings left little doubt that sexual abuse involving breach of trust is pervasive in Canada. Many of the perpetrators are members of self-regulatory professions such as medicine, dentistry and law" (CL 239). This section has not a single footnote or reference to any study or statistic to support its contention that "there has been a recognition that a more stringent level of safeguard must be imposed on self-regulating professions" (CL 240).

Many of the responses in the *Scrapbook* have been truncated to the point where they lack meaning. For example, in the section labelled "Draft Material," under the heading "Things to Change" (52), all we get is: "Denial: public, parents, police." Another kind of inexplicable peculiarity is in the form of the letters themselves. Several hand-written letters have been included, presumably to authenticate the *Scrapbook*, and make the women's voices seem more "real." However, this publication is produced in two parts, one French and one English. Both parts contain the same materials. Both versions are the same in content, though some grammatical or spelling errors in the one are not reproduced in the other. In two of the English-language letters, the handwriting changes wildly, from one place to another, to two different styles in one case (25, 26, 33). Evidently, the "original, hand-written" submissions have been hand-written in the other language by someone working under the direction of the panel. This little artistic licence is not identified anywhere.

What is more troubling is that there is no indication anywhere of how extensive the editing has been. The first three lengthy letters, which are said to be "edited versions" contain no ellipses or brackets to signal where. What is worse, this *Scrapbook* material, said to be in its "original form," does not match well with the purple fragments in the CanPan's final report, though those are described as "unedited, unadorned." Where it is possible to match up a fragment from the report with an item in the *Scrapbook*, there are significant and numerous changes to punctuation and paragraphing, as well as to content.

In one case, a four-page letter in the *Scrapbook* from a deeply, possibly clinically disturbed individual (14-17) is truncated and compressed into one purple paragraph in the report (CL 46). There is evidence in the full letter that would suggest caution in assessing its contents. These include references to herself as two or more people, unique personal systems of reference, and the erratic, fantastic organization of exotic material. The panel omits large chunks of the letter, mixes up the order of the words and sentences, tidies up the prose, and puts the whole thing together in such a manner as to make the author of the letter sound like a rational survivor of some horrible things. The context is one of ritual abuse, gang rape, buying and selling people, cannibalism, sodomy, group sex, human sacrifice.

Look at some of the changes (italics added in each case). The woman's letter begins: "My abuse started *at birth*, no noise was allowed in our house, no crying not even from a baby." The CanPan's purple excerpt starts: "My ritual abuse began *when I was 7 or 8.*" The letter reads: "The cross was inserted in my vagina, making me ready for a higher position." In the CanPan fragment: "A cross was inserted into my vagina *at these ceremonies,* making me ready for a higher position" There are numerous other discrepancies; the body of the letter is about inner perceptions, which the panel simply omits. Into her list of abuse suffered, from molestation to breeding a child for later sacrifice, the panel introduces the additional abuse of "being photographed." And the woman never says she is or has been in a hospital. In fact, she says she currently has a job and is bettering her education. She does say that she does *not* need hospitalization: "I don't need to be hospitalized with drugs and shock treatment to help me live." The CanPan fabricates the following, however: "I spent most of my time in and out of hospitals."

In the end, the CanPan concludes that ritual abuse "urgently requires recognition in Canada" (45). The section on ritual abuse appears to rely entirely on the testimony of patients under treatment for "multiplicity," and it does not make reference to a single publication or any hard evidence that ritual abuse is any more a reality, much less a widespread reality, than the "snuff movies" to which reference *is* made in the same section in one of the purple passages (CL 46). In all of this, it is hard to avoid a sense that the evidence is being tampered with, and this casts suspicion over the rest of the "voices" in the report.

Since the CanPan did not include in the *Scrapbook* all the original letters, submissions, and testimonies which it received, it is impossible to know in what ways it may have tampered with the other things it was given. On the other hand, not everything that is actually collected in the *Scrapbook* found its way into the report. At the same time, *some* material is used more than once. The first letter in the *Scrapbook* is used in the report at least six times; in fact, it is quoted five times in four pages (CL 30-34).[6] The text gives the impression that different stories, with different male perpetrators, are accumulating toward a massive volume. But the same one husband is responsible for all the crimes alleged in these six fragments. Without an attribution list, one cannot allay a suspicion, formed on the basis of the use to which this letter is put, that the testimony on the pages of the CanPan report might be attributable to a small number of women.

One Cracked Lens

When all is said and done, the CanPan's work leaves us *not* knowing what is going on. The panel has not actually done any research of its own. It has consulted volunteers, asked some questions, and conducted a literature review. It has gathered a variety of studies that were susceptible to being taken out of their own context and to being recontextualized by the biofeminist "lens" of resentful polarization. The panel actually uses the available research to obscure and cloud the reality of women and men.

First, it *overstates the drama of women* by carelessly mixing apples and oranges. Most of the public quite rightly do not think that we need crisis centres for verbal and psychological conflicts, for spiritual or economic frictions, for grievances about language, humour, or other new thought crimes and crimes of expression, or even for things like unwanted looking at the beach or unwanted touching at youth dances, which together make up the bulk of the statistics used to victimize the general female population and to indict the general male population.[7]

Second, the panel *forgets about men.* I am referring to more than the fact that the panel does not take into any consideration the research evidence that interactive abuse is actually a two-way street, and that many men are in fact victims of brutal violence from women, as well as from other men. The ideological and statistical drive of the panel is simply and obsessively narcissistic on behalf of women. It makes an implicit *uniqueness* claim. For example, much of what the panel says in chapter 7 on the vulnerabilities of the disabled, including the economic disadvantages of disability, and the barriers to independent living that are found in education, the labour market, health care, and the law, applies equally to men, but is not so applied in the report. Its conclusion, in what amounts to the casual brutality of careless self-involvement, is simply that "women with disabilities continually receive the message that they are merely tolerated" (CL 70).

In chapter 6, when the panel talks about homelessness, it laments only the plight of homeless women, though these women make up only a fraction of the homeless population of men and women (CL 64). Likewise, one of the gross errors in chapter 14, on Inuit women, is the assumption that the problems mentioned are uniquely women's problems. The problems detailed in the sections on housing, education, employment, health and health facilities, alcohol and substance abuse, suicide, the media, elder abuse, abuse of trust, and customary adoption may apply equally, if not in greater proportion, to Inuit men. It is hard to see how the effort thus to divide disadvantaged populations of men and women on sectarian biopolitical lines can do any good for the cause of those populations.

Thirdly, the panel compounds its partial blindness by adding to it an egregious *double standard*. Where it notices men at all, it wants to punish them. In chapter 15, the report's premise is that aboriginal women in conflict with the law are not responsible for their actions. Their "prison sentence is the final act of violence imposed on them by a society that has oppressed them since birth" (CL 161). In addition, according to the panel, "women often serve a longer period of their sentence in prison than do men" (162). Prison "is not the answer for Aboriginal women; for many it is a death sentence" (162). It is clear to the panel that aboriginal women must have an alternative justice system just for them (162), based on the principle of healing, within the context of their own culture; a good start is the new jail for women in Fort Smith, which is basically a community centre.

Jail for men, on the other hand, is "like a holiday," according to one of the panel's interviewees. Men in jail just play softball and "live like kings" (168). And while there should be a whole separate justice system for aboriginal women, the cultural background of aboriginal men "should not be considered in determining whether or not to lay criminal charges" (169). In a bizarre turnaround, the panel finds itself arguing that if aboriginal men's cultural background were considered a factor by law enforcers, that would constitute "systemic racism because different standards of treatment are applied to Aboriginal people than to non-Aboriginal people" (169). Nevertheless, aboriginal women should have special services which are attuned to *their* cultural differences. Moreover, crimes against aboriginal women and children must be considered more serious than crimes against men: "Aboriginal women oppose lenient sentencing for Aboriginal male sex offenders whose victims are women and children (169)." In the end, in chapter 18 on the legal system, the panel extends this double standard with one stroke to all women and men: "Women who have committed crimes need healing models identical to other women ... They have more in common with other women than with male perpetrators of crime" (224).

These sections are excellent demonstrations of the staggering weakness of biopolitics in the face of social issues. It refuses to treat them as *social* issues, preferring to make them into issues based essentially on some ineluctable feature of nature or biology. The divisiveness in this mindset induces an inflationary desperation, and calls forth infectious delusions of alarmed perception and panic response. The biofeminist lens is cracked. That this blindness in one eye destroys the panel's depth perception is beyond doubt. It vitiates the entire report, and any sense of due proportion which is needed for the formation of policy. It is an object lesson in both ethics and practical social reasoning. Any insistence on unequal compassion, on setting up a competition of suffering, with predetermined favourites, corrupts compassion and discredits the distorted claims advanced on its behalf. Corrupt compassion gets in the way of community.

V
The Ones that Got Away: the CanPan Goes Fishing

"The first word," she said, "is 'bandaged and wounded.'" ... "Run together," she said. We mentally reviewed the great themes in the light of the word or words, "bandaged and wounded." "How is it that bandage precedes wound?" (Donald Barthelme, Snow White 59)

CanPan Fragments: Researching for Panic

In the previous chapter, I discussed the conceptual premises that undermine the CanPan's final report. A pressing question still remains, however: what about the figures? My own attempts to investigate the panel's scandalous approach to research have left me disturbed about the deceptive statistics it has unleashed on an unsuspecting public. In this and the following chapter, I investigate a few of the more dramatic numbers, to show that not one of them can make a claim to general reliability and validity. Nor do they mean what is claimed or implied for them by the panel.

Aboriginal Women and Panic Statistics (Chapter 15)

The panel uses a number of different statistics to convey "the pervasiveness of violence against Aboriginal women and children" (CL 156). They show no awareness of the nature of the original studies from which they take their figures, and not the least concern that these studies cannot support the case that the panel builds by casual reference to them. Without appropriate evidence, often on the most casual basis, the panel holds up a mirror to this community that can only sow the seeds of desperation and division. For example: "A study by the Ontario Native Women's Association found that eight out of 10 Aboriginal women had personally experienced violence. Of those women, 87 percent had been injured physically and 57 percent had been sexually abused" (CL 156).

The ONWA study is cited six times in the chapter. On consulting it, one finds that it takes as its premise the idea that violence in aboriginal communities is caused by the Canadian government and patriarchy (ONWA 8), though individual men are to be held responsible for their actions (ONWA 9). The questionnaire ONWA developed for this study was distributed to women "via the network of our local affiliates" (ONWA 13). That is, to feminists, and to women who were already abused and seeking social services. This makes for a biased and unrepresentative sample group. Furthermore, although 680 questionnaires were distributed, the total number of fully or partially completed questionnaires received and collected was 104. This (15%) response rate is very small, and far below the 60-85% desirable for reliable representativity in a random sample.

In addition to the questionnaire, the ONWA conducted consultations by telephone (127) and personal interview (40). These contacts were made through organizations such as transition houses, crisis centres, the police, etc. No men were interviewed or invited to fill out questionnaires. The most interesting aspect of this questionnaire is that it is not based on personal experiences, but rather on witnessing. A typical question is "Does Family Violence occur in your community? Yes/No/Don't Know" (ONWA Appendix 1). Only one question asks, in a very general way, about personal experience: "Have you personally ever experienced Family Violence? (Appendix 1)" Also, the definition of violence includes mental and emotional "violence," which "is when someone believes they are going to be hurt because of threats or gestures and it is when someone feels depressed, hopeless or even suicidal because another member of the family continues to put them down, and has convinced them that they are no good, useless, or always wrong" (Appendix 1).

Here is something else: "The suicide rate among aboriginal women is more than double the national average for other Canadian women" (CL 179, 186). This is from a decent study in 1990 by Catherine McBride and Ellen Bobet for the Department of Indian Affairs and Northern Development, called *Health of Indian Women*. They use data from respected organizations such as Statistics Canada. The panel cites the study 5 times in this chapter. What is interesting here is that the CanPan twice cites the same fact from this document, about the suicide rate among aboriginal women, without ever acknowledging the preceding contextualizing sentence, which is as follows:

"Women are less likely to commit suicide than men: in the Indian populations, the female suicide rate is about one-quarter the male rate" (McBride and Bobet 11). The male aboriginal suicide rate is therefore not only significantly higher than the rate for aboriginal women, but also more than double the rate for all Canadian men.

Some of the most distressing information about the prevalence of woman and child abuse comes from the *National Family Violence Abuse Study/Evaluation* (NFVAS), conducted in 1991 by Claudette Dumont-Smith and Pauline Sioui Labelle for Aboriginal Nurses of Canada. The study itself, like that by ONWA, was about witnessing experiences rather than personal experiences. Its claim to being a "national" study is quite limited. For a start, its 9.5% response (203 of 2,126 questionnaires returned) is very low. Furthermore, the sample is far from representative, consisting as it does of the following: courtworkers, police officers, social workers, treatment-centre workers, band-employed nurses, regional nursing officers, non-Native nurses (by request only), and community health representatives. *There was no attempt to reach Native women themselves.* Most importantly, the definition of violence is extremely broad, including material and financial exploitation, neglect, and such psychological and emotional factors as belittling, degrading, not showing love, intimidating, insulting, pressuring, destroying property, expressing jealousy.

Despite these limitations, the panel, impressed by the shocking numbers reported in the NFVAS, simply quotes from it without qualification. On page 150 of the report, the NFVAS is cited for four different figures, only one of which refers to the NFVAS's own research. The three others come from studies noted in this study's literature review. Let us look at these three, and how information finds its way from the NFVAS study into the panel's report:

1) "A study entitled *Native Women's Needs Assessment Survey* (Riddell 1986), conducted in the London, Ont. urban area and Oneida reserve populations, reveals that

71% of the urban sample and 48% of the reserve sample experience assault. Current or past partners are responsible for the abuse" (NFVAS 18).

2) "In an article called 'Dragging Wife Abuse Out of the Closet' (*Wawatay News*, November, 1989), it is estimated that between 75% and up to 90% of the women are battered in some northern Indian communities" (NFVAS 18).

3) "Daily (*Windspeaker*, 7, No. 2, 1989: p.12) estimates that up to 90% of aboriginal families are touched by child abuse and substance abuse. In the Northwest Territories a survey finds that 80% of girls less than eight years of age are sexually molested and 50% of boys are also sexually abused (Ibid)" (NFVAS 25).

Did the panel actually consult these sources before borrowing the information about them from the capsule citations in the NFVAS? Did it form an independent judgment on the validity of the numbers that it would use to raise alarm? It is hard to believe. In the case of these three, only the document by Riddell is even included in the bibliography of the National Family Violence survey; there is no further information about the other two sources.

Riddell's NWNAS was difficult to locate, but it did turn up, finally, and only by chance, uncatalogued, in the resources of the Ontario Women's Directorate. Jane Riddell and Pauline Doxtator's study was prepared for the Women's Education and Research Foundation in 1986, with the intention of serving as the first study of the experiences of battered aboriginal women. They hoped to get a random sample of women from the reserves near London. However, only 19 women agreed to be interviewed of the 200 to be sampled. The authors state, therefore, that "the response was too poor to draw any concrete conclusions about prevalence" (NWNAS 13). They added 45 self-selected volunteers from the reserves, and got another 105 interviews by advertising in aboriginal centres in the city of London. Their attempt to get 35 health-care professionals as well yielded only 18 more questionnaires.

It took a year to interview the 169 women. The questionnaire used a CTS type of scale, and included verbal forms of abuse along with physical and sexual. The NWNAS offers the 71% and 48% composite figures for their self-selected London, Ontario, group. What these figures mean is that a total of 106 women in and around London were voluntarily self-identified as battered, under a set of definitions that include some form of possibly quite mild, verbal, physical, or sexual unpleasantness. The authors note a number of times in the study that no reliable statistics on prevalence were generated by their project. The panel reports none of this—not sample bias, not definitions, not disclaimers—only the numbers.

The second reference, the article in *Wawatay,* proved impossible to find. Did the panel actually get it? Should it have mentioned how obscure this was? We checked the Native Studies Department at Trent University, the Peterborough Friendship Centre, two other friendship centres, the Sexual Assault Support and Information Centre, a couple of band offices, various libraries, and other organizations. All without success.

The third reference is the article in *Windspeaker,* the source of the dramatic information that 80% of girls and 50% of boys under 8 are sexually molested. This figure started us on a fascinating investigative trail, which provides indispensable insight into the complexity of communities, the problematical nature of social studies, the fragility and impermanence of evidence, and the venality of panic sensationalism. To begin with, the article was written not by Daily, as the NFVAS had it, nor even by Brenda Daley, in the CanPan's inexplicable correction of the reference. Its author was actually Elaine O'Farrell. Quite evidently, the CanPan did not go to the source materials for these fantastic and frightening numbers. The numbers appealed to their perverse biopolitical agenda, and they grabbed them. Well, it turns out that the

O'Farrell piece is not the source of the figures either. It refers us back down to a fourth level: CanPan, to NFVAS, to O'Farrell in *Windspeaker,* to a Northwest Territories child-sexual-abuse study that O'Farrell refers to but never names.

According to O'Farrell, the study was co-sponsored by the NWT Native Women's Association and the NWT Social Services Department. We phoned her at *Windspeaker,* but she is no longer working there. A secretary there said that she would get the editors to call, but no one from the publication has ever done so. We phoned the NWT Social Services Department, and spoke to Robert O'Rourke, who takes care of matters pertaining to child sexual abuse. He could not immediately recall the study, and then thought that perhaps he had heard something about it. He could not remember any details, and certainly could not suggest where to look for it. He said he had checked all the records and information in his department, and was sure it was not there.

We got in touch with the NWT Native Women's Association, the other co-sponsor, and spoke with Michelle Boon. She said that she had heard vaguely of the report, but that it was no longer in their records. She thought it had been lost during a move. We phoned Alice Hill, the former executive director of the NWT NWA. We seemed to be in luck. She actually recalled the report, and said that it was in a red folder in the NWA office, titled something like *The Delta Study on Child Sexual Abuse.* She said, however, that at some point the Social Services Department had decided to withhold the report from the public. We wondered why. She said she did not know. She was sure that it was still in the NWA office; she said that when she left, she had entrusted it to Helen Hudson-McDonald, former president of the NWA.

So, we called the NWA back, but once again they said that they thought the report had been lost. We called Ms. Hudson-McDonald, who was no longer with the NWA, and left messages. When she kindly returned the call, she said that she vaguely recalled the study, but would have to look through her files over the weekend in order to locate it. She said she would get back to us in three days. She did, had not found the report, but agreed to search further. We eventually received from Michelle Boon the proceedings of the first conference held in the N.W.T. on child abuse, "Communities' Voice on Child Sexual Abuse" (1989). The Proceedings contained a talk by Mary Beth Levan *about* the study, which she (and unnamed others) had conducted for the NWA and the Ministry of Social Services in the summer of 1988.

The conference account, which gives fair detail about the study, shows that it was a laborious interview of a small sample of about 50 people in six communities within the Delta and Sahtu regions. Levan and others interviewed the few people in service agencies and native organizations who were willing to speak to them about child sexual abuse, as well as adult survivors of child sexual assault, and offenders under treatment. They worked from a standard questionnaire that is not described in the account. The picture presented is strictly anecdotal. The RCMP charge at most one or two people a month. "Generally the perception, outside of the number of charges that were made, was that there was a great deal of it going on ... Victims and offenders themselves say that it happens a lot" (Levan 29). The interviewers also heard, however, that "it doesn't happen here" and the elders and leaders expressed "a genuine sense of disbelief" (31). In spite of this, Levan guesses at the figure eventually picked up by the panel. Her anecdotal source for the 80%-50% figures for the sexual abuse of young girls and boys under the age of 8 is the "estimate" provided by the "offenders themselves and most of the service agencies that had direct contact with this particular crime" (Levan 30).

We called Mary Beth Levan in the Northwest Territories to ask if she could provide us with the original report on which her conference account was based. She could not. "I don't have a clean copy of the study," she said, having passed it along to the Social Services Department. She thought perhaps they had decided not to circulate it because it painted too negative a picture. We asked if she knew that the study was cited, in a roundabout way, in the final report of the panel? She said that she did not know, but she hoped they knew that the figures in her study were "just estimates," "scraped together" from a few community health nurses.

Did the panel know or care that it was printing "guesti-mates" based on limited information as though they were scientific fact applicable to a whole native population? Could they or should they have known? Which is more irresponsible: to vacuum up any and all scary data into their fear machine, without attempting to verify the sources? Or to consult the actual sources, discover their obvious limits, and cite them anyway, without contextual-izing their weaknesses?

Quite recently, we did receive a copy of the original report from Mary Beth Levan herself. She generously appended some additional source materials. It turns out that the study was conducted in the summer and fall of 1988 by the Native Women's Association, under contract with the Department of Social Services of the NWT gov-ernment. The report, called "Needs Assessment Study for Victims and Perpetrators of Sexual Abuse in the Inuvik Region," was prepared in October 1988 by Levan, acting for K'alemi Consultants, and by Marja van Nieuwen-huyzen, of the Native Women's Association at the Inuvik Training Centre. The latter suggested the list of inter-viewees, who in turn suggested others. In all, the 45 interviews consisted of 5 RCMP, 6 social workers, 3 health nurses, 2 doctors, 1 school counsellor, 5 elders, 6 counsel-lors, 9 clinicians, 5 victims and offenders, and 3 people in native organizations.

What the study shows is that front-line service workers in the field believe there is a problem that needs attention. It also reveals, even more clearly than the conference account, that it would be unwarranted to take any of the figures at face value, and quite irresponsible to generalize them to the population at large. It turns out that the RCMP only prosecute 1-3 cases a year (2)! All the rest of the numbers are based on anecdotes and extrapolations, resting, in turn, on an assumption that is standard in this field, that most offences are unreported. It is a long way, however, from an annual official incidence of 1-3 charges to a sexual-abuse prevalence rate of 80% of all young girls and 50% of all young boys. The people who thought that "there's a lot of it going on" were the community-health nurses (3). Their hardest data was that 5% of reported venereal disease infections were in children under 14. Each nurse also knew personally of a few incidents and had heard of a few more.

The most inflammatory figure, as it turns out, comes from a single medical person, who arrived at it strictly from seeing his patients. According to the study: "One doctor, who has practiced in the Delta for several years, estimated that 80% of all young girls (under 8) were abused either with fondling, exhibitionism, and/or sexual intercourse ... This doctor estimates that 50% of the young male population is offended against—usually by older teenage boys (4). Alcohol counsellors meanwhile report a high level of victimization among their clients, and say that "often males report having been assaulted by older females, e.g. mothers and sisters" (5). How often is not revealed, nor what percentage of the population are alcoholics treated by counsellors. The school counsellor speculates, on the basis of "children exhibiting symptoms that could be linked to child abuse"—like failing grades, adult-like work behaviour, and unresponsiveness—that the incidence of abuse "affects up to 45% of the children in the community" (5-6). She says she "understood that in earlier days" father-daughter sex was considered acceptable if the mother was ill. The elders, however, say that sexual abuse "was not part of pre-colonial culture," although "its growing prevalence" is shocking (6).

The rest of the picture emerges in the same way. The native organization personnel, "while they didn't have exact numbers ... agreed that a large percentage of children in the settlements were victims of abuse" (6-7). Social workers give details from their own caseload which "serve to portray the nature of the problem," say the authors of the study. For example: "Male children under 11 have, under the direction of older boys, been raping women 'passed out' from alcohol." Or, "five children were 'indoctrinated' into a range of sexual activities by two older teenage girls." In one community, "there is reportedly a game called 'hunt and fuck,' where groups of teenage boys cruise the settlement at night looking for a female to rape." And, reportedly, in another community, there is a game where "younger boys race and the winner performs oral sex on the older boy in return for alcohol and gifts" (7-8). Family and psychiatric counsellors also report evidence pointing to widespread childhood sex (8-10), as do the offenders and victims interviewed (11).

Interestingly, there is a double projection: both a sense of the pervasiveness of the activity, and also that individuals are shunned and scorned if their involvement becomes known (9). Indeed, the authors argue that "public awareness itself acts as a prohibiting agent for offenders" (12). But if the activity is pervasive at the level of 50%-80%, how does the community come to be so disapproving of it? There is no explanation for this tension in the account. Likewise, there is a sense, reported by both the school counsellor and the clinicians, that "there was less of a taboo against it in the past" (9) but that there is now an increasing modern guilt and shame (6, 9). This historical pattern of changing boundaries of normality is not explored in the study, but clearly must be on the agenda of any serious cultural review of a situation that is currently being addressed only as a moral and criminal pathology. The cycle of depression-alcohol-sex-suicide is also one that calls out for social attention and remedy in a context that is far different from the biofeminist formulas.

What is most interesting is the aftermath of the study. The study was never published, nor was it released to the media. The Department of Social Services suppressed it, for reasons unknown. The way in which it became publicly known, nevertheless, was through Mary Beth Levan's account of it a few months after its submission, at the January 24-26, 1989 child-sexual-abuse conference in Yellowknife. The conference was planned by a large committee that included community and government representatives, the two sponsors of the study among them. The day after the conference, the story and the biggest numbers—the ones the panel uses—were all over the broadcast media like the CBC, as well as the front pages of regional and national newspapers (e.g. "8 in 10 native girls sexually abused, study finds," *Toronto Star*; "Sex abuse hits 80% of Arctic girls under eight," *Edmonton Journal*). The headlines never mentioned the boys, although the copy did. The story went out over the wires of the Canadian Press.

This much the panel perhaps knew. Why did it pay no attention to the rest of the story? At the time, then minister of social services Jeannie Marie-Jewell reprimanded reporters for their coverage of the consultant's report, and dismissed the stories as inaccurate. The numbers were mere estimates by a Mackenzie Delta physician, and no evidence has been produced to support them. The victims were not identified as native or non-native; and moreover, conditions in the Delta communities that were studied do not necessarily reflect conditions in the western Arctic. Besides, there were only 45 interviewees, and the report contained no "conclusive statistical analysis" ("Media reports"). "The use of one man's estimate as a percentage that strongly suggests it has been accurately calculated for the entire western Arctic is just not good enough," said Marie-Jewell ("Child sex-abuse"). The minister was doing damage control. The data have to be contextualized to the sample and its methods, and it is irresponsible to generalize them beyond the limits of the study. This was one kind of response, from a responsible official, that the panel could have taken to heart.

Another response came from the Native Women's Association, who also commented on the news reports in a press release of their own. Alice Hill, executive director of the association, adopted the strategy of downplaying the sensational 80%-50% (girls-boys) numbers. At the same time, she tried to draw attention to the problem itself. "It is not alleged that this is a statistic based on scientific research; the scope of the study was not broad enough nor was it intended to encompass such research. It may well be that the incidence is not as high as 75-80% ... We feel that the focus now should shift; whether or not one is prepared to accept that the incidence of child sexual abuse in native girls under the age of ten is as high as 80%. The problem exists in this region and in other regions of the Northwest Territories and we must take steps immediately to address the problem." The association, she says, will vigorously lobby the government for action programs. Notice, by the way, that the boys have now disappeared from the picture and from the program she goes on to propose.

Elsewhere, Hill is quoted as saying that she had been told by the Department of Social Services not to comment on the report (as the department itself declined to do when the *Native Press* inquired). She adds, "I can believe that if they were to visit every individual that they would come out with statistics like one or two out of every ten girls have been sexually molested. But to say that it's eight out of ten is pretty hard to believe" (Pritchard, "Sex Abuse" 1). Trying to put the controversy and the incredulity about the sensationalized findings behind her, Hill argues that there is indeed a serious problem. "Let's look to the future and try to do something about it" (3). So what does the CanPan do?

Oblivious to or uncaring about the nature of this matter, including the way its controversies played themselves out just four years earlier, the final report of the panel casually revives and recycles what is a sensational and unwarranted assumption: "A Northwest Territories survey found that 80 percent of girls and 50% of boys under 8 years old were sexually abused" (CL 156).

Older Women and Panic Statistics (Chapter 5)

The panel provides the following scare statistics at the start of a very brief and uninformative chapter where very few statistics are cited: "Elder abuse is not gender neutral; older women are the main victims of violence. As many as one in 10 elderly people experience abuse, and, according to the Ontario Advisory Council on Senior Citizens, at least two out of three victims are women" (CL 61). As if this were not enough, the panel goes on to add: "Other anecdotal sources give a higher estimate." This little paragraph provides a very good glimpse into how the panel marshals its data to fit its preconceptions.

The panel attributes the 1-in-10 elder abuse figure to two well-respected researchers in the field of family violence, Karl Pillemer and David Finkelhor, of the Family Research Laboratory at the University of New Hampshire. But the panel cites their study second-hand: not the original version in *The Gerontologist*, but the reference to it in a Winnipeg publication, *Elder Women Speak Out on Abuse* (1988) by the Senior Women Against Abuse Collective. But either the Senior Women got it wrong, and the panel once again took it over without checking the sources; or the panel falsified the information in its sources. Either way, Pillemer and Finkelhor do *not* give the figure that 1 in 10 elderly persons are abused. Nowhere in their study is that figure, or any like it, to be found. The figure that they give for the prevalence rate is 32 in 1,000, and for the incidence rate it is 26 per 1,000. In fact, they show that more elderly people suffer from Alzheimer's disease or related disorders (60 per 1,000) than from abuse. In other words, the panel *triples or quadruples* the findings provided by the very source that they cite as the authority, and conducts this inflation without explanation.

The actual Pillemer and Finkelhor study, as published in *The Gerontologist*, is one of the few solid studies in this area. They argue that earlier studies, which are based on highly selective samples "of cases that have come to the attention of a social agency or reporting authority" (PF 51), are highly unreliable. This study, on the other hand, is "the first large-scale random sample survey of elder abuse and neglect"(PF 51). Their final sample was 2,020; the response rate was 72%. The survey was conducted in the Boston metro area on persons over 65 living in the community. Respondents were interviewed over the phone, unless they could not use a phone, in which case they were personally interviewed. The study used a modified CTS to determine who the victims of elder abuse are and then re-interviewed those victims in order to get information on the context of the abuse. The definitions used are liberal without being ridiculous.

There is another striking fact produced by Pillemer and Finkelhor's random-sample representative study: the risk of abuse for elderly men is double that for elderly women (51 per 1,000 versus 23 per 1,000). Moreover, elderly men are most likely to be abused by their female spouses, and to a much greater degree than elderly women are abused by their male spouses. Instead of reporting this, however, the CanPan chose to cite a different study for its gender data, one done six years before Pillemer and Finkelhor's, by Donna Shell, *Protection of the Elderly* (1982). It is a mark of the CanPan's sloppy procedures that it attributes Shell's figures to the Ontario Advisory Council on Senior Citizens.

The Shell study that the panel uses, but does not correctly cite, for its "2 out of 3 abused elders are women" statistic, is an obscure study done in Winnipeg for the Manitoba Council on Aging. It uses the "snowballing" technique criticized by Pillemer and Finkelhor to make projections from the severe cases to a larger population. This is a dubious practice, with a very low likelihood of validity. Making general statements on the basis of nonrandom studies of reported cases runs a high risk of distortion. There is no need for it, and the panel has no excuse for perpetuating the clinical fallacy when a solid representative sample study is available. This is clearly a case in which the CanPan chose to ignore the best research in the field because it did not accord with the biopolitics favoured by the panel and its sponsors.

Women With Disabilities and Panic Statistics (Chapter 7)

There has never been a large-scale, random-sample survey of people with disabilities. The designs and sample biases of the available studies raise significant barriers to wide generalization. We asked Dick Sobsey, one of the leading academic experts on disability, and one of the panel's sources, about the state of the research. He told us there is no good, reliable information on the prevalence of violence or abuse, so that studies in this area which rely on one another are merely reproducing the same flaws.[1]

The panel cites only six studies in its entire chapter (CL 97, notes 25-31): McPherson, Sobsey, Morin and Boisvert, Ridington, twice, and Stimpson and Best. None of these, singly or in combination, can support the weight of generalized interpretation that the panel loads on to this modest research base. To say so is not to criticize, much less denigrate, these studies, which provide important information, and which can be useful if understood within the framework of their own limits. They just do not do what the panel suggests they do, once the panel has woven them into its panic narrative.

Cathy McPherson writes as an activist, not a researcher. She cites no sources anywhere in her article, "Out of Sight, Out of Mind." Her definition of disability is astonishingly broad, and includes women who are seeing a therapist, and women who have cancer, epilepsy, Alzheimer's disease, or low vision. On her authority, the panel says that "eighteen percent of all women in Canada have a disability" (CL 67). By contrast, the most recent Statistics Canada figures in the *Disabled Persons in Canada* report (1990) offer a lower figure: 13.8%. The Statistics Canada figure amounts to 1.8 million women; the panel's 18% is 2.3 million. This inflates the number of women with disabilities by .5 million, or 28%.

Dick Sobsey's article is not an actual research study either, but a summary of a literature review, and a discussion of a small number (94) of abuse cases selected from the available literature, without disclosure of method of selection or nature of the sample. The panel treats it as though it were an actual study, and cites it as a reliable authority for generalized anxiety: "An Alberta study found that 88% of the victims with disabilities knew their sexual abusers ..." (CL 69).

The Morin and Boisvert submission to the panel on mental impairment, by contrast, is not published at all, and available only through the National Archives, by permission. It is the panel's source for its assertion that "close to 40% of women with developmental disabilities (including those with learning disabilities and intellectual impairments) will be victims of sexual abuse before the age of 18" (CL 68). There is no easy way to discover what sample, definitions, and methods were used to generate this figure. The numbers always depend on the definitions. "Sexual abuse" does not correspond to the Criminal Code term "sexual assault," and is meaningless to the reader without definition. It is most probable that the sample is a clinical sample selected by social agencies, and almost certain that, in the absence of a large random survey, the prediction of 40% abuse is without warrant. There can be no justification for launching it on the public, or building policy around it, without exposing the research methods and findings to public scrutiny.

The two Ridington reports are based on a study of responses to 245 questionnaires (20% of the 1,200 in the original distribution through DAWN affiliates, disabled consumers' groups, and feminist contacts). The results of interviews with 50 women invited to meetings about sexual assault and other feminist issues were combined with the questionnaire data. Nineteen percent of the sample experienced violence before the onset of disability but not after; these cases remain included in the study. There is no control for how developmental or learning disabilities may have affected the responses. "Some of the respondents with developmental disabilities did not fill in their own forms" (Ridington, *Beating the "Odds"*), but no indication is given as to whether this is because they did not understand the forms, or could not write, or some other reason. There were no definitions used in the study; results depend, then, on the respondents' interpretations.

The panel uses percentages from this selective study: "Of the 245 women with disabilities who responded to a 1988 survey, 40% had been raped, abused or assaulted." This finding refers to the first question of the survey: "Have you ever been abused, raped, or assaulted?" Verbal abuse is counted as a form of violence against women. And there is no indication of the sex of the perpetrators of abuse. Another study (cited by the panel in the chapter on women living in poverty, but not here) shows that women are the most frequent abusers of children with disabilities (Doucette, *Violent Acts Against Disabled Women*).[2] The Doucette study is small, self-selective, and unreliable as a basis of generalization, but not more so than the other studies from which the panel draws its numbers.

The panel makes no effort to contextualize the limits of the sample, the methods, or the design of the Ridington study, *and* gives none of the actual numbers. The biases in the study constrain the extent to which it can be valid to generalize its results, and the numbers are much too small to serve as the basis for any reliable generalization to a population larger than the study itself. For example, the panel insists dramatically: "Most women with disabilities are underemployed and restricted to low-paying jobs. A 1988 survey found that 58 percent of women with disabilities were living below the poverty line in Canada" (CL 68). The panel does not mention that nearly a quarter of the respondents chose *not* to answer the question on income, showing more reticence about disclosing income than about discussing violence, nor that the 58% is an unwarranted projection from information about only 109 women in a study of self-selected respondents.

In Chapter 6 on poverty the panel simply affirms: "In 1986, 74% of women with disabilities reported an annual income below the poverty line of $11,000" (CL 64). Does this mean that around 1.5 million women with disabilities declared poverty? Not at all. As its authority for this bald assertion, the panel reports the Doucette study that I mentioned above. The disabled women that Doucette studied were a self-selected group of delegates to the DAWN provincial conference in 1986, further self-selected as those delegates (not all) who were prepared to answer the questionnaire. The panel does not disclose that Doucette studied only 30 disabled women. The reader would never know from the final report that 74% of Doucette's sample is *22 actual women.* Moreover, 5 of these 22 women reported no source of income at all, which may mean that they are dependent on spouses or parents, for example, but does not necessarily mean that they are poor.

The Stimpson and Best study, *Courage Above All: Sexual Assault Against Women with Disabilities,* acknowledged by researchers like Sobsey as one of the better studies, begins with the premise that no study can be objective and that it makes no attempt to be objective. The researchers interviewed disabled women at meetings held to discuss sexual assault, and mailed out some questionnaires to a selected list of Ontario women drawn from the files of disabled-women's organizations (such as DAWN). In other words, this is no random sample, but rather a small and highly self-selective one. The study is based on 85 questionnaires (28% response to the 300 distributed). The checklist of "violence" includes "verbal" as well as "neglect." I will pass by its own results, because the panel never cites any of them. The panel does, however, refer to the Stimpson and Best study as its authority for a sensational result that is not one of their own findings. Here again, the panel did not go to the original source. This trail is worth following in detail, because once again it shows the research incompetence of the panel, and the susceptibility of a biopolitical agenda to the lure of panic hyperbole.

The 83% Hoax (Women with Disabilities)

With the notable exception of the 98% figure for sexual violation(see chapter VI), the most shocking statistic in the report is the following: "There is certainly no question that women with disabilities are more vulnerable to violence. According to one source, approximately 83 percent of women with a disability will be sexually assaulted during their lifetime" (68).

What source would claim such a bold and frightening finding? It must be an unimpeachable, reliable and valid, presumably public, widely available source of information, if a national inquiry accepted its results and chose to produce them in a public report. Only the sober truth could justify risking the race against time, as the policy makers of a nation rush to find remedies for the epidemic of sexual assaults against the 2 million women with disabilities, before the whole community of the disabled sinks into fearful despair in the face of the hopeless prospects of violated helplessness. As the reader already anticipates, the reality could not be further from this ideal picture of civic and research responsibility.

The source cited by the panel for the 83% statistic is the Stimpson and Best study. With a panic statistic like 83%, I had no choice but to look for the original source; but it turns out the report is not readily available in libraries. Even the University of Toronto's Robarts Library does not have it. We got in touch with the publisher, the Toronto DisAbled Women's Network (DAWN Toronto), to see where we could purchase a copy. Alas, the publication is now out of print. Moreover, neither DAWN Toronto nor

DAWN Ontario could provide us with a copy. Ginny at DAWN Toronto informed us that she was not prepared to make us a photocopy. It turned out, in fact, that no one at either agency could even find this report, although Ginny felt sure it was there somewhere. Her advice was that we should go to Toronto and do the search ourselves. So, the next day, Ginny let Mary Ritter, my research assistant, into the resource library but would not help her to find anything. She offered more recent material instead. She implied that it was silly and pig-headed to persist in trying to find *Courage Above All.* Indeed, the library was in disorder; there was no coherent filing system, and boxes and papers were strewn everywhere. Mary stumbled on *Courage Above All* almost by accident.

We checked the first page, which the CanPan had noted as the source of the 83% statistic. It matched the CanPan document almost exactly: "The numbers of disabled women who are sexually assaulted are horrifyingly high. According to one source, approximately 83% of disabled women will be sexually assaulted during their lifetimes." In short, Stimpson and Best were *not* the original source of the 83% number. We would have to go to another level, and our trail was just beginning. We had a clue. In their endnotes, Stimpson and Best attribute this figure to Dorothy Griffiths, Lecture at Conference at Northern College, Timmins, Ontario (June 21, 1991).

We then phoned DAWN Toronto and DAWN Ontario, to find the numbers/addresses for Griffiths, Stimpson, or Best, in order to track down the paper given by Griffiths at this conference. We also called Northern College to see if they had Griffiths's address.We were volleyed for days between DAWN Toronto (contact: Tari Akpodiete) and DAWN Ontario (contact: Robyn Artemis), as we tried to find this information. Finally, Tari kindly ran a number of database searches. No addresses or phone numbers came up for Griffiths or Stimpson; there was an address for Best but DAWN could not give it to us. In the end, Tari gave us two numbers, which she culled from the phone book, for

L. Stimpson, one of which turned out to belong to Liz Stimpson's son, who gave us her number.

We then phoned Stimpson at her home, to ask her about Dorothy Griffiths's paper. Stimpson said she did not have a copy of the paper; moreover, as she is blind, she had never seen a copy of the paper. We asked her if she knew the original source of the 83% figure. She said she did not know. She added that she had asked Griffiths the same question and that Griffiths had told her that she could not remember. In other words, Stimpson framed her report with a figure she attributed to Griffiths, knowing that Griffiths was not the original source of the information, and without verifying the original data herself. Moreover, how could Griffiths have been using the 83% figure in her lecture? *How could everyone in this chain have been so casual about a figure so extraordinary?*

We tracked down Griffiths, and spoke with her briefly. She said she remembered having the 83% figure on an overhead which she used to use, and which perhaps she showed at the conference at Northern College. She thought it came from a book called *Vulnerable*, published by the G. Allan Roeher Institute, which has some statistics on abuse of women. She told us to contact the Canadian Association for Community Living for the book. On further probing, Griffiths clarified that, actually, the 83% came from a study by S. Hard, who had published some research with statistics like that in 1986. Griffiths was kind enough to look up her own copy of *Vulnerable*, check the source, and relay that S. Hard had presented these findings at a conference at Omaha on Oct. 22, 1986. It was a study of 95 men and women with disabilities; 83% of the women had been abused. Griffiths noted that Hard's research was not very good now, but it had been good at the time. I still do not know what that means, but apparently the research is still good enough in the eyes of the panel to have its findings featured without reserve. In any case, it seemed that at last we had found the original source. Omaha was a little far away, but the Canadian

Association for Community Living could perhaps be authoritative. As it happened, we had to go down another level or two before we could properly review the original study.

We phoned the Canadian Association for Community Living and ordered *Vulnerable: Sexual Abuse and People with An Intellectual Handicap.* Unfortunately, *Vulnerable* does not contain Hard's research paper, as delivered in Omaha. Nevertheless, in chapter one, in a discussion of the "Prevalence of Child Abuse," we found a summary reference to Hard's research: "Hard (1986) conducted a study of the case records of 95 adults with developmental disabilities enrolled at a work activity centre. She then interviewed 65 of the individuals using a questionnaire she developed to obtain more detailed information. Hard (1986) reported that 83 percent of the women and 32 percent of the men had experienced prior sexual abuse. The ages of the subjects of this study ranged from 17-48 years. Of the 38 individuals for which age at the time of abuse was available, 17 or 45 percent were under 18 years of age when the abuse happened. Again, 99 percent of the victims were assaulted by a perpetrator known to them. Although the results are generalizable only to people involved in work activity centres, Hard's research is probably the best estimate we have at the current time on the prevalence of sexual assault and abuse in the population with developmental disabilities" (1).

The sample seemed small, but the numbers looked so authoritative. Yet, at this point, we still did not know where this research took place, what questionnaire or other instrument of research was used, or how Hard got access to the information. We had to find Hard's study. The reference in the bibliography in *Vulnerable* was: Hard, S. (1986) "Sexual Abuse of the Developmentally Disabled: A Case Study". Paper presented at the National Conference of Executives of Associations for Retarded Citizens, Omaha, Nebraska, Oct. 22. We phoned the Roeher Institute at York University, and asked whether they had a copy of Hard's 1986 paper in their files. We spoke to Miriam Ticoll, who informed us that they no longer had a copy, although they had it in their files at some point. We were lucky, however, because Ticoll phoned back the next day to say that she had found the paper. We finally had the full original source for the 83% figure.

The study took place at the Indian Wells Valley Association for Retarded Citizens (ARC) work activity centre in Ridgecrest, California, where Hard was executive director for 13 years. Hard does not indicate how her 95 subjects were chosen: perhaps they were chosen randomly, perhaps this was the total number of files available to Hard, or perhaps she hand-picked these subjects, thinking them to be appropriate subjects for this study. She states: "During the first study phase each of the subjects' individual case records were examined and analyzed, many of which contained documentation of prior sexual abuse. Subsequently, during the second phase a questionnaire was developed to elicit more specific information, and administered to 65 of the 95 subjects" (1). She goes on: "The remaining 30 individuals were not included in the second phase questionnaire nor the study conclusions for the following reasons: several were non-verbal, a few chose not to be interviewed, two did not understand the questions, and the others had left the ARC programme prior to the interview" (1).

Hard interviewed her 65 subjects "in a private setting, on an individual basis" (1). She adds that "terminology appropriate for the individual was utilized"(1). This not only means that each person may have been asked different questions, but that the questions might have been asked by Hard in a number of different ways and several times. Clearly, this introduces the possibility of leading questions and responses tailored to please the interviewer. In total, Hard interviewed 34 retarded women and 31 retarded men. Their functioning level was as follows: 18 of the women and 24 of the men were mildly retarded (IQ 50-70); 12 of the women and 5 of the men were moderately retarded (IQ 35-49); and 4 of the women and 2 of the men were severely retarded (IQ 20-34). In the case of the severely retarded especially, the accuracy of their answers must be questioned.

The respondents were asked to remember instances of sexual abuse in their past. The age range at first abuse for the females was 6-34; for men it was 11-36. Sexual abuse was defined for this study as "sexual contact with the victim which has resulted from force, coercion, manipulation, exploitation or otherwise entered into unwillingly or un-kowingly [*sic*] or without understanding" (2). Incest for this study "refers to a relative by first or second degree engaging in oral, anal, or vaginal intercourse, or touch-ing/manipulating of the breasts or genitals" (2). According to these definitions, "83% of the study subject females and 32% of the males had experienced prior sexual abuse"(2). That is, 28 women and 10 men had experienced abuse. Ninety-seven percent of the abusers were male.

Hard compares her findings with those of other researchers: "These findings compare with other research studies in the literature indicating that sexual abuse occurs with persons with developmental disabilities anywhere from 70% (Department of Developmental Services, 1985) to 99% (Seattle Rape Relief Project, 1979). Rush (1980) reports that 80-90% of the sexual abusers are male, and O'Day (1983) reports that 90% are male." Hard mentions a few other studies which are comparable to hers and emphasizes that her own study finds a much higher rate of incest than Briere's 1984 study, for example. Since she gives no information about these other studies, however, it is impossible to judge how well they can be compared with hers.

Hard and others have mentioned that retarded people and people with disabilities in general must be given proper sex education. She notes that 72% of the individuals in her study, for example, had received no sex education. She does not identify characteristics of the abusers in her study, apart from whether or not they are family members. In a similar study by Dick Sobsey, cited in *Courage Above All*, 41.2% of the offenders who perpetrated sexual abuse were handicapped in some way; 22.1% of the offenders suffered from intellectual impairments. We might conjecture that the combination of no or little sex education with low IQ on the part of both the man and the woman who are participating in some kind of sexual act might well produce some unwanted or uncomfortable acts being perpetrated against or being experienced by both the man and the woman participant. Of course, it is not possible to determine in the case of Hard's research whether or not this was the case with some of her subjects.

So, there we have it. An executive director of a work centre for retarded citizens in rural California interviews a portion of the residents. She compensates for the low IQ and lack of sex education of her subjects by leading questions and descriptions that refashion the interview to suit each respondent. She tries to find out if they have ever had unwanted sexual experiences. She finds 28 institutionalized, retarded California women (leaving aside the 10 men in whom the CanPan shows no interest) who can be described as having had, on some occasion, some experience that they can describe as unwilling or unknowing.

On this evidence, and on this evidence alone, the CanPan accepts and announces that 83% of Canadian women with disabilities *will be* sexually assaulted. The panel is prepared to generalize from 28 retarded women in a California institution to the whole Canadian population—not just women in work camps, not just women with IQ between 20 and 70, not just women with developmental impairment, not just California women or U.S. women, but actually 83% of all Canadian women with disabilities. This is the most fabulous example of the clinical fallacy that I have ever seen.

And that's not enough! When the CanPan issued its training video, "Without Fear," it *raised* the figure from

83% to 90%, citing the DisAbled Women's Network (DAWN) as its source. We asked Professor Sobsey, whom DAWN considers an expert in this area of research, what he thought about this spiralling inflation.[3] He said that numbers always depend on definitions, and people like to throw around all kinds of numbers. In particular, he said, people like to throw around his figures for sexual abuse, but the 90% figure touted by DAWN definitely does not come from him. A 90% figure, he said, is "misleading and dangerous." It makes the problem out to be hopeless; it may be good politics, but it is not good research. On my account, it is also very bad politics, as time may show. In due course, it is likely to be repudiated by both the disabled community and the public at large.

VI
No Safety in Numbers:
Panic Utopia and the CanPan

" ... in a hundred years, I thought ...
women will have ceased to be the protected
sex. Logically they will take part in all the
activities and exertions that were once
denied them. The nursemaid will heave
coal. The shopwoman will drive an engine.
All assumptions founded on the facts
observed when women were the protected sex
will have disappeared — as, for example
(here a squad of soldiers marched down the
street), that women and clergymen and
gardeners live longer than other people. Remove that protection, expose them to the
same exertions and activities, make them
soldiers and sailors and engine-drivers and
dock labourers, and will not women die off
so much younger, so much quicker, than
men that one will say, 'I saw a woman
to-day,' as one used to say, 'I saw an
aeroplane.' Anything may happen when
womanhood has ceased to be a protected
occupation, I thought ... " (VirginiaWoolf,
A Room of One's Own 40)

The CanPan notes that the 1970 *Report of the Royal Commission on the Status of Women* did not mention the issue of violence against women (CL 14). I can add that the 1983 anthology of Canadian feminism by Miles and Finn, *Feminism in Canada*, has nothing to say on that topic either, anywhere in its thirteen essays, or in its bibliography of nearly 150 titles (with the possible exception of just one of Finn's own articles). The violence-against-women industry, hard as it is now to believe it, is merely a decade in the making, and there is no evidence to suggest that there has been a dramatic increase in any kind of violence during that time, except the *rhetoric of violence against women*. The Panel participates in this escalating rhetoric of panic.

The 98% Invention: the Women's Safety Project

"When all kinds of sexual violation and intrusion are considered, 98% of women reported that they personally experienced some form of sexual violation. This finding, in particular, clearly supports our assertion that violence against women affects virtually all women's lives" (CL 10). Virtually all women are victims, and therefore virtually all men are summarily indicted as perpetrators. Such seamless universality, rent only by the relentless bipolarity of biopolitics, is the goal and the desired result of biofeminist panic, and the foundation for its draconian, "safety"-oriented policy initiatives which threaten the liberal egalitarianism of expressive freedoms and due process. The Women's Safety Project (WSP) is quoted at least 15 times in the text of the CanPan's Final Report, where other reports are mentioned only once or twice. All of page 9 is devoted to the results of the WSP, which are used to support the CanPan's claims about the prevalence of violence against women in Canadian society. The WSP's results are further discussed in extensive detail in the eighteen pages of Appendix A. This is the only study which receives so much space and attention from the CanPan.

This survey, conducted by Lori Haskell and Melanie Randall, is clearly the centrepiece of the CanPan's demonstration polemic, the cloak of scientific proof in which it wants to dress its argument. Haskell is a graduate student at the Ontario Institute for Studies in Applied Psychology (OISE), and Randall is a part-time researcher there. Sincere biofeminists, neither has major scientific or academic publications. In spite of its reassuring, collective title, the Women's Safety Project (WSP) is the epitome of sloppy, amateur advocacy. Scientifically worthless, the WSP exhibits sampling errors, idiosyncratic research tools and methods, erratic coding, poor arithmetic, faulty projections, inflated numbers, and misleading arguments. And yet Haskell and Randall acknowledge the support of a dozen women's organizations, from Education Wife Assault and the Elizabeth Fry Society of Toronto to the Federation of Women Teachers' Associations of Ontario, the Metro Action Committee on Public Violence Against Women and Children (METRAC), the National Action Committee on the Status of Women (NAC), and the Women's Legal Education and Action Fund (LEAF). They are also funded by public agencies, such as the Ontario Women's Directorate, the Ministry of Community and Social Services, the Ministry of the Solicitor General (Ontario), the City of Toronto, the Ministry of Health, Ontario, and Health and Welfare Canada. And, of course, the Canadian Panel on Violence Against Women (CL A15).

What the CanPan tells its readers is that it funded Haskell and Randall in order to get some accurate figures, "in the absence of nationally tabulated statistics on the full scope of violence against women" (CL 8). What Melanie Randall told us, however, is that the WSP was completely autonomous from the CanPan, which hired them to do some analysis near the end of their project. By incorporating the WSP findings, the panel evidently got the numbers they wanted, but from the point of view of any responsible outsider, they backed the wrong pony. It is a scandal that the panel should have advertised these results to policy

around OISE and the University of Toronto, physically located in and around the Annex area in Toronto. Is this in fact the "community" referred to in the subtitle of the Women's Safety Project: *A Community-Based Study of Sexual Violence in Women's Lives?* Did the authors knowingly select, or permit the self-selection of, an entirely biased and unrepresentative sample of the kinds of people they were themselves most familiar with, and yet conceal this knowledge from their sponsors and from the public?

An urban sample like Toronto is probably much more highly affected by violence and casual sexual activity than rural populations, so that extensive generalization from a Toronto sample to all Canadian women would be in any case suspect, because it would produce figures considerably higher than the actual national averages. In addition, the sample here is specifically biased toward a university-educated generation that has been unusually sexually active and also highly politicized about women's issues and sexual issues, in ways that are not representative of the Canadian female population at large. There is no scientific justification whatever for extrapolating from the reports of these 420 women to the experiences of all Canadian women.

The WSP numbers are striking, and higher than the numbers reported by other researchers, including Russell. In addition to the 98% sexual violation number, Haskell and Randall claim that 67% of all women will be sexually assaulted sometime in their lifetimes, that 56% will suffer rape or attempted rape (vs. 46% for Russell, 25% in some popular studies, and figures ranging down to 2% and less in other reputable studies), that 54% will be abused before the age of 16, 42% with forced sexual contact, and that 40% will be victims of completed rape. You have to scrutinize the definitions carefully to discover that the rape and attempted rape figures include oral sex. For example, the commonplace experience of most young women, of feeling a downward pressure on her head when in the vicinity of his genitals, could be classified at least as attempted forced intercourse, or actual rape, if successful. Rape and attempted rape also include lack of consent from "helplessness": attempted sex with a partner asleep qualifies; as does sex or attempted sex with a woman who is drunk or drugged. Drinking or smoking as preludes to sex also permit the classification of forced intercourse. So does the insertion of a finger. Sexual assault, meanwhile, is taken to include the necking and petting behaviour of teenagers—something Russell, for example, explicitly excludes. Since 60% of what is described as childhood sexual abuse falls into the age groups of early adolescence (as the actual tables show), and more than a third of reported adult sexual assault occurs between 16 and 18 years of age—and fully two thirds between 16 and 21, indeed, 81% by the age of 24—the fact that the study does not distinguish between the unwanted awkwardnesses and ambivalences of peer dating and some other kinds of sexual coercion makes its numbers useless for measuring violence in a meaningful way. There is no way to know, once all the padding is removed, and the numbers deflate considerably, what residue of actual violence remains, worthy of public concern.

Finally, the 98% figure is not only built on all this, but additionally includes unwanted hugs and kisses, as well as interactions that do not involve physical contact of any kind: for example, exhibitionism, being followed, obscene phone calls, verbal propositions, or any suggestive or otherwise unwelcome sexual comments. And even that is not all. The 98% figure for sexual violation turns out also to include any and all acts of "physical abuse" in an intimate relationship, such as pushing, shoving, or slapping. Is there anybody whose life has been completely devoid of any uncomfortable sexual language or sexual ambivalence and even the slightest physical friction? It is astonishing that the number is *not* 100%. Indeed, the 98% is not at all disturbing, considering the definitions. This grab-bag of everything, from the uncorroborated and perhaps even imaginary follower on the street, and the unwanted sexual banter, all the way to brutal and violent stranger-rape, effectively insulates us from concern: it conceals and trivializes the real victimization that exists.

It is impossible to tell from the WSP presentation whether the women surveyed agree with the way their experiences are characterized. Like Koss, and Russell, Randall and Haskell classify female experiences on the basis of how they satisfy the researchers' definitions, not according to the respondent women's own assessments. Unlike Koss and Russell, however, Randall and Haskell do not tell us at all how the respondents themselves described the behaviours they encountered and experienced. Nor do they mention that they did actually collect this information from the respondents (as Randall told us). Since 50% of those whom Russell classified as rape victims, and 73% of those whom Koss classified as rape victims, did not classify their own experiences this way (see chapter II), it becomes an important principle of research *at a minimum* to indicate the respondents' own descriptions alongside the researchers' manipulation of the data (Schoenberg and Roe 16).

It is also crucial to provide the researchers' definitions and the questions to which the respondents reply. It has become standard in the genre of survey research to begin the presentation by describing sample size, response rate, and methodology (including the questionnaire). We all know that the questions you ask shape the answers you get. The WSP is unusual in *not* having done this. So, not only did they conceal their response rate and the bias in their sample, but they also provide no insight into the questions they asked. This is most peculiar, especially since they struck out on their own, and do not seem to have set out to apply either the CTS or the SES, or any widely known variant of these question sets. What is astonishing to me is that the panel would have accepted the findings of the Project; indeed, that it would have paid Haskell and Randall $50,000, without looking at the questionnaire. Certainly, my first impulse, on seeing the central role of the

WSP in the final report, and learning that their findings were way out of keeping with other results, was to double-check their methods and measures. The first thing I needed was access to the questions and access to the tables that tabulate the answers. Unfortunately, these were not made available by the CanPan in the final report.

Not Yet Ready for Prime Time

By June 1994, one year after the final report was released, the panel was no longer in existence. The Canadian Advisory Council on the Status of Women had no information on the Women's Safety Project. Status of Women Canada had no information either, even though they inherited the extensive and ongoing follow-up to the panel's activities. There was no trace of any publication by Haskell or Randall in any of the libraries I could consult; and, beyond the summary of the WSP in the CanPan final report, no report seemed to be available anywhere. Indeed, the findings of the WSP appeared to have made no impact even on feminist pamphleteering. Randall acknowledged as much when we spoke with her, but she added that what is in the Appendix is not the full report; that is still unfinished, unpublished. In fact, all the information we were seeking is in a 150-200 page manuscript that she would send us, to be returned to her as soon as we made a photocopy.

This information was puzzling, as well as gratifying. The panel refers to the Women's Safety Project in a footnote as self-published (CL 54, n.2). But there has been no publication. It refers to the final report of the Women's Safety Project in the endnotes of the *Facilitator's Guide* to the video *Without Fear*, and also in the credits to the video (FG 33, nn. 1, 7, 8). Yet, we are told that the WSP is unfinished. The various references that the panel makes to tables of statistics from the WSP (CL 54-55) do testify to the existence of a document beyond the summary that is published as Appendix A, so we had some hope that the manuscript Randall was sending would be the same document the panel had seen. It would certainly contain the questionnaire, she told us. The status of the document, whether final report or work in progress, remained troubling. After all, how could the panel have published unfinished work with such finality and fanfare? Alternatively, if the work was finished, why was it still unpublished and being revised? What was being revised? Surely not the tables whose highlights had been published by the panel and which we were looking for?

A month later, there was still no sign of the manuscript. We had left messages for Randall, reminding her to send the text, but had no response. When we finally reached Randall againin mid-July, she said that many other people were asking for the ms. as well, and this had delayed her, but we could expect it in a week. What we got instead was a call from Randall's research assistant, Elizabeth Chen, to say that the ms. would not be mailed to us, after all. It would be available, however, at the Women's Resource Centre at OISE. This turned out to be another disappointment, however, as the Women's Resource Centre, according to Paula Bourne, had never had a copy. They had often been asked for it, but she did not know of anyone who had received a copy.

This was a very different picture from Randall's story of being delayed by the pressures of multiple distribution. Since we were advised that the source materials for the panel were divided between the Women's Resource Centre at OISE and the collection at METRAC, we checked for the WSP text at METRAC. No luck. We checked Robarts Library at the University of Toronto, the York University library, the Toronto Public Library, and the Prevention of Child Abuse Centre. No text. We called Cathy McRae at Status of Women Canada. Struck out there as well. Health and Welfare Canada, one of the financial sponsors of the WSP, had never seen a full report either. Another call to Chen clarified that nobody other than Haskell and Randall has a copy, not even herself. The authors were making revisions in preparation for publication, and had decided not to give it out to anyone until they were ready. What Chen had meant to tell us, in her earlier message, was that the document might be at the Women's Resource Centre in about a month. In the meantime, both authors were out of town.

This seems quite extraordinary, considering that the summary results—98% of Canadian women sexually violated, 40% of adults raped, 54% of children abused—had all been in the public domain, courtesy of the CanPan, for over a year. Virtually all of the press commentary on the CanPan results focussed on the WSP portion. How could the supporting documentation be withheld from the public? How could its evidentiary basis not be readily available to scrutiny? How could the whole culture of public inquiries, advocacy groups, funding agencies, policy makers, and the media all be so casual about the way information of this kind enters the culture?

We followed up one more lead. It seems that Haskell and Randall marketed their project to the Solicitor General of Canada as well, and got financial support for analyzing unprocessed data. They submitted a report just this spring, April 1994. We recently talked to Jacques Deverteuil at the Solicitor General's office. He told us he could not release the report (which they will consider for publication), because they had not yet reviewed it. Apart from one reporter, we were the first to inquire after it. At our request, he checked, and determined that no survey instrument—no questionnaire—was included with the WSP report. Since the questionnaire was not one in standard use, it could be a welcome innovation in the field, or it could mean that the WSP had not used a reliable instrument. The Solicitor General's office seemed properly interested in the possibility that the research might be flawed, though it does not seem to have occurred to them that this cannot be determined without due examination, among other things, of the survey instrument.

Throughout August 1994, we kept leaving messages for Haskell and Randall. We still hoped to see the tables that had been submitted to the panel, and the questionnaire, as we had been promised. If revisions were to be completed imminently, we hoped to see the original or the revised text as soon as possible. On August 24, Mary Ritter, my assistant, succeeded in reaching Randall for the first time since the mid-July promise of a text within a week. Randall said she was busy and virtually hung up on her. A little later, in early September, Mary received a letter from Randall, dated August 17, 1994. It referred to "extensive" revisions being undertaken, and forecast the eventual depositing of a copy at OISE. "We do not know exactly when that will be, given other commitments." Finally, it advised: "It is not necessary for you to contact us further at this point as we have no additional information to offer you."

It seemed that, after three months of effort, we were not to be able to look at the tables that are cited in the CanPan final report, nor the questions that solicited the much-publicized results. A bizarre situation and, in my view, a scandalous symptom of irresponsibility by the panel, in failing to ascertain that the research was indeed ready for the public.

Black Folder, Red Folder

Fortunately, the story has another chapter. In September, we tracked down the relevant files in the Canadian Panel deposits in the Government Archives Division of the National Archives in Ottawa, applied for clearance to review them, and, with the help of Danielle LaCasse and Michel Filion, managed to inspect the materials in the Women's Safety Project file. No questionnaire on deposit. We saw, however, the 150-page text that was submitted in March 1993, identified on the title page as *Final Report to: The Canadian Panel on Violence Against Women.* This was in a black folder. We saw another text, with revisions, marked as Second Draft: this was in a red folder. We saw some 5 versions of revisions, some correspondence between the authors and Bonnie Diamond, the panel's research director, and some faxes of queries and answers. The text that was published appears not to have been finalized until June 1993. Both the black folder and the red folder contain a full set of tables, and the texts and tables are identical for the first two chapters (30 pages). They differ in chapters 3 to 6. The red folder appears to have the tables which are excerpted in the Appendix A summary in the CanPan final report. The tables make it a little easier to see what is going on here than the summary does, because they provide numbers of women to go with the percentages. Four items of interest are worth highlighting here briefly.

First, the major discrepancy between the black folder and red folder documents, apparently both produced in March 1993, is that the sample numbers 400 in the black folder, and 419 or 420 in the red folder. The number given in the panel summary is 420. The entire text of the black folder (like the unchanged first two chapters of the red), refers to "a random sample of 400 women from Toronto" (BF 1 and RF 1). The description of the sample at p. 12 has the following curiosity: "The size of the sample for the main study was intended to be 400." There is no mention of the letters sent to the actual random sample of 1,200 addresses. A footnote offers only the following cryptic amplification: "However, the figures will be adjusted slightly when an additional number of approximately 15 interviews are integrated into the data set."

What 15 are these? Why are these to show up only after the final report has been submitted in March 1993? On p. 18, to complicate matters, the authors say: "There are an additional 18 cases in excess of the 400 reported on here, to be entered and analysed into the final results of the project." They talk of "data cleansing" still to come that will repair the problems of coding and inputting errors, as well as missing cases, all of which will amount to only minor statistical adjustments (RF 18). In any event, what is marked as "New Draft," starting with chapter III, "Sexual Abuse in Childhood," and running through to chapter 5, inclusive, in the red folder, recalculates all the tables on the basis of 419 women, that is, 19 additional interviews. Chapter 6, however, offering a variety of summary prevalence tables and explanations, bases the tables on a sample of 420 women. This is the number—420—that is reported in the panel's Appendix A, without comment.

Secondly, the additional 19 women, as they figure in the tables in chapters 3, 4, and 5, or the additional 20, if we look at chapter 6, appear to have different profiles from the 400 who preceded them into the tables. Comparisons between the black folder (400 women) and the red folder (419 or 420 women) make this clear. For example: the increase of 20 women over the sample of 400 is an increase of 5.0%. But the number of all cases of sexual/physical assault reported rises from 1,359 to 1,554, an increase of 195, or 14.3%. Where the 400 women reported 3.4 cases each, the 20 women added account for 9.9 cases of assault each! As a group, then, they are nearly three times as prone to assault as the first group (table 6.1.2). In the same way, every one of the 19 additional women seems to have reported childhood sexual abuse, compared with 1 in 2 of the 400 women (table 3.2.1). The recorded rate of incest in the group of 19 was twice the level (36.8%) of the rate (16%) for the 400 women (table 3.2.2). The group of 19 also reported far more cases of adult rape or attempted rape for each assaulted woman than the group of 400 (Table 4.2.1): 5 cases each (54 cases for 10 of the women), in comparison with 1.8 cases each (202 of the 400 women). Maybe these were the most complicated cases, with the longest interviews, part of the original sample but set aside for especially careful tabulation? Or maybe this is an additional sample of some sort? There is no way to know from any of the documentation.

Thirdly, erratic data entry, faulty arithmetic, and shifting categories make some of the tables unusable, and generative of false arguments (e.g. the perpetrator tables 3.5.1 and 3.5.2, or the revictimization tables 6.2.2 and 6.2.3). Even more unsettling is that, in the course of the revision of numbers between the black folder and the red folder text, strange things happen to the numbers that are not accountable by the addition of 19 or 20 women to the sample. In the prevalence table for sexual assault, the increase in the sample from 400 to 419 has inexplicably pushed up the number of raped women by 34, from 134 to 168 (table 4.2.1). Elsewhere, grandfather rape or attempted rape *decreases* from 2 to 1, and sexual touching increases from 1 to 4 (table 3.5.1). The increase might come from the new arrivals, but if the decrease is a reinterpretation between, say, attempted rape and sexual touching, then the reliability of all the interpretations, not to mention all the quantifications, may have to be called into question. For example, with the addition of 19 women, including 37 cases of child sexual abuse, the overall tabulation of uncle incest mysteriously goes down, from 26 to 25, including a reduction in rape/attempted-rape from 8 to 5 (table 3.2.1). Incest by other male relatives declines from 19 to 9.

For extrafamilial perpetrators, from dates to strangers, the discrepancies between the black folder and the red folder, some two weeks apart, are even less comprehensible. For example, the overall number of reported cases of sexual abuse by acquaintances and neighbours goes *down* from 115 to 51, including a reduction of sexual touching from 63 to 8. At the same time, the number of acquaintance/neighbour rape or attempted-rape cases is increased from 23 to 33. In this chart, the overall pattern of revision is a sharp drop in the aggregate numbers of cases, combined with a decrease in the sexual touching cases, from 116 to 58, and an increase in the rape/attempted-rape cases, 48 to 76 (table 3.5.2). Are these reinterpretations? The volume of them is very disturbing. And what happened to the cases that have been now removed from the charts? How did they get there in the first place, and where have they gone? How did the number of cases of sexual assault by strangers *drop* from 200 in the black folder to 91 in the red folder (table 4.3.3)? Was this a deliberate attempt to reinforce the fashionable argument that dates and acquaintances (146) and boyfriends/lovers (126) account for more sexual assault cases than strangers (now only 91)? Strangers may not be "the most likely perpetrators of sexual assault" (RF 33), but they seem much less active in the red folder than they had been in the black folder. What happened to the cases? How did husbands go down from five cases of attempted intercourse (3.1%) in the black folder, to *no cases* (0%) in the red folder and the published summary (table 4.3.5)?

Fourthly, the WSP work is inconclusive, inconsistent, and often chaotic. What is visible in the tables and the shifting categories and numbers is the tip of an iceberg. The qualitative data must be virtually unmanageable, and certainly not easily reducible to numbers. The project signals inexperience, and the arguments rest on biopolitical advocacy more than on scientific insight. The authors acknowledge that "a detailed account of the methodology, including the response rate, has yet to be prepared" (BF 19; RF 19). And the survey instrument, the questionnaire, is nowhere to be found, although there are two or three references to specific types of questions asked, implying that there was some kind of regular routine. There are also enough references to Diana Russell to suggest that her questionnaire may have been adapted in some way for the use of the WSP.

Two points are worth making in closing this review of the WSP and the CanPan. The first is that the WSP material should never have been rushed into print. Haskell and Randall took advantage of the panel's need for something that looked like scientific proof of the general indictment of men that it wished to offer to the Canadian public. The panel's preference for whatever might cause maximum alarm induced them to buy the WSP and blow it all over the front pages. Together, they chose to exploit the public, and together they caused incalculable harm to the deserving cause of those who genuinely suffer.

What makes all this possible is the myth of the unconvicted rapist, the idea that the lives of women are full of perpetrators and nasty incidents that never reach the public ear or the police record. The glory is the researcher's who can ferret out the untold volume of pain, by getting past the women's censor ("denial") which refuses to call rape rape or sexual assault assault, and which keeps women from reporting what is supposedly known and suffered in silence. That's why all these clever researchers invent strictly behavioural questions to describe incidents which are apparently prevalent in women's lives. Catalogues of unwanted incidents, over a lifetime. What these catalogues and tables do not do, however, is to set the unwanted incidents against the wanted incidents of sexual and physical interaction in women's lives. Were they to do so, they would have a very different measure of the *meaning* and *proportion* of unwanted incidents. What percentage of women's sex lives and interactive lives are "unwanted"? Did they ever have "wanted" sexual touching? How sexually active have been these lives, and over what period of time?

In short, the contexts of experience might very well disclose the crucial difference between the clinical population of battered or violated women and the general population of women. The former have chosen to report "unwanted" experiences to the police and to other agencies in order to seek protection from what they consider pathological. The latter, on the other hand, do not report unwanted experiences, because they can and prefer to cope with them on their own. In fact, we have to assume that most of these experiences, though not specifically wanted, go unreported because they are normal, and not pathological. Nobody is entitled to or capable of a life free of all unwanted experiences.

Indeed, the discovery of preference is strictly speaking a construction resulting from a sorting of experiences into wanted and unwanted. This precisely is the process of learning, growing, and maturation in the general population, and it is as much the case for sexual matters as for any other. The medium of our interactions is ambiguity, ambivalence, and a mixed economy of initiative, responsiveness, and reticence; and our own motives are no more unequivocally transparent to ourselves than they are to others. This psychological dimension is given shape by the particular sexual economy of our time, but not replaced by it. The expectation of female monopoly over the management of sexual contact is a horizon in relation to which the whole range of personality variances can play itself out. The pretension of the empirical social scientist, that she or he can simplify the whole world of meaning and value down to unambiguous labels for unambiguous incidents of conduct, conceals an aggressive program to straitjacket the play of human motivations and expectations. Biopolitical moral panic just happens to be the mental disease of our day, masquerading as mental health and social welfare.

The CanPan Recommends: Biofeminism at the Helm

The panel does not mince words when it comes to spelling out its perspective. The advocacy, the one-sided organization and presentation of data, testimony, and argument, and the manipulation of emotion and logic are all gathered in a single purpose: to churn up an irresistible wave of moral panic, and to ride it to a safe haven. The bigger the panic about security, the bigger the clout that needs to be wielded, and the bigger the change that must be effected, in order to make the world "safe for women" (CL 195). Virtually all women are victimized everywhere in Canadian society. Any who are not are nevertheless expected to internalize a universal anxiety: "the only reason I am not in an abusive relationship is by luck—not because of my race, class or ability" (CL V: 103). Accordingly, virtually all men are indictable perpetrators of violence (broadly defined as a "continuum" from words to murder, including physical, sexual, psychological, financial, and spiritual dimensions—CL 3). Virtually all Canadian institutions are organized around hatred for women and hostility to women.

Social services, "except for those delivered from a feminist perspective" (CL 200), fail to understand violence. The police "hold stereotypical views of gender, race, and class" and show reluctance "to respect a feminist analysis" (CL 214). The courts blame the victims for the offence (CL 220); and where women commit the crimes, the courts fail to see that they are still the victims in need of healing: "They have more in common with other women than with male perpetrators of crime" (CL 224). In fact, says the panel, "no aspect of the legal system is innocent"; "the legal system reflects and enforces the sexist and racist structures of Canadian society, and serves those interests, not those of women" (CL 242). Women are not really parts of society, then, as much as survivors in it. Even in the universities, women students and teachers are faced with "abusive, belligerent and dangerous environments" and hostile administrators and colleagues (CL 262). Finally, what society learns from the ubiquitous media is in support of men's power over women and "threatens women's sense of well-being" (CL 268). "There is no question that the media are all too often a misogynist force distorting women's realities in Canadian society" (CL 273). Band-aids, therefore, are not enough: everything has to change from top to bottom. Only biofeminists have the wherewithal to rise to the occasion, and have to be given total power to turn everything upside down.

The panel's work is scandalously irresponsible, and deluded. It is hard to describe its recommendations without an element of parody, since they are deeply self-caricaturing. There are 105 pages of more than 400 recommendations, and most of the media have so far ignored them. One exception is Ted Byfield ("$10M violence report plans an Orwellian utopia"), who highlighted some of the changes the panel wants to introduce, including some of the following. All social services would be expected to change over to "a feminist intervention approach" (CL V: 41) and to a "gender, race and class analysis" (CL V: 43, 46). Similarly, anybody who has anything to do with the law would have to be indoctrinated in "gender and race sensitivity" (CL V: 8). Being of "good character," as defined by women's organizations, would become an eligibility criterion for a legal career (CL V: 55), and all law courses would be developed "in partnership with women's organizations" (CL V: 54).

Law enforcement would become a feminist activity. There would be special courts and judges for cases of violence against women, with training in "the parallels between torture and woman abuse ... including psychological and emotional abuse" (CL V: 52). Men would not get off on "legal technicalities" and their defence lawyers would be constrained by protocols designed to protect the female victims (CL V:54). DNA evidence would be collected from anyone *accused* of a sex offence (CL V: 50), and sex offenders would be prohibited from looking at *Playboy* in prison (CL V: 57). There would be mandatory inquests for female homicide victims (though not for murdered men) (CL V: 60); and there would be a new "victims' advocate office and a victims' bill of rights" (CL V: 58).

In government, the Status of Women portfolio would be a senior cabinet post, with the power to review "all federal government policies, programs and legislative proposals" (CL V: 11). In the military, women would take part in all major decision making, but would also be guaranteed that they "can leave any situation of violence, regardless of where the base is located, in Canada or abroad." The training of men for combat readiness would have to be balanced with training in non-aggressive interpersonal relationships; and pin-ups would be prohibited on military base premises (CL V: 65, 66, 67). In the workplace, post-traumatic stress disorder would be recognized as "a form of injury" resulting from sexual harassment (CL V: 63).

In schools, the safety of girls and women would be made a priority, and only staff with appropriate attitudes would be hired. Awareness of inequality would become a factor in performance appraisals (CL V: 70, 72). "Violence prevention" would find a place in all curricula. In fact, all educational institutions would have to reform their course contents significantly. In universities, all professors would have to be trained by the staff of rape-crisis centres, while feminist "methodology" would have to receive "recognition." Universities, in general, would be required to "provide support for feminist faculty" (CL V: 74, 75). All teachers would have to be taught to "maintain warm, nurturing relationships with students," while recognizing that no student has sufficient power to consent to having sex with a teacher (CL V: 76).

There would have to be, of course, rigorous, legislated enforcement of a prohibition on stereotyping in media, and elimination of anything that demeans women. No program would be prepared without consulting feminist experts. Print media would be expected to "dedicate print space as frequently as possible to the issues of violence, women's safety and equality" (CL V: 80). In fact, the media, like the schools, would be expected to mount constant comprehensive propaganda campaigns over biofeminist issues. The self-regulation of the media would be abandoned for stiffer measures, if they failed to provide a "realistic portrayal of women" (CL V: 82). Finally, the churches, too, must be feminized. They would have to "work to revise religious teachings," incorporate feminist theology, abolish ecclesiastical authority, "adopt democratic structures," and eliminate sexism, racism, and homophobia from all religious instruction (CL V: 88, 89).

One central point needs emphasis. The point of the inflation of a problem to the level of an all-embracing totality is to recommend total abolition. *Zero tolerance.* It has no cognitive content; it is tautological and self-referential. It assumes such complete reversal of its own picture of reality that it is more about redemption than remedy. The panel's view of the situation of women is comprehensively bleak: "Violence against women is a product of a sexist, racist, heterosexist and class society and is perpetuated through all social institutions and the attitudes and behaviours of members of all Canadian communities" (CL V: 23). But then, blithely: "The elimination of violence will best be achieved through the adoption and rigorous application of a policy of zero tolerance" (CL V: 24). How can a policy negate the entire fact basis of its global situtation? Where is the *sequitur*?

Zero tolerance has become the leading formula for prescriptive intrusion by government in the 1990s. The panel here is part of a fashionable trend toward authoritarian intervention. The appeal, like the snake-oil vendor's appeal, is to the gullible, who believe in the quick fix, the easy cure, and the prospects of zero risk. The appeal is also to the power fantasies evoked by the images of magic solutions. Total power, absolute intolerance. Intolerance of violence spreads to intolerance of verbal harassment. That expands outward to intolerance of stereotypes. Then intolerance of explicit sexuality. Intolerance of humour. Intolerance of beliefs, attitudes, ideas. Intolerance of difference and, finally, intolerance of tolerance itself. Intolerance of unregulated life, of inappropriate life. Intolerance of life.

The panel announces: "The National Action Plan introduces the concept of zero tolerance and a policy framework for its implementation" (CL V: 3). There is no doubt here about the role of the state: "Governments have a major role in protecting women's rights, promoting equality and providing leadership to the application of the Zero Tolerance Policy" (CL V: 3). Nor is there any hesitation about the scope of desirable social control. "Zero Tolerance Policy underscores the importance of accountability at all levels and in all sectors" (CL V: 4). Actually, the panel wants to set up zero-tolerance accountability boards at the federal level as well as at every provincial and territorial level (CL V: 99). The panel's utopia, the dictatorship of biofeminist morality—its remedy for biofeminist panic—rests on the same totalitarian mindset that has devastated our century, again and again. False hopes, false values, false analyses, false policies, false authorities.

It is appropriate for us to remember, *à propos* of mental dispositions and utopian perspectives, that the biofeminist literary utopia of the 20th century, particularly the lesbian utopia since the 1970s, is a radical intervention in a genre that has been historically dedicated (with mixed results) to the perfection of human life. The utopian writings by a number of biopoliticized women, from Charlotte Perkins Gilman's *Herland* (1915) to Joanna Russ's *The Female Man* (1975), Suzy McKee Charnas's *Motherlines* (1978), and Sheri Tepper's *Gate to Women's Country* (1988), however much they are praised by a readership that includes male admirers, share a problematical innovation. They make up the only public discourse in our time that is openly organized around a positive view of separatist and genocidal fantasies of a world where men are not just disposable but systematically disposed of, leaving women to flower to independence, full humanity, and perfection, all on their own.

After all this, I wanted to know how extensively the panel's materials were being distributed through its primary network. Perhaps we would not have to come up against the CanPan's misinformation campaign in every school, and office, and county newspaper. Cathy McRae, the chief public environment analyst in the Communications Directorate of Status of Women Canada, had the answer, and she was kind enough to take the trouble to impart it:

"There was very wide distribution of the panel report; it can be borrowed from over 900 public and university libraries that participate in the Federal Government Depository Services Programme. We've also distributed it free of charge to national women's organizations and other non-governmental organizations (there's about 70 national women's organizations), members of advisory councils on the status of women in all provinces, relevant provincial and territorial ministers and senior officials, members of Parliament and senators, selected media, other federal departments and all participants in the panel's work. The video was shown nationally on CTV in July 1993, and it is available from the National Film Board which has offices from coast to coast.

On the numbers ... let's see ... there was the final report in English, 3,512; in French, 2,516. There was a summary—the executive summary—6,323; in French, the summary, 2,906. There were 2,910 copies of the kit in English, 1,535 in French. There was a *Facilitator's Guide* that went with that—we didn't print as many—there were 605 in English and 385 in French. Now, the vast majority, or a good percentage, were given away or available through the libraries across Canada and there are still small quantities available for sale. The videos can be rented from 35 offices of the National Film Board across the country so they've got quite wide distribution. As well, Status has done a marketing plan for the Community Kit and advertised it in most organizations, like teachers' organizations, nurses' organizations and their newsletters, and that sort of approach. *So there has been a very wide distribution in all the social service areas, in all the women's communities, and to the general public.*" (italics added)

So there it is. It will filter into the arteries of the culture. Unless it is confronted before it can download itself into the manifold channels of biofeminist transmission. Its numbers and stories have already begun to make their appearance in publications of the Ontario Women's Directorate, and other intermediate distributors. The panel, meanwhile, "proposes that all actions begin immediately, with results to be achieved by the year 2000" (CL V: 33). Millennial thinking. *Caveat emptor.*

VII
Zero Degree of Tolerance:
Policy Schooled In Panic

"Horace Walpole once said that the world is comic to those who think and tragic to those who feel. I hope you'll agree with me that Horace Walpole somewhat simplifies the world by saying this. Surely both of us think and feel; in regard to what's comic and what's tragic, Mrs. Poole, the world is all mixed up." (John Irving, The World According to Garp 233)

"It was not one of Garp's better points: tolerance of the intolerant. Crazy people made him crazy. It was as if he personally resented giving in to madness — in part, because he so frequently labored to behave sanely... Tolerance of the intolerant is a difficult task that the times asks of us." (John Irving, The World According to Garp 537)

Biopolitics in Education Policy: the "Equity" Agenda

Panic thinking makes panic policies, and panic policies have panic implementation. As biopolitics issues forth in one regulative policy after another, in one field of human affairs after another, the effects of adversarial thinking can be seen directly in the practical marks that they leave. We are still, as a society, at a relatively early stage of this incipient mental disease. If we pay attention, we may be able to shorten its course.

The institution at the cutting edge of moral panic is that of education. Universities are busily producing the social science underpinnings that provide some academic credibility for the biopolitical program. At the same time they are being made the first laboratory for the current phase of the regulative march of "virtue." They are well on the road to damaging their educational mission by subordinating it to the pressures of panic. In addition, they are committing serious injustices against some of their members. In this chapter, I am going to look at the nature of biopolitical "policy." In the next two, I will present some case studies of biopolitical panic in action in the universities.

Legislative backlash in the past two years has begun to overturn the great liberal achievements of previous generations of progressive social activism since the Second World War. Some of the most damaging instruments of government policy currently in play in the domain of education, which I mentioned briefly in the first chapter, are described below in somewhat more detail.

The employment-equity legislation (Bill 79), the first of its kind in Canada, became effective in Ontario as of September 1994. This highly intrusive and prescriptive law specifically proposes to move beyond the existing human-rights legislation, by imposing positive reforming obligations on employers. It is not just a case here of requiring numerical plans for the preferential hiring of preferred groups (women, racial minorities, aboriginals, and people with disabilities). Nor of requiring their auditable retention. In addition, it calls for the implementation of explicitly positive, supportive, and accommodative measures, addressed to the designated groups. No care has been taken to buffer the *intellectual* life of universities against the as-yet-unexamined impact of a legislated, therapeutic requirement (that the creation of a "supportive" environment be given priority).

The Ontario Council on University Affairs, at one time a buffer body between universities and government, but lately the craven tool of ministry policy, has begun a major review of the financing of Ontario universities. The objectives of the review are not only to save costs and find ways to underfund the system even more dramatically than underfunding in the past (which, according to OCUA's report about underfunding in the 1970s, has already put the "System on the Brink"). No, OCUA is setting out to overhaul the universities and transform them into instruments of government policy. Its objective is to make universities fundamentally redirect themselves to serving the government's short-term "equity" agenda.

The OCUA document, absurdly called "Sustaining Quality," attacks the universities and the academic profession, separates teaching from research, and insists that "equity" is not satisfied by equal opportunity or equitable access to education. Universities are to be expected to provide "equitable outcomes" for students. This is short-hand for saying that merit is an obsolete, elitist conception.

This conception may well turn out to be deeply dysfunctional from a social point of view. Our lived reality cannot be built on purely ideological standards; it must relate to practical things. This is not to say, nor even to imply, that minority individuals do not have merit. Nor that many more cannot develop it. Far from it. My point is exactly the opposite. Unable to understand or address the limited imaginary horizons that serve as barriers to universal participation in higher education, and yet affronted by a sense of a certain lack of access, the "progressive" agenda opts to go *against* the grain of what universities may properly offer to society, and prepares to change the rules of the game, instead of developing programs to assist more people to become better players.

In July, 1993, the MET issued minister Dave Cooke's policy guidelines on "Antiracism and Ethnocultural Equity in School Boards." This was accompanied by deputy minister Charles Pascal's "Policy/Program Memorandum No. 119" on developing and implementing the appropriate policies to comprise all the elements prescribed under the guidelines. In time-honoured fashion, the implementation plans are required to be five-year plans (Memo 4; "Antiracism" 8). Every school board is currently turning cartwheels to comply. The guidelines provide mandated formulas for *racializing ethnicity*. This, precisely, is the biopolitical program: to take *cultural* differences, and treat them on the model of biologically defined, *racial* differences. The net result can only be a culture where perspectives are dominated by racial typologies to a far greater and more damaging extent than is currently the case.

Like the guidelines, which state that much of the traditional curriculum is discriminatory because it focusses on white Europeans (13), the deputy minister's policy memorandum attacks the European perspectives in Ontario education, and deduces that the school system suffers from "systemic inequities." In an extraordinary statement, the directive advises educators that their institutional policies and individual behaviours are objectively racist, regardless of what they may think: "Racist in their impact, if not in intent" (Memo 1; "Antiracism" 5). They have to be made to change. If the educators themselves do not know or intend their "racism," however, who will educate the educators? The biopolitical ideologues? The guidelines involve an immense amount of monitoring—by communities, boards, and the ministry—of teachers' lesson plans, performance evaluations of staff, annual reports of supervisors and principals. Says the deputy minister: "In this regard, antiracist and ethnocultural equity education goes beyond multicultural education, which focuses on teaching about the cultures and traditions of diverse groups" (1). Does the Ontario public have the slightest idea of what is being planned in its name? Have the parents in Ontario given this government a mandate to do all this to their children, and to their children's teachers?

"Beyond multicultural education" means far more than providing comparative cultural information, sensitivity training, and lessons in tolerance. Its commitment to "equitable outcomes" reaches into what students are taught, and also who teaches them. Apart from commanding the reorganization of every aspect of schooling, the government's obsession with racial differentiation will differentiate kids in an entirely inappropriate and unnecessary way. Racism with benign intentions is still racism, however you dress it up. As part of the process, students can expect to be catalogued with unilluminating racial identifiers such as "skin colour, shape of eyes, texture of hair, and facial features" ("Antiracism" 5). In the name of promoting racial harmony, individual kids will be divided from other kids, labelled in ways contrary to today's standards of respect for the individual, deprived of the right to exercise personal choice of association, and involuntarily assigned to an institutionally defined social group (Bled 2).

Teaching children to label themselves, or others, as "disadvantaged" by virtue of race or ethnicity is teaching them to label themselves or other kids downwards. Even if "the cultural and racial identities of all students are affirmed" ("Antiracism" 14), according to one of the core objectives, the children are effectively racially differentiated. Race-thinking is not erased, but validated. As a direction in education, this is far worse than teaching kids that the whole world of accomplishment is open to them (unreferenced to racialized role models and "identities"). Benign racism will produce separate education; and the chances are that "separate education means separate futures" (Bled 3).

The NDP's Orwellian superministry of education and training (MET) also issued in 1993 the government's official policy, "Framework Regarding Harassment and Discrimination in Ontario Universities and Colleges," to mandate immediate policy development and implementation. I will review its direct attack on freedom of expression in higher education at some length below. All of these ministry initiatives require the establishment of action plans by 1995; all of them require submission to government for audit and, in most cases, approval. All of them have the potential to ruin education in Ontario for a generation.

I should add that there is little chance for even-handed implementation of these policies. The new equity bureaucracies in the government will likely be staffed by extremist advocates, in the fashion of the Ontario Women's Directorate, the Anti-Racism Secretariat (formerly the Race Relations Directorate), or the Human Rights Commission. Policies designed for designated "disadvantaged" groups are staffed by personnel from those groups. Biopolitics is intrinsically and aggressively adversarial, and there is no competition more fierce than the struggle over oppression credentials. The designations carry enormous status value, as well as access to influence, authority, and power, at least over some people. They mean also income, careers, and security in the new equity growth industry.

It would be naive to overlook the momentum of symbolic and rhetorical escalation, especially where discourse is the only link to reality. The hostilities and intolerances that will emanate from the equity agencies will surely match the aggressive discourse of biofeminism, and far outstrip anything in the culture at large directed against the minorities. Indeed, the potential for internal division among the "disadvantaged" is just as great as the potential for separation from the "dominant white male." Group thinking has a nearly unlimited potential for subdividing into narrower and narrower concentrations of some essential bioquality. The fragmentation of the new left into competing groupuscules in the late 1960s and 1970s provides the probable model and destiny of the equity politics of the 1990s.

The designated groupings are already exclusive of other "disadvantages"—religious minorities, for example, or economic. The poor fisherman's son from Newfoundland would hardly fare well in the equity race against a well-educated, East Indian woman from a wealthy family. There are hierarchies inside the designated groups, as well. Asians do not have the same oppression status as blacks do. No equity progressives cried for the Korean-Americans who were savagely attacked by black Americans in the Los Angeles riots in 1992. In Canada, NDP guru Stephen Lewis advised Premier Rae in 1992, in a letter that was to become a keystone of the government's policy agenda for its first and probably only term in office, that blacks were more deserving of the government's anti-racism attention than other racial minorities. Lewis wrote: "Just as the soothing balm of 'multiculturalism' cannot mask racism, so racism cannot mask its primary target. It is important, I believe, to acknowledge not only that racism is pervasive, but that at different times in different places, it violates certain minority communities more than others."

Anyway, one does not have to theorize. There are also the participant-witness accounts. Julie Mason, a feminist activist, and former director of communications for the federal NDP, worked for a year at the new Employment Equity Commission in Ontario. According to journalist Thomas Walcom, she called it the most racist workplace she had ever experienced. In his study of the follies of the NDP, Walcom quotes Mason: "I've never seen anything like it. It was absolutely vicious ... The blacks hated the Indians; the Indians were the most anti-Semitic; everyone hated the lesbians and gays ... There was a real pecking order. At the bottom were people with disabilities. Next to the bottom were white women. There were no white men, not until they had to bring in John DeMarco (a senior bureaucrat in Citizenship) to fix up the mess" (B4). Walcom also adds that "white bureaucrats within Citizenship were encouraged, in scenes reminiscent of Maoist self-criticism sessions, to admit publicly to their inherent racism" (B4). A modicum of caution will remind us that people who set out deliberately to erase the liberal forms of civil liberties in favour of systematic preferences are likely to rediscover and repeat all the patterns of illiberal ignorance and intolerance available to those in positions of power.

Biopolitics and "Human Rights"

All of this is relatively recent, although it is galloping through our social institutions and education policies at a breakneck pace. It would be a grave error to think that this policy direction is entirely driven by the government of the day. The bureaucracy in the ministry itself seems to be committed to keeping up the pressure over the "equity" agenda, regardless of which politicians are in power at a given moment. As I will review below, the moral panic I have been detailing in connection with violence against women is now being absorbed at the administrative level into a larger program of panic about what is called *human rights*. The assumption is that "human rights" can trump any other argument, and settle policy debates before they get off the ground.

I happen to believe that this agenda rests on an abuse of a noble term in order to advance an authoritarian program. Whatever its intention, its effect is to gut the legal and moral institutions of due process and of fundamental freedoms. Moreover, its end result will not be inclusion, multiculturalism, and equity, but rather polarization between biologically demarcated formations: men and women, black and white, able and disabled, original and aboriginal. I believe also that the social-engineering agenda flying under the banner of "human rights" will exacerbate what sex, race, and class tensions there are in

Canadian society. It will get in the way of progressive social reform. It is a wolf in sheep's clothing.

Words like "rights," "equity," and "inclusion" have become control terms, and their use is increasingly a code for regulation and for the upward transfer of social power. Panic fear about symbolic safety, harassment, or discrimination, about *violation* in a broad or virtual sense, is being metonymically jacked up, just *as if* real violence were being perpetrated. Panic engineering relies on expanding the boundaries of fear to engineer an ever-growing demand for protection that only the state can satisfy. The state's gain, of course, is society's loss. The looser networks of private remedies, tacit communal sentiments, and collegial relationships are hollowed out to make way for discipline. In universities, the greatest threat is to free inquiry and expression.

The two most pernicious aspects of the CanPan are its *imperialism* and its *automatism.* Everything in social and cultural life is to be brought into a single perspective, subordinated to the main biopolitical objectives and remedial methods. The problem with this method is that each domain of culture has its own governing values and objectives, and its own privileged agencies, which set up frictions or conflicts with those viewed through biofeminism's single cracked lens.

More specifically, "women" as a group may not be the most important group for social attention when it comes to compassion. Women are not the primary victims of violence, homelessness, or occupational health hazards. More generally, "safety" may not always be the most significant priority, especially as we get away from direct issues of physical safety to such *indirect* threats to safety as unwelcome comments, discomforting language, and troubling perspectives. When it comes to education or, say, journalism, freedom of expression, curiosity, getting the story, finding the difficult and unsettling truths, and so on, may all loom larger. Diversity of human expectations and interests, conflicts of values, and frictions between expressive rights, equality rights, and security rights all call for a complexity of human sorting.

The biopolitical program has no patience, however, for complexity. Its efforts are dedicated to sweep away all other representations of a given situation than its own; and to downgrade or eliminate all other values and priorities than those that serve its own objectives. Its method, in every case, is to demand the non-discretionary automation of its own program.

How has this biopolitical program taken hold in every field and every situation? How can it triumph over every other personal and political consideration? How can it operationalize its fundamentalist binary logic: on-off, right-wrong, appropriate-inappropriate? The formula is very simple: fuelled by the fear of violence, all obstacles and barriers in the way of the biopolitical program are to be transmuted by force of description into *violations* of *human rights*. And human-rights violations cannot be tolerated, right? These are absolutes, not matters of degree. Rape or "inappropriate" sexual jokes can both be described as manifestations or symptoms of the underlying "inequality" of women, and therefore *equally* violations of the human rights of women to full equality.

In the view of true believers, every such violation, however modest, is entitled to trump every other concern. Anything that is objectionable to "women"—or rather, to the biofeminist usurpers who claim to speak for womankind—qualifies as *discrimination against women*. Any culture that loses the ability to distinguish meaningfully between rape and humour is in deep trouble. And yet, it is this increasingly pervasive cultural logic of the continuum that is entering our laws and transforming our institutions.

The vicious character of continuum thinking, of thinking without distinctions, is compounded by its imperviousness to *intentionality*. Adversarial biofeminism sees only victims and perpetrators. How could the perpetrator's intentions matter? Why should the perpetrator enjoy freedom of speech, and get recourse to due process, at the expense of the victim? Now, most human interactions that take place in a cultural setting of any sophistication do not fall neatly into such typological moulds. The conceptual language of violent crime does not assist the analysis of cultural friction in the general population. And even where a situation might ultimately lend itself to characterization in terms of such stark polarization, we cannot decide who is victim and who is wrongdoer, unless and until due process has run its course, and certainly not until free speech has brought into play the divergent self-presentations of the players.

Biopolitical automation dispenses with such refinements of fair play. Its principle is: *guilty if accused.* Tidy little formulas like "don't blame the victim," once moved into the domains of general behaviour, beg every single important question of adjudication. What is most troubling is that the principle is compatible with Canadian administrative law, and capable of exploiting the latter in unanticipated ways.

Biopolitics and the Law: The Supreme Court in Janzen (1989) and Butler (1992)

The Canadian constitution has a concept of substantive due process, which prevents a finding of criminal responsibility in the absence of a finding of criminal intent. The standards of protection for the accused are less rigorous, however, outside the frame of criminal law. Human-rights law falls into the domain of administrative law, and operates with lower levels of protection for the respondent to a complaint. The burden of proof is often a "balance of probabilities," rather than "beyond a reasonable doubt"; and the intentions of the accused are often disregarded altogether. Administrative law, dealing with disputes rather than crimes, directs itself toward dispute resolution; a settlement rather than incarceration. Neither the consequences of the resolution achieved nor the stigma attached to wrong-doing are expected to be as severe in the case of an administrative dispute as in the case of a criminal offence.

These expectations fail, however, in the case of discrimination issues that acquire a high social profile. They fail utterly in the case of sexual harassment, under conditions of a sex panic. A finding of sexual harassment today in a university, for example, or even an accusation of it, can damage lives and careers beyond repair. The level of stigmatization far exceeds the comparable levels for minor criminal offences. Yet, the leading case law in the area of sexual harassment has established, and the Supreme Court of Canada has confirmed, that the law excludes intention as a relevant factor in connection with inappropriate behaviour (*Janzen et al. v Platy Enterprises*, 1989). Intention is irrelevant in cases of sexual harassment, inasmuch as sexual harassment is considered an abuse of power and discrimination against women, with a negative effect on the work environment.

A principle of this kind may make some sense in dispute resolution, where it is a matter, perhaps, of improving some employment practice. It makes no sense, however, where sexual harassment is treated as a crime, where the outcome is expected to be disciplinary, and where the result of conviction is moral and social disapprobation, as well as long-term stigmatization. There is a fundamental injustice in the making here, and it is imperative that the blind automation, a prominent feature of most harassment policies and policy implementations, be reversed. It is false to human realities and expectations and, if left unaltered, will not only produce injustices, but will also in time utterly discredit the problem of sexual harassment itself.

The method of biopolitics in policy making is to insist on the linkage of the concepts of violence, violation, and harm. These terms are rapidly becoming interchangeably operational, *not with reference to established consequences (actual injury), but with reference to estimated origins (inferred source of risk).* Unfortunately, one of the worst decisions that the Supreme Court of Canada has made in recent memory amounts to authorizing this kind of thinking in Canadian administrative institutions. An obscure video store owner in Vancouver provided the biofeminist lobby with the opportunity to win perhaps their biggest North American legal victory. Butler was the immediate loser; freedom of expression in the direct, immediate situation was the second. But perhaps the greatest consequences are yet to be felt from the entrenchment in the law of a characteristically biopolitical logic of harm.[1]

The Butler decision of February 27, 1992, often called the "first MacKinnon law"[2] in the Western world, plays a large part in Canada's international reputation as the leader in feminist jurisprudence. It circumvents the traditions of protecting freedom of speech in order to install prevention of harm to women as a higher and more imposing value.[3]

The way the Court argues has wide ramifications. In order for materials to qualify as "obscene" under Canadian law, the exploitation of sex must not only be its dominant characteristic, but such exploitation must be "undue." The most important test that the courts use to determine when the exploitation is undue is the "community standards of tolerance" test; that is, not what Canadians will not tolerate for themselves, but rather what they would not tolerate other Canadians being exposed to. Here is where the court breaks new ground. They write: "There has been a growing recognition in recent cases that material which may be said to exploit sex in a 'degrading or dehumanizing' manner will necessarily fail the community standards test, not because it offends against morals, but because it is *perceived by public opinion* to be *harmful* to society, particularly *women.* In the appreciation of whether material is degrading or dehumanizing, the appearance of consent is not necessarily determinative" (3-4).

According to the highest law in the land, then, not fact, not knowledge, not objective evidence, not clear and convincing argument, not expert scholarship, and nothing like proof beyond a shadow of a doubt are to be the decisive arbiters of harm. It is public opinion, and its perception. This sounds democratic, indeed, and possibly unavoidable, or at least better than the alternatives. But the value of this democratic criterion, as a principle of *justice*, not politics, depends heavily on the *quality* of the public *opinion*, as well as the fair-minded care with which *perception* is studied. But in a democratic society, where consensus is not required, and uniformity of perception and opinion are not the norm, who speaks for public opinion? Who determines what is decisively the perception of public opinion? The danger is that, instead of finding the best path through the conflicts in the public will, we simply concede to the most powerful lobbies of the moment.

The Supreme Court takes the view that the objective of the obscenity law is "the avoidance of harm to society" (5). But surely the earlier concern with the offence against morals was also a concern with the prevention of harm? What has changed? The Court gives a new meaning to harm from exposure to "degrading and dehumanizing" sexual materials: "It *predisposes* persons to act in an anti-social manner" (italics added) and adds that "the stronger the *inference* of a *risk* of *harm*, the lesser the likelihood of tolerance" (4; italics added). Not just harm now, nor even the *risk* of harm, which is already an estimate, but an *inference of a risk* of harm, is the standard of legal intolerance. This is the realm now of speculation, and several degrees of speculation, moreover, about what could be inferred to pose a possibility of harm.

The special target, moreover, of when the full terror of the law might be brought down to support speculative public opinion, is a *predisposition*: anything that might predispose someone toward anti-social action. Predispositions are attitudes, beliefs, motives: the inner texture of our minds. According to this principle, anything that promotes anti-social mental activity, as imagined by public

183

opinion, is illegal! I don't need to spell out here the deep implications and alarming consequences of the Court's reasoning.

end

But there is another element. The Court is concerned with what is "harmful to society, *particularly women*" (4; italics added). In this entire judgment, in fact, society is identified with women, women are identified as society, society is considered only from the point of view of "particularly women." In short, the decision sets out the principle that legal decisions about sex are to be made on the basis of making guesses about what kinds of expressions may have the effect of promoting mental attitudes that may in turn possibly result in some behaviour that could potentially be harmful to women.

In rejecting the civil liberties arguments put to it, the Court specifically held that "the objective is the avoidance of harm caused by the degradation which many women feel as 'victims' of the message of obscenity, and of the negative impact exposure to such material has on perceptions and attitudes towards women" (60). And what impact does this exposure have on women? The final paragraph in the summary of the majority judgment spells it out when it points with the assurance of self-evidence to the "serious social problem" of "violence against women." It becomes pretty clear here that the arbiter of this neo-Victorian obsession with the corruption of men and the protection of women, particularly from sex and sexual symbols, the arbiter euphemistically described as "the perception of public opinion," can be none other than those who claim to represent "women": the biofeminist lobbies.[4]

It is well known that there are numerous Canadian laws which restrict speech, including laws concerning official secrets and emergencies, contempt, hate propaganda, broadcasting, human rights, civil defamation, and the different forms of criminal libel: seditious, defamatory, obscene, and even blasphemous libel. As legal observers also know, however, all these rest on some approximation to an *objective* standard of harm, rather than subjective feelings or theoretical speculations (see Adam). It has been the dramatic achievement of the biopolitical interventions of the past decade to have shifted these standards, to the detriment of the legal system. As a result, the historical traditions that have protected expression have been displaced as well.

Any strategy to circumvent the traditions of legal protection for thought and expression by turning to the law on torts, that is, on wrongful harm, is already a dangerous deviation. But the authority to curtail expressive freedoms on the strength of an *inference*, without even a demonstration of actual harm, must surely in time be recognized as failing to meet the test of "reasonableness" (which is a requirement of the Canadian Charter of Rights). The obsessive processing of *inferences of risks of harm* testifies to irrationality fuelled by anxiety: a panic phenomenon. The Butler decision is most important for the way it will contaminate all sorts of other policies and decisions with practical consequences. The MET Framework, and the evolution of harassment policies generally, are examples of just such contagion. Indeed, the Framework uses the formula that gathers up the sense of the entire biopolitical lobby about its comprehensive claims and all-embracing remedies: "zero tolerance."

Zero Tolerance, Zero Risk

The CanPan hollers for zero tolerance of violence against women. The Ontario Ministry of Education and Training (MET) demands zero tolerance of sexual harassment in universities and colleges. Governments have introduced zero tolerance of domestic assault, zero tolerance of violence in the schools, and no doubt zero tolerance of many other objects of disapprobation. The term, borrowed from the Reagan era war on drugs, has become the favourite of politicians. Nothing looks more decisive than declaring war on a problem. Zero tolerance of drunken driving, loitering in subways, loud house parties (Barclay). And who, after all, is likely to defend the persistence of the problem in question? Nothing seems more natural and reasonable than the innocent question: Don't you think schools should be free from violence? Don't you think women are entitled to live in a society free from violence? Don't you think students have a right to a learning environment free from harassment?

No, I don't think so. Not if it is a yes-or-no question. The answer to a policy-related question is always: "it depends." Peter Gzowski asked me this last question in a *Morningside* interview on CBC Radio (February 3, 1994), and I had to say no, or rather, it depends. For a start, what view we take of "harassment" is very much a question of what we can agree to mean by it. Harassment may be an offence, but not everything that gives offence can be considered harassment. In universities, for example, "harassment" is becoming a code word for any form of speech, behaviour, attitude, or sexual manners that deviates from a narrow band of orthodox fashion. Zero tolerance would censor and suppress, and promote self-censorship, to a degree unimaginable in generations. It is impossible to concede to such a profound intrusion into privacy and fundamental individual freedoms.

We live, moreover, in a society that does not have a practice of zero tolerance even for the most contemptible and tragic criminal deviancy, like killing another human being. We want to know the context. Are we talking about war—against the Nazi horror, for example? Or is it a case of the police using deadly force to save lives, like killing an armed terrorist who has already killed several hostages and threatens to kill more? What about abortion? And self-defence? Intention, motivation, provocation? We distinguish between murder and justifiable homicide. And even in the case of murder, there are degrees of criminalization, according to the nature of the intent and the circumstances, and there are extenuating circumstances that can be cited as a defence. Indeed, the battery syndrome has been recently invented for women, precisely as a way of getting away with murder. So, if we do not have zero tolerance of murder, how can we imagine that we will institute zero tolerance of physical friction in the schools, or sexual humour in the universities?

Zero tolerance. Quite apart from whatever particular moral targets it is aimed at, this is in and of itself an ugly slogan of intolerance. It promotes an absolute, with relentless righteousness. But let nobody be fooled. You cannot get to tolerance by getting more and more deeply immersed in intolerance. Illiberalism will never expand the horizons of freedom and diversity.

It is commonplace nowadays for censors to preface their edicts by stressing their opposition to censorship, and for those who are about to curtail someone else's freedom to profess their commitment to the greatest degree of liberty. But there is always a *"but."* It applies to whatever falls outside the censor's limits of acceptability, and it does not strike the censor as censorship at all. It seems to be in the nature of orthodoxy to consider itself pure virtue, and to treat its own act of censorship not as an infringement on another's liberty, but as simply the sensible suppression of vice.

Zero tolerance is about lack of discretion, as well as lack of tolerance. Its special contribution is to strip discretion out of situations. As I suggested earlier, it aims to automate the implementation of its own program. Any institution that accepts legal or moral liability for a zero tolerance policy is setting itself up to police its entire domain without relief. Zero tolerance is about enforcement. Often, its proponents pretend to be unaware of the born-again authoritarianism that is concealed behind the moralistic subject matter of zero tolerance. They speak virtue, but they prepare to do vice. Zero tolerance is the dark side of utopian absolutism; it is tyranny militant, even if it views itself only in the mirror of its intentions, and not pragmatically, in the mirror of its actions and their consequences.

It is only too easy to forget that zero tolerance, regardless of how its friends describe it, is a deliberate effort to move beyond morality to setting practical policy with heavy-duty force behind it. But however much its supporters want to transfer discussion to the virtue it is said to serve, or to the mechanisms of its implementation, policy must be *debatable*. The struggle which is beginning to take public shape over the zero tolerance policies regarding sexual harassment, or violence against women, is first of all a struggle to extract these issues from the moral rhetoric of biopolitical panic, and to reframe them within the horizons of social policy debates about procedural alternatives.

Framing the Offenders

A case in point is the controversy over the MET's ill-fated effort in October 1993 to direct universities into rigid self-regulation and self-censorship. It is not likely that this was merely a failed, one-shot venture by a laughably arrogant and incapable one-term NDP government. It was much more in the nature of the tip of an iceberg that signals a new cultural ice age in the expressive culture of universities. More broadly, the cultural institutions of Ontario and Canada (including, besides education, the arts, the media, and the whole system of information) may also be under threat. Is it likely that the carelessness about expressive freedoms and due process which characterizes the "caring" agenda, to which governments are lately paying much lipservice, is merely an oversight? Or is it, instead, the censorious habit of a puritanical anglo establishment urgently trying to recycle sexual reaction in the form of "women's safety" and ethnic parochialism in the guise of multi-ethnic virtue?

On October 7, 1993, the Ontario Ministry of Education and Training (MET) issued its negative utopia for universities, the now notorious "Framework Regarding Prevention of Harassment and Discrimination in Ontario Universities." The same framework has been unceremoniously imposed on Ontario's 23 colleges, whose administrative leadership had actually suggested the basis for the Framework, through the Council of Regents' Task Force on Sexual Harassment in 1992. Based on subjective standards of potential harm, the Framework sets out to cleanse the culture of universities and colleges of any instances of "unwelcome/unwanted, offensive, intimidating, hostile, or inappropriate" comments or conduct (Framework 4). Will the state now legislate what is "appropriate"? Putting jokes, gestures, and graffiti into the same category as physical and sexual assault, the Framework sets out "the Ministry's minimum expectation of the elements that should form both the process and product of institutional policy" (1).

Leaving no doubt as to its sweeping and commanding character, the document spells out its purpose and its authority simultaneously, in its very first sentence: "The Government of Ontario has adopted a policy of zero tolerance of harassment and discrimination at Ontario's universities." Indeed, on the assumption that higher education could be described as the provision of goods and services, the policy requires from universities the full set of concerns occupying the Ontario Human Rights Code, and therefore applies to "any university in its employment, educational, and business dealings" (3).

In fact, the policy framework goes far beyond the Code, as the Canadian Association of University Teachers (CAUT) pointed out in its reply to the government. For a start, it takes in too much of human affairs, including normally protected speech. It expands the categories of offence to any "negative environment" at the same time that it lowers the threshold of offence from the Code's "course of vexatious conduct" to any *single* comment. Most surprisingly, it tries to muzzle free speech and to control free association even off campus and in private life and study. In short, it is far more intrusive than the Code was ever expected to be.

One of the most troubling aspects of the policy framework is the lack of any objective standard, either for judging what conduct actually qualifies as harassment, or for evaluating the reasonableness of a complaint. The framework promotes policies that are strictly complaint-driven; that is, pushed along solely by the subjective perceptions of grievance of a complainant (8). This is the revenge of the "victim," and it is a departure from all but the most recent legal tradition. Its only unforeseen irony arises from the fact that the policy is framed in universalistic language, with references to the dignity of every individual. This entitles individuals who are not members of the government's preferred groups to exercise the huge prerogatives granted to complainants under this policy; and to exercise them, moreover, against members of the preferred groups, feminist or aboriginal instructors, for example, whose consistent and militant advocacy positions frequently offend a number of their students, often deliberately.

Other government policies, such as the Employment Equity Act, make it clear that the policies are for the benefit only of preferred groups (women, racial minorities, aboriginals, and people with disabilities), and explicitly establish double standards under the law. It is worth noting that advocates even more zealous than the government, like Saul Ross, president of the Ontario Confederation of University Faculty Associations (OCUFA) during the gestation period of the framework, stressed that harassment and discrimination policies should *not* be for the protection of everyone! They should state explicitly that their purpose is to protect and redress victims of "systemic discrimination" (i.e. the preferred groups). "This is important so as to protect the individuals that the policy is indeed trying to protect. It should, for example, protect underrepresented groups from charges of 'reverse discrimination,' and gay and lesbian faculty from charges of harassment by homophobic students" (see Brown, "Response Expected").

Even if its larger analysis of systemic disadvantage were correct, this outlook fails to distinguish between the *systemic* level of social dynamics and what is more properly called *interpersonal* interaction, where individuals may harass or be harassed, and where they have to assume personal responsibility. It is precisely this type of deductive, syllogistic idea of class morality that kept Marxism from developing a viable ethics, and vitiated its moral standing in the eyes of all but its most cultic devotees. The relationships of effective power, and the ability to damage another person, may be quite different at different levels, depending on circumstances; and relative responsibility cannot be deduced from sociological premises. Female teachers will tend to have a great deal of institutional authority relative to their male students, for example. Female students who can destroy a man's career and life through a casual accusation are also in a very powerful position.

Ross's thinking is unfortunately typical of a devastating new trend in legal thinking, which promotes double standards under the law, and diminished responsibility for some groups.[5] Apart from the disadvantage that is thus created for grievants who are not members of the groups designated for special privileges, the greatest damage is suffered in the long run by exactly those specially favoured women, minorities, disabled, and aboriginals who thus learn to conduct themselves without bearing the same legal responsibilities as other citizens. It is doing them no favour. They will be diminished, even as they benefit, in exactly the same way that feminists now complain about the diminished status of women under the umbrella of special protection elsewhere and elsewhen—in Victorian times, for example, or under the rules of the Islamic *sharia.*

The government's zero-tolerance policy constitutes a monster plan, dense with prohibitions, incoherent lists of examples, indirect and systemic infractions, prevention and re-education provisions, interminable complaint and adjudication procedures, and numerous sanctions. It would have required universities, under threat of legal liability, to police every aspect of their interactive lives, from posters and student journalism to lectures and texts. But there is nothing in law that says a university must become a surrogate commission, or board of inquiry, and there is much in educational tradition that suggests that it should not. Universities should think twice, and more than twice, before they start shifting the balance of the university's cultural activities from the classroom to the courtroom, before they start giving up controversy for discipline, and before they start to compromise the university's educational mission by permitting intellectual problems to be defined by therapeutic values. Zero tolerance means a reduced opportunity for exposure to ideas, and lowers the value of education.

By the spring of 1994, the ministry had performed a tactical retreat from its initiative. Separate letters to universities and to the press, from minister Dave Cooke (Feb. 9) and his deputy, Charles Pascal (April 25), set aside the March deadline for compliance, and set a new target date a year later. This was designed to beat the heat from academics and journalists. Even the ministry's friends at the time, like OCUFA, began to condemn government "imposition" (see April 8 resolution of OCUFA Board). After a long period of silence, the CAUT, representing nearly 32,000 faculty, also called on the ministry to withdraw its "Framework," without planning to redraft or revise. The CAUT's position is backed up by a devastatingly critical "Reply to the Ontario Government," drafted by the Standing Committee on Academic Freedom and Tenure. This report argues that the framework fails to square with academic freedom and free speech; threatens the legal autonomy of universities; exceeds the legal provisions of the Ontario Human Rights Code; and even transgresses the case law evolving under the Code. University administrations, one after another, have voiced their own, well-modulated misgivings. To be sure, all this followed a grass-roots movement of faculty, which started at Trent University (with wide faculty endorsement of my public statement "On Free Inquiry and Expression") and spread to Carleton, Ottawa, and other universities in Ontario. It followed, as well, the persistent work of an alert and concerned press and broadcast media, all of which blew the whistle on the framework.[6]

At the same time, there is evidence that the government was only responding to what academic activists had been demanding for nearly a decade, through a variety of statements and submissions from OCUFA, CAUT, status of women committees, conferences on sexual harassment and "the inclusive university," and an ever-expanding articulation of a concept of "equity" along the lines of zero tolerance. In other words, the program of cultural and economic equity activism is already quite deeply implanted in the universities. The government's initiative was not only unnecessary, but also ironic; it may have acted as a lightning rod for a new kind of resistance.

In fact, as I write, in the fall of 1994, it seems that there has been a perceptible breach in the previously relentless progress of biopolitical authoritarianism; indeed, that a season of real debate may lie ahead of us. This seems a good time to highlight prominent features of the issues at stake, starting with the zero-tolerance policy, designed for universities with respect to sexual harassment.

Harassment, by definition, is a matter of interpersonal friction, brought to legal attention only under administrative law dealing with "rights," particularly in employment. It falls short of assault, or any other criminal act, much less a violent criminal act. It is not the crime of the century, though sex panic more and more stigmatizes it as though it were. What should be of unmistakable interest in the subject matter of this chapter, and the two that follow, is the cancerous progress of infectious sex panic, and panic remedies, as these fan out from the discourse on physical violence against women and metastasize in previously robust areas of culture, through the lymph nodes of symbolic expression. In the absence of an effective counter-agent, the progression of the disease can only end up with the contamination of the whole symbolic body of culture.

One issue ought to be foregrounded from the start: namely, that the matter of sexual harassment is a *policy* matter. There is no question of *whether* discriminatory or sexual harassment are acceptable. The debate is over *what* constitutes harassment, and how that can be distinguished from legitimate conflicts of value and conviction, differences of taste, theoretical and moral controversy, or variant appetites for sexuality and eroticism. Harassment may always be offensive, but most kinds of "offence" are not reasonably considered harassment. There is a near-infinite range of legitimate expression at which individuals may *take* offence for one reason or another. The distinction between these and the sanctionable offence of harassment must be made clear. Indeed, this is what supporters of zero tolerance are most reluctant to spell out; and yet it is what defenders of expressive freedoms must insist on with the weight of the entire liberal-democratic tradition, which permits curtailment of expression only in the narrowest and most specifically delimited regions, on the basis of specifically established warrants. A failure to establish careful distinctions, limits on the scope of "harassment," and protections for expression will expose the culture of universities to rapid degradation.

The other main aspect of debate, aside from definitions, is not *whether* harassment must be addressed, but *how* this is best done. Here again, the zero-tolerance model opts for the grossest teleology: *the ends justify the means.* In practice, this means that its supporters forgo all scruple about extensive policing, a judicial system of tribunals, and draconian sanctions. Zero tolerance implies procedures driven by pre-emptive censorship and facilitated complaint. For universities, it means that the classroom gives way to the courtroom, and that the internal culture is administered and policed more extensively than any other institutional culture, with the possible exception of the armed forces and the prisons. The obvious fact that universities are not capable of carrying through on this, and would be destroyed in the process if they were, does not offer relief from the implications of zero tolerance. It simply indicates the inviability of this kind of single-minded overreaching. It also suggests why zero tolerance so rapidly ran into trouble when it finally went public.

In fact, the debate over *how* to provide protection from harassment is precisely and properly a debate over how to make those protections consistent with the other organizational and cultural values that are fundamental, prominent, or functional in the complex ecology of liberal-democratic cultures and their institutions—including due process. Alternatives to zero tolerance stress informal conflict resolution over rule of law, and they prefer to mix administrative remedies with a greater confidence in the normal functioning of tacit practices of civility, informed by vigorous cultural and political process.

It is this last point that takes us perhaps to the heart of the motivational forces behind both the advocacy of zero tolerance and the resistances to it. The issue is the *extent* to which cultural and political process should be translated into, or supplemented with, or decided by legislative or regulative power. Zero tolerance rests on a chain of assumption and argument: the world is radically wrong; it must be radically changed; its culture and attitudes must be transformed; and finally, *this cultural reform is best carried out through the force of regulative measures as its primary instrument.* Nearly all parties to the debates agree to *some* extent of regulation, but zero tolerance is *not* discretionary, and therefore, by definition, not political and cultural in its primary application. The opponents of zero tolerance may demur from any or all the links in the chain of propositions on which it is based, but all are hostile to its final link: the idea of a command culture.

Hence, the sharp debate over the profoundly undesirable environmental terminology that supports the zero-tolerance agenda: negative environment/positive environment. Penalizing the former means introducing both behaviour controls and prohibitive censorship over expression. Requiring the latter is even worse, because it introduces hortatory censorship: *the requirement of orthodoxy in communicative interactions, pedagogy, and curriculum.* Several years' worth of OCUFA position papers about the code phrase "educational equity" make it clear that there is another agenda behind the foregrounded concern with allegedly derogatory verbal exchange in universities. This is fuelled by a desire to control the teaching and research culture, and to impose on it, by legislation and regulative measures, a particular *political* shape and content.

In its February 18, 1992 *Brief to the Employment Equity Commissioner on Educational Equity*, OCUFA proposes legislated mandatory programs: "Educational equity programs will help change political consciousness ... Without a social and political commitment from all workers, employment equity programs in the workplace can easily be sabotaged" (2). It goes on to spell out some of the "necessary changes" with respect to the *curriculum*, e.g.: "ensuring that the curriculum incorporates multicultural, multi-racial, multi-abled and gender issues, addresses sexist, racist and homophobic myths and stereotypes, and notions of gender and racial inferiority and supremacy, and generally examines the legitimate role of the designated groups in our society. This includes both special courses in Women's Studies and Native Studies, and the transformation of curriculum to include materials by and for members of designated groups"; and also, more specifically, "requiring a course on race, class and gender as part of graduation requirements at post-secondary institutions. This has already been done at some colleges and universities in the United States" (7-8).

In addition, OCUFA calls for legislation to impose orthodox *pedagogy*, under penalty of law. "Anti-sexist and anti-racist pedagogical strategies are critical to curriculum transformation. Class, race and gender dynamics are very much present in the classroom, and pedagogical practices *which do not actively take them into account will be discriminatory*" (italics added). Moreover, it will be "necessary" to create "a code of appropriate and inappropriate behaviours and attitudes within the classroom" (8).

This move to regulate the classroom is part of a disturbing new trend toward censorship and law 'n' order policies affecting cultural expression. In fact, minister Dave Cooke's letter to universities and the media, which attempts to do damage control, refers in its five short paragraphs more than a dozen times to government, law, policy, and "legal responsibilities," but only once, and then disparagingly, to the concern with free speech and academic freedom. The minister moves to dismiss the charge that the policy "would somehow limit free speech and academic freedom" by trumping it with what he claims is nothing more than the legal *status quo*. Zero tolerance, according to the "Framework," is to be regarded as nothing more than the existing legal responsibility of employers under the Human Rights Code. In effect, all of Ontario is put on notice that, as soon as education has been made an island of total virtue, the rectification campaign may move on to the newsrooms, the editorial departments, the arts, advertisements, other sites of symbolic activity, and ultimately to any and all sites of social interaction.

There is no evidence that society would be rendered thereby more virtuous (and Milton's warning that it is conflict which purifies us and not cloistered virtue is still wise guidance), but our culture would certainly become less capacious, less robust, and less free. There is another type of problem as well. If the investigative and adjudicative practices evolving under the Code legitimate the ministry's zero-tolerance framework, then the Code must be publicly reviewed as soon as possible, with respect to constitutionality in relation to expressive freedom guarantees. Or else, the Code must be uncoupled from the practices evolving under it, including the ministry's "Framework," and these latter must sink or swim on their own.

There is no evidence that the zero-tolerance initiative is capable of delivering significant benefits to socially disadvantaged or marginalized groups. Indeed, historical evidence suggests that increased intolerance is not in the interests of these groups. The lobbies which have come to expect the support of government and other power institutions of society are, by definition, not *marginal*, but, in fact, emerging parts of the institutional formation of the dominant culture itself. Their concerted moves, through state agencies and the courts, to restrict expression and introduce systematic discrimination into the law fly in the face of the basic human rights and strategic needs of the powerless. For the truly marginal, the universality of fundamental freedoms (under the Charter), including the freedom of expression and association, provide the most direct access to the prospects and practices of a level playing field.

The real backlash in our culture is the backlash of ever-polarizing biopolitics: the backlash of a new censorship and a new authoritarianism against the precious freedoms and tolerances which are the basic distinguishing features of the culture of Western modernity. Trading in the wisdom of two sides to every story, different strokes for different folks, one person's meat is another's poison, and what is sauce for the goose is sauce for the gander—all for the flat and flatulent formula of "zero tolerance"—is a bad trade.

VIII
Professors on Trial:
Universities Exercise
their Demons

> "...your sincere conviction has touched me even though it cannot influence my judgement." (Franz Kafka, "In the Penal Colony" 217)

> "Guilt is never to be doubted. ... If I had first called the man before me, and interrogated him, things would have got into a confused tangle. He would have told lies, and had I exposed these lies he would have backed them up with more lies, and so on and so forth. As it is, I've got him and I won't let him go. —Is that quite clear, now? But we're wasting time, the execution should be beginning..." (Franz Kafka, "In the Penal Colony" 199)

Instinct For Censorship: the New Religion

When panic fuels policies, and policies are put into practice, no one should be surprised that trouble follows. In this chapter, I look at some cases of professors on trial in universities, to review the fallout from the violence-against-women industry. In American jurisdictions, hundreds of universities have imposed speech codes in the past ten years, and the courts have begun to throw them out. Canadian institutions are in mid-immersion; they only got going in the late 1980s, but they are also more ambitious, and market their disciplining efforts under the guise of protecting "human rights." This apparently permits them to attack faculty more than the Americans can; there, it is more often the students who get hit.

It is instructive that the University of Wisconsin, the first to set up a code, has now rescinded it. As Wendy Warburton tells the story in the *Ottawa Citizen* ("Code"), crafters of the code expected it to deal only with the "vilest, meanest conduct," perhaps one complaint every decade. Instead, complaints flooded in: about a painting of the Pope with a condom pinned to his lapel; about a cartoon in the student newspaper; about calling a student a primitive dinosaur. Only nine complaints elicited disciplinary action. In 1992, after two court rulings against it, and two attempts to fix it, the university got rid of the code. Associate dean Roger Howard, who pioneered the code, told the *Los Angeles Times Magazine* that setting rules may make intellectual sense, but it is a disaster from a practical point of view. "I absolutely have come to the conclusion that it's better policy not to have a code. The human instinct—or the American instinct—for censorship is just too strong."

The Canadian instinct for censorship need not take a back seat to the American. While James Joyce's *Ulysses* was banned in Britain from 1922 to 1936, its importation into Canada was banned until 1952. Canadian film censors treated *The Tin Drum* as child pornography. At the University of Toronto, works by Sigmund Freud, Havelock Ellis, and Richard Krafft-Ebing were kept under lock and key until the 1960s, made available only to advanced students with special permission, if they could certify being free of "mental problems" (Marchand, "Threat"). More recently, the press ban on the Homolka trial has made international headlines as a symbol of the suppression of information. Canada Customs has been holding up books and magazines at the U.S. border, for such crimes as demeaning women. The police have seized Eli Langer's paintings from the Mercer Union Gallery in Toronto, as demeaning to children. The theatrical production of *Showboat* was subjected to a campaign of racially motivated hostility, as demeaning to black Americans and Canadians.

This last example opens up a new front. Leftist politics of intrusion are joining up with rightist habits of suppression. Where censorship from the right attacks as immoral any deviation from the "normal," censorship from the left attacks the norms as themselves deviations from morality. Sexuality often provides a target for both, as in the coalition against erotic art, video, and magazines. Biopolitics, drawing on left and right, is everywhere on the move, mobilizing against smoking or drinking, against medical research on behalf of animals, or against impolite humour. In 1992, the *ushers* in the theatre where Andrew Dice Clay performed successfully demanded that Vancouver City Council adopt guidelines to determine which acts can be banned from the city-owned theatres. They were supported by Mediawatch, LEAF, and Feminists For Healthy Humour (!). The city agreed to prepare guidelines based on anti-harassment and human-rights policies. Vulgarity, apparently, is to be treated on the model of denying someone a job; discrimination statutes, designed to regulate selective behaviour, are to be misapplied to matters of manners and taste (Dafoe, "Ushers as censors").

Mattel Canada, Inc., a giant corporation, has had to replace Teen Talk Barbie, which admitted that girls (like boys) think that "math class is tough." Although Barbie also says she is studying to be a doctor, would like to start a business, has fun doing homework with her computer, and needs to "study hard tonight," she was ritually denounced by the Canadian Mathematical Society, the Alliance for Children, and the NAC, for reinforcing negative stereotypes about women. Mattel managers rapidly acknowledged that the math sentence was "inappropriate," pleading that Mattel only "reflects society's values, but doesn't try to set them." Their market likes them: Barbie's sales in a single year total $840 million. The business is a business, and it satisfies its customers. Not good enough, says Dr. Glenda Simms, president of the advocacy group, Canadian Advisory Council on the Status of Women, inventing a new mission for entrepreneurs. "They have a responsibility to society" (Smith and Mitchell).

Texts and movies come in for the same treatment. Librarians in Guelph schools are ripping pages out of books of poetry by Robert Louis Stevenson, on the grounds that they are racist. They treat allegedly sexist or anti-gay books in the same manner (Thompson, "Left joins right to censor schoolbooks"). Librarians in Toronto public libraries have removed the popular children's books by Roald Dahl, such as *Charlie and the Chocolate Factory* and *James and the Giant Peach*. Dahl stands accused of glorifying the elitist English school system, and slandering women by portraying witches as malevolent (Gildiner, "Banning"). Don McKellar, star of Bruce McDonald's road movies *Highway 61* and *Roadkill*, makes an erotic short film, *Blue*, and finds that friends and colleagues refuse to see his movie because it contains explicit sexual material. He says "he knows there's a widely-held notion out there that *any* depiction of heterosexual intercourse is by definition an act of misogyny" (MacInnis, "Don" C3).

All this is symptomatic of a cultural current which involves, in most manifestations, a series of public frictions and public irritants. As a movement, however, it is headquartered in universities, where it is conducting its most sinister thought experiments, and having its most direct disciplining impact.

Biopolitics is a cold war state, ever flirting with hot war, supercharged by the excess energies of panic. The violence-against-women scare, more than any other, is the model reference point for putting the internal life of universities in jeopardy.[1]

The biopolital war, cold or hot, is a holy war. With their anti-harassment, anti-discrimination, and anti-misconduct codes, universities are on their way to becoming doctrinal institutions. What used to be considered disagreements are increasingly treated as heresies, deviating from orthodox beliefs. The new litany of "isms" to be exorcised—racism, sexism, ablism, speciesism—provides instant biolabels for identifying the sins and sinners to be cast out from the circle of virtue. This is the *fundamentalism* of biopolitics.

The new piety is organized around abstractions like equity and inclusion—very broad terms, dripping with the pathos of injustice and exclusion, and open to changing definition by those who claim the authority to speak for "disadvantage." In the widest protestant interpretation, such authority can be given entirely *subjectivist* meaning. In practice, however, biopolitics is Calvinist, and links disadvantage to "the disadvantaged," that is, to elite groups, assigned privileged standing by virtue of their putatively oppressed condition. As we have seen, biopolitics is given to *formalism*—the designation of elites through elementary, biological demarcation (women, disabled, racial minorities, aboriginals)—as an instrument for turning disadvantage into group advantage. As formalism turns into orthodoxy, protestantism can also turn infallibilist and militant, on the analogy of catholicism. It can find appealing the methods of *inquisition.*

The university, with its "anti-..." codes, and with its new and expanding policies of positive obligation, is coming to resemble a creed-state, heading toward maturity on the model of medieval Christendom, the Iran of the ayatollahs, Nazi Germany, or the Stalinist USSR. Creed-states impose state-creeds; they profess and practice zero tolerance of other creeds. Universities as creed-states are increasingly coming into conflict with the over-arching procedural principle that has underpinned their intellectual and social expansion throughout this century and that has guaranteed the liberal character of their educational mission: academic freedom. It is true that academics have often had to resist pressure from church, government, and business interests, in order to make an independent contribution to public welfare and human society. But now the pressures are mounted from within the universities, by students, administrators, and the academics themselves.

Panic Contestation: Discipline and Punish

Universities have revived the "star chamber" for the 1990s. Contrary to universities' customary habits of openness, the harassment hearings have initiated a departure into the heart of darkness. The alibi, as usual, is that privacy will protect the women, and perhaps also the accused. But in fact, universities constantly try to gag and muzzle the accused, and make a mockery of their professed desire to "educate" the community about the reality of sexual harassment. In the past few years, an enormous investment of time has been sunk into various harassment policies and training functions. Yet, there seem to be too few complaints of sufficient substance to justify the machinery being developed. On the other side, young accused faculty often feel too vulnerable to tell their stories, and well-established professors, used to being articulate about their work, or on behalf of other people's causes, often find it difficult to write on their own behalf. Nobody knows how many disputes have turned into "cases," much less how these were finally decided.

Meanwhile, the public is given the impression, from the few cases that do find their way into the public eye, that universities are rife with sex crimes and abuses of power, and that these new procedures are dealing with cases of sex-for-grades blackmail or some other serious corruption or coercion. The public can have no idea—university colleagues themselves are just beginning to discover— how far this is from the truth. Where there is any sexual component at all, it is likely to be no more serious than suggestive material, humour, or looks. Many of the disputes involve no sexual content whatever. That is, no sex for grades or other benefits, no sexual coercion, no sexual touching, no sexual advances, and no sexual propositions or even implied invitations. Many of the disputes do not involve one person doing something to another person! Often, there is no evidence of harassment at all, in the common sense of the word.

In other words, "sexual harassment" is increasingly a euphemism for general disputes over language, ideas, and manners, in a wide sense that has no closer connections with sex than simply the "relationship between the sexes." It is about biopolitics, pure and simple; it is about relationships of power and contestations of power in the general cultural settings that form the crucible of our activities. *A remarkable and increasing amount of procedure is being devoted, not to some course of one-on-one vexation, much less to sexual coercion, but instead to charges of creating a negative environment, or some version of it (hostile, offensive, or intimidating).* As though one person, in a community of thousands, could be held accountable for creating a whole environment! The secrecy serves often to conceal fraudulent accusations, shoddy processing, and, more generally, workplace politics.

The stuff about encouraging vulnerable people to report injuries, protecting "human rights," and removing inequities is an alibi; it is not the real stuff of which daily experience around these issues is made. Least of all is the "human rights" concept expected to be applied universally, even though policies are almost always written in the language of universality. In practice, these policies are conceived to be preferential instruments for the benefit of selected groups. Only "members" of designated groups, favoured with preferential treatment by a range of currently fashionable laws and regulations, are expected to avail themselves of the machinery of complaint and remedy.

More specifically, nobody expects to see "members" of groups actually *on the offensive* charged with harassment for giving offence: biofeminist student journalists who defame "male" cultural institutions and individuals; radical s/m lesbian students like those who destroyed gay professor James Miller's class on the literature of homosexuals at the University of Western Ontario ("Harassment Police"); radical sovereigntist aboriginal spokespeople who criticize "white" history and its prominent elements; radical black culturalists, like those who intimidated and threatened Professor Jeanne Cannizzo while the University of Toronto watched, or those who attacked the producers of *Showboat* in Toronto with anti-semitic slogans; or any other self-styled underdogs with a credibility that only biopolitical credentials can provide. It is outrageous that universities should use the pretext of privacy to conceal from scrutiny the practical politics of workplace and cultural regulation. Disciplinary strategies are not the best ones for controlling the culture of the educational workplace in any case; but secrecy in these cases is less a protection of confidence and more a cover-up for new historical inequities.

The university is precisely a place in which diverse, sometimes agreeable and sometimes disagreeable (intellectual, emotional, introspective, and interactive) stimuli add up to a complex educational opportunity. There is no other social environment with as much recourse to second opinions, appeals, counselling, mediation, or alternative resources and responses, and where individuals are more free to learn who they are by experimenting with their own responses. As long as the university remains secular and non-discriminatory in providing access to its offerings, as it is required to do by law, it need not worry about individuals creating environments. Crucially, universities have to abandon the misguided aspiration promoted by their biopolitical factions to reform the "climate" or "environment" by quasi-*judicial* means. Where these are to be contested, let them be contested by political and cultural means.

Professors, like the public, remain largely unaware of the potential that anti-harassment and ethics codes and policies have for acting more like a weapon to win advantage, settle scores, or attack adversaries than like a shield to protect vulnerable individuals. In some cases, professors have been accused in a grade-appeal process. Other charges are directed against innocent remarks that happened to cause displeasure, often for ideological reasons. Some of the false process has been launched in order to punish individuals for their ideas. The codes serve all these purposes faithfully, and the panic secrecy in which they are applied covers up the scruples that observers might bring to the persecution. What is striking in each case is how long the unfair process goes on while supposedly good people stand aside. Universities are massive institutions, now embarked on a contemptible course of institutional harassment of their long-standing employees.

Cases

I report here on a number of cases in brief form. These are all Canadian cases from the past six years. In the following chapter, I will endeavour to report at greater length on three currently ongoing cases which display important features: Professor Alan Surovell at Dalhousie; Professor Ken Westhues at Waterloo; and Professor Warren Magnusson at the University of Victoria—all savaged by institutional harassment. There is at present no clearing house for this information, and it is painstakingly hard to come by. I am not saying that there are no bona fide cases of sexual or racial harassment in universities. As in any other social institution, there may well be some. The veil of secrecy keeps us from knowing. Nor do I say that substantive and procedural injustices have become the order of the day in Canadian universities. Far from it. Faculty associations, the CAUT, and my own efforts here as well, are committed to ensuring that this never happens. Nor do I know, on the other hand, just how much miscarriage of justice, corruption of intellectual and moral value, and compromise of free inquiry and expression actually do go on daily under conditions of biopolitical moral panic. The cases of ungrounded overreaction that have surfaced, and that I list here, have cost millions of dollars, and have caused measureless distress. I hope that accounts like the ones below will stimulate the surfacing of further information and, generally, will do some good.

The key concept that we have to flesh out as we contemplate the instances of mistreatment is the concept of *institutional abuse* or *institutional harassment* of employees by the employer. Reputable members of the academic profession, left wing, right wing, of every traditional political inclination, male and female, and ethnically diverse, are being subjected to serious courses of vexatious conduct by their employers and colleagues. The abusive processes into which they are dragged by the implementation of new harassment codes interrupt professional work and devastate personal lives over lengthy periods, sometimes as much as two to five years. The damage to careers and reputations is incalculable; the stigmatization from the charges alone, never mind conviction, is indelible. In the case of termination of employment, re-employment is impossible, and careers are finished. No one takes responsibility for these costs. No one is held publicly accountable.

Sexual and racial harassment complaints are prosecuted under university policies as though they were all crimes of hate and violence. And yet they are often based on purely subjective attitudes, poorly remembered or misremembered, misreported or falsely reported incidents, and even inadvertent or innocent behaviours given unfriendly characterization. Often, sex has nothing to do with it; the objections are based on simple disputes about values, styles, personalities, as these are made manifest and expressed *in the course of the normal discharge of duties.* Universities are permitting or undertaking attacks on their employees for just doing their jobs.

To make matters worse, the adjudications are so organized as to subordinate both the university's educational values and the social values that obligate universities to their employees, to a narrowly defined set of social values that pertains chiefly to the harassment procedures under way and, in many cases, chiefly to the narrow interests of the accusers. University officials often lack the legal expertise to guarantee proper handling of evidence and due process. Universities cannot duplicate the courts without becoming the courts, and they should not be expected to substitute themselves for the courts. Their endeavours in this area may amount to little more than institutionalized forms of *vigilante justice.*

Since harassment must be defined as short of criminal assault, it is hard to see what forms of harassment of one person by another would be the equivalents of the institutional harassment that begins the moment a formal charge is laid against an employee inside the imposing harassment machinery operating as an emblem of the employer's misdirected sense of "responsibility." The unpleasantness experienced by complainants is often of very brief duration and of slight impact. Injury is not expected to be demonstrated. And in some cases, the very pursuit of satisfaction is an extracurricular political project, more than an exercise in pain reduction. Meanwhile, the stress and trauma, and the severe consequences and damages, are on the side of the accused.

Anyone who has ever spent five minutes in a performance evaluation that was tense can begin to imagine the experience of being accused of harassment-related job misconduct, of having to face hours, often months of clarifying, making submissions, explaining one's behaviour and motives, over and over again, and of facing up to all the threats, anxieties, disappointments, betrayals, and deep uncertainties of the process. In my view, the striking *disproportion* between the experience of this kind of suffering and risk by the accused, and the accuser's discomfort in taking offence, between the perpetration of institutional abuse by adminsitrators against the accused, under the cover of formal policies, and the perpetration by the accused of some version of alleged symbolic harm against the accuser, is spawned and legitimated by biopolitical panic, and takes shape through the assent that institutions give to undue pressures. The disproportion is so great, in fact, that it brings this whole machinery to the edge of a historical irony: the reversal of the overheated medium. Panic excess will discredit the very causes that rely on it for advantage.

Professor Jeanne Cannizzo, University of Toronto

Censorship has gained new momentum in the 1980s, then, with backing from a tidal wave of biopolitical activism, not only against expressions of sexuality but also in support of wholesale symbolic *cleansing* of everyday communications. The objective is to produce significant structural and behavioural changes in the institutions of culture, from mind-set to curriculum, pedagogy, and public exchange. Individuals caught in the gears of this panic machinery may get badly mangled. A case in point was Jeanne Cannizzo, now on extended medical leave. The exhibit that she curated for the Royal Ontario Museum in 1990, "Into the Heart of Africa," designed deliberately as a critique of white colonialism, was nevertheless plagued by protests that it was "racist." Cannizzo, a well-known anthropologist, was persecuted out of her academic position at the University of Toronto by insults, physical intimidation, and classroom disruptions, all under the gaze of the authorities, who wanted to occupy the middle ground (Fennell, "Silencers" 42-43). Martha Latta, another anthropologist, openly criticized the administration, and insisted on the importance of "reject[ing] bigotry of all kinds, including the bigotry which masks itself as anti-bigotry" (Hurst, "Politically correct?" A12).

Professor Richard Devlin, Osgoode Hall, York University

Cannizzo was a casualty of administrative timidity. Other professors have fallen victim to a disciplinary zeal, and have had to face pressures and penalties ranging from warnings and admonishments to termination of employment. It is hard to know how many professors have been under attack by the institution itself, because most proceedings are in secret. It is also hard to know how much coerced accommodation, self-censorship, and curricular change have been produced by interference behind the scenes or the reasonable anticipations of interference. The Canadian Civil Liberties Association relates, for example, that in the late 1980s, at York University's Osgoode Hall Law School, Richard Devlin, a young male law teacher, asked students to prepare a legal factum challenging the constitutionality of a hypothetical anti-pornography law. Some women in his class sought counselling because of their discomfort over having to argue against their own point of view. They were suffering identity crises. The teacher was then admonished by two of the university's sexual-harassment counsellors, who warned that "if a similar situation were to occur again, there would be a possibility of an investigation to determine whether sexual harassment was actually taking place" (CCLA 3).

What would happen to the system of law if defence lawyers took only cases that made them comfortable, and if lawyers were assumed to share the actual and implied viewpoints of their clients? What would happen if law students were not prepared to anticipate the arguments they will have to face on the other side of issues? What *is* happening when the emotional responses of young people, under the unique educational pressure of having to encounter ideas foreign to their background, expectations, or "identities," are made the gauge of the ideas themselves and the standards for their permissibility? Why are we training and encouraging young women to develop and indulge in emotional incapacitation? How have we come to approve of disciplinary force to turn emotional incapacitation into emotional tyranny?

In this case, reportedly, the young teacher has changed his teaching practices. How many others are reacting in the same way? Alan Borovoy, the Director of the CCLA, writes: "Devlin acknowledges that he was frightened, 'indeed sick' because of what this could mean for his reputation — 'and career.'" Borovoy adds: "Something very real had made him afraid. And something very real had made him recant rather than fight back" ("Campus"). Not a minor matter. What is remarkable about this case is that Devlin attacks Borovoy for his "feminist baiting" and says that Borovoy's comments demonstrate "the incapacity of mainstream, fundamentalist liberalism to tolerate the emergence of anti-sexist education" ("A counter-attack in defense of political correctness"). I seems that, having found true religion — with a little help from the threat of discipline — Devlin is not ready to recant again.

Professor Richard Hummell, University of Toronto

Some of the early cases became famous too rapidly, and attitudes jelled on them before we could see how basically crazy they were. Professor Hummell was labelled for posterity as the "leering professor" when Hart House was required to pass part-time student Beverley Torfason's complaint of October 11, 1988 upwards, to be processed through the university's brand-new sexual harassment policy, just released that March. It was to take countless hearings before a hearing board, an appeal board, and judicial review, to the tune of an estimated $200,000, processed the accusation that Richard Hummell stared at Beverley Torfason in the Hart House swimming pool where he had been swimming for 28 years. There was no effort to resolve the complaint informally. The transcript of the hearings runs to hundreds of pages and makes for extraordinary reading. For example, Torfason was allowed to introduce a series of sports photo-

graphs taken by Hummell of synchronized swimmers—
world class athletes, rising out of the water to their waists.
According to the transcript, she found the pictures "inappropriate." "To me they do not look like pictures of swimmers, they look like pictures of legs and crotches and
buttocks, they do not look like pictures of swimmers. When
competition pictures are normally taken, they normally
take pictures with their faces in them, so that you can tell
they're people" (Hummell 3).

The Board found Hummell guilty, but drew the line
short of awarding Torfason the $4,000 that she wanted in
damages. They did, however, ban him from Hart House
for five years, and required him to take counselling from
someone approved by the Sexual Harassment Office. This
kind of forced re-education has since become a staple of
biofeminist power-tripping. They also ordered that their
decision be kept secret. Hummell appealed. The university's appeal board released its decision, upholding the
earlier decision, on December 8, 1989, two days after the
Marc Lépine event. Although the decision was split 3-2,
the administration explained at a press conference, according to Hummell, "how this decision would prevent a
repeat of the Montreal massacre." He adds, "How they got
from staring in the pool to murder and why, if they truly
believed this, they preferred I received amateur rather
than professional counselling escapes me" (2). Hummell
asked for judicial review, which then went on for years.

To this date, "leering" is a prime entry in the lexicon of
sexual-harassment offences. When I taped a segment of
CBC Newsworld's new program, *Face-Off*, in September
1994, the first question host Judy Rebick asked was about
a leering professor. But really, a look is just a look. The
leer is in the mind of the complainant as much as in the
eye of the accused. And looking cannot be controlled,
least of all at a beach or in a swimming pool, though a
range of responses is available for it, far more effective
than regulation and punishment.

Professor J. Philippe Rushton, University of Western Ontario

Professor Rushton's case has been even more of a sensation, and attitudes have polarized rapidly, without much sense of the mistreatment he suffered. Rushton is a research psychologist at the University of Western Ontario. He has authored or co-authored six books and a hundred and fifty articles, and has received a long list of awards, including a Doctor of Science degree from the University of London and a fellowship in the prestigious John Simon Guggenheim foundation. A paper he read at a science symposium in San Francisco, on January 19, 1989, exposed him to years of abuse, and to the threat of potential job loss and even criminal incarceration.

He examined social-science data related to social behaviour, sexual habits, personality traits, performance indicators, physical characteristics, and numerous other traits, and concluded that the data clustered in such a way that three different racial groups, "Negroids," "Caucasoids," and "Mongoloids," could be distinguished. With the help of knowledge about population biology and reproductive strategies, he argued, hypotheses could be formed about the evolution of races. He has become especially well known for his findings on race differences in brain size and levels of intelligence. He did not claim that these hypotheses can predict individual variation, however, or that they can serve as the basis for any social, legal, or political policies that would single out members of a racial group for discriminatory treatment.

Nevertheless, questions about the competence of his scholarship will continue to be raised, for both intellectual and moral reasons. Only intensive and rigorous scientific scrutiny and debate can settle this kind of issue. At the same time, Rushton's work, with its challenge to the taboos on talking about a possible relationship between genetics and intelligence, is one of the limit cases of free inquiry and expression. Popular ideas do not need protection. As soon as there is a move to censor speech and thought, however, that speech becomes an underdog in need of fundamental rights.

An article by philosophy professor Barry Gross has documented the chronology of the Rushton persecution. On February 2, 1989, David Peterson, former premier of Ontario, denounced Rushton's work as "offensive to the way Ontario thinks" and demanded that he be fired. Rushton was pilloried in the press, and linked by metaphor with the Nazis, the Ku Klux Klan, and the Anti-Christ (Gross 35). A month later, the Ontario Provincial Police launched a six-month investigation, questioning him and his colleagues, to determine whether he had violated the Criminal Code (Ch. C-46, 319, par. 2) by promoting "hatred." *The Attorney General of Ontario decided that his scholarship was incompetent but not criminal.* One does not have to support Rushton's work or agree with his views or conclusions to see how frightening this is.

The chair of Rushton's department gave Rushton an "unsatisfactory rating" on his 1989 performance evaluation and deprived him of his annual salary increment, in a context where three such reviews could lead to dismissal. This was in the same year that Rushton was awarded the Guggenheim Fellowship and "had more scholarly entries on his annual report than any other member of his department" (Gross 43). Subsequently, the department ordered that Rushton be removed from direct contact with students, and lecture only by videotape, and that students be permitted to watch the tape only individually, "under supervision at a location in the [psychology] department" (Gross 45 n. 23). Rushton began to receive a great deal of support from colleagues internationally and, eventually, the restrictions on his teaching were lifted. Since 1991, there have been no further infringements on Rushton's academic freedoms and on normal working conditions at the University of Western Ontario. The university appears now properly supportive of his rights.

The Rushton case, however, is not dormant in the legal arena. A complaint that seventeen students filed with the

Ontario Human Rights Commission in 1991 is now being activated (interview with Rushton, October 15, 1994). The Human Rights Commission sent Rushton on August 12, 1994, a letter dated June 19, from the "case coordinator in the South West region" who has apparently been assigned the lead role in the investigation of the complaints. The coordinator advises Rushton that many other staff will be involved in the investigation, and lists something like a dozen different individuals by name. The complaints have to do with "poisoning the work environment" and "academic racism."

Rushton, meanwhile, continues to produce scholarship that draws wide attention. His most recent book, *Race, Evolution, and Behavior*, an expansion of the conference paper that got him into hot water in 1989, drew the lead review in the *New York Times Book Review*, Sunday, October 16, 1994 (Browne, "What Is Intelligence"). Dr. Walter Massey, who is black, was president of the American Association for the Advancement of Science at the time that Rushton gave his paper there, and argued that no scientific organization has the right to censor scientific debate (Browne 45). Yet Rushton has not been able to get a research grant from standard academic funding sources, such as the Social Sciences and Humanities Research Council, has difficulty publishing his work, and has no graduate students, for their own well-being. He worries that we are perpetrating a fraud on ourselves. "It's very scary," he says (interview with Rushton, October 15, 1994). "This is unheard of in science, that something should become forbidden. The history of science is riddled with events where prejudices are overcome and truth wins out. This is the first time in history that the taboos are being put in place by the scientists themselves."

Between them, Hummell's case and Rushton's case introduced both sex and race to the *punitive* trends in the management of university controversies, as well as the two variables that have come up again and again over the past five years in the institutional overreaction to faculty speech

216

and conduct: complaints based on subjective perceptions of offence, and ostracism of non-conforming belief or behaviour. Both threaten academic freedom and the prospects of an open university culture far more than the violations that they purport to regulate threaten either the culture at large or the welfare of groups or individuals within it. The end results may range from near-dismissal to near-exoneration, but the processes and issues have in each case excited on the different campuses the widest range of disagreements. In each case, too, some portion of the institution has acted significantly badly, with troubling implications for the future, even if the situation turned out better than it might have, owing to countervailing pressures.

Professor Larry Belbeck, McMaster University

Larry Belbeck was a professor of pathology in the Faculty of Health Sciences and director of the Central Animal Facility at Hamilton's McMaster University. In November 1989, he was accused by two students and a member of the technical staff, all women, of a pattern of academic misconduct of a sexual nature, up to the level of sexual assault, in addition to the use of abusive language. They said he had created an "uncomfortable and even hostile environment" ("Chronology"). At least, the university's public chronology begins in November. But the ordeal for Belbeck started earlier, in May 1989, when he was suddenly ordered to turn in his keys and leave the campus. No reason was forthcoming until a week later, when the dean's letter told him that he was recommending his dismissal to the president.

Belbeck was not told why. He was not informed of the nature of the complaints against him. He was kept waiting for six full weeks before he could get a copy of the complaints in July. Belbeck answered the allegations. He received an official letter from Alvin Lee, the president, in the fall of 1989: his reply was not believed. The president would recommend his dismissal to the board. As he was entitled, Belbeck asked for a hearing to contest being fired. A hearing committee of three legal amateurs then took two years to conclude, by a vote of 2-1, that he was guilty of "unethical academic behaviour," such as to "impair his usefulness as a member of the University." This matched the exact wording required to show "adequate cause" for dismissal under clause 2 (a) of the university's policy on dismissal (1977).

What does a senior professor have to do to "impair" his usefulness so deeply that he has to be suspended or fired? The hearing committee noted, with respect to Belbeck's professional responsibilities as director of the facility, that "there is plenty of evidence of praise from the University for the work he has done." Also, student evaluations "are full of praise for him as a teacher" (36). They seem to fault him mainly for participating in the conviviality of a loose and sometimes crude workplace culture, instead of engaging in exemplary behaviour. According to Alexander Darling, McMaster's vice-president of administration, the hearing committee specifically found that Belbeck had used vulgar and abusive language, made uncalled-for and inappropriate sexual and personal comments, failed to make eye contact with students and staff while fixing his eyes "on other parts of their bodies," and "made sexually suggestive comments" (Peters, "McMaster reinstates"). However, according to Belbeck's CAUT lawyer, Mariette Blanchette (at a CAUT/CALL seminar on college and university law, May 13, 1994), all they *proved* legally was that he had said "fuck" 16 times in 10 years. Meanwhile, one of his accusers kept referring to him as "that fucking fat pig."

For most of the accusations against Belbeck, there was contrary evidence. The hearing committee's majority conclusion, by Dr. D. H. Carr, chair, and Dr. M. Kristofferson, does not come anywhere near to a finding of sexual assault, which had been the serious part of the original, and apparently false, charge against Belbeck. The dissenting, minority report of Dr. T. Hulland concedes that Belbeck's behaviour was flawed, but far from so severely flawed as to warrant suspension or removal. In fact, the majority conclusion makes no finding of sexual misconduct at all—not only not sexual assault, but not even sexual harassment of any kind! "Some of the behaviours which formed the basis of the complaints against Dr. Belbeck were clearly not of a sexual nature (for example, his outbursts of temper) and some were not clearly of a sexual nature (for example, his disregard of the proprieties of dress), and others, while clearly experienced by the complainants as of a sexual nature, may or may not have been so motivated by Dr. Belbeck (for example the physical examinations)."

Not sexual at all, or ambiguous, or without sexual motive: apparently, sexual misconduct had not been demonstrated. Why did the majority not conclude that they should leave him alone, perhaps with some injunction for improvement, since he had already been through an ordeal of more than two years of process? Because they were able to rationalize their mission: "We do not believe that it is our task to determine in any legal sense whether Dr. Belbeck sexually harassed any or all of the complainants. Rather it is to determine whether Dr. Belbeck's conduct toward them was such as to constitute unethical academic behaviour as to impair his usefulness as a member of the University" (45). In short, they cannot prove any of the sex charges, which had lent the prosecution its biopolitical urgency and apparent gravity, and cannot find any other violation of the university's policies, much less any legal culpability.

Therefore, the two professors sitting in judgment rest content with non-specific disapprobation of Belbeck's moral conduct. It is not surprising that the minority position scoffs at the punitive majority: "If the conduct which is not acceptable is neither described nor (apparently) describable in law or university code, those who sit in judgement of their university peers sit on a very precarious perch indeed" (58). It seems that a presumption of innocence should have given Belbeck the benefit of the doubt.

So, it was a hung panel on November 29, 1991: one member recommended termination of employment, one (the chair) recommended six months' suspension, with conditions, and the third, dissenting, recommended no penalty. In January 1992, the university senate, without hearing any evidence, voted to fire him. Professor Belbeck had no recourse to appeal. The board of governors voted to fire him as well. "It has now been made abundantly clear that appropriate behaviour is an expectation of *all* those employed by this University," said Vice-President Arthur Heidebrecht in a news release.

This was the first dismissal of a tenured faculty member in McMaster's history, and it was from beginning to end a form of institutional abuse of an employee. He had given 20 years of service to the university, but that had not enough weight in the balance against the rush to purify the work culture. In May 1993, the Divisional Court overturned the dismissal on a judicial review. Senate and board had no jurisdiction to impose a penalty more severe than the chair of the hearing committee recommended ("Court quashes" 2). McMaster did not accept the Court's decision. In September 1993, the Court of Appeal denied McMaster's appeal motion ("University loses"). It took another half a year before the board, in March 1994, confirmed a six-month suspension without pay, back-dated to 1992, and reinstated Belbeck, then 50 years old, subject to conditions that include counselling, treatment, and an undertaking to guarantee good behaviour (Peters, "McMaster reinstates"). Professor Belbeck is now back at work, five years after he was forced out. The damage to his life in those five years is incalculable. The university has not yet agreed to turn over the back pay for the two-year period of his removal.

Professor Jacques Collin, University of Manitoba

Jacques Collin, professor of architecture in the graduate program at the University of Manitoba, was suspended for a year without pay in April 1992, for "reprehensible conduct in relation to students" (Santin, "Prof fights"). He was accused of using profane, sexist, and racist language and of drawing inappropriate analogies in his classes. There were objections to his slides of nudes. There were objections to his baiting of feminists. Also to his sexual humour, swearing, and blunt pedagogy. And there were objections to his deliberately or casually provocative examples to demonstrate perfectly reasonable points. For instance, to show that design architects had to learn the art of efficient action, he once said: "If you want to rape a woman, you don't stick it in her armpit" (Freedman 8). Collin explained that the principle of efficiency applied even to "misdirected action" (30).

In his appeal, which went to labour arbitration, Collin acknowledged that his use of language was "offensive" to students, pleaded for pedagogical contextualization, added personal circumstances, and asked for a reduced penalty, preferably a reprimand. His penalty was reduced by arbitrator Martin Freedman to a six-month suspension (May 13, 1993). The university, meanwhile, fired him in September 1992, on the basis of new evidence that he had slapped a student (whom he was trying to stimulate to brighter attention). Arbitrator David Bowman set aside the termination (December 16, 1993), since Collin had never had a warning. Indeed, he had received teaching awards. He was given a second chance, effective January 1994, with one year of probation. Collin was 66 years old at the time and had given 30 years' service.

What is most interesting here is that students were sharply divided between those who brought and supported the charges, and those who thought Collin was the best teacher they had ever had. From all around the world, testimonials poured in to the outstanding pedagogical skills, architectural insights, and basic humanity of the man, whose behaviour was, at least according to his admirers, in no way racist. Accomplished architects all, male and female, they paid tribute to him as an untypical and exceptional teacher, whose provocative and sometimes outrageous teaching methods expanded their minds. He had been nominated by the dean for a teaching award just a few months before the incidents in the complaints. Strong language had been a feature of his style throughout his career.

Nevertheless, Martin Freedman finds Collin's conduct "grossly inappropriate, manifestly rude and insensitive" (Freedman 72; "Architecture prof."). Meanwhile, psychiatric assessment suggested that Collin may not have realized he was being insensitive. In any event, he was an easy target in a political climate of conformity and rectitude. In a noticeably parochial statement, Freedman adds: "It is not, I think, relevant whether Professor Collin's teaching methods were or were not effective. What is relevant is that his teaching methods to a measurable extent were offensive. He may have been recognized for the effectiveness of his teaching, and yet may properly be subject to sanction for the offensiveness of his teaching methods ... Prof. Collin's conduct and behavior undermined the dignity, self-esteem and productivity of some of his students, and certainly in that sense it was a contradiction of the University's sexual harassment policy" (75-76). Intellectual values are utterly subordinated to therapeutic values in Freedman's argument. This is the new line among censors: it is not what you teach, it is how (i.e., how "sensitively") you teach it.[2] Fetish of etiquette; pedagogical tyranny.

Collin, of course, had had a flamboyant, theatrical style throughout his teaching life. One of the students testifying on Collin's side, Ken Goodman, noted the biopoliticization of the current climate of perception: "Changes in the world in the last ten years," with respect to sex and race, set new limits on what appeared to be permissible comment in the classroom (35). Freedman himself goes with the grain of the narrowing sensibility. He accuses Collin of creating an unsuitable learning environment for *some* students. Apparently, this is a complaint-driven observation. Those who found the learning environment not only suitable but outstandingly successful simply do not count. "The fact that a number of students appear to have understood the message which Prof. Collin may have intended to convey is a tribute to them. It is not a tribute to him or his methods, which for other students hindered and impaired their ability to function freely and without fear or apprehension" (84; "Architecture prof."). In short, if students get it, it is to their credit; if they do not get it, if they "shut down," it is not their fault. Praise the victim, scapegoat the teacher.

I do not have to judge Collin's lifetime of achievements to recognize that he is not everybody's cup of tea. But since he is clearly not everybody's villain either, the proceedings display a damaging sententiousness. They convict Collin of not being a "right-thinking" staff member (72). They pander to a sanctimonious idolatry of the innocent student, whom in fact we see being trained to perceive and punish offence, where she might just as well be trained to perceive difference. They also pander to the biofeminist student, like the complainant Deborah Shewaga, who felt abused and angry at "the system that let this happen" (Freedman 15), and attacked Collin for rendering her environment "intimidating, hostile, and offensive" (7).

Shewaga took a one-week course from Collin in February 1991, found his language offensive, and was "caused to 'shut down' and not listen, because she did not care to listen to what he said" (5). She started a studio course with him in September of 1991, and by October, when he said she was "another Anita Hill," having to put up with "all us sexist bastards in this school," she "decided to start writing things down" (11). While others were coping with architecture and pedagogy, she was also building a case to get him. She had enough to have him charged by December. She said she "learned very little from Collin," but she was assigned a grade of A+ in the course by another professor.

A series of disputable assumptions and a great deal of double-think are driving a machinery of intolerance. It is easy to forget, in the midst of the pathos of victimization stories, that everyone in university is an adult. Shewaga was a 25-year-old graduate M.A. student at the time of testimony. Her reaction to Collin was not the norm. According to the intriguing testimony of Ms. Sharon Green, Collin once called Green "you goddamn pagan Jew" (Freedman 23). But she would imitate him and refer to him as "you fucking French frog" (24). She adds that he reacted well.

This will not be to everyone's taste, but in combination with testimony that Collin taught with a passion, yet encouraged students to form their own opinions, that he put in more effort than most professors, and tried to motivate the students, and that "he was always available and accessible to students and was committed to them" (23), the picture becomes far more nuanced than what the quasi-judicial procedures and the puritanical assumptions currently built into them can handle. Not only women but, by extension, students in general, are coming to be considered infants, in constant need of special protection. This is to the detriment of higher education, and it will prove to be to the detriment of university students, and ultimately the society at large.

The question in this case is not whether Collin went too far, but rather whether he went too far to merit response in anything but disciplinary terms. This issue divided the union; many of its members, some executive members included, thought Collin was the exact example of a hostile environment. But obviously, many students *did* find Collin's work stimulating. A more judicious conclusion would be that we simply do not know enough about learning to be sure about the effectiveness of a given pedagogic style for different types of student populations. The faculty association, in any event, took a middle road, made the case that the administration had overreacted, and argued for a reduced penalty. It spent $118,000 for the two arbitrations ("UMFA objects"). If the administration paid out similar sums, then it cost close to a quarter million dollars to find punishment for a very senior scholar. He should instead have been helped to come within the orbit of the norms of employment, such as they are, protected in his eccentricity, and appreciated by the institution to which he gave much of his life.

Professor Lucinda Vandervort, University of Saskatchewan

Lucinda Vandervort is a law professor at the University of Saskatchewan. She is frankly honest, pro-gay, and pro-feminist. The Ontario Women's Directorate lists one of her articles (on sexual-assault legislation) in its bibliography. Between 1992 and 1994, the university spent nearly $200,000 unsuccessfully trying to fire her. Vandervort was unceremoniously suspended in May 1992, recommended for dismissal in August 1992 by President George Ivany, and then reinstated in May 1993, immediately following the end of 21 days of hearings, by the interim order of arbitrator Innis Christie, a former dean of the Dalhousie law school, who, in his final decision in April 1994, called for only minor warnings about her technical duties to be added to her file.

She joined the law faculty on July 1, 1982. In the next year, her peers judged her work "superior." The following year, her department turned against her. Three consecutive years of negative decisions followed (1984-87); three times she was denied promotion, and the third time, her colleagues in the College of Law recommended that she be denied tenure as well. Late in the fifth year (April 1987), a university-wide tenure appeal committee unanimously (6-0) rejected the recommendation of her law colleagues and she was awarded both tenure and promotion. Her sixth year was uneventful, and she went on sabbatical leave in her seventh (1988-89). In the fall of 1988, however, the new dean, Prof. Peter MacKinnon, offered to buy out her tenure. She refused, and spent two further years away on research leave (1989-91). In the first year back, 1991-92, her tenth at the University of Saskatchewan, the dean recommended that Professor Vandervort be fired. This was the fifth year of unpleasantness for her. She then had to undergo one year of litigation before being reinstated and a further year's wait before the final decision of the arbitration committee was released.[3]

The point here is that Vandervort apparently did not fit in, and there was a long-standing desire to get rid of her. But her file contains no disciplinary warnings. Even in 1991-92, the dean found only minor failings of duty to complain about: rescheduling some classes, oversleeping a supervisory assignment, breaking a rule by rescheduling one class into the last two weeks of term. None of these added up to anything remotely like adequate cause for termination of employment; nonetheless, the university characterized them in the aggregate as *insensitivity* to students. Fortunately, the arbitrator, who found Vandervort had made at most minor errors in judgment, would have nothing to do with this charade, and refused the argument "that a single theme runs through the failings established by the evidence" (Christie 71). Indeed, there is much evidence to show that Vandervort is a caring and sensitive teacher. But the master code of protecting the underdog is what surfaces in the Vandervort hearing, as in the Collin hearing, as the central issue. Typically here, as elsewhere, a weapon pretends to be a shield for the needy; but it is the weapon that the case deploys, and it is the accused who suffers damage.

There is one other piece of colour in the Vandervort proceedings, that highlights its biopolitical character. The usual faculty backbiting stuff of which this case is full could not get off the ground until it found a way to connect itself with the new proprieties (repressions) entailed in the "changes in the world in the last ten years" (to cite from the Collin case). The "backbone of the university's argument" against Vandervort (Hoffman, "Key incident") became the taint of homophobia, though everybody was careful to insist that Vandervort was not homophobic (Christie 33). In the usual double-talk, it was not her allegedly "homophobic speech" that was culpable; it was her alleged insensitivity to the lesbian student in her class that was unconscionable. Accordingly, neither party made arguments about free speech, and the arbitrator was therefore, unfortunately, entitled to assume that the charge of *pedagogic* culpability "means that there is no issue of academic freedom of expression here" (34).

In her Critical Legal Studies seminar, Vandervort naively used the term "limp-wristed" to describe a judge as indecisive. Student "B" was offended, and wrote to her to demand an apology (14). Vandervort, remarkably enough, had no knowledge of the pejorative use of that term to refer to male homosexuals; she worried that she might have offended a physically handicapped student. She asked and was enlightened by colleagues; she confirmed what she was told by checking two slang dictionaries. Professor Beth Bilson, soon-to-be chair of the Saskatchewan Labour Relations Board, and then associate dean, and another senior professor both advised Vandervort to confront the matter in class (34). Vandervort did. B's objection was raised in the class; Vandervort explained her unwitting use and said she regretted causing offence. In the lengthy discussion, B became overwrought by considerations of graffiti and general homophobia on campus, burst into tears, and disclosed to the class that she was herself lesbian. She said it was the only way to make her classmates understand her extreme distress. The class was a small, intense grouping of only six students.

Six months later, the dean's charge, leading to dismissal, proposed that Vandervort's behaviour (somehow triggering, assisting, inviting, or permitting the student to "out" herself) was "both invasive of the student's privacy and an act of humiliation toward the student" (14). The university's nominee on the panel, Nancy Hopkins, argued that Vandervort's actions were "astounding in their disregard for B" (89), and had serious potential consequences for B, considering discrimination and violence against homosexuals. Suzie Scott, the faculty association nominee, argued that Vandervort had done the right thing pedagogically by talking openly to her students about the issues. Christie, the chair of the arbitration panel, thought that Vandervort should have avoided "personalizing" the matter, or should have dealt with it in private (62). A matter of judgment.

In any case, there was evidence before the arbitration that B had previously identified herself publicly as a lesbian when she spoke at a University conference in 1990. Between the incident in class, moreover, and the time when the dismissal charges were laid, B ran successfully for office as student body president in the College of Law and identified herself as a lesbian in her campaign (101). B herself had not complained to the dean. When she was asked by the dean to relate her story in March, and subsequently heard of the charges against Vandervort, she wrote to the dean to say that, as "every week i'm [*sic*] challenging someone's views or their language," she wants to see them educated, not to have their employment status reviewed. She stressed that she opposed the dean's action. The latter can only lead to fear among professors, and silence or revolt among students (38). In general, B was a strong student, got an A in Vandervort's class, and clearly did not see herself as a victim in need of *administrative* protection from this teacher. Her story highlights the opportunism of powerful interests which take advantage of the climate of panic, and of the designation of official underdogs in need of protection, to mask oppressive administrative actions behind fake altruism. Some of these issues will be dealt with in the grievances on discrimination and breach of academic freedom still outstanding in the Vandervort case.

Not every such case gets to the point of dismissal proceedings. Nevertheless, faculty can get chewed up in lengthy proceedings where they are the only ones at risk, the only ones to suffer pain and stigma—though, of course, the general tension and trauma of an elaborate investigation and hearing can draw in and damage a whole academic community. The University of Western Ontario had two such cases in recent years, and has had reason to look seriously to revising its policies and understandings. What strikes the outside observer of cases such as these most forcefully is that they were allowed to go on as long as they did. Once the machinery starts, internal administrative commitment to the action, plus ignorance and neglect, can allow it to keep moving relentlessly along, regardless of how little sense it makes to continue. Every such case raises serious questions about the general quality of academic decision-making, and further tarnishes the reputation of the entire academic community.

These irresponsible persecutions, driven on by administrators or complainants who often have little to lose, suggest both the need to build discretion and public accountability into these procedures at much earlier stages, and also the need to build in *costly disincentives* to frivolous complaints and administrative abuse. The latter runs in the face of the belief system that imagines vulnerable students continually abused by powerful professors and, further, that extensive underreporting is a reality rather than an opportunistic biopolitical hypothesis. Nevertheless, if the panic that is comprised in the excessiveness of these proceedings is to stop, a different understanding will have to emerge and take charge of a situation that is already sometimes out of control.

Professor Marjorie Ratcliffe, University of Western Ontario

Marjorie Ratcliffe, a professor of Spanish in the Department of Modern Languages at the University of Western Ontario, ran into a nightmare problem with an Iranian student who wanted better grades than he was getting. In the fall of 1991, in the course of a grammar lesson, where he was mistranslating verbs with the root "con," she made her point about correct usage by giving him an example. He had translated four different English words, all as *condinar*, the Spanish for "condemn." She reminded him that he had once said in class that, in Iran, "they condemn everyone" (Leishman, "Professors shackled"). Her words: "*Condinar* means, as you said, 'in Iran they condemn everybody'" ("Harassment police"). In London, Ontario, Canada, she came very near to being condemned herself. Later, when he plagiarised an essay, she let him rewrite it. Then, the day after he got a poor mid-term grade of 62%, the student complained of racial harassment to Matthava Rau, the race relations officer, who went directly to the dean. The student said Ratcliffe had offended him. She said it had been inadvertent. Eventually, after three hours of mediation, the student withdrew the racism allegation, but insisted on a lesser accusation: she had been "insensitive." The race relations officer, to Ratcliffe's total surprise, initiated a formal complaint (Sullivan, "Too Much Heat"). Here began the University of Western Ontario's very first racial-harassment complaint process under their shiny new policy. It was to take two and a half years of Ratcliffe's time, full time, $7,000 of her lawyer's time, and who knows how much other time, before the case would be dismissed as unfounded ("Harassment Police").

Ratcliffe found herself charged with a form of racial harassment and was dragged before a Human Relations Tribunal, in the person of an external adjudicator from the University of Windsor (Prof. Emily F. Carasco). This was crazy. Nobody put a stop to the lengthy process that a single student was able to unleash with just a few words of complaint, and that a designated administrator could keep going on the basis of an advocacy impulse. "Sensitivity" is a term so broad that, unless the expressions covered by academic freedom are protected, the whole life of universities can become subordinated to the vagaries of one unhappy individual's state of mind. What are we supposed to do, wonders Ratcliffe, "in September, ask our students for a list of topics that might offend, then make sure we never cover those topics?" ("Harassment Police").

Part of the problem is that the equity bureaucracy at Western is bloated and insatiable. There is a half-million dollar staff, including, in addition to a full time race relations officer, an ombudsperson position, a sexual harassment officer, and a male alternate sexual harassment officer, all supervised by a director of equity services, and all shadowed by a duplicate bureaucracy in the student union (vice-president student issues, women's issues coordinator, race relations coordinator, campus safety coordinator, commissioner for gay, lesbian, and bisexual issues, and a students with disabilities commissioner). There are simply not enough serious complaints to go around!

Ratcliffe was under repeated pressure to apologize, with the incentive that all charges would be dropped. The administration offered to write the apology for her, if she would only sign it (Leonard). It was five months after the formal charges were laid that Carasco dismissed the complaint (June 8, 1992). And it took another nine months, and strong pressure from the faculty association, before the university would agree to compensate Ratcliffe for her legal expenses (Canadian Civil Liberties Association 4). They would not do so until she agreed to waive her right to sue the university (Leonard).

It is not clear to this day whether Ratcliffe has been properly exonerated by the university which clearly abused her. The president has not offered an apology. The race-relations officer has remained unrepentant, up to the time when she left her position, in the fall of 1994. Professor David Mullan, of the Faculty of Law at Queen's University, reviewed the race-relations policy of the university at President K. G. Pedersen's request (back in 1992), and found that the race relations officer acted as advisor, investigator, mediator, and prosecutor, stacking the process in favour of complainants (CAUT, "Reply" 18-19 n. 32). The race relations policy has recently been changed, but not to Ratcliffe's satisfaction. The officer remains both informal mediator and formal prosecutor. Meanwhile, the general response of the equity bureaucracy at Western to the utter fiasco of the two wrongful prosecutions of professors Ratcliffe and Klatt was to recommend to the university—not protections for the accused, discretion in reviewing complaints, new definitions of serious offences, open process, safeguards against institutional harassment? No, not at all. They recommended that there be penalties for "breach of confidentiality" by the accused, and also that the use of lawyers by the accused should be prohibited in Western's proceedings.

Professor Heinz Klatt, King's College, UWO

Professor Klatt is a psychologist in his 50s: European background, multilingual, professional, dedicated to education, proud and cultured. His prosecution is perhaps even more offensive to a sense of natural justice than Professor Ratcliffe's. It involves an astonishing level of mismanagement, which Klatt's own reports articulately detail. It is generally difficult to get information on what is going on behind the veils of secrecy; Klatt is rare in having courageously detailed his mistreatment to his colleagues at large. This is another case of wrongful accusation, vague definitions, weak intellectual values, zealous morality officers, benefit of every doubt to accusers, timid administrations, lapse in obligation to long-serving employees, inability of amateur academics to perform the roles of police investigator and judiciary with due process and due observance of the rights of those who fall under suspicion, faulty assumptions that blind everyone in the process to how excessive and panic-driven it is, and how damaging to justice and educational ideals.

In April 1991, after his second-year child psychology course was finished, Klatt was accused by some of his weaker female students of sexually harassing them in class. The accusations were without any substance, and would have looked silly to anyone outside an overly receptive university environment, where regulations and officials stand ready at times to validate even feeble, subjective complaints. King's College is a small school, where student unhappiness would loom large in the eyes of overprotective administrators. What Klatt's accusers claimed bothered them was that Klatt got too personal with one of the sixty students in the class, simply by calling her by a nickname, "Lucky Lucy."

The accusation has a particular irony in the case of Klatt. He is quite formal in his demeanor, strongly dislikes North American familiarity, and never has nicknames for students. The epithet "lucky" actually came about, untypically, when Klatt tried to remember her name, Lucrecia, but could only recall that it started with "look" or "luck." Lucy herself was not complaining: she appreciated the rapport with her professor and wrote to the one-man tribunal, Douglas Letson, to defend him. In other correspondence to the college, she signed herself "Lucky Lucy"!

The accusing students also complained that, in their view, Klatt used language and analogies in the classroom that were inappropriate. In Psychology 140, he once said, in the context of developmental milestones, that, in its emotional significance, a girl's first experience of menstruation is comparable to the first steps of a toddler (Klatt, "Kowtowing"). In a lecture on perinatal psychology, dealing with breast-feeding, he referred to women's breasts as "exuberant" or "Twiggy." (Women with large breasts or small can equally feed their infants and bond with them.) It is hard to see how anybody who is not already disturbed could take offence, much less how anybody could imagine that such expressions of personality could be prohibited and excised from professional style.

On receiving a complaint from the students, the King's College sexual-harassment advisors, Camiletti and Jaco, consulted with them, and only with them, in violation of college policy. They reached a conclusion. They advised the principal that an accumulation of such incidents "amounted to sexual harassment in which a negative psychological environment for study was created" (Sullivan and Munoz). This is a good example of why the CAUT advises that "the words 'comfortable' or 'negative environment' should normally set off alarm bells when they are applied to the classroom situation" ("Reply" 14). There is of course no law in society which prohibits talking about menstruation or breasts, nor any regulation of that kind in universities. It is unimaginable that one could or should teach child psychology and abnormal psychology, as Klatt does, without touching on the human body and sexually related topics. It is only the intensity of the current sex panic that creates the moral presumption that such matters are immediately suspicious, and it is only the pandering to immature and unsettled or vindictive students which jeopardizes the careers of serious and dedicated professionals with so little scruple.

The harassment advisors never informed Klatt of the complaints, nor consulted with Klatt himself about his classes; nor did the students take their complaint to him directly. Klatt wrote once that the process should have taken no more than an afternoon's discussion ("Censorship" 1). In fact, Klatt now thinks an hour should have been enough (letter from Klatt, October 14, 1994). As it happened, there was no informal effort to clear up what the students claim were their concerns. Why not? Did the college authorities really accept these claims at face value? Or did they punish Klatt to settle other scores, knowing full well that in this case he had not misbehaved as charged? The persistence of this kind of ambiguity is the reason for the principle that justice must be *seen* to be done.

Klatt's case, instead, was conducted with the maximum secrecy. The harassment officers convicted Klatt before informing him of the charges, and so reported to the principal. He was never to see the evidence or get the opportunity to confront and cross-examine his accusers. On June 20, 1991, two months from the date of the complaints, when Klatt was finally apprised that something was happening, it was in a letter from the principal, advising him that he was facing formal disciplinary action that could lead to his dismissal. The college took another full year—a year full of harassing procedures—before conceding, in another letter from the principal, on June 24, 1992, that Klatt had *not* violated any rules and was not guilty of sexual harassment.

During that year, the college made a mockery of its own procedures and bungled every aspect of fairness. The principal, Philip Mueller, appointed an outside adjudicator, Douglas Letson, president of St. Jerome's College at the University of Waterloo. Letson collected a huge amount of information about Klatt over four months, by way of secret interviews with deans, chairs of departments, secretaries, and the registrar, none of whom had attended Klatt's classes (Sullivan and Munoz). Although Letson would eventually concede, with apparent reluctance, that "there was no sexual harassment in Psychology 140," his report would also dwell on irrelevancies, and suggest that Klatt should be monitored more closely and evaluated more frequently than usual. Klatt found Letson's investigating procedure repugnant and abusive (letter from Klatt, October 14, 1994).

Letson had, for example, assured the interviewees that Klatt would never find out what they said, "in the interest of greater accuracy" (letter). This is a bizarre, though not unusual, rationalization, widely built into academic assessments: the idea that secrecy somehow encourages frankness and improves the quality of information. Many of us, however, have seen evidence that secrecy can just as readily cover up abuse and irresponsibility, and degrade the quality of information. Wherever there is a chance of discipline, moreover, these matters should not be left up to administrative preference. Our judicial traditions provide for cross-examination as the fairest test of the reliability of information, and the fairest protection of the accused, who is to be presumed innocent until proved guilty. Letson's proceedings, like so many harassment proceedings in universities, appear to have proceeded on an unwarranted presumption of guilt. Since Letson was given the power to fire Klatt, the secrecy of the proceedings that denied Klatt the fullest opportunity to confront, cross-examine, and respond to the evidence amounts to a particularly grievous violation of natural justice, because the King's College policy provided for no appeal against Letson's decision. The fact that, even under such conditions, no finding of sexual harassment could be made against Klatt, is to Klatt's credit, but not to the credit of the proceedings.

Some of the interviewees themselves objected. Klatt's own objections, of various kinds, and also those of his lawyer, were ignored. He himself spent the summer collecting student testimony. Lucrecia Demelo ("Lucky Lucy") wrote early during that year (June 28, 1991) to express "outrage" at the "vicious and slanderous attack" on Klatt. About her nickname, which was used perhaps three or four times over the entire year, she stated that she was pleased, and "at no point during the year did I feel it was offensive or sexual in nature." She rebuked Kimberley Lees, one of Klatt's accusers, "in no uncertain terms," for using Demelo's name against her will to attack a teacher whom she herself recommended to "everyone who is interested in children and particularly my women friends." In fact, 24 of Klatt's students rose to his defence and wrote individual letters on his behalf.

Finally, in June 1992, 14 months after it began, the inquisition was over. Letson had already reported in October 1991. Klatt was not guilty of sexual harassment. Principal Mueller, for reasons still unknown, sat on this finding for another eight months, from October to June, before letting Klatt off the hook. Klatt was never removed from the classroom while all this was going on, but he was very badly bruised. There had been pain, but no light. There was no apology from the principal, and no compensation. Klatt was not guilty, but, the principal said, against all apparent evidence, the complaints had not been frivolous or malicious. This too is a characteristic abuse. The belief that student complaints are always sincere, and that sincerity has significance and a relevance for judgment, is often the face, or the mask, put on by the authors of institutional harassment. On October 16, 1992, in another letter closing the door on Klatt, the principal expressed his confidence in the sincerity of the complainants, and in the fairness and ability of the harassment advisors. Nobody was to be held accountable. The solicitor had apparently assured the principal that they had "no further obligations" to Klatt (Klatt, "Censorship" 3-4)!

Eventually, in March 1993, two years after the affair began, the board of directors of King's College, having been heavily lobbied on behalf of Klatt, overruled the principal and agreed to destroy the secret, tape-recorded testimony that Letson had collected and Klatt had never heard, agreed to pay his legal fees (over $5,000), and agreed to a one-year paid study leave (Sullivan and Munoz). There was still no apology. Indeed, the deal was that Klatt had to agree not to pursue matters any further. The offer, in fact, was open to him only for a few minutes, while he was in the office where it was presented. Take it or leave it. He was not permitted to think it over, sleep on it, or consult his wife. He signed under duress. What kind of gangsterism operates like this? What objectives are university administrators really pursuing?

One final irony is that the eventual and inevitable overhaul of the college's sexual-harassment policy was to take place under the pressure of the "Framework" directive from the Ministry of Education and Training. The zero tolerance direction can only make an already bad policy much worse. The new policy at King's College has not yet been approved as of the fall of 1994.

Klatt himself found the indifference of many colleagues unimaginative and disturbing. The continuing intensity of his perspective on these events, a year and a half after the final settlement, is particularly instructive, in as much as it rests on the historical dimensions of personal biography. He writes: "Born in Nazi Germany, where I lost seven members of our extended family due to fascist ideology and procedures, and raised in Communist East Germany, it is devastating to experience the effects of reckless denunciation, unscrupulous investigation, disrespect, if not contempt, for due process, natural justice and reasonableness all over again in a Catholic, academic institution in democratic Canada. When would the epithet 'perverse' be used if not in a situation where a policy that is supposedly formulated and implemented to contain harassment is used to censor, control, and, above all, *to harass?*" (letter from Klatt, October 14, 1994).

Professor Irwin Silverman, York University

In some institutions, the conflict between the new moralism and the traditions of academic freedom is played out within the organizational structure itself, which is to say that the whole organization has not yet collapsed into the morass of anti-intellectualism. York is an interesting case in point, because it has one of the most anti-libertarian sexual-harassment operations in the country, but also strong traditions to protect the freedoms of faculty. These latter traditions have support within the faculty association, the departments, and the administration.

Like Rushton and Klatt, Silverman is a psychologist, and vulnerable in the way professors in that discipline nowadays seem to be, because their work at the interface of culture and biology is open to controversy. In 1989, his lectures on biology and sex differences came to the attention of the sexual-harassment people. Suddenly, there were strangers sitting in his classes. On being challenged, those officers said they wanted to tape-record what he said, in order to evaluate whether concerns about sexual harassment were in order. Silverman eventually launched a grievance about this, which is still to be heard. In the immediate, what he did was refuse permission to tape, and ask the watchdogs to leave. They would not. He said he would not carry on classes in their presence. They did not care. He cancelled his class, and cancelled it again the next time they showed up. Silverman told the associate dean that he would not teach until the "observers" stationed in his class were out.

This went on for a couple of weeks, until finally, on Silverman's request, the associate dean, Professor Tom Traves, posted security guards at the doors, to keep out the intruders. A remarkable case of an early skirmish, and an unusual willingness by one arm of the institution to safeguard its academic mission against undue interference from another arm. I recently asked Silverman whether he would get the same help now, five years deeper into the biopolitical era (October, 1994). He expressed no confidence that any administration would respond so swiftly and effectively today.

Professor Reg Whitaker, York University

Another York dispute, from the current calendar year, suggests the continuing gap between the academic mission and the sexual-harassment organization. The outcome of the dispute got a chance to be satisfactory, because Whitaker's response was exemplary, and the colleagues in his department supported him. A more timid or apologetic response, or a department divided on the basic issue or compromised by other considerations, might have had different results.

Whitaker is a senior professor of political science who publishes on contemporary issues in the political formation of society. On January 6, 1994, the *Globe and Mail* ran his article on employment equity, with the title "The cutting edge of Ontario's bad law." Whitaker argues against Bill 79 (which has since become effective on September 1, 1994) on the grounds that it is a bad law, a *biopolitical* law. He criticizes the law's contradictory premise that, since discrimination on the basis of biology is wrong, the answer is to entrench biological characteristics as advantages. He also challenges the confusion of fairness in process with equality of results, and "the dubious notion of mirror representation." Instead of creating fair, non-discriminatory procedures, and removing barriers to equal treatment in the workplace, the legislation will create new forms of entry-level discrimination.

On January 31, Dr. Selma Zimmerman, advisor to the university on the status of women (and professor of natural science), wrote to Whitaker to call him to account. "I have received reports of concern in the York community that this article reflects your opposition to the concept of affirmative action and may compromise your position as

Chair of the Political Science department's hiring committee ... Could you please clarify for us your position ... so that I can set to rest any doubts that are raised." A brief summons, one paragraph.

Whitaker got mad, and wrote back to Zimmerman (February 5), with a copy to the academic chain of command, chair, dean, vice-president, and president. He was only an elected member of the hiring committee and not its chair, in any case, but the central issue was Zimmerman's "assault on academic freedom and freedom of expression." He does not owe her a loyalty oath (about the "concept of affirmative action"); if anyone wants to debate on the substance of Bill 79, "let them express these views in public." The idea that intimidating interventions of this kind might be approved by the university (given Zimmerman's official position) was a particularly galling concept in the light of the Ministry of Education and Training's policy directives on "zero tolerance" of "harassment and discrimination" which were becoming matters of controversy at this time, particularly since they would require inquiries whenever anyone registered feeling offended, particularly if the feeling of offence related to biopolitically defined disadvantages. Whitaker indicated these concerns in his covering memo to President Susan Mann (February 5).

That was pretty much that. The chair, Professor Leo Panitch, wrote to Zimmerman "to defend the integrity of this Department" against interference (February 7). The department voted to endorse Whitaker's position. Zimmerman replied once, to lament having her intentions misinterpreted; her role is not to suppress but to clarify. It is an advocacy role, meant "to address issues of concern to the York women's community" (February 14). She provoked a sharp retort from Whitaker: "If this means advocating on behalf of anonymous persons who fail to challenge my arguments in public debate, but resort to privately raising 'doubts' about my [ideological? political?] suitability for participating in academic self-government, then the role of your office should be reviewed, and the implications considered, as I have asked the President to do" (February 16). The president, for her part, wrote Whitaker on February 23: "I take the point of your letter of 5 February and will raise it with Professor Zimmerman." Zimmerman is at this time no longer in the advisor position (for whatever reasons), and Whitaker has suffered no repercussions. Academic freedom was, if anything, reinforced in the encounter, and one may read the situation as indicating the *weakness* of the biopolitical forces at York in this particular encounter. But this is a cautionary tale nevertheless.

Professor Paul Lamy, University of Ottawa

Not all disputes have the same shape or quality. Some involve less light and more heat, and also a far greater readiness on the parts of the authorities to interfere. Professor Lamy's situation, like Professor Matin Yaqzan's, detailed below, indicates the climate of biopolitical hysteria which precipitates rapid overreactions from over-sensitive administrators. Lamy made a casual remark that got him some student complaints, a quick reprimand from the dean, and a lot of media attention. Both the sensation and the punishment had to do with our current fascination with biopolitical issues and, at the same time, the desire of certain authorities to limit and regulate the range of possible attitudes and expressions in relationship to these issues.

This is classic censorship, masquerading as consensual virtue. Of course, it is an endeavour to pre-empt the diversification of views around contemporary cultural agenda items. The more these items become matters of both culture and social policy, the more dangerous it is to require normative conformity in public discourse, or, put differently, the translation of etiquette into formal regulation. In universities, in addition, these regulative efforts run against the grain of the institution's intellectual mission and its expressive preconditions.

241

On January 4, 1994, in a Department of Sociology lecture on the family, in the introductory sociology course 1401A, Lamy was describing types of family structure, traditional and non-traditional. He has been teaching for twenty years, and his style of work is highly structured, with spontaneous elaborations added (Lamy, letter to the dean, January 9, 1994). He always exposes students to different viewpoints, before coming to his own. In this instance, he showed a half-hour TVO video on the family, followed by an array of theoretical, conceptual, and empirical information. He described the monolithic model of the family, as well as its critiques. He described alternative lifestyles, and the moral choices societies face in defining what is and what is not a family. He described both heterosexual and homosexual families. He worked with a tripartite classification: "traditional family" (legal marriage, usually children), "quasi-family" (cohabiting couples, gay and lesbian couples, single parents), and "non-families." He described the trend toward dropping the "quasi" designation, and extending the concept of "family" in the way feminists, for example, have suggested, and that social program delivery agencies are coming to accept.

Lamy also examined bisexuality, in the form of serial monogamy involving partners of different genders, and noted that empirically, at any one time, these persons would be in either a heterosexual or a homosexual relationship. Sociology and psychological or political identity may have entered into friction here and caused some sparks. Lamy saw no problem in extending the concept of family to these relationships, at any rate. Where he got into trouble was where he said, in an aside, that "having an ongoing relationship with a person of the opposite gender while engaging, as a lifestyle, in a series of sexual encounters with persons of the same gender and this without the partner's knowledge or consent sounded more like psychopathy than bisexuality" (Lamy 9-10). He went on to clarify, in response to a question, that he would take the

242

same view of similar behaviour by heterosexuals, but not every student heard him. Six of the 180 students had walked out of the class in protest.

An official complaint was filed the next day, and a petition of signatures was collected the next week. Student radio and newspapers spread the complaint to other media. Sensationalism surrounded the story ("professor calls bisexuals psychotics"). What indeed would the university do? They tried to compromise. They did not pull Lamy out of class. But they did discipline him through a formal reprimand. They tried to look responsible by gagging him. A little bit, anyway.

A few students represented to Professor Henry Edwards, Dean of Social Sciences, that Lamy was homophobic and that his lecturing is pervaded by "intolerant attitudes." He was criticized as unfriendly to Marxism and feminism. Where he undeniably presented feminist materials, and even endorsed some of it, he was attacked for "hiding behind a false veil of feminism in order to deflect many feminist criticisms from students." They argued that his lecturing was unprofessional and defied "the positivistic academic traditions of truth and ethicality upon which our institutions of higher learning are founded" (letter from students to the dean, January 8, 1994). They asked for an administrative review. The student petition, meanwhile, demanded "strict disciplinary action" for failing to provide an environment conducive to learning.

How does he create a negative environment? His opinions "offend the personal, moral and ethical sensibilities of the class." Few students signed the petition; many others argued with them. But the dean, having looked at the student letters and Lamy's extensive replies in defence of his intellectual integrity and professional sociological knowledge, opted to discipline him as demanded—by the handful of students, and the opportunistic pressures of a biopolitical public moment. Was he spooked by the student militants, or by the press attention?

Lamy did not arrive at the University of Ottawa yesterday. He has established his teaching and scholarly credentials over a long career. He has strongly positive teaching evaluations. Like all faculty, his work has been under constant scrutiny: for tenure, promotion, research grants, annual teaching evaluations, and the like. The dean acknowledges that he cannot verify the student recollections of what Lamy said. He agrees that there was no evidence that Lamy harassed or discriminated against minority groups. This leaves only speech, and the *perception* of speech. Anyone who has seen student notes on lectures or student performance in assignments and exams knows well that these are not a reliable index much of the time of what material has actually been presented. The dean, however, makes much of the fact that *some* students "perceived some of your classroom comments as insensitive, offensive, and/or indicative of intolerance on your part"—especially the expression of personal opinions or asides. The dean then invents the principle that "academic content" and opinions must be kept separate for lower-year undergraduates. On the basis of this pedagogic and methodological bias, and without any investigation beyond the complainants, the dean concludes that Lamy has violated his contract, which requires him to foster and maintain "a productive and orderly learning environment" (letter to Lamy, January 28, 1994).

Within three weeks from a complaint, the dean has convicted a senior professor of the expression of comments that some have perceived as insensitive or offensive to them. What makes this casual tyranny so interesting is that it highlights how arbitrary are the concepts used to punish. The dean has not undertaken any study of Lamy's classroom environment. The language cannot be taken at face value at all. What is the connection between perception of offence by some students and a classroom environment? The point is that the dean did not think that he had to find out. It was enough for him that some students disagreed with their professor's views. Punish the prof.

As it happens, Lamy's course scored very high in a comparative study of classroom environment undertaken by a doctoral student in psychology just before the incident. And Lamy's course was evaluated by students, in the annual course evaluations that took place after the incident, more highly than in the preceding year. Clearly, there was nothing wrong with Lamy's learning environment, at least not as far as the large majority of students was concerned. Crucially, in a way that this whole new genre of injunctions shares, the concept of negative environment refers, not to the classroom at all, with reference to some objective, statistical, or otherwise meaningful standard, but solely to the perceptual world of any single student—particularly a student whose perceptions are modishly connected with public orthodoxy about necessary virtue.

Ought Lamy to have known that an aside would produce a small minority perception of offence? Perhaps. Should he have refrained from making the aside? His choice. Should his asides be subject to dispute? Of course. Should they be forbidden? Definitely not. Such a prohibition offends academic principles, freedom of speech, and also the entitlement of other students who do find Lamy educationally stimulating to have access to his uncensored teaching. The prohibition is too indefinite, in any case, to be enforceable.

Nevertheless, in his formal letter of reprimand (January 28, 1994), which will sit in Lamy's file, the dean wrote to Lamy: "I direct you to refrain from expressing personal opinions which are inflammatory or likely to be harmful or offensive to students or groups of students." "Harm" was never demonstrated; "inflammatory" is uncertain of meaning. Arousing emotion? The dean knew that Lamy had twice retracted the offending comments. Nevertheless, he took the trouble to endorse the retraction in a public statement. He issued a public document advertising that Lamy has been directed "to refrain from expressing non-academic personal opinions which are likely to have counterproductive effects on the students."

Apart from the freedom-of-speech issue, the notion of counterproductive effects from personality raises also a danger to other educational values. It is notable that professors are being re-imaged as indoor maintenance workers, responsible for environmental comforts. It is also worthy of note that the key to the presumption of productivity is forged from the notion that academic expression is divisible into professional and personal, and therefore professors can be made to refrain from "personal" expressions. This is conceding too much to biopolitical lobbies; and it is also false to the libidinal erotics of education. Students *crave and demand* the personal touch; they do not want teaching machines, either at the undergraduate or graduate level.

Administrations are running up test balloons to see what kinds of restrictions on expressive freedoms will fly, and professionalism-without-personality is one of the bogus thought experiments that they are trying out in public. One does not have to agree with Lamy's comments to see that the muzzle does more damage than the bark. Self-presentation is inseparable from teaching, and communicates in volumes, even when it is stripped down toward a zero degree of self.

Professor Vedanand, University of Manitoba

Following from the reprimand against Professor Lamy, for "unproductive" asides, it is instructive to see that the notions of etiquette, which are excessively, if asymmetrically, validated in a biopolitical climate, have also a fallout for the general protection of free inquiry and expression in a university setting. A recent labour arbitration in Manitoba (february 11, 1991) produced an unsettling decision on the permissible scope of expression, and on the latitude allowed for institutional censure. Professor Vedanand is an associate professor in the Department of Marketing in the Faculty of Management, with a special interest in Japanese marketing strategies. He joined the faculty in 1969. On Sept. 28, 1988, at a Faculty Club reception hosted by Xerox Canada Inc. for members of the Faculty, in connection with employment prospects for students, attended by 15-20 people from the faculty and the company, Professor Vedanand had a verbal exchange with the presenter, major account sales manager Mr. William Morrissey, at one point involving Mr. Lovie, Mr. Morrissey's superior. Professor Vedanand argued that the Japanese, Canon in particular, had a superior marketing strategy, and that Xerox had lost and not regained its leading market share in the home-copier market. The exchange appears to have lasted 3-5 minutes. It was casual and cordial, according to both Professor Vedanand and a colleague. It was embarrassing, challenging, inappropriate, rude, aggressive, unpleasant, and/or antagonistic, according to the company and Professor Vedanand's superiors (chair, associate dean).

No one took him to task at the reception or in the days that followed. In a memo dated Nov. 4, 1988, however, dean W. Mackness wrote to Professor Vedanand: "I have been disturbed by several reports of your comments ... The tone of your challenge concerning their report on share of market was unpleasant, and your 'grilling' of sales representatives on company strategy inappropriate. The Faculty is working very hard to cultivate positive relationships with the business community and your remarks were counterproductive." The dean later said this was not meant as a form of discipline. Professor Vedanand always insisted he was only putting matters in perspective, as a scholar must. In a second memo (January 17, 1989), the dean argued that "these observations are a matter of politeness and have absolutely nothing to do with academic freedom."

This matter was tested through grievance and arbitration. The university stipulated that the memo was not disciplinary and would never be used that way. The arbitration heard representations from Donald Savage and the CAUT, as well as Pierre-Yves Boucher for the AUCC, plus assorted other experts. It reviewed a variety of articles, statements, and model clauses on academic freedom, as well as related court judgments from the U.S. (Sweezy, Keyishian, Tinker, Pickering, Mabey, Bishop, Rigg). It considered whether "remarks" referred to Professor Vedanand's content or his manner, and whether the dean's memo related to his conduct or his scholarship. The CAUT's argument that the limits on academic freedom were only to prevent abuse of authority regarding students, and to ensure that nobody else's argument is shut down, were held to be too narrow, with respect to other social and community limits to academic freedom.

The award by arbitrator Perry Schulman, Q.C., was related to the terms of the University of Manitoba collective agreement, but it had some general considerations to offer as well: "In some circumstances, rudeness, short of shutting down the presentation can exceed the bounds" (Schulman 59). He acknowledged that it would be illegitimate for administrations to harass professors, or to express disapproval as part of an act of institutional censorship (60). But he accepted the "distinction between institutional censorship and the remedying of a matter of decorum by a suggestion rather than by penalty" (60-61). Professor Vedanand's conduct "comprised a breach of etiquette which entitled dean Mackness to make some comment" with a very limited circulation (63-64).

Professor Matin Yaqzan, University of New Brunswick

Matin Yaqzan, a professor of mathematics for 27 years, was savaged by his institution, in one of the worst examples of abject surrender to a panic climate ever witnessed in Canadian higher education. In the past thirty years, academic freedom has become the central normative framework of university level research and education, positioning universities as central institutions of a liberal culture.[4] Because academic freedom imposes obligations of tolerance on university authorities, and protects minority rights, it serves as a countervailing power against orthodoxy. As a principle of diversity, it does more than any other device to prevent the formation of creed-states and to equalize structural inequities (Kubara).[5] Today, not only is tenure—the safeguard of academic freedom—under pressure,[6] but academic freedom itself is again under sharp attack, this time from biopolitical advocates of minority power. The difference, in the 1990s, is that academics themselves are badly divided, and some academics are leading the charge to curtail and diminish academic freedom and subordinate everyone's research, teaching, and cultural expression to specific social objectives.

One way that a wedge is introduced into the unity of free expression and free inquiry established in the academic freedom tradition is by insisting that the two are separable. Academic freedom can be reserved therefore for academic expertise, narrowly understood. Beyond that, free speech can be simply subordinated to other values in the university "community"—for example, hospitality, purity, comfort, self-esteem, encouragement of designated minorities, women's safety. A kind of elitism about the prerogatives of expert expression is combined with a populist authoritarianism about speech in general. The university is then seen as a little tribal enclave that can be empowered to limit the legal rights of the adults who work there, on the implied argument that academic expertise (narrowly conceived) and progressive social values serve a university better than the full range of legally available expression.

Yaqzan had unpopular, right-wing views, and he was punished for them, as was Rushton in a different context. Non-conforming views and attitudes can equally bring professors on the left into trouble with the biopolitical orthodoxies and the authorities hiding behind these control devices, as happened with professors Cannizzo, Vandervort, Whitaker, Westhues, and Magnusson. But Yaqzan seemed really out of touch with colleagues. He defended

Malcolm Ross, the Holocaust-denying Moncton school teacher. He took the Arab side against Israel in debates. He was not on any fast track; for example, he had remained an assistant professor since the 1950s. He was a fringe character: a conservative former Muslim, who made many enemies, but whom nobody could quite get, until his brush with biofeminism. There was a culture clash, an ethnic clash, and multicultural variations in perspective, as well as some clumsiness in phrasing, which may have all been factors. None of this got sorted out. When Yaqzan waltzed into the date-rape controversy, he had to be carried out flat on his back.

Things happened with lightning speed. Like Whitaker, but without the professional credibility and without the support networks, Yaqzan wrote an opinion piece for the student newspaper, *The Brunswickan,* on November 5, 1993. By November 11, he was pulled out of classes. By the time the second term began in January 1994, Yaqzan was gone from the university. What he argued, in a one-page piece called "Opinion: 'Rape' Past and Present," was that the revolution in the realm of human sexuality during the last 30-40 years, related to technological, economic, and cultural factors, including changes in the family and in the expectations of young women, has brought with it changes in language and meaning, including the meaning of "rape." His article is actually a reply to Laura Penny's "Recognizing Date Rape When It Happens," published in September 1993 in the Canadian Federation of Students' *Student Advocate.*

He argues that sublimation of the natural sexual urges requires social controls and cultural supports, all of which have been attenuated with the removal of such devices as chaperones, veils and body coverings, the prohibition on premarital sex, and the stigma on youth sexual activity. It seems to him, therefore, that men, for their part, will sometimes rape, when the self-controls fail to rein in the natural passions (particularly when they are specifically aroused on dates). It also seems to him that sexually active women, for their part, will experience coercion under dating circumstances differently from the utter, traumatic terror of rape for girls in traditional societies (whose loss of virginity means disqualification from marriage, fear of pregnancy, life-long shame and guilt, sinfulness, and stigmatization by family and society). He thinks boys are after sex more than girls are, and accordingly should be educated to restraint, while girls should be educated to due caution.

Finally, he argues that for sexually active, non-stigmatized young women today, the only damage from unwanted sex is "discomfort" which, he suggests, deserves compensation in the form of monetary "damages." Such compensation strikes him as more appropriate than moral outrage of the kind that the word "rape" evoked "in yesteryears." Now, this is not a perfect viewpoint, but neither is it outside the orbit of human understanding. In fact, Yaqzan is in accord with many feminists about the aggressive proclivity of men, as a biological given. He supports education about perceptions and expectations of a kind that counsellors often provide. He accepts that sexual violation is doing harm, and he believes there should be not only a penalty, but a compensation for the victim. He calculates this on the American model of financial damages for discomfort, and there may be, though it is not spelled out, an unconscious subtext connection with female prostitution as well. The same subtext probably operates in the vitriolic responses.

But his main point is about cultural change. And his main difference with the biofeminists is that he wants to downgrade the meaning of unwanted sex on dates by contextualizing it: to a biology, to a cultural history, and to an interpersonal interaction. His unpardonable sin, in the biopolitical understanding, is that he refuses outrage. At the deepest levels, he clashes with the program of biofeminism, which is to create sex panic, and to amplify it through the violence connection. Yaqzan's view is that sex itself is not damaging, apart from the coercion itself, which is a culpable act of causing discomfort. The biofeminist machinery is dedicated to decontextualizing and restigmatizing sex by borrowing from the perennial, traditional stigma against rape. Yaqzan's cultural historicism means to deny biofeminists access to traditional claims. No compromise between them is possible. In any event, Yaqzan's views are labelled "opinion," and he is entitled to them. The biofeminist sacred cows are just opinions too. The reader remains free to look for other alternatives, away from both.

After publication of the article, feminists stirred things up in the student press. Yaqzan was accused of condoning violence, inciting to rape, and making the campus unsafe for women. Then the local press got into it. After five days, there seemed to be enough frenzy that the vice-president (academic) wrote to Yaqzan on November 11, 1993: "This is to inform you that you are hereby suspended from all your duties as a faculty member at the University of New Brunswick with effect from 12 November 1993. You will remain on full pay and benefits until I complete an investigation of numerous complaints about your conduct and performance of your duties. Until this investigation is completed you shall not come to the university campus to use your office or any university facilities. During the period of this suspension you will be replaced in your current courses so that the students enrolled will not be disadvantaged." It is noteworthy that the vice-president had not been long at the University of New Brunswick. This was the same Tom Traves who had posted security guards to protect Irwin Silverman's classes from sexual harassment officers back in 1989, when he was associate dean at York University.

The local press supported the university. The national press tore it to pieces. It was clear to the faculty association that the suspension was a form of discipline, possibly a step on the way to termination of employment. Traves wrote Yaqzan another letter, a face-saving letter, a mere week later (November 19), to say that the suspension was not disciplinary, but necessary for "public safety and an orderly academic environment." He lifted the suspension, effective immediately. But he added, without irony, "in order to prevent any further disruptions for students," Yaqzan would not return to the classroom for the rest of the school term. This too was "not a disciplinary action." After all this, the letter concluded on a predictably false note: "It is my understanding that you have indicated ... that you do not advocate or condone violence of any form against women. This has been a difficult time for all of us and I hope this letter clarifies our position on these event."

The time was more difficult for Yaqzan than for Traves. The university public-relations machinery put out the idea of public safety for all it was worth. But Yaqzan had gone to classes in the week between the publication of the article and the letter of suspension without any difficulty. There were no mass demonstrations or disruptions. Only after Yaqzan was banished from campus did the media circus start, with exotic celebrities offering their views and arranging interviews: CNN, the *Donahue* show, Camille Paglia ("outrageous infringement"). Robin Armstrong, UNB president, denounced Yaqzan in the press: "Free speech does not equal irresponsible speech. Prof. Yaqzan has abused his position by excusing and encouraging behaviour that is not only unacceptable by the standards of human decency but also subject to criminal charges" (Bergman, "Conflict on campus" 18). But only Yaqzan was in danger, from the biofeminist lobby and the local press, which cried for blood. The university reassured the faculty association that it supported the policy on academic freedom. The faculty association reassured the university that it supported the policy about sexual harassment. Yaqzan, however, was going to be sacrificed.

After a brief hysteria, the situation calmed. But after November 19, a mere two weeks from the start of the affair, the university felt it could not let Yaqzan back in class. Yaqzan, meanwhile, insisted on an apology. It was agreed he would not go back before January 1994. And he would have gone back happily with an apology, even one without much fanfare or *mea culpa*. The university would not have it. The faculty association made the options clear: settle with Yaqzan, or face a huge law suit by him for defamation, maybe worth $500,000. It was cheaper to keep him on the payroll until he reached the age of 65 in less than three years. The university considered paying him a salary, without assigning teaching duties. In the end, they decided to buy him out and retire him early. This suited the faculty association as well, since they wanted to avoid lengthy and costly grievance and arbitration hearings, where the chances were that Yaqzan might not be a good witness.

The association was divided in any case. A number of influential and well-known feminists wanted to see Yaqzan fired, or at least humiliated and committed to "sensitivity training." There was a vigilante notion afoot that the courts cannot deal with these things, and so the universities *must*. Professor Jack Vanderlinde, the faculty association president, stood by the idea that a member of the association had to be defended against arbitrary suspension and termination. In the end, the association in effect wound up in the role of broker, more than advocate. They got Yaqzan an independent lawyer, and it turned out that the early retirement plan suited Yaqzan too. Oh yes, the usual muzzle clause. Yaqzan had to sign an agreement not to sue, and also not to disclose the terms of the agreement. Very quickly, it got very quiet, and the public lost track of the case. Perhaps it had never been much more than a tempest in a teapot. Perhaps neither Yaqzan, nor the institution of academic freedom, nor the fundamental right to freedom of expression would be irreparably damaged by the end of Yaqzan's academic career. But the venality of the biopolitical climate, and the teeth its advocates are hoping to acquire, was amply on display.

IX
Riders in the Storm:
Cases from Coast
to Coast

"But under the beards—and this was K.'s real discovery—badges of various sizes and colors gleamed on their coat-collars. They all wore these badges, so far as he could see. They were all colleagues, these ostensible parties of the right and the left, and as he turned round suddenly he saw the same badges on the coat-collar of the Examining Magistrate. 'So!' cried K., flinging his arms in the air, his sudden enlightenment had to break out, 'every man jack of you is an official ...'" (Franz Kafka, The Trial 47)

In this chapter, I relate three ongoing cases that demon-strate important features of the havoc unleashed by giving biopolitics a free ride on university campuses. All three cases have at their centre an individual whose self-image is "progressive," who supports causes like anti-racism, anti-sexism, feminism, equity. These three people have been surprised to discover that the dominant culture seems to have changed while they were not looking. In fact, the biopolitical, specifically biofeminist, capture of the very causes they had espoused has become a leading menace to their personal beliefs and security. All of them serve as outstanding examples—as do the cases in the previous chapter—of the indispensable role and continuing signifi-cance of tenure in protecting academic freedom. Without it, all the worst in human nature (and culture) would overwhelm the universities, and individuals who failed to conform to some prevailing norm would be readily purged.

Professor Alan Surovell, Dalhousie University

Alan Surovell comes to Dalhousie from a private-sector background as a software developer, and a New England background as a strong civil libertarian. Like others with a left history who have got caught in the gears of the panic machine, Surovell has discovered that biopolitics, using rhetoric borrowed from both left and right, rolls over the old left-right politics altogether, in order to repolarize social issues and group affiliations around different cen-tres of identification. These do not acknowledge, much less respect, progressive credentials acquired in the frame of other definitions. Surovell's case has received little publicity to date, even among his own colleagues, because his trials have been cloaked by confidentiality. This will change.[1]

Surovell has been at Dalhousie since 1987, promoted to senior instructor in 1992 on the basis of positive teach-ing evaluations. His duties are split between the Depart-ment of Math, Statistics, and Computing Science and the

Transition Year Program. He teaches math in both. TYP is a one-year preparatory program run for the benefit of African-Canadian and aboriginal students; it is staffed by Surovell and five other instructors, two of them black. Surovell's last two years have been consumed in the bio-political mirage. He suddenly had to deal with an investigation of racial harassment in TYP, and a charge of sexual harassment in the Math, Statistics and Computing Science Department.

A social activist since his youth, Surovell says he joined TYP with "anti-racist" motives. The program has been unsettled since the appointment of Beverley Johnson, an African-Canadian social worker, as its director, effective 1992-93. With no previous experience in an academic department and an autocratic bent, the director was soon caught up in increasing conflict with participants in the program. By the end of the year, she was asking president Howard Clark to investigate the possibility of gender and racial harassment by faculty and staff. When in difficulty, reach for the morals charges.

The president appointed Mayann Francis, former employment-equity officer at Dalhousie, to investigate. Francis was a friend of Johnson's, and had lobbied for Johnson's appointment while a member of the search committee that had hired her. According to Surovell, the investigation was a witchhunt. The accusations were not disclosed to the accused; individuals were interviewed in secret; black teachers were advised against a common front with the white teachers; the objectives were confessions of guilt or promises of compliance.

Surovell tells the disturbing story of his meeting with investigating equity officer Francis in her office, where Francis told him that if Johnson acted vindictively toward Surovell, it would be "understandable" because, after all, as a member of Johnson's search committee, he had failed to support her candidacy (letter from Surovell, August 26, 1994). The investigation went on over a few months in the spring of 1993. A year and a half later, Surovell is still waiting to see the report. Francis, meanwhile, has been gone from Dalhousie since December 1993.

The race charges are interesting chiefly as evidence of the excessive readiness of individuals to slander each other casually, and to blame every friction on systemic causes with designated scapegoats. They show the extent to which *authorities*—from the director, through the equity officer, up to the president—stand ready to invoke the heavy artillery of moral panic in order to establish social controls in university settings. The duplicity of human behaviour will not soon disappear from the arenas of social conflict; but it is crucial to reduce the level of atmospheric panic in order to reduce the automatic supports for biopolitical opportunism. The board of governors at Dalhousie may have taken a small step in the right direction by turning down a new omnibus harassment code on racism and sexism (called Policy on Discriminatory Harassment) that had been prepared by a group that includes Mayann Francis and Barbara Harris, both of whom figure prominently in Surovell's story. The policy was adopted by the Senate with a two-thirds majority in February 1994; but it was then "overwhelmingly" defeated at the Board on March 15 (Watson, "BoG rejects").

Surovell takes his teaching very seriously and likes to make a connection with the students. In 1992-93, Lynn Bradley, a nurse enrolled in Surovell's Math 1000C class, showed interest in occasional social contact. The two met twice at Surovell's house over the Christmas holidays: the first occasion was a dinner in mid-December, attended by Surovell's ten-year-old son; the second was a lunch in early January, in the presence of the boy as well as Surovell's visiting brother. Bradley apparently enjoyed these occasions, but afterwards found that her "interest in having social contact with Mr. Surovell outside of class waned" (Bradley, "Complaint" 2). His recollection is that they exchanged a few phone calls as well as brief hallway pleasantries after class, especially when she waited for him. They also discussed getting together for lunch or coffee over the spring break, but he was busy and declined. Both agree that there was a minimum of actual social contact between them in the second term.

On March 23, after class, Bradley "politely, clearly, verbally stated my disinterest in any social contact with him"—no extra attention or telephoning. "Mr. Surovell agreed to this" (2). On the advice of three professors, however, she then went to the Dalhousie Advisory Committee on Sexual Harassment to "take the matter up," but decided to wait for her final grade before taking action. She got a D grade, which signals poor performance, but she apparently considered this a fair grade (*Report of the Hearing Panel* 8). On June 28, she filed a formal complaint, using the language of Dalhousie's harassment policy to allege that Surovell "engaged in sexually harassing behaviour." She accused him of (1) implied threat of reprisal for refusal to comply with a sexually oriented request (specifically—social contact outside of the academic setting); and (2) sexually oriented behaviour which created a negative psychological and emotional setting for study (unwanted attention, negative comments).

These accusations—threats, sexual coercion, negative environment—would strike intense fear into the heart of any professional in today's punitive university milieu. What followed was six months of ordeal for Surovell. He experienced long periods of sleeplessness, loss of appetite leading to significant weight loss, irritability, lack of focus, difficulty with personal relations, all resulting from the acute stress of being charged (letter from Surovell, October 7, 1994).

In January 1994, a formal hearing panel(chaired by Jane Spurr) unanimously dismissed Bradley's complaint. She herself said in her own summation to the panel: "Professor Surovell is *not a sexual harasser.*" And the panel concluded: "There was no evidence of anything sexually oriented. The parties were clear in their evidence that they were initially mutual 'social interest' *[sic]*. There was no evidence from either party that this 'social interest' involved any physical or sexual activity, that there was any intent that it develop to this state, that there was any express or implied request from either party for sexual contact, or that either party made any sexually-oriented remarks or behaviour" (*Report* 9). But if there was no evidence of wrongdoing, why were charges launched against Surovell in the first place? To answer this question, we have to backtrack to Bradley's initial approach to the Advisory Committee on Sexual Harassment.

Bradley's complaint was initially received and evaluated by Barbara Harris, the president's adviser on women's issues and the prominent chair of the Advisory Committee, from which the hearing panel was selected. Harris went on to act as advisor to and advocate for Bradley throughout the whole affair. Surovell objected to the propriety of Harris, the chair of the committee, accompanying Bradley to the hearing; but the panel flatly dismissed these objections. The Dalhousie policy, which allows for this fusion of roles, is clearly flawed in this respect. It is likely that Surovell's actual exoneration by the panel is testimony less to the lack of potential bias than to the abject weakness of the accusations against him.

A larger issue here is that Harris, with all her experience, should have known better than to bring such a worthless case forward, only to have a panel of five members drawn from her own committee reject her client's case with unanimity. Had she exercised simple discretion, a staggering unfairness to the accused Surovell could have been avoided. Harris had to do nothing more than recognize, as the panel did, that there was no sexually oriented content whatsoever to Bradley's complaint, and that there was simply no jurisdiction under the policy to proceed with it. Why did Harris not exercise such discretion? Is the university prepared to harass its professors recklessly?

The answer to this question may be "yes," at least "thoughtlessly," if not recklessly. And it may not be Harris's fault (as case officer), though she must bear some responsibility. After all, she set up the policy like this in the first place. Unless clause 14 (ii) of the policy, which authorizes case officers to "advise the complainant of possible courses of action" (*Plan* 6), allows for excluding particular cases, it may well be that neither the case officer nor any other person can actually stand in the way of the complainant's will to go all the way through "Informal Process" and "Formal Hearing." Automated and complaint-driven, Dalhousie's policy, like many others, has no built-in discretion that would weed out either frivolous and malicious complaints or misdirected ones that do not meet the definitions. This is the zero-tolerance conception: discretion is rejected on the unacceptable premise that any individual with a complaint should be encouraged to test her grievance in front of a tribunal, regardless of the costs to the other party. It is as though neither the police nor the Crown attorneys nor the courts were ever to screen the nature of accusations before organizing and holding trials.

In her complaint, Bradley details three sets of concerns, all of them examples of purely subjective perception. All pertain to the second term, after her second meal with Surovell in January. First, she was, quite rightly, worried about math, and was never quite clear about the grading scheme. She thought the C- grade she got at mid-year was too high in light of her performance, and worried that Surovell might be favouring her for social reasons. She began to avoid him and to miss classes. Noticing her absences, and being aware of her difficulties, he once called and left a message on her machine, expressing concern about missed classes. Later in February, he spoke to her prudentially after one class, as any good teacher would, to suggest she should not miss too many classes. She never talked to him about it. She claims she took his comments for a veiled threat: using the language of the policy, she calls it an "implied threat of reprisal for refusal to comply with a sexually-oriented request."

The fact is, her grades remained steady, so there was no basis for inferring a grading threat. She could never produce a single example of a sexually oriented request from Surovell that would have tested her unwillingness to comply. Her fantasy that, after a couple of casual and chaperoned meals, she was so important to him that if she missed classes he would throw professionalism to the winds just to get back at her, was quite unconvincing to the panel. However, although the panel finds no fault with Surovell on this, it surrenders to the temptation to set up some kind of equivalence of confusion: "The complainant alleged confusion in her mind about the Respondent's actions and comments and chose to look at them from the perspective of sexual harassment. The Respondent was equally confused about the change in the Complainant's behaviour during the second term. Neither party spoke directly to the other about their concerns or utilized any other appropriate mechanism to resolve their difficulties" (9).

This is most peculiar. Surovell and Bradley were not a couple with "difficulties" to resolve. Here was a student heading for obvious trouble, with no obvious reason why. His alleged "confusion" was no more than that he had no explanation for her missing classes, apart from the usual mid-winter overwork. Her complaint and her "confusion," however, nearly destroyed Surovell's life. There is no symmetry between her accusation-producing imaginings and his good-will concern about her performance, which did her no harm of any kind. When she came to tell him in March that it was not his business if she was not in class, and she did not want to continue any social relationship, he thereafter respected her wishes without fail, even though he was surprised by this unanticipated outburst of anger. After all, the nature of her inward, mental evolution during this period was not communicated to him. It was all in her head, and this was the first he had heard of it. As Surovell told the panel: "I was not particularly concerned about any changes in her behaviour which in any case did not occur until March. After only two social encounters with her almost two months earlier, I hardly knew her well enough to intuit what she claims to have been conveying non-verbally. If anything, my impression of her was that of a mature, forthright and confident person who would certainly not hesitate to discuss openly with someone any confusion she may have, whether to question a grade or to request discontinuance of a friendship" (Hearing Summation 2).

Secondly, Bradley alleged two staring incidents, in late March and in April, the first in the hall and the second in class. The panel notes that there was no pattern here, and that the allegations were not corroborated by witnesses (*Report* 7). Thirdly, Bradley reports her complaint that, on two occasions, Surovell spoke to her private math tutor about her. Once, in February, when she was missing classes, he inquired casually about how she was doing. Then, in late March, after she told Surovell out of the blue of her "disinterest" in contact with him, Surovell asked the tutor if the latter knew why Bradley might be upset with him. The tutor did not volunteer any information. The panel goes off the rails on this point. Just before exonerating Surovell on all charges of sexual harassment, they find that talking to Bradley's tutor was unprofessional, because of the tutor's "unequal, inferior" standing in the department relative to Surovell (8). They insist that Surovell ought to have pressed Bradley directly to find out what was causing her distress, or else that he should have consulted the Department Head.

It's damned if you do and damned if you don't. Imagine what Bradley and the panel would have said if Surovell had insisted on confronting Bradley directly, in person or by phone! And imagine what they would have said if he had gone to report her to the head of the department, missed classes and all, and undermined her standing in the department. She was already imagining grade reprisals as it was, without Surovell doing anything to warrant it. The panel does Surovell a great injustice in this section (8). What planet do they live on to have such twisted notions of professionalism? Faculty talk about students all the time, and just in this way, when they run into each other in the halls. Most of it is done with integrity, and out of fair interest and concern. Surovell did not seek out Bradley's tutor deliberately, and it made sense for him to inquire about Bradley from someone who knew her and was in contact with her, rather than from a stranger, or by forcing her into a conversation she did not want to have. The evidence is that Surovell did not pressure the tutor, and in fact the tutor was fully able to choose whether and how to respond.

The panel admits that it has "no authority to adjudicate on behaviour of this nature," yet without authority, it accuses Surovell of harassing someone in a less powerful position. Not only is this assertion gratuitous, but the accusation of "unprofessional" conduct is damaging and slanderous. In the light of the actual, palpable power abuse being enacted by virtue of the unequal power between the university and Surovell, the hearing panel and Surovell, even Bradley (with the machinery on her side) and Surovell, it is obscene to attack the accused, who is about to be cleared, and who has been badly harassed under the system. The panel owes Surovell a retraction, on the face of it; or the university does.

There is no evidence of wrong-doing. Surovell had two meals with Bradley, both in a family setting. He took a casually friendly interest in her until, for no reason apparent to him, she turned hostile. The moment he discovered that further academic or social attention from him would be unwanted, he respected her wishes. Twice, he inquired of a colleague if he had any insight into her situation. There is not a hint of sex.

For her part, she considered her final grade of D fair, but invented a purely unprofessional sex-for-grades motivation to pin on her professor for her C- grade at Christmas: as the panel said, the difference between C- and D is negligible. She falsely accused him of a sex crime and an academic breach of ethics, without a shred of evidence. She dragged him through mediation, and expected him to agree to a number of conditions in order to settle her complaint: written apology, attendance at a sexual-harassment workshop, refraining from talking to her or about her, and (adding insult to injury by the very suggestion) no reprisals against her tutor. Of course he could not meet her conditions. Then she dragged him before a hearing panel of two students, one professor, one staff person, and one administrator, to defend himself against the prospects of ("guilty-if-charged") stigmatization.

Surovell is not a powerful senior member of the faculty. He does not have tenure, although he does have a continuing contract. He does not have the support of a powerful research network. He was not defended by the faculty association. Most of the people who testified for him were his students. The people who testified against him were Bradley's professor friends, in the main (2 out of her 3 witnesses). The panel does not relate the testimony of the witnesses, but generally found all but one of them credible. Hard to believe. Bradley's formal complaint says that she approached the harassment office on the advice of some of her professors (*Report* 6-7; Complaint 2). Two professors were witnesses for her. One of Bradley's professor witnesses, as Surovell tells the story (Letter, October 7, 1994), was there to tell the panel that Bradley's distress was obviously symptomatic of sexual harassment. Another professor witness said the same. With Bradley's distress his only evidence, he told the panel that they were dealing with a "classic" case of sexual harassment. When asked by a panel member what qualified him to make such an expert assessment, he revealed that he had taken a sexual harassment course the previous year.

Surovell's own rebuttal witnesses were dynamite. He remembers that one female student recalled seeing Bradley waiting for Surovell after numerous classes. Another student told the panel that he had gotten to know Bradley well, and she had revealed to him that she enjoyed socializing with her male professors. At the present time, she was having a relationship with a professor whose class she had been taking at the same time as Surovell's. Moreover, the student identified him as the same professor who had testified about Bradley's experience of "classic" harassment from Surovell. This had real impact. When the panel inquired how the student could be sure it was this particular witness, he calmly replied that he happened to live across the street from the man, so there could be no mistake.

Surovell's prosecution is a nearly perfect example of the flaws of the complaint-driven process, built on an idiosyncratic perception of offence by an individual. If it were not for recent biofeminist success in establishing entitlement to monumentally excessive protections for "women's safety," the case against Surovell would never have gotten to first base. Indeed, if it were not for the climate of moral panic, I doubt that his accuser would have thought to bring charges against him, or indeed, that she would have been encouraged to do so by friends and administrators.

The formal hearing panel was struck on October 1, 1993, three months after the official accusations. The hearing was started on November 29, and completed in early December 1993. Since the complaint was dismissed in the hearing panel's report of January 24, 1994, Surovell has been trying, with the aid of legal counsel, to reach a settlement with the university for compensation. Nine months later, there is still no settlement. He is thinking that a lawsuit may be his best option. There have already been real costs to him, in terms of both pains of body and anxieties of mind. There are no official repercussions for Lynn Bradley, his accuser. Barbara Harris too has meanwhile left Dalhousie voluntarily, with honour. His own job, however, was on the line, and the university acted without reasonable and probable grounds. What had to be driving the machinery therefore was some small thing like malice, or some large force that would treat him like a pawn in a game. Surovell is currently on medical leave. It looks like the force of biopolitics is what put him there.

Professor Ken Westhues, University of Waterloo

Professor Westhues's situation, which has been spiralling out of control for a full year now, is a case study in the breakdown of an institution's ability to regulate and resolve its internal disputes. I cannot review here the more than 500 pages of documentation that the case has generated as it has moved from one arena of discord to another. Nor can I speak to all the issues and distortions of normal interaction. Speaking to my theme, however, I can say that the shriek of biopolitical panic is an undercurrent throughout the case, which has all the signs of a tragedy in the making, without any remedy in sight.

Westhues is a senior scholar with commitments to a humanistic vision of sociology that differs from the quantitative and statistical approaches of many of his colleagues. His book, *First Sociology* (1982), is widely regarded as an important text. Over 25 years of a teaching and research career, he has built up a strong reputation that draws graduate students to Waterloo to work with him. He is fiercely protective of these students, in what he regards as a potentially risky intellectual environment. He was awarded Waterloo's Distinguished Teaching Award in 1985; his research is acknowledged beyond the borders of Waterloo; and his service work to the academy and the wider community is prolific.

Over the years, Westhues has chaired the department, and has served as its graduate studies officer. He has also been embroiled in numerous controversies with his colleagues and deans, over a range of departmental and other university matters. Those who like him have a high regard for his integrity, intelligence, and generosity, even when they acknowledge that his passion for causes can make him prickly, abrasive, and relentlessly adversarial. He acknowledges that he is "not easy to live or work with" ("Dear Gail" 6). But nobody has ever convicted him of violating principle or university policy.

It is commonplace in university departments, as in small families, for hostilities to develop among the permanent staff, who have to live and work together, year after year. Usually, the hostilities are multidimensional and multivariate; they do not line up along any one particular axis. On occasion, when they do, terrible things can happen. In this case, the fallout from decisions and actions taken or omitted, by everybody in the chain of command up to the president, is on the way to ruining Westhues's career and life. It is not that he is an innocent bystander in all this. On the contrary, he is a combatant-participant, often painted by others as an aggressor. In reality, however, it is only Westhues whose rights and prerogatives have been curtailed; and only Westhues who has been made to endure institutional censure. The main problem is that there appears to be nobody in a position of authority with enough character, wisdom, courage, or organizational intelligence to sort the situation out fairly. What follows is only a small part of Westhues's story.

In the fall of 1993, one of Westhues's Ph.D. students is facing a comprehensive methods exam that he has previously failed. There have been two years of heated controversy, especially between Westhues and the current chair of the department, Professor Ron Lambert, over allegations of irregularities and bias in the administration of the first exam. If the student fails this second exam, he will be finished in the department, even though he already has one doctorate in hand, and some respectable publications. On Thursday, November 11, 1993, Remembrance Day and, strangely enough, the same day that, far away in New Brunswick, Professor Matin Yaqzan meets his students for the last time before being suspended, the student is failed by a unanimous vote of the examining committee. His career is now, indeed, finished in the department. In the weeks to come, his funding is terminated. His request to review the audio-recording of the exam is denied. He files an appeal. Lambert informs him of an unidentified professor's (never-proven) allegation of plagiarism against him with regard to one of his books, but he is not allowed to see any evidence for this allegation, nor to know his accuser. He asks for inactive status in the department and is refused. He drops out of Waterloo.

When he learns that the student has been failed, Westhues explodes in grief and frustration. On November 11, and again on November 12, he is rude to the chair of the examining committee. The decibels, like the sentiments, are not particularly different from the amplitude of previous clashes in this matter between Westhues and various officials of the department and faculty. "I'm not saying you're evil, but the system is," he tells the chair of the examining committee. Westhues subsequently apologizes for his emotional outbursts but, even though he apologizes again and again, his apology is never accepted. He is simply not considered sufficiently contrite; mainly because he refuses to drop his claim that his student was mistreated, and that there ought to be a review of the whole examination procedure.

In any well-functioning community, Westhues's apology should have ended the matter. His act was minor, understandable, and excusable. At most, the chair might have talked to Westhues about the strain put on collegial citizenship when normal tasks like chairing examination committees are made preludes to controversy and sharp criticism. What made this particular altercation different was that biopolitics came into the picture. Westhues was not dealing, in this instance, with any of the colleagues with whom he had had conflict before. This time, he was dealing with Adie Nelson, young, untenured woman; feminist powerhouse; instructor of a course called "Victims and Society." All the men in the department, and particularly the chair, rushed to her defence. She rushed to the attack.

To continue the story. On Lambert's invitation, Nelson writes a ten-page report about the exam, and the conversations she had with Westhues before and after it (November 24). This is a revealing document. She relates her contempt for the student's failure to learn statistics, given the department's requirements. She also claims to have tried to set the student at ease at the beginning of the exam by calling him to account for his published views on feminism. In fact, she challenges him to show how there could exist any viable "nonsexist" alternative to feminist research. This introduces the *feminism theme* that permeates the whole Westhues case.

In discussing her 15-minute argument with Westhues, Nelson claims that Westhues questioned her professional credentials; led her to believe that she was regarded as marginal in the department; and chastised, belittled, and intimidated her. She suggests that she thought her job was in danger, although a phone call to Lambert reassured her that Westhues did not speak for the department.

Lambert circulates Nelson's memo to members of the department's promotion and tenure committee. Westhues is not provided with a copy, and only learns of its existence from Roman Dubinski, chair of the faculty association's academic freedom committee. He asks and fails to get it from Nelson and Lambert, and finally receives a copy through Lambert two weeks later, after an appeal to the Dean. On that same day, December 10, Lambert summons him to a meeting of the promotion and tenure committee to answer to complaints that he exerted unacceptable pressure on the examiners of his student. Lambert says the meeting will go ahead with or without Westhues. Dubinski writes to Lambert to express his "abhorrence of the process you contemplate," in violation of due process and natural justice (December 14, 1993). Westhues declines to go, unless advised of what university policies he might have contravened and what jurisdiction the committee has over such issues.

He has already had a telephone call with Nelson on November 12, when he had meant to apologize, but instead found himself in a shouting match. Now he wants to make the apology official, by way of his letter to Lambert (December 13, 1993): "Adie Nelson deserves an apology from me, and I am pleased to set it down in writing." In this letter, Westhues disputes the legitimacy of the planned proceedings, however, and notes that the chair might do better to facilitate a reconciliation. On December 13, Westhues also apologizes several times in a private letter to Nelson. He affirms the sincerity of the apology in the letter to Lambert, confesses his anger, asks her forgiveness, regrets his comments: "Adie, once again, I am truly sorry for the grief I've caused you." He also tries to explain the general motives and the history of experiences that led him to lose his temper in the first place.

As evidence of both confession and lack of repentance, Nelson circulates this letter widely in the university, to the sociology department, the Waterloo administration, and officers of the faculty association, along with her memos to the chair of November 24 and December 16. In this latter, which Westhues only sees through Dubinski, she dismisses Westhues's apology as "at best, a pious justification for his earlier offensive behaviour which, in his letter, he admits to." She regards his letter as neither apology nor resolution, but further insult, and lambasts it for three pages, for what she says is its bullying uncollegiality. She says that she "no longer would view any apology tendered by Professor Westhues as meaningful." She asks the chair to act as her intermediary in any necessary departmental contact she must have with Westhues. "I will receive no further communication, oral or written, from him."

As in the November 24 memo, she again sounds the feminist theme around her presumption of vulnerability. Westhues says in his letter to Lambert that he had not intended to intimidate Nelson, and anyway lacked the resources to do so since he held no administrative office. Nelson replies (to Lambert, no copy to Westhues): "First, I assume that Professor Westhues recognizes that the 'chilly climate' includes sentiments expressed casually in conversation and within informal spheres of influence. From my position as an untenured person, this possibility has to be of concern." She goes on: "How can a senior member of the university, a tenured full professor, former Chair of the department, and current member of the executive of the Faculty Association claim that he 'lacks resources' to intimidate a junior, non-tenured faculty member?" This case makes apparent to me one of the ways the "chilly climate" is maintained at the University of Waterloo. Professor Westhues's actions are not merely testimony to a "chilly climate" but to a "deep freeze."

In universities, all too often, this is a call to arms. Female faculty feel under tremendous pressure to fall into line, for fear of breaking ranks with the biological group of women who allegedly share a common fate. If they withhold consent to this kind of emotional blackmail, it is silently or privately. As a result, their actions and inactions confirm the biofeminist model of the world as one where women are ranged against men, rather than like-minded people of all sexual types and orientations, in conflict with other mixed groups clustered around other variables. One of the worst distortions in contemporary political relationships is this false coalition of women, which sometimes permits falsehood to claim the day, in the name of some greater end. The call to arms nowadays tends to be even more effective in the way it works on academic men. The old, reactionary, protective structures of chivalry have been transformed into new, reactionary, protective structures of chivalry on the part of male faculty "sensitive" to feminist claims. Nobody is so immoveable as the feminist male in defense of a feminist female. It's a perfect justificatory circle: sealed, comfortable, rewarding, and deluded.

It is not surprising, then, that when Lambert writes a second letter to Westhues, detailing his complaints against him (December 17), he accuses Westhues, among other things, of creating "... in the Department the 'chilly climate' that women academics sometimes deplore, and which any fair-minded academic must abhor and denounce." This is quite painful to Westhues, who thinks of himself as a life-long champion of sexual equality, who has often given lectures on the topic, reviewed feminist literature, and repeatedly criticized in departmental politics and wider university correspondence the "chilly climate" that other faculty, committees, chairs, and administrators were creating for feminist scholars. Biopolitics has no memory.

Lambert asserts, in this same letter, that Nelson "declined to attend the Department's Christmas party on the grounds that she was physically intimidated by your volatile and hateful behaviour." At this point, with the entire syndrome of the violence-against-women panic laid at the door of this *man* who has admitted being rude to a *woman*, Westhues's prospects do not look very good. Nor is there any way that Westhues seems to be able to work himself out of the trap. Lambert makes it clear that Westhues's behaviour—including his apology to Nelson—is not only unacceptable, but sanctionable. Protection for women is the objective, punishment is the practice, and Westhues's "power" is not about to protect him from the wrath of the officially weak and vulnerable, and their not-so-weak friends.

Without Westhues's knowledge, his exchanges with Lambert and Nelson become matters of discussion for most of the department, and indeed for officials beyond the department. His colleagues, too impatient to wait for the decision of the committee Lambert wishes to consult, get into the act, and demand that Westhues be punished. Despite warnings from faculty association president, Professor Jim Brox, that the actions of the department are "without due process" (December 22, 1993), Westhues's colleagues insist that his behaviour was so bad that he should be cast out of the graduate program.[2]

Westhues, still unaware of the extent of the consensus building against him, tells the dean, in a letter dated January 4: "You can be sure that I will not let myself be discredited in the Department to which I have given almost two decades of my life, without one hell of a fight." He will indeed make a heroic effort in the next few months to document his case, but the situation is rapidly slipping away from him. On January 4, he writes to the two doctoral students he is supervising: "You cannot afford to have as your supervisor a professor who is the object of this degree of hostility." On January 10, he seeks the dean's exemption from submitting to the annual performance review in the department, and asks for a direct decanal review instead. The dean rejects his request, with strong emphasis on Lambert's fairness and impartiality. Shortly after, Westhues is informed that Lambert and associates have failed him on his performance review, in spite of excellent teaching evaluations, research productivity, and service to the community.

On February 14, 1994, Westhues receives a third letter from Lambert. He has been convicted and sentenced. The complaints detailed in the earlier letters are repeated, with some variations, but the focus remains on Nelson's complaints about the "pressure" she was subjected to, and on the "demonstrably uncollegial" behaviour. He questioned her integrity, intimidated her, and interfered with her academic freedom. The penalties, says Lambert, all fall within the authority of the chair: an official reprimand, placed in Westhues's file, and copied to the dean of arts and dean of graduate studies, with a threat of more severe sanctions if there is further offence; removal from the graduate program (teaching, examining, and advising students) for five years, until 1998, when he may apply for resumption of duties; unsatisfactory performance review, to reflect his unsatisfactory conduct. This latter is confirmed in a letter from Lambert on March 14, 1994.

So, Westhues has been severely disciplined for rudeness during two private conversations with a colleague! Nelson has shown enough confidence to make the conversations public, distribute them in writing, lampoon his personal addresses to her, and stand on ceremony as a weak victim of a powerful attacker. Within a month, if not sooner, the department, including the chair, are set on a course whereby the "powerful" Westhues is ostracized. He stands alone, outside the magic circle of collegiality, officially reprimanded, without graduate students, and disbarred from access to graduate teaching for at least the next five years. For a research scholar, this is a dramatic set-back in his expectations and career. Indeed, he is also failed on his performance review, not for his performance in doing his job apart from this incident, but for his conduct toward Nelson.

The story has barely begun. Westhues's student has left the university. His own work and career have been damaged. Extremely harshly worded petitions and memos about him have been circulating and attacking his reputation (see note 2). And reports of the terrible harassment of which he must have been guilty in order to suffer such strong penalties have begun to reach other universities. Westhues is now trying to clear himself, and restore sanity and normality to his life. He gets into deeper and deeper difficulties, the more he struggles. The department, indeed, the university, seems unable to hear anything he says except as further proof of his apostasy, as further aggression against collegiality; or, more importantly, against a helpless young woman.

While his department carries on as usual, Westhues languishes in a cloudy land of grievances and efforts to find some redress. To date, this has been denied him. When Lucinda Vandervort's colleagues ganged up on her three years in a row, at the University of Saskatchewan, she could turn to the university at large, with some help from outside supporters, and have the department overruled and her tenure and promotion awarded. When Philippe Rushton, at the University of Western Ontario, was given an unsatisfactory performance rating on his research by his departmental colleagues, during the media attacks on his work, he was able to turn to a university-wide committee, which overruled his colleagues and lifted the penalties and sanctions against him. Waterloo has so far not been capable of providing a comparable review by some independent group of faculty.

When rumours of Westhues's punishment spread to other universities, his friends start to ask questions. On

March 14, Westhues sends a skilfully written, somewhat understated, five-page report of his story to a former student, Professor Gail Grant, now employed at Guelph University. He carefully conceals the identities of his student and his colleagues; in fact, these names remain confidential until Lambert supplies them, in the summer of 1994, to the University of Waterloo newspaper. Grant circulates the report to about 100 people who know Westhues. Many of them are shocked. Some 75 professors from outside Waterloo write to president James Downey to express their hope that something can be done to restore some sense of proportion to the situation. Most of the letters are in the nature of testimonials to Westhues, with little or no analysis of the proceedings at Waterloo. They barely mention Nelson, much less criticize her. Their intention is to help Westhues in some way. Unfortunately, their intercession will be used as evidence against him.

In late January, Westhues had filed a grievance, under Policy 63, on due process grounds. On February 18, after receipt of the February 14 letter of punishment from Lambert, Westhues revises the grievance to include references to the sanctions. He still hopes that he will be able to sort out the matter informally with the chair, and also with his colleagues. Attempts at reconciliation, combined with all sorts of procedural wrangling, drag the process out for months. The grievance itself is ultimately to be directed only against the actions of the chair in imposing such severe sanctions on him. But Westhues is not to get his fair hearing.

Westhues's grievance has nothing to do with Nelson. On March 3, however, Westhues writes to Nelson (care of Lambert) to alert her to the fact that her memos to the chair of the department form part of the relevant documentation in his grievance. This is simply a matter of courtesy on his part; a misguided courtesy, as it turns out. Nelson's response? She drags Westhues before the university's ethics committee under Policy 33, which is designed to handle sexual harassment complaints, as well as other allegations of ethical misconduct.

The university, astonishingly, permits Nelson to hijack Westhues's grievance; and, in fact, during April and May, this committee rapidly gets on with hearing and deciding Nelson's complaint, despite Westhues's vigorous objections to the overlapping jurisdictions and issues of the grievance procedure and the ethics procedure.[3] The ethics committee simply decides that its report will be provided in due course to the grievance panel. Without ever getting close to having his own complaints heard, Westhues is compelled to answer to Nelson's. Even more remarkably, the ethics committee permits Nelson to base much of her complaint against Westhues on quotations from a confidential grievance document he has filed under a different policy, to a different panel, and which has not yet been heard!

Nelson files a complaint, on March 25, 1994, that Westhues has attacked her professional integrity. Less than half of her six-page complaint is based on her own memos and history review; 13 of her 24 paragraphs are devoted to rebuttals and criticisms of Westhues's grievance document. She cites from Westhues's complaints in 14 different places in her text, mostly taking issue with his emphases. For example, Westhues protests against being described by his chair and colleagues with words like "harassment, intimidation, particularly vicious verbal attacks." He rejects the slander, "while admitting and apologizing for the intemperance of my own behaviour" (Westhues, Statement of Grievance, Part One 4). Writes Nelson: "As the subject of Professor Westhues's attacks, I reject the use of the term 'intemperance' as a euphemism which sheathes his intolerable behaviour in soft poetry."

She goes on to describe his conduct as "intimidating, degrading, and insulting" (Nelson, Complaint 1). Further on, she adds other words to describe what he had allegedly done (denigration, deprecation, denunciation), as well as many adjectives to characterize his expressions (hurtful, repugnant, cowering, fallacious, reprehensible, lugubrious, unfounded, whifty, unprofessional, threatening). Her un-equivocating self-assurance, belying her self-presentation as a vulnerable victim, is conveyed in a further string of such amplifying adverbs as *terribly, entirely, absolutely.*

Nelson's special fury, however, is reserved for West-hues's observation that "she seemed to me to be overre-acting" (Westhues, Statement of Grievances, Part Two 18). She attacks this more than once, providing for it a feminist context which is her special signature: she reads into Westhues's one-word lament about overreaction the im-plication that she is "an 'overreacting' *female*" (italics added): "Apparently we have to remind Professor Wes-thues that feminism is the radical notion that women are people too—not 'overreacting' hysterics" (Complaint 4).

Nelson asks the ethics committee to "help make this situation stop." Westhues might agree. But how? "I request that sanctions against Professor Westhues be called for" (6). Here, we see the untenured and *vulnerable* Professor Nelson carrying the ball for the whole department. The remedies she asks for are that the original sanctions against Westhues should be ordered to stand, and that the matter be "forevermore laid to rest." She wants Westhues's grievance against his mistreatment and punishment *to be suppressed, without ever being heard by the grievance panel.* She also wants his complaints about her examining role to be *forbidden,* and any future criticisms of her to be pre-empted in advance. A very extensive program of demands indeed, especially coming from a "junior" person against the al-legedly powerful and intimidating "senior" Westhues.

The ethics hearing committee (Professors Sally Gunz and Don Brodie, and Ms. Patti Haygarth—hereafter EHC) decides its jurisdiction does not extend to the methods examination failed by Westhues's student, nor to a review of interactions between Westhues and his chair and col-leagues. In other words, they will not address Westhues's actual complaints. They do decide, however, to expand the scope of the inquiry in one respect. At the first meeting, April 15, they allow Nelson to extend her complaint to cover Westhues's letter to Gail Grant, which has by then been circulated to others. In their report, the EHC will indict Westhues for writing this letter, which potentially exposes Nelson to colleagues all around the country. In truth, there is no evidence Nelson could be identified from Westhues's letter. Furthermore, as Westhues tries to point out, the letters that poured in to the president of the University of Waterloo from his supporters do not cast aspersions on Nelson. Damage to her had *not* been his intention, or his achievement. In fact, these letters have not yet had any pro-Westhues effect, much less any anti-Nelson effect, on the proceedings to date.

The whole EHC approach to Nelson's complaint turns out to be based on a rather simple formula that overrides every other consideration: "The comments must be placed in the context of ones made by a senior colleague to a junior, untenured one" (4). In other words, Westhues is powerful, and he intimidates a younger, and more vulnerable colleague; more particularly, a woman. With this *ritual formalization* as their guiding principle, Westhues has no chance of a fair hearing.

The EHC finds against Westhues in every respect. The committee members convict Westhues of breach of ethics for his two conversations with Nelson around the exam, and for the March 15 "Dear Gail" letter, all of which "fall outside the bounds of acceptable academic discourse" (8). They say he attacked her competence and her character. They say he interfered with her ability to discharge her academic duties, although they never attempt to show that there was any actual effect on her performance. They say the circular letter may "damage her ability to perform her academic duties at the University of Waterloo or elsewhere" and extends "misinformation" beyond Waterloo. All this, despite evidence that the whole episode has done nothing but strengthen Nelson at Waterloo, while weakening Westhues.

One of the most extraordinary features of the EHC report is its preoccupation with the subject of Westhues's apology. The committee members convict him for bad behaviour, primarily by quoting from his own letters of apology. Even he admits it, they say. Then they turn around and indict him for not writing good enough apologies! "Has an adequate apology been tendered? The Committee believes not" (4). In its recommendation that "strong measures be taken," the committee recommends that Westhues "be required to write an apology" (8). What was wrong with Westhues's apologies up to this point? They say his first apology, in the December 13 letter, was coupled with an explanation of why he questioned the examiners' decision. Therefore, it was "not unequivocal"(5). Why not? Westhues was unequivocally sorry that he had lost his temper and offended his colleague and (he thought) sometime friend. He reserved his criticism of the exam. Why shouldn't he? It is his own professional opinion. It may even be his duty as a supervisor whose student's career has been unceremoniously ended. Maybe if the department had been more collegial, and disclosed to him directly the tapes and other records concerning the exam, he might have been satisfied to the point of dropping his criticism; he might have been able to withdraw from the field. As it was, the whole institution has consistently refused to address his substantive concerns; on what basis could he be expected to change his beliefs?

To go back to the apology: the committee fails to consider the apology in Westhues's other December 13 letter, to Lambert, which was also copied to eight other people: "I am guilty of misjudgment, insensitivity, and rude behaviour to a colleague ... Adie Nelson deserves an apology from me, and I am pleased to set it down in writing" (4). They quote this passage *as a prelude to convicting him of intimidation.* Again, even though his apology seems to be unmistakable, apparently it does not qualify because he has not surrendered on all the issues in dispute. Therefore: "No clear apology had been provided"

(5). Even when Westhues offers to let Nelson and Lambert draft an apology, he is faulted for making the "inappropriate" offer, since he has not done "the one thing that might resolve the dispute with the Complainant, namely apologize."

It is clear that Nelson, Lambert, and other colleagues want from Westhues a "more complete, abject, and unqualified apology" than he is prepared to make (Statement of Grievances, Part One 3); not an apology for incivility, but regret for having questioned the decision of Nelson's examination committee. The EHC seems to agree with them, which is especially peculiar in light of Nelson's indication on December 16 that she will refuse any further apologies from him.

In any case, the EHC requires, not only an apology from Westhues, but also that this apology be distributed to the recipients of the March 15 "Dear Gail" letter, to the University of Waterloo *Gazette*, and to the Internet. But first it has to be right. "Prior to its distribution/circulation, the response would be vetted by this Committee" (Report 8). The Committee's report is accepted by provost and vice-president Jim Kalbfleisch on May 18. Westhues clarifies with the provost that he will be deemed to have complied with the decision if he signs the appropriate apology, regardless of whether Nelson accepts it.

Accordingly, on May 24, Westhues submits his written apology, noting that he has been directed to prepare it. The EHC, finding Westhues's apology unacceptable, insists he rewrite it by May 27. Westhues makes some slight modifications, by inserting a reference to the failed exam at the beginning of the chain of events, and asserting the right to disagree. The apology is in final form (May 31). On June 1, the provost acknowledges that Westhues will have complied with the EHC recommendations once the apology has been distributed, by signed copy to Nelson, and copy to all recipients of the Gail Grant mailings. He accepts Westhues's undertaking to behave toward Nelson according to university policy and standard norms of civility and collegiality.

Following the recommendation of the EHC, he also directs the publication of the apology in the *Gazette*, and on the Internet. This is the first time in Waterloo history that a professor has been required to make a public apology in the newspaper. The provost goes further. He demands a listing of the names of all the Westhues-Grant friends who received the March 15 circular letter. He never gets this list. Some of the individuals object to the demand to turn over the mailing list as McCarthyism. Lambert, by contrast, complains vigorously to the grievance committee as late as August 10 that Westhues "has steadfastly refused to honour these penalties, at no apparent peril to himself." Kalbfleisch eventually accepts that he will not get the names, and releases Westhues from the requirement to provide them (September 26, 1994).

That should have been it, then. On June 3, however, the day after Westhues sends out his public apology to his friends, he hears from the provost that he need not bother. Nelson will not accept it; she has launched an appeal to the president. In addition, Kalbfleisch himself takes exception to Westhues's communication with his friends. In sending out the one-page public apology to Gail Grant's list, Westhues attached a cover letter, thanking his colleagues and friends for their life-support during "the most difficult months of my quarter-century of university teaching." The letter simply updates people on events since the March 15 letter. He asks if people wish their names turned over to the provost. He also reiterates that, apart from the matters covered in the apology, he is not repentant, and has done nothing sufficient to warrant disbarment from graduate teaching.

Provost Kalbfleisch's response is quite extraordinary. He *denounces* Professor Westhues in an "Open Letter to the University of Waterloo Community," dated June 6, and published in the *Gazette*, June 8 ("Written apology"). He contends that Westhues's cover letter to his friends is "not an acceptable response to the Report of the Ethics Hearing Committee." He describes it as a "onesided public statement" that causes damage which is only reparable, if at all, by publishing the full text of the confidential EHC Report which had condemned Westhues. Kalbfleisch now demands that the ethics report be sent to everyone who got the cover letter, or else he will send it to all sociology departments in Canada. Apart from the bizarre escalation in institutional harassment that is involved in this response, it is remarkable that Kalbfleisch consulted with Gunz and Nelson before impugning Westhues's integrity in public, but never gave Westhues himself an opportunity to respond to his allegations. The chair of the faculty association's academic freedom committee also points out in a letter to the *Gazette* that the public condemnation "may make it impossible for Professor Westhues to get a fair hearing of his case" before the grievance committee (Dubinski, "Words").

Westhues has now had the dean refuse to mediate his dispute in April, preferring to let the sanctions stand, which debar him from graduate teaching, downgrade his performance review, and rob him of salary. He has gone through a gruelling ethics hearing, under duress and over his protestations, and has complied with undertakings and public apologies. He has been publicly defamed by the vice-president and provost. He has been humiliated and damaged in the media. And now the institution threatens to destroy him in the eyes of the entire Canadian profession of sociology. He has been punished for ethical misconduct, with maximum publicity, and has had his work curtailed. All this in response to two private conversations with a colleague, and two letters to friends. What is going on at Waterloo? How could one imagine more chilling disincentives to the exercise of robust academic freedoms and collegial commitments than the example that has been made of this senior professor, former chair of the department, pillar of the graduate program?

The story continues. Once the EHC report is issued, Dr. Greg Bennett, chair of the grievance committee, demands a formal statement of Westhues's grievance within 5 days (May 19). Westhues is not allowed to wait until he can appeal the EHC decision to the president, so he complies by May 24. He laments the collective attack on him, as well as the EHC defamation now forced into his grievance hearing. He asks the committee to set aside the penalties imposed on him. He does not ask for apologies from or penalties for his chair or his colleagues. He does, however, ask for a presidential criticism of due process violations against him; for direct performance evaluation by the dean or his advisors, rather than Lambert, over the next three years; for release from teaching duties in the fall of 1994, to make up for his lost research leave which was entirely consumed by the conflict; and for an outside review of the department.

There is a great deal of wrangling over procedural and jurisdictional issues which drags out the process for months, in ways too detailed to describe here. One of the more sinister delays is over the question of *confidentiality*. Lambert, who has already held up the grievance hearing committee (Greg Bennett, Lee Dickey, Bruce Mitchell—hereafter GHC) with a number of demands and objections, at one point refuses to participate in the proceedings unless Westhues and Dubinski make an "unequivocal commitment" to confidentiality. He says he cannot demonstrate the fairness of the sanctions he imposed without confidential documents and testimony (July 11). He provides legal advice from Clarke Melville of Haney, Haney, and Kendall, to the effect that Westhues and Dubinski must agree to confidentiality and, should they refuse the direction of the GHC, the grievance should be dismissed for contempt and the sanctions stand. West-hues agrees to *in camera* proceedings, but not to be gagged once it's all over. Nor will he agree to restricting his private consultation during the process to Dubinski and one lawyer. This is, in Dubinski's view, an issue of Westhues's civil rights.

It is probably safe to assume that, had the grievance ever got under way, the episode with Nelson could have been the focus, once again, of the proceedings. In a kafkaesque series of procedural complications, however, the GHC's process is derailed over and over again. Its first meeting is on June 20, 1994; by July 20, the GHC *disbands*. It reconvenes, at the request of the president, on August 3rd, over objections from Lambert. Nothing happens. Westhues, on August 17, writes to the GHC, with copies to Downey, Brox, and Dubinski: "I simply do not understand what is going on, or why the committee has become so reluctant to proceed." He asks the committee to decide if the case will be heard.

On September 6, the GHC quits for the second time. They have not been able "to establish rules for the resumption of hearings." They blame Westhues for failing to get his grievance into the right format for their purposes. Their frustration turns on their ultra-legalistic interpretation of a few lines in Section 2 of the policy, under "Objectives," which Westhues reads as a section of general aspirations that he has well satisfied. Bennett never meets with Westhues to clear up their misunderstanding. He prefers to adjourn the committee and close the investigation of the grievances filed by Westhues against Lambert. Nearly a year after the incidents, nearly eight months after the grievance was filed, and nearly four months after the formal stage began, it's all over for Westhues. From Westhues's point of view, the breakdown of order in the sociology department has been followed by the breakdown of the grievance proceeding. On September 16, he writes to president Downey: "This memo is to ask what action you, as president of the university, propose for the resolution of this matter?"

As of this writing, that is where things stand. The president and Westhues are both waiting for the report of the grievance committee, which is being held back until Lambert's return from sabbatical absence in mid-November, 1994. Nothing has been worked out, but there has been a lot of damage. Westhues is worried about his future. In his moments of anxiety, he is 90% sure that his career as a graduate professor, supervising graduate theses, is over. Unless publicity or the academic freedom committee of the CAUT can help him, he fears his employment may be in danger.

Remarkably, wherever Westhues turned for redress, Nelson was there. Before she arrived in the department, there was a long history of antagonisms in an intense little unit of a handful of people: under conditions of academic freedom and tenure, everyone felt they could push pretty hard, from time to time, since it was just words. There would usually be somebody with sufficient authority or sense to say, cut it out. They got at each other, and they put up with each other, as people do in marriages and university departments.

Ten years ago, it would never have gone like this. Nelson's presence changed all that, and Lambert's response to her. She drew him to her, in some way that was as strong as what pushed him away from Westhues. The two elements combined. At the centre of it all, everybody came to treat this whole thing as a case of sexual harassment, but without calling it that. In the midst of so much history, how could she have been allowed to think it was all about her? How could so many others outside the department join in this transparent delusion? Biopolitics. Conditions of moral panic.

Professor Warren Magnusson, University of Victoria

Universities are at the cutting edge of biofeminism rising; and the Political Science Department (hereafter DPS) at the University of Victoria is the ravaged battle frontier of a prolonged confrontation between warrior biofeminism and its academic targets. Two stories converge in one here: a classic "chilly climate" take-over bid, and a fraudulent harassment proceeding. Warren Magnusson is caught in both.

A contemporary narrative, this case provides a rare insight into the inner workings of universities, under the pressure of biopolitical panic. It is Victoria today, but it could be any other university tomorrow, and any other institution at any time. Like Professor Westhues at Waterloo, Professor Collin at Manitoba, or Professor Vandervort at Saskatchewan, Magnusson is suddenly rendered vulnerable by the new issues of moral panic. Like professors Klatt and Ratcliffe at Western, he is charged by a student, and dragged through lengthy procedures in a case that should never have been allowed to go forward, and that is eventually dismissed. Like Professor Yaqzan at New Brunswick, he is challenged for the expression of ideas which run so deeply counter to biofeminist orthodoxy that they are read and treated as nothing but provocation. And, finally, like Professor Whitaker at York, his integrity in faculty administration is improperly called into question by an assault on his biopolitical credentials. Unlike all of these, however, Magnusson is also caught in a frontal attack on his department and on many of his colleagues.

What is at the centre of both the collective skirmishes and the private persecution is, quite openly and explicitly, a punitive and insatiable biofeminist fundamentalism. By fundamentalism, I mean the effort to place biofeminists and biofeminist theories at the absolute centre of evaluation and meaning, fully protected from criticism, and with its program accorded the force of self-evidence.

Magnusson is a senior professor in the DPS who, like Westhues, never expected to see himself at the receiving end of feminist hostility. He is a former Rhodes Scholar, with a doctoral degree from Oxford. He has been at Victoria for fifteen years, and has directed the Interdisciplinary MA Program in Contemporary Social and Political Thought for the past five years, since 1989. He has co-edited three books on Canadian politics, and published numerous articles in learned journals and collections. He has played a national role in his profession. He is highly regarded by friends and colleagues across the country. Such sterling credentials, and the flawless reputation accumulated over nearly two decades of work, count for nothing, however, once the biopolitical mud begins to fly.

It belongs to the historical irony of the situation that Magnusson has been in the forefront of support for social movements and, in particular, for the advance of equity considerations in the employment and support of a new generation of activist women. He chaired the gender equity committee of the DPS and the ad hoc committee on child care in the university. He served on the status of women committee of the Faculty Association, and he has been supervising a variety of feminist graduate theses. He has a left-feminist reputation in the scholarly community. Today, this "progressive" image makes him a natural target of biofeminist fury because, though a "fellow-traveller" up to a point, he draws the line somewhere short of the full program of preferential double standards in the all-power-to-feminists scenario. It is this resistance that got Magnusson into trouble with his adversaries, Professor Brodribb, and her student, the biofeminist student accuser (BFSA). But what is perhaps most telling about his case is that, once under attack, he has been virtually incapable of attracting the degree of liberal support that would have been his due by reputation, achievement, and integrity; and more especially by his current course of unimpeachably decent and courageous action on behalf of liberal and progressive principles.

Somer Brodribb joined the DPS in 1991-92, hired on merit, of course, but also in a deliberate and good-faith effort by a previously male-dominated department to improve its gender balance. The university got more than it bargained for. Brodribb, extremely attractive to a number of people, is a genuine biofeminist warrior, whose language is full of incitement to violence. In her text, *Nothing Mat(t)ers*, for example, Brodribb attacks postmodern philosophy in the name of feminism, and builds a bridge from the weapon of criticism to the criticism of weapons. She holds up as a positive example the "gesture" of Valerie Solanas, who wrote the SCUM (Society for Cutting Up Men) Manifesto, and who shot and nearly killed "pop-misogynist Andy Warhol" (ix).

In an instinctive response to an office conversation about the high suicide rate among teenaged boys, Brodribb apparently once said, "I wish they'd all kill themselves" ("UVic convulsed"; Magnusson, "Feminism" 10). Writing in a feminist symposium on academic freedom, she is the only negative critic of the lead article by Drakich, Taylor, and Bankier of the CAUT's Status of Women group. Their line is already over the edge: they defend the Supreme Court's Butler decision as well as Catharine MacKinnon's tirades against freedom of expression. It is an index of Brodribb's fundamentalist frame of thought that she describes this article as *too* soft and pluralistic. She says, the article is defensive, fearful, and intimidated; it is a "retreat into conservatism" ("Apolitical Correctness").

On May 11, 1992, on the recommendation of a committee chaired by Magnusson, the DPS struck a "Committee to Make the Department More Supportive to Women." Brodribb, in her second year in the DPS, was named to chair this committee. Under her direction, it came to be known as the Chilly Climate Committee (CCC). A year later, on March 23, 1993, the Brodribb committee submitted a six-page report to the department, which reads like a short version of the final report of the Canadian panel on violence against women (see chapter VI). The CCC report laments the condition of women in the department, who are, they say, subjected to: harassment and hostility; "sexist and racist treatment" in class; "derogatory comments about 'the feminists' and 'feminism'"; and "sexual advances at social gatherings." It suggests, though without any specifics, a pattern of corrupt and violent behaviour ("Report of the Climate Committee to the Department of Political Science").

As Magnusson later pointed out, 12 of the 20 complaints listed were specifically related to the treatment of feminism. "The other charges are thrown in," he suggests, "in order to create the sense that negative attitudes towards feminism are symptomatic of a pattern of behaviour that involves men in sexual harassment and discrimination against women. The hope is that people will slide down the continuum, get shocked at the idea of professors making sexual advances to students, and double back to express their outrage that these professors have not been more sympathetic to feminism" ("Feminism" 10).

At a meeting on March 29, the department began to consider the 34 recommendations in the report, but eventually adjourned to April 15. The recommendations, requiring the commitment of all the members of DPS to anti-sexism, anti-racism, and feminist pedagogy, as enforced by "the chillies," were never to be legitimized by the department. The report might have had a more receptive hearing if it had not been set in a discourse of hostility and generalised accusation, and if it had been more cautious about setting forth dubious requirements, such as: "The department should regularly gather and compile data by race and sex," on everything from salaries to workloads and committee assignments.

The whole proceeding was surrounded by heightened excitement. Already in January, the recently formed Women's Caucus of the Political Science Course Union had been considering boycotting classes taught by male faculty. In February, these women were demanding that the department hire only women until it has a 50-50 balance. Twenty female students apparently wrote angry, anonymous letters to the department early in February, attacking one particular department meeting. These letters were never sent, but the CCC included them in an appendix to the CCC report. The students had also planned to occupy the chair's and the dean's offices, in connection with a false alarm about a problem with Brodribb's promotion.

Brodribb followed up the release of her "general" report with direct "personal" actions. In a reminder of the improper targeting of Professor Whitaker at York University with civic penalties for the expression of ideas that departed from biofeminist true beliefs, Brodribb demanded that the chair remove Magnusson from the faculty's research grants committee for "conflict of interest." She demanded also that the Faculty Association remove him from the Status of Women Committee. She was unsuccessful in these moves. She declared in conversation that she was "at war" with the department, and in particular with Magnusson ("Feminism" 6). In early April, the CCC circulated the Chilly Climate Report across the country, making the internal controversy public before the department could proceed to consider the report in detail.

The eight tenured male faculty, including the department chair, prepared a public response on April 8, to register their concern about the unjustifiably unconstructive tone, contents, methods, implications and distribution of the climate report. They drew attention to the already existing gender equity policy in the department and in the university, as well as all the existing procedures to deal with harassment complaints. They recalled the department's recent good-faith efforts: 3 of 6 regular appointments since 1988 had been women, as had been 10 of the last 13 candidates interviewed. In one competition, only women were allowed to apply, and all three women hired have been feminists. The proportion of women on staff is near the Canadian average (25%), and near the proportion of women among graduating doctoral students. There is a policy of maintaining the rate of female hiring at 50% or more. Several feminist courses have been added to the curriculum ("Gender Equity in the Department of Political Science").

They also sent a calm but forceful private letter to Brodribb on April 8: she should retract the non-specific accusations of sexist and racist behaviour and serious sexual misconduct; or supply supporting evidence to some impartial authority; or else face "further steps to protect our reputation." Much was subsequently made of this last comment, as an unforgivable legal threat, even though Professor Jeremy Wilson, the chair, Magnusson, and the others made it clear, as early as April 14, that they were not considering legal action. For Brodribb and her supporters, this letter was to become the very proof of the chilly climate they were trying to reform: an example of hostility from the men. This is an intriguing and precise fulcrum of biopolitical perception. Actually, it was just a case of men saying: "We're here too, real people, with feelings, reputations, and rights, with our own story: don't malign us; don't damage us." In the biofeminist scenario, their only role would have been to figure as perpetrators, to be reformed. Instead of erasing themselves, or at least withdrawing into the background, they insisted on some measure of equality and reciprocity. At the least, they wanted an inquiry; and they were ready to submit to any university procedure that could effectively test and, as warranted, counteract the widely circulated allegations. After all, these, however generally put, could not help but implicate the small group of eight men who made up the target of the CCC report.

All this shipwrecked because the other two female members of the department wrote (April 13) that they were "shocked and deeply troubled" by the "hostile and confrontational nature" of the letter to Brodribb, and lined up with Brodribb. They withdrew from collegial departmental administration. The conflict thus acquired the worst possible public image: men against women. And the situation just got bigger and bigger. Just as the starting point for moral outrage in the Westhues case was sparked by his expression of resistance to the "untenured woman," no matter what actions on her part had provoked it, at Victoria as well, the warranted firmness of the response by the tenured men to the emblematic untenured woman (Brodribb) forever overshadowed any recognition that the Climate Report and the surrounding agitation were themselves real provocations.

Over the next year, the university was progressively more damaged by the clashes promoted by an aroused minority of faculty and students. By April 19, the *Globe* carried a front page story from Brodribb's point of view (Wilson, "Sexual-politics"), for which the paper apologized, but only much later ("Correction"). The secretaries, a female part-time teacher, and a host of female students supported the male faculty and the department, on the argument that the Climate Committee had not consulted widely, and that it had misrepresented the experience of women in the department. Other feminists closed ranks behind Brodribb. Faculty from other universities wrote to offer their comments. In time, the CCC started to receive demonstrations of moral and financial support from feminist students and faculty around the country, as well as from academic societies, like the Canadian Sociology and Anthropology Association and the Canadian Women's Studies Association, feminist journalists, community organizations, the University's Steelworkers Local 9288, the National Action Committee on the Status of Women, and a variety of politicians. A Chilly Climate Committee Support Group was formed. By September 1993, Professor Dorothy Smith, one of Canada's leading feminist luminaries, was circulating an alarmist three-page call for support and donations to the Chilly Climate Committee Support and Legal Defence Fund. The title of her piece was "Backlash at the University of Victoria: Women Need Your Support."

In response, the eight tenured men in the DPS also looked for support from the wider university community, though on a much more modest scale, and without a fraction of the organizational capability of the pervasive network of women's caucuses. The most comprehensive analysis of their situation was a 12-page piece called "Feminism, McCarthyism and Sexist Fundamentalism" (May 13, 1993) by Warren Magnusson, which circulated in the university, and to colleagues outside, many of whom would have seen the *Globe* story, or heard about it on the CBC. The difficulty that the maligned men encountered in getting support is exemplified by the high-handed manner in which Magnusson's own colleagues on the editorial board of the journal *Studies in Political Economy* responded to his document. Eight of his fellow editors (Caroline Andrew, Himani Bannerji, Gillian Creese, Roberta Hamilton, Jeanne Laux, Barbara Neis, James Sacouman, Daiva Stasiulis) wrote a letter to Brodribb: "We are writing to let you know that we reject the misogynist values underpinning this document. We also wish to affirm our support for all efforts to deal with the chilly climate in universities" (June 4, 1993). Magnusson resigned from the board.

Contrary to the way it has been described in official report after official report, Magnusson's account of biofeminism in action ("Feminism ...") is a narrative about a significant, collective disorder in our time. It belongs in the annals of the best in political sociology. Its unrepentant self-respect is refreshing amidst the chorus of *mea culpas* that dominate the academy, above all in the social sciences. In his polemical discussion of events, Magnusson tries to dispel the sensational "scent of sexual misconduct and cover-up" that the media seized on, as well as the idea that a radical feminist professor was being persecuted because of her beliefs. He argues that the sex-crime charges Brodribb makes are false, and that the anti-feminist remarks in the department, such as they are, are no different in status from critical remarks about neo-conservatism, liberalism, Marxism, religious fundamentalism, or Quebec nationalism. They are not unfriendly to women, but only to a particular ideological trend. Indeed, it would be patronizing to assume that women, or feminist women, are more vulnerable than anybody else to the put-downs of academic life.

What is even more important, and unforgivable to his adversaries, is that he turns the tables, in an acute critique

294

of the biofeminists. Writing as a political theorist deeply committed to equality, human rights, and the welfare of women, Magnusson argues that the Brodribb faction represents a kind of fundamentalist sexism, "parading under a feminist banner" and attacking the left in the name of a politics of identity. The point he urges is that feminism, like any other movement, is capable of developing a damaging fundamentalist variant, which is dangerous and undeserving of the support properly owing to the main, progressive tendencies. "It is a story that feminists especially would prefer not to believe. However, it is one we should attend to, because it carries with it so many of the cautions we need for politics in the 1990s" (1).

These themes will come back again and again in the Victoria dispute, inasmuch as the place and treatment of feminism are accepted by virtually everybody as the defining framework for the conflicts. At least three studies commissioned by the Victoria administration (Callahan-Pirie, Lessard, and Bilson-Berger) have a direct bearing on the messy dispute in political studies, as do activities of the British Columbia Ombudsman's Office and the British Columbia Council of Human Rights. As of this writing, in October 1994, a year and a half after they erupted at Victoria, these matters are still under continuing active review. The mind boggles at the amount of energy expended, the amount of anxiety generated, and the amount of paper filled with argument, partial insight, and misinformation.

All the meddling, one has to observe, has been loaded from the start. All of it accepts the environmental assumptions (see chapter X) promoted by the Chilly Climate Committee as primary building blocks: that the "climate" worth addressing in universities, as a matter of first priority, is a "chill" affecting feminists. Each successive intervention has been designed to make these assumptions more forceful and effective, and to perfect their operational application. Magnusson's argument, that the CCC report did not point out any derogatory remarks about *women* in the DPS, whatever may have been the conflicts in which

295

feminists felt themselves engaged, is very significant. Nevertheless, this distinction was nearly totally lost in the ongoing frenzy of discussion, so contrary are its implications to the biopolitical shifting of ground from the well-being of women to the well-being of feminists, and, ultimately, from "sexism" to biofeminist fundamentalism and a regime of orthodoxy.

The first study that the administration called into being (April 14, 1993) was an internal review that satisfied nobody. Professor Marilyn Callahan, of the School of Social Work and Advisor to the vice-president Academic on Faculty Women's Issues, and Professor Andrew Pirie, of the Faculty of Law and the director of Victoria's Institute for Dispute Resolution, reported on May 11. They annoyed the male faculty by offering a solution to the problems that depended on their giving up demands they had made in their April 8 letter, and acceding to external supervision of the department. Incredibly, Brodribb and her supporters seem to have rejected this gift for not going far enough. Within two weeks of the report, vice-president Sam Scully had to acknowledge that it had "done little to remedy the present impasse" (May 26, Scully to the department).

Of particular interest is the explanation that Callahan and Pirie give for their recommendation (#3-5) that it is best to avoid a formal inquiry into the allegations of sexual harassment, and instead substitute a series of individual consultations with experts in harassment and sexual harassment. "Given the present atmosphere," they say, "it would be very difficult for anyone to come forward with harassment or sexual harassment complaints yet *the air would not be cleared if no one pressed charges at this time*" (italics added; "Findings" 7-8).

What is the role of a passage like that? Is it a speculation, a solicitation, a provocation? What resonances does it evoke in the overheated atmosphere of the weeks of intense controversy following the release of the report? What we know is that the Callahan-Pirie "Findings" were released May 11. Magnusson circulated his "Feminism" piece on May 13. Exactly three weeks later, on June 3, 1993, the biofeminist student accuser (BFSA), submitted a "Formal Charge of Harassment and Sexual Harassment Against Dr. Warren Magnusson." The narrative now forks over to this new trial for Magnusson, though it will rejoin the main branch of controversy before long.

In the spring of 1993 when the climate controversy breaks, the BFSA is a fourth-year student writing her honours paper on radical feminism. She is a first-class student, like Deborah Shewaga at Manitoba who accused Collin, or "B," who confronted Vandervort at Saskatchewan (see chapter VIII). She is headed for graduate studies in the interdisciplinary MA program in contemporary social and political thought headed by Magnusson. She wants to work on feminism, and even her application is phrased in terms of climate issues. A week after her application, she writes Magnusson, the head of her prospective graduate program, a bizarre letter (May 20). She refers to his "Feminism" document and describes it as offensive and disparaging to her, patronizing to feminist students, and vitriolic toward feminist theory. She demands a public retraction and apology. "All previous recipients of your paper must be informed in writing of your retraction and apology to me." She demands, further, that he step aside from his position as director and have someone else review her application. She "requires" his compliance by 5 p.m. one week later, or else she "will be forced to pursue sanctions, institutional and otherwise, against you."

It is worth reflecting on the evidence of this letter. Like the rest of the proceedings, and much like Nelson's behaviour in the Westhues case above, it testifies to a characteristic duality and duplicity. On one side, there is the *claim* of vulnerability, particularly with reference to relationships of formal power (e.g. student/professor, junior/senior, untenured/tenured). On the other side, in the actual *enactment*, the action manifests an assumption of invulnerability. For all their talk of marginality, biofeminists know full well that they are in the driver's seat in universities, in the social sciences in particular, as well as in relation to the calculus of administrative decision making. Wherever biofeminism engages in hostilities, or in rule and policy formulation, it never occurs to its proponents that their hostility could find a hostile response, or that any of the rules could be applied against them. And yet, such response would be fair play. The desperate surprise and wounded lashing out that greet the rare instance of a Magnusson who actually stands up for himself are expressions of sheer panic. In this case, the aggressive BFSA quite obviously does not think she is in danger. She is just playing her politics through. She is on the attack.

The BFSA sent copies of the letter to the chair of the DPS, and also the vice-president. In addition, she sent copies to the director of equity issues, and to Brodribb, as chair of the Chilly Climate Committee. When Magnusson failed to comply, she then made good her threat and filed a formal harassment charge with Sheila Devine, director of the Office of Equity, with whom she had already met on May 20, the day of her initial letter to Magnusson, to discuss possible sanctions against him by the university. This is a portrait of the modern Canadian university, and it will get uglier if left to this dynamic. This young woman's complaint is a document that belongs in a museum of the 1990s: it is full of puffed up "anger and righteous indignation," which she "unflinchingly" embraces as her creed. She is a trainee warrior, imaginatively absorbed in the lives of her role models, especially her honours supervisor, Dr. Brodribb.

Her personal complaint is indistinguishable from the larger climate wars around her. Indeed, her use of the discipline system against Magnusson is a good demonstration that the male faculty were right to be concerned about the personal implications of the general accusations that filled the CCC report. The BFSA imagines that, having already "threatened" Brodribb, Magnusson and his colleagues "might use my oral defense as one battle-ground for the hostile and intimidating spectre of mi-sogynous backlash" (BFSA, "Formal Charge" 2). Magnusson, like other male faculty members who had no obligation to be in attendance, did not in fact show up to her oral thesis defence on April 22, 1993. Surpris-ingly, she attacks him for that too. She insists that her aim is to disrupt "the dominant discourse," and she claims the right "to articulate women's voices and expe-riences to other women without interference," which would imply she did not want men there to "interfere." But she also complains bitterly of "a politically motivated patriarchal boycott of my defense." Damned if you do, and damned if you don't.

Apart from his voluntary non-attendance, she faults Mag-nusson for a paragraph in his "Feminism" account, in which he analyzes the dynamics of the polarized moral universe of biofeminism, with reference to the "climate" in which the graduating students' oral presentations took place in April, three weeks before his paper was issued. A mere two sen-tences are devoted to her, as one of a number of presenters. In spite of the fact that she is neither named nor identified, she charges that Magnusson's comments "are irreparably damaging to my academic reputation and personal integ-rity." He has hurt her academic future: "It will be very difficult for me to gain admittance to graduate school and have unbiased access to funding, grants, research positions, scholarships, etc." (5). These are of course merely idle words, selected to raise alarm and to evoke protection. They are also more than a little narcissistic. She pulls a couple of sentences out of a lengthy analysis, whose proper context is a conflict among her elders, being played out way over her head—except to the extent that her role models have turned their students into a kind of infantry in their own fantasy wars. It's not about her.

How far is the conflict over her head? She is not a good reader of Magnusson's text. As far as one can tell from her complaint, she has little appreciation of metaphor and less sense of irony. Magnusson writes: "One of Somer Brodribb's students [this is the BFSA] led off with a paper celebrating women's ways of knowing. She had the *Globe* story ["Sexual politics battle rages in university," April 19, three days earlier] and related publicity in front of her as she celebrated women's ways of knowing, and the examination turned into an orgy of self-congratulation for members of the Women's Caucus" ("Feminism" 10).

What the BFSA singles out from these sentences is what she regards as a sexual slur. She says that calling her defence an "orgy" for women is "homophobic" ("Formal Charge" 3). It conjures up a negative image of women having sex with each other. She ignores Magnusson's repeated employment of the "orgy" metaphor to evoke a libidinally invested excess of some kind, not literal sex, much less among women. On the same page, just eleven lines earlier, in describing the biofeminist picture of what might be an appropriate moral standpoint for men, for example, Magnusson likens it to Christian repentance, "repeated in orgies of self-laceration" ("Feminism" 10). The BFSA also ignores the sense of the whole paragraph, which concerns itself more with audience group behaviour than with the individual presenter's intellectual focus. She treats his *political* criticism of the biopoliticization of scholarship as a case of *sexual* harassment, confirming his point, and mine as well.

Magnusson follows the account of the self-congratulatory feminist orgy with unmistakeable irony, describing the presentation of "an earnest young man who had learned his political lessons. It consisted of a long condemnation of Foucault and Baudrillard for their sexism, combined with an extended *mea culpa* for men in general" ("Feminism" 10). The BFSA manages to miss the irony and complains: Magnusson "implies that only young men are earnest (serious, legitimate?) students of political theory and that he had learned his political lessons and I have not" ("Formal Charge" 4). She carries on in the same literal vein throughout the complaint, inventing grievances against a text that she does not really understand, but knows that she hates.

The BFSA is literal-minded, and intent on running a pre-written script. Like too many other bright students, she has been trained to a learned ignorance that threatens to gain the upper hand in universities, behind a screen of ideology and fanaticism. People outside the university would find themselves hard put to imagine just how much the university is beginning to surrender to therapeutic values that encourage the primal scream of offended egos and empower the protective repressions of the vengeful superego. Everybody who cares about women, and about mental life, society, and the future of culture and civilization, has a real stake, by contrast, in insisting that universities should remain adult places for adult intellects and emotions, and higher education should be a training ground for more intelligent adulthood, not indulgent and dangerous infantilism. Forget about pampering the child within; grow the creative and robust adult.[4]

Another of the BSFA's charges, worthy of particular attention, is that Magnusson creates "a hostile environment for women within the Department" by issuing a paper consisting largely of "hateful statements about women, women students and women as scholars (all subsets of 'feminists')" (3). Magnusson, of course, insists that neither he nor his colleagues do or say anything negative in connection with "women," at the same time that "feminists" cannot be sacrosanct inside some protected circle. This distinction is thematic in the paper, and crucial for Magnusson. It is a distinction that is incomprehensible and intolerable for the BFSA. There is no such thing, in her estimation, as non-feminist women. A former DPS graduate student, now part-time teacher, who listened to the BFSA's presentation, was surprised to hear that women who study male authors were considered "transvestites" by the BFSA, that is, in some way not really women at all (Judith Stamps letter, May 18, 1993). Feminism becomes the primary concept, the primary collective noun, blinding the BFSA to the knowledge that female feminists *are* actually a subset of women.

The nature of this mind-set could be described as strange, exotic, silly, frightening, sad, tragic, absurd, idealistic, exaggerated, experimental, naive, and a variety of other qualities—if it were not that it has access to an investigative and disciplinary proceeding. Nelson had carried the ball for Lambert in front of an ethics hearing against Westhues at Waterloo; here, it is astonishing to what extent the BFSA's formal charges against Magnusson hope to accomplish in the arena of personal discipline what Brodribb had failed to extort in the arena of public politics. The BFSA demands "non-negotiable sanctions and remedies": public retraction and apology "for his wrongdoing"; removal of Magnusson from his position as director and teacher in the program he heads, wherever her own career is concerned; censure by the university "for his actions against me and other women," including loss of a portion of salary and removal "from any decisionmaking committees, particularly with respect to graduate students, scholarships, grants, funding, teaching and/or research assistant appointments, and hiring issues"; and, finally, the "assembly of a hearing panel to hear the charges of harassment and sexual harassment against Magnusson that would be composed of equity officers from outside the University of Victoria" (7-8). In addition, she reserves the right to take further action.

On July 28, the equity officer recommends finding Magnusson guilty of harassing the BFSA. He had made full and articulate answer on July 2 to the BFSA's charges, in a single-spaced, 13-page reply, longer than the initial "Feminism" document, with appendices. He was courteous and professional in his reply, and said that he had intended no adverse comment on the BFSA in the course of a general analysis. He remained resolutely supportive of women and also of feminism, except for "sexist fundamentalism," as he had argued all along. Feminism, he clarified, is not monolithic, but complex and contested, and "it is certainly not the Equity Office's job to settle such issues" (Letter to Devine 6). He noted, in conclusion, that it was hard not to regard the BFSA's complaint "as another salvo in a political conflict," especially in the light of her assertion of the absurdity of tempering women's "rage" in the interests of civility. With remarkable restraint, he added that, in the midst of trying to "improve the working and learning environment" in the DPS, "proceedings such as these are an unnecessary and unhelpful distraction" (11).

Devine disagrees, in a 27-page document. She accepts that Magnusson's non-attendance at the BFSA's presentation was not harassment or sexual harassment. She also accepts that the "Feminism" piece cannot amount to sexual harassment of the complainant. She finds, however, that the part of that document which described the student presentations and the audience behaviour constitutes harassment: "Unfair and demeaning treatment of the Complainant that had the effect of creating a hostile educational environment for her, and demonstrated a lack of awareness of the power and authority the Respondent had over the Complainant" (Devine, "Report" 25).

Magnusson had had no dealings with the student, was not her supervisor, was not grading her, did not identify her in his piece, and his piece was not intended for her as its target audience. There has been no discrimination against the BFSA, and no appreciable or demonstrable effect on the actual educational environment. In fact, the BFSA had graduated by the time Magnusson wrote his document. Yet his "fair comment" rights, his "true comment" rights, and his academic freedom are all curtailed, on the argument that his analytical comments of a cultural and political pattern were considered offensive. And yet, finding "offence" is no demonstration of demeaning unfairness; and the references to power differential are simply vexatious. Where is the senior professor's "power" if he cannot even write an analysis of a controversy, with cogent and appropriate examples, without being disciplined for it on the complaints of his political adversaries, by an Equity Office which relies on those same adversaries for its own support? Harassment policies, in this respect, are continuations of politics by other means—unacceptable means, in the context of a discursive university community. In this case, their use appears to have violated Magnusson's basic human rights, his speech rights, and political rights.

Devine's recommendations to the president concede that no further hearings are called for. But they would order Magnusson to retract and apologize, and to publish the apology to his mailing list. They would also remove him from decision-making and pedagogical responsibilities with respect to the BFSA. Magnusson's 30-page reply is a tour-de-force of detailed reasoning about the harassment policy at the university, due process, intellectual integrity, and political pluralism. He also takes pains to place the complaint in the framework of the very heated ongoing campaign to discredit him and advance the climate agenda. A harassment charge triggered by that extraneous agenda appears an abuse of process. He points to the summer issue of the student newspaper *The Emily (The Chilly Climate Issue,* vol. II, no. 3), where the BFSA can be seen to describe the complaint ("complaint is a weak term, an OUTRAGE?") in relation to collective rage, and not personal fear about her career. Magnusson is just a convenient target of a campaign about systemic discrimination, that has a dark and potentially violent dimension.

The Emily supplements the BFSA's article on her complaint/outrage with inflammatory suggestions, in a piece called "Suggestions to Warm Up a Chilly Climate." Magnusson cites the following passage, which is not only personally threatening, but also a disturbing feature of the direction in which student passions have been inflamed by the biofeminist agitation: "Build a bonfire! Materials needed gasoline, lighter, waste paper such as, Machiavelli, *The Prince,* Plato *The Republic,* Aristotle *The Politics,* Jean

Jacques Rousseau *Emile,* anything by Freud, Malleus Male-
ficarum (text written by witch hunters), D.H. Lawrence,
Sons and Lovers, any work by Phillip Rushton, Hobbes,
Leviathan, Locke's *Second Treaties on Government,* Robert
Bly, *Iron John,* Magnusson, 'Feminism, McCarthyism and
Sexist Fundamentalism,' and countless others. Also re-
quired eight white tenured males to huff and puff." [Er-
rors in the original.]

In the same issue, Magnusson's "earnest young man,"
who uttered all the *mea culpas,* shows that he knows how
to hurl blame and castigation at "Magnusson's juvenile
piece of vapid propaganda." He calls Magnusson neurotic,
deluded, paternalistic, disrespectful, reactionary, self-
righteous, condescending, silencing, and freedom-
limiting, with "privilege-defending rhetoric." The BFSA's
article describes the DSP professors as "violent misogynists" filled with "irrational hatred" who engage in "dia-
tribes, invectives and emotional outbursts" (BFSA v.
Magnusson 19-21).

In short, Magnusson makes the case that he is being
targeted, singled out, and stigmatized in a proceeding that
is really a stand-in for a political battle that continues to
heat up around the proceedings, to the point of overheat-
ing. The entire equity structure, indeed, the entire feminist community, in its organizational forms and biases,
and in its political engagements, has to bear some real
measure of responsibility for the overall character of the
campus "climate" and its potentials for civilized reform.
Meanwhile, the equity officer's report damages Magnusson's working environment, interferes with his status and
performance, and will predictably be used in a public
campaign to smear him.

The BFSA also finds fault with the equity officer's
report (August 10, 1993). Magnusson should have been
found guilty of sexual harassment for the "orgy" comment,
a sexual slur that damaged the status and treatment of
women. And it should have brought disciplinary action
against Magnusson, not just apologies and the rest. "Clear

punitive action is required" (5). She revises her demands: he must not only retract and apologize, but also acknowledge sexual harassment, and any future distribution of his paper "must be disallowed." He must be disciplined by: removal from decisions about female students, a letter in his file, and consideration of suspension and financial penalties. The university must denounce the ongoing hostile climate for women in the DPS, educate the faculty, pay for her lawyer if these demands are not met, and reimburse her for wages lost and expenses incurred in pursuing her complaint (6-7). She should be paid punitive damages as well. And she wants exemption from all the requirements of the graduate program.

Clearly, the various exchanges through September between the two parties and the harassment machinery, including letters to the president, were not going to sort the matter out amicably. On the other hand, the documentation evidently made enough of an impression on the president that he did not want to make a judgment based solely on the Equity Office report. In late September, he decided to solicit outside advice. He turned to Professor Margaret E. Hughes, family law specialist at the University of Calgary. In November, he advised both parties that he accepted Hughes' conclusions. These would represent both good news and bad news for Magnusson, and would leave the situation unresolved.

Hughes's 18-page "Report" (October 31, 1993) dismisses all the harassment charges against Magnusson, including the one that Devine accepted. The challenged words are not abusive, unfair, or demeaning to the BFSA (13), or to women (14), and they are demeaning only to the group of presenters on April 22, but they may be true and fair comment (14). In addition, they do not interfere with anybody's status or performance, and did not create a hostile or intimidating environment. The environment was already divisive, emotionally charged, and hostile (15). There were no threats, no intimidation, no discrimination on the basis of sex, no abuse of power over the

BFSA (16). So far so good. Hughes gets stuck on the last little bit of her painstakingly analytical review of the Victoria policy. She can't let Magnusson off. She finds that he misused his authority as a faculty member. Not so as to demean or abuse the BFSA or any particular group, however, and not so as to create a hostile environment (17). No harassment has been established, and the complaint is therefore dismissed.

But now, here's the bad news. It is true that Magnusson is now cleared of all charges under the university's harassment policies. But the misuse of authority, according to Hughes, violates the Professional Ethics Code of the university—its policy on academic freedom, in fact. Hughes concludes that Magnusson's paper "Feminism" "did not constitute constructive criticism, even when viewed in the context of what the Respondent saw as libellous, unfair, and anonymous accusations of sexism and systemic discriminatory practices directed against him and his colleagues in the Chilly Climate Report" (17). In effect, the DPS was held up to public ridicule "for its politicization and debasement of academic scholarly learning and evaluation standards and processes" (17).

This is terrible, and more than a little bizarre. Academic freedom at Victoria "carries with it the duty to use that freedom in a responsible way" ("Tenure Document" I.1.4). Being "unconstructive" and contributing to divisions are considered violations of ethics, and therefore *not* a responsible use of academic freedom. So now, Magnusson, who had been claiming all along that he had the academic freedom right to write down his political analysis, stands accused of violating his own academic freedom obligations. And how did he do that? By telling the truth about the politicization and debasement of the exam process, which had the *effect* of holding up the department to ridicule. Shoot the messenger.

This is in any event wrong on three counts, at least. It is perverse to consider that truth-telling does not satisfy the "responsibility" obligation for the use of academic freedom as well as a newly fabricated "constructive" speech doctrine does. Constructiveness, collegiality, cooperation, and the other civil virtues cannot become the primary standard of intellectual behaviour, at the peak of the relevant value hierarchy. Secondly, the truth-telling description of an ongoing, otherwise unchecked, political debasement of scholarship can be considered precisely the appropriate and most constructive balancing performance that could have been offered under the circumstances. To say otherwise, *a priori*, is to deny Magnusson his fundamental right as a political and moral agent to define his own contribution to the prospects of general well-being. His integrity, as a tenured faculty member, entrusted with long-term trusteeship of the university's well-being, through the structures of academic self-governance, must be presumed, unless it is proved corrupted. The superficial view, that his analytic contribution was unconstructive in the given context, suppresses his politics, and overdetermines the interpretation and progression of the political conflict from the start.

Finally, if the messenger of departmental problems is to be faulted, how much more must those be faulted who are responsible for the substance? Arguably, if the department is the object of ridicule, it is not because the story is told, but because of the story that is there to be told. Magnusson has been saying since the beginning that there are grounds for disciplining Brodribb. Whatever may be the merits of a disciplinary route, at a minimum her responsibility, or at least co-responsibility, for the climate of hostility has to be recognized and assessed. It is arbitrary to single out Magnusson, and unfair to subject him to further individual process, in a fundamentally political situation.

It is worth noting this tendency by lawyers to meddle in affairs of the university where they have no better expertise than any other professor, and less than the experts in the area. Academic freedom is one of these matters, and universities should beware of imagining that lawyers, just by virtue of their profession, are going to have better insight into this area than, say, philosophers, or indeed, any rank-and-file professor who cares about the issues, not to mention the accumulated expertise in faculty associations, and the CAUT, especially its academic freedom committee.

In early November, then, president David Strong formally dismisses the charges against Magnusson and makes no move to open up the ethics issue with which Hughes concluded her report. For the moment, the personal process against Magnusson is at an end, and his case rejoins the wider climate controversy and the steps that the university takes to resolve a festering dispute that is drawing more and more of the university into it, in the way a fire consumes the oxygen in a room. For example, president Strong's re-appointment proceedings are under way, when complaints about his lack of action on harassment matters surface in the news. On December 14, the Graduate Students' Women's Caucus demands the resignation of the president, for alleged deficiency in pursuing an anti-harassment agenda. The students distribute three chronologies of events (about the Chilly Climate Committee, Student Harassment Experiences, and the BFSA's Equity Proceedings). These go to a couple of dozen individuals, including a CBC TV journalist, two provincial cabinet ministers, the provincial ombudsman, the provincial Council of Human Rights, and a variety of students, faculty, and administrators at Victoria. It would appear that someone also distributes excerpts from the supposedly-confidential harassment proceedings to the media, including the Devine report and the Hughes report.

On December 31, in response to the December 14 distributions, Magnusson raises detailed objections to the Hughes report with the president, and raises the issue of institutional harassment with unmistakable clarity. On March 8, 1994, this issue of the Hughes report raises its ugly head again, when a mass of women's institutions on campus write jointly to the president to demand that he should immediately set up an inquiry into Magnusson's alleged violation of professional ethics. The letter is signed by the Faculty Women's Caucus Steering Committee, the Graduate Students Society, the University of Victoria Students Society, the University of Victoria Caucus of the National Association of Women and the Law, the Student Representative on the Board of Governors, the University of Victoria Women's Centre, the Support Staff Women's Caucus, and the Graduate Students' Women's Caucus, and it is copied to the BFSA, who also writes on the same day to the president to ask for the same investigation. President Strong writes back to everyone on March 24 that there has been no actual "finding" of professional misconduct, and that it would be unfair to open another venue of investigation until the B.C. Council of Human Rights has finished with these issues (see below).

In short, even while Magnusson's own dispute with the BFSA was unfolding, the larger dispute swirling around the DPS, Warren Magnusson, Somer Brodribb, and the university continued apace, with no immediate resolution in sight, except for the possibility that fatigue at Victoria would simply prove decisive, and the theatre of conflict would shift to another Canadian university site. In the midst of his harassment case, in other words, Magnusson had to stay busy simultaneously with the continuing climate investigations in which he was a major player. I can only touch on the highlights in the balance of this account.

From April 1993 onwards, the tenured male faculty in the DPS keep trying to get a university process to inquire into the production and distribution of the CCC report, and to provide an opportunity to clear the department of the damaging allegations. They never succeed in getting such an inquiry. The university does however keep setting up initiatives to look into matters, and articulate advocacy by Magnusson and his colleagues has at least the effect of protecting their interests from being completely swept away. Over time, the administration, which vacillates between competing claims and perspectives, begins to lean toward normalization, and it is clear that only the male faculty are interested in that. After the failure of the Callahan-Pirie efforts to resolve the dispute in the DPS, Brodribb and supporters carry on a relentless campaign to persuade everyone that there is no credible administration inside the DPS, or indeed, in the university as a whole. This campaign climaxes with Brodribb's letter to the CAUT in May 1994, more than a year after the Climate Report, demanding the resignation of the president of her university. This is an act of desperation that may show her increasing isolation. But there are many steps before this one.

In early June 1993, Brodribb's group file a complaint with the B.C. Office of the Ombudsman, alleging that they have been subjected to administrative mistreatment. They omit the full political context, of course, and complain that the Climate Report has not been handled properly inside the DPS, or subsequently, and that the administration's conduct renders an internal avenue of appeal illusory. The complaint is against the administration. The male faculty in the department never find out exactly what the complaint is, and the ombudsman's office does not consult with them, on the assumption that the dispute is strictly between the chillies and the university officials.

During June and July, there is a lot of discussion between the university and the ombudsman's office about the nature and conduct of a committee of inquiry that the university will strike to look into the dispute. The ombudsman, Dulcie McCallum, virtually dictates terms to the university. The DPS men are unable to get agreement to inquire into the full politics of the situation, or into the contents of the climate report: its initial legitimacy is always somehow to be taken for granted. To this day, the ombudsman's office is occupied with the matter in some fashion that has not been disclosed to the DPS, and it now appears that it will report in the near future, perhaps before the end of 1994.

On August 25, president Strong appoints Beth Bilson, chair of the Saskatchewan Labour Relations Board, and Thomas Berger, former justice of the B.C. Supreme Court, to make recommendations "respecting the learning and working environment" in the DPS. They issue a 9-page interim report on September 29, 1993, and a 70-page final "Report of the Review Committee" on January 21, 1994. The committee takes for granted the usefulness of the climate audit; and, in the end, they make ten recommendations. They endorse climate studies, and recommend increased resources for it. At the same time, they want climate studies to be much improved over the CCC version, in composition, methods, terms of reference, language, and contents, and also in the separation of what belongs in a climate report from accusations of misconduct that must be channelled through a complaint procedure. They recommend improved collegiality, a separate code of ethics, and a senior, external chair for the DPS, preferably a woman. They recommend clarification that the letter of April 8 is withdrawn and there is no legal threat hanging over the authors of the CCC report.

President Strong gets behind the report immediately, praising all ten of its recommendations. The male faculty accept its recommendations and set about normalizing relations and getting a procedure set up to find the external female chair. The faculty women's caucus endorses the report with some caution. In their view, it does not have enough teeth to compel the administration to get going on full implementation. The chillies denounce the report. A group press release from the CCC, the UVic Students Society, Graduate Students' Women's Caucus, the Women's Centre, the Chilly Climate Support Group, the Student Representative on the Board of Governors, and Instructors in Women's Studies, acknowledges that the report has some merit, but then blasts it for a "fundamental flaw": "The Berger-Bilson Report systematically suppresses the Chilly Climate Committee—its members, its work and its worth." They don't think that climate issues get their due importance, and they attack the report for "numerous evasions, contradictions and spurious arguments" ("Viewpoints"). This is one month after the students demanded the president's resignation.

More trouble is to come, however. On February 2, 1994, the president issues a press release in response to claims broadcast on the CBC that the Bilson-Berger report has endorsed the CCC allegations of sexual harassment and sex discrimination in the DPS. He defends the department, its track record, and its learning environment, and supports its normal procedures, within the framework of the report's recommendations. He gets hit pretty hard for the announcement. On February 14, the Faculty Women's Caucus meet and react negatively. Strong was too soft on the DPS; his statement undermines the women's confidence in the administration's commitment to deal proactively with climate issues. They won't take part in implementing the Bilson-Berger recommendations until Strong takes new measures to reassure them. Some of these will be hard to get. They want the women in the DPS to have a veto over the appointment of the new chair. As it happens, both Brodribb and the other female faculty member (who heads the support committee for the CCC) decline to stand for the search committee for chair, and the search is getting along nicely. The Women's Caucus also want a new letter retracting the April 8 letter to be published, addressed and delivered to Brodribb.

The history of this letter is worth a closer look. It is like the obsession at Waterloo with making Professor Westhues apologize—again, and again. On May 26, vice-president Scully wrote to all DPS faculty, after the failure of the Callahan-Pirie initiative, requesting a reciprocal compromise: the male faculty to withdraw their letter, and the CCC to withdraw a brief section of their report alleging sexual misconduct. On May 28, the men complied, by letter to the vice-president; the women never did. On June 10, Scully wrote to Brodribb, to ask for a reply, and to inform her that the male faculty had withdrawn the April

8 letter. On June 21, Brodribb declined to withdraw the accusatory section. The women supporting Brodribb had made the April 8 letter the centre of their propaganda campaign, and had been quite successful in persuading people that the real issue was that women were being intimidated into silence about their real grievances by powerful male faculty. Their own refusal to have their indiscriminate allegations investigated never properly emerged into clear public focus.

As a consequence, there was tremendous pressure on the men to withdraw the letter of April 8, as a precondition of progress. The letter was that widely regarded as inappropriate. In the end, the vice-president agreed to make a public statement (in his May 26 letter) to the effect that he had not seen any evidence to support the CCC allegations, and saw no reason for an investigation. This was acceptable to the men, and they withdrew the letter. The vice-president, under some pressure apparently, kept the withdrawal quiet for a long time. He never published the May 26 letter. As a result, though Brodribb knew better, the Women's Caucus put out the story that the men had not withdrawn the letter, or not properly. The withdrawal, on terms satisfactory to the chillies, then became a permanent rallying cry. The misinformation leaves its mark even on the Bilson-Berger Report, which consigns a whole recommendation to getting a letter clearly withdrawn, although that had already been done eight months earlier.

In February 1994, then, the president's press release confirmed publicly that the letter had been withdrawn in May 1993. Still, the Faculty Women's Caucus demanded that a *new* letter be sent to Brodribb. Meanwhile, in March 1994, in the course of interviews with Brodribb, and Professor Constance Backhouse from Western, the CBC repeated the defamatory allegations. It is clear that until the chillies withdraw the allegations, or prove them—certainly while they keep repeating them—there cannot be peace on this matter (Morley, "Political science prof speaks out"). But the agitation on Brodribb's side has not stopped. The Faculty Women's Caucus took their demand for further withdrawals to the Faculty Association on April 18, 1994, and got support for it (though the association balked at chipping in to the CCC's legal costs).

As of the fall of 1994, the male faculty in the DPS have not agreed to this obsessive request to acknowledge to Brodribb directly that they had somehow misbehaved. And more than a year and a half into the matter, the CCC has neither withdrawn its accusations, nor supported them with evidence, nor agreed to any sort of inquiry that could investigate the conduct of the accused male faculty and have a chance to clear the innocent of the spectre of wrongdoing. It is very hard to see why the CCC should get away with it.

There is a large issue in all this that the CCC have not conceded, but that university commissions have grappled with: the issue of due process in relationship to climate reports. The chillies are chewing over the men's adversarial response as though it had been a cardinal sin, and a divine manifestation of the justice of their complaint. But nobody has to be the passive target of accusations of sexual misconduct, professional misconduct, and illegality, without the right to some kind of remedy. A legal recourse may not be necessary unless there is no other. The university has tried to think of another. President Strong established an Equal Rights and Opportunities Committee to report on the harassment policy. Professor Hester Lessard, of the Faculty of Law, chaired the committee and reported back on October 15, 1993. Her report urged that climate complaints be differentiated from individual complaints of harassment, and that systemic issues should be addressed with systemic solutions. This was a formula for expanded climate studies and interventions, but at least it might have avoided the DPS problem that general investigations brought back results that implicated individuals and impeached their character and reputations. In fact, Bilson and Berger criticize Lessard sharply for failing to find an adequate solution to the problem.

"It is argued that if a report is a 'climate' report, *considerations of due process have no place* [italics added], even if allegations of misconduct which impugn an individual faculty member's character are made. The faculty member must, if identified, or if identifiable to family, friends and colleagues, be prepared to accept the report, for to dispute it is to invalidate the experiences of the women who made their disclosure to the authors of the report .... Due process has no place, because it effectively channels discussion away from the real complaint, which is the condition of women" (Bilson-Berger 33). The ordinary citizen, who rarely gets her share of due process, will be amazed at the readiness with which women in universities—lawyers, even!—will sacrifice due process on the altar of their political program. To their credit, Bilson and Berger close this loop: "We think it right therefore to affirm due process. It is a fundamental human right"— even if it is at the expense of the climate investigations.

Brodribb cannot win in the long run, although she may still put people through a lot with the ombudsman and the Council of Human Rights. The university has its own traditions and missions that it cannot hand over to either of these agencies. It may have to renew its sense of these, if it wants to negotiate successfully with other organs of public policy. But the Victoria case shows up as clearly as any other that human crises and conflicts can go off the rails, given even a very few determined people, and the right "climate." Brodribb is not on the level about climate issues. She has not been swimming against the current; she has just been swimming faster than the current can carry her. No one person could have had the impact that she has already had on the modern university if she had not had the "climate" on her side. She would have just been brushed aside. As it is, the experience permits colleagues at Victoria and elsewhere to see from the crisis that things tend to be more complex than is first assumed, and that every new complexity is an invitation to learn more about what we are risking, what risks are worthwhile, and at what point you say enough is enough.

It is not clear how settlement will be reached. There is still the outstanding issue of the withdrawal that Brodribb wants. She also wants the dean and the president to resign, and the vice-president to be censured by the CAUT (Brodribb, "Submission"). The ombudsman will soon report. The human rights case is pending. The male faculty have sued the CBC for libel, for falsely reporting that the Bilson-Berger Committee had confirmed the findings of the Chilly Climate Committee. There is a broad struggle on a broad political front, and many venues remain open for further interventions and negotiations. Victoria is now in its third academic year since this began. The troubles may be spreading elsewhere in B.C. The political season over the next twelve months may refocus everybody's attention. Warren Magnusson, meanwhile, is temporarily far from the madding crowd, quietly at work on his sabbatical leave—uncompensated for his troubles, but also, at the moment, unharassed. Only, however, until the seemingly interminable abuse of process catches up with him again.

In December 1993, the BFSA specifically accused Magnusson's "Feminism" article of violating her human rights. The investigation of that particular allegation by the B.C. Council of Human Rights is a dubious pleasure that awaits Magnusson in the near future. Indeed, in December 1993, Brodribb and the chillies filed several complaints with the B.C. Council of Human Rights, alleging that the university had sexually harassed them and sexually discriminated against them. The Chilly Climate Committee's most contentious allegations, accusing the male faculty in the Department of Political Science of widespread sexual harassment, sexual discrimation, and sexual misconduct, in class and in social settings, are restated for the council. Brodribb alleges that "all female students" and "all female employees" at the university are subjected to "a working and/or learning environment that is poisoned by harassment based on sex and sexual discrimination," and fur-

317

ther, that women employees "are being subject to discrimination because of our feminist political beliefs" (Brodribb's complaint, file #930482). All of this has yet to be processed.

There are so many different opportunities—counting all the venues for complaint and all the avenues for appeal—for any determined accuser to stress and devour the life of even the most innocent accused person, that the whole system of complaint-management, not only at Victoria or in B.C., but in most comparable jurisdictions in Canada, must be indicted as abusive. There seems to be no capable discretionary power and no mechanism for saying, "enough is enough," and for cutting off the complaint process before it does more harm than good. Those who have a concern for procedural and substantive due process have to face up to the need to reassess and readjust the proportions of risk and damage, and find ways to build into the system some serious and practical disincentives to the exploitation of claims of "vulnerability" as weapons. We have to turn attention to this, as a matter of the most urgent priority. The "sincerity" of the accusers cannot be an overriding influence on our judgment of fair process.

X
Righteous Panic and Sinister Fallacies

"Alice began to get rather sleepy, and went on saying to herself, in a dreamy sort of way, 'Do cats eat bats? Do cats eat bats?' and sometimes, 'Do bats eat cats?' for, you see, as she couldn't answer either question, it didn't much matter which way she put it." (Lewis Carroll, Alice in Wonderland 7)

"When I use a word," Humpty Dumpty said in rather a scornful tone, "it means just what I choose it to mean—neither more nor less."
"The question is," said Alice, "whether you can make words mean different things."
"The question is," said Humpty Dumpty, "which is to be master, that's all." (Lewis Carroll, Through the Looking Glass 238)

In this final chapter, I want to look at the cognitive features that make the rhetoric of zero tolerance, biopolitics, and moral panic culturally effective today. Only if we can recognize the shapes of the logical fallacies, the statistical spins, and the supporting myths of biopanic, are we likely to become sufficiently immunized—and sufficiently reasonable—to resist the "mind-forged manacles."

Zero tolerance of violence against women—extended in the universities to zero tolerance of "sexism"—is promoted as the right of every Canadian woman to an environment free of violence and a climate free of "chill." This has three characteristic components, in addition to zero tolerance itself as an intolerant enforcement scenario. "Environment" is a totalitarian code word in biopolitical usage. It means the whole world—all the conditions of a woman's life. When the whole world of social interaction is treated as *environment,* human life is utterly objectified, and made subject to definition and manipulation from a particular standpoint. What is particularly central in this conception of the whole world as environment is that other people are brought into the picture only as features of the environment. Not intersubjectively; not as autonomous beings who have as much title to their needs, desires, attitudes, and expressions as the female focal point of the claim to a pacified environment: simply as part of *her* environment. Society has become less than social in this formulation; it is just a biological niche. A demand for an environment "free of" the code word "violence," then, or for a cosy or hospitable "climate," is a demand for safety and protection from all discomforts arising from other people.

This is all that freedom means in biopolitical code: safety, protection. Women are not expected to be looking for freedom and the fullness of life's adventures. On the contrary, they are to look for safety and protection from anything in their "environment" which might pose a risk or a hazard, any discomfort, anything unpredictable: in short, protection from any eruption of other people's self-expression. A desire for total safety is insatiable, of course, and calls for ever more radical interventions. The environment is to be purged, literally, of unsafe elements—purged in the way (if not yet the style) that Stalinists kept purging the counter-revolution that they projected as their very shadow. The radical echoes of the same old power-lust are audible in the language of *rooting out*[1] popular evils, such as harassment, discrimination, homophobia, or Eurocentrism.

"Violence," meanwhile, stands for everything biofeminists do not want. For a start, it never means violence according to the common-sense understanding that permits the word to have an emotional impact in the first place. It does not mean the use of physical force, much less physical injury. This latter is what Canadians fear, and this fear is exploited by biopolitical rhetoric when it expands the definitions, as the CanPan does, to include not only physical matters, but also sexual, psychological, spiritual, and financial conflicts of every kind. Violence is made all-inclusive of every form of unwanted interaction, including the unwanted attitudes of other people. The first rule of confronting biofeminist rhetoric is to scrutinize the definitions; the second rule is to challenge their totalizing character.

Remember that biofeminists speak of rape as worse than death, and speak of due process as a form of violent rape. Pat Marshall went to the Parliamentary Subcommittee on the Status of Women in 1991 to argue that the presumption of innocence in law had to be reconsidered, along with other basic principles of democracy, including the freedom of speech, in order that women should have "the freedom to feel some safety and security" (Lees 102). We saw, (in chapter IX) that "climate audit" advocates explicitly reject due process, as an inappropriate distraction from their concerns. In biopolitical discourse, freedom of expression and due process, two towering achievements of liberal democracy, become, simply, threats to women's safety. Safety has become the Trojan horse of the biofeminist assault on the liberal-democratic order.

There are numerous logical manoeuvres, methodological strategies, myths, and stereotypes that underpin and amplify the totalitarian sweep of the safety against violence projection. I hope that it is clear from the earlier chapters how much of the rhetorical case rests on *dubious evidence*. The research is bad, the conclusions unwarranted. I have argued that the particular move that stretches out falsely from palpable instances of violence to the society as a whole is the *clinical fallacy*, a version of the *fallacy of hasty generalization*. There are two other versions of hasty generalization which are particularly prominent in the mindset associated with biopolitical totalitarianism: *the corrupt continuum*, and the *cancerous cause* (for short). The latter is a complex form of the *slippery slope* fallacy, and its full name might properly be *cancerous cause by contaminating correlation and inversion*.

The Fallacies of the Corrupt Continuum and the Cancerous Cause

The slippery slope refers to a sequence of steps, where taking the first step amounts to an unstoppable slide down the slope to the very bottom step. When applied to human affairs, this is a stategy for linking up a huge range of widely separated attitudes and behaviours. For example, the French Renaissance believed that drinking will lead a man to womanizing, and womanizing will in turn lead him to homosexuality. This was the slippery slope of progressive degradation (see de Musset's *Lorenzaccio*). The slippery slope is a vertical scale; it is about progression through time, in a sequence where the undesirable consequences get worse and worse along the slide. The horizontal equivalent of the slippery slope argument is the continuum argument. In this case, the concept links up a huge range of divergent attitudes and behaviours which coexist at the same time, by focussing on some characteristic that they can be alleged to share. It is said that they share this quality on a graduated scale, from light to dark, soft to hard, or mild to extreme, for example, but their essence is the same. On the model of a spectrum of light waves, a physical continuum, people postulate, for example, a psychological continuum of fear, as though moderate and healthy caution were essentially the same thing as irrational phobia and paralyzing panic.

What the slippery slope and the continuum have in common is the hasty generalization that is inattentive to distinctions in gradation. In biopolitics, this becomes ideologically fixated and impervious to persuasion or falsification. If the differences in degree between steps on the slope and positions in the continuum are washed away, all that is left is a schematic structure. Steam and ice may both be composed of water molecules in a continuum of transformations, but if we lose the distinction between hot and cold, and the divergent consequences of changes of state, all brought about by differences of degree, then we are indeed drowning in confusion.

The biopolitical usage of these strategies rests on two deceptive moves. First, the slope and the continuum are described in each case as having an essential quality that is given a *moral* characterization. Second, the moral quality assigned to the entire sequence of steps and all the points on the scale is derived from the most extreme and morally contemptible position on the slope or in the continuum. This is why I refer to the pre-eminence of the *corrupt continuum* and the *cancerous cause* in biopolitical rhetoric. This is a dual triumph of biopolitical duplicity. Not only is the entire scale given a negative value, but this negative attribution is twice inflated: by spreading the defining qualities of the worst case to all cases, on one hand; and, on the other, by boosting the infrequent incidence of the worst cases with the sheer volume of all the variations of human life dragged into the schematism.

Thus, on the "continuum of violence" defined by Marc Lépine, all men are monster killers and all women are innocent and helpless victims, "*just because [they] are women*"

(Collins 1). Moreover, the raised voice or the sarcastic tone, a joke or a put-down, are enlisted as evidence of the same *syndrome* of "violence": a "continuum which includes a range of behaviour from harassment and offensive comments which undermine people's dignity to sexual attacks and murder" (CAUT, "Educational Handbook" 6: 3, 1). Jokes and murder sit side by side, as manifestations of the same thing. The character of murder inflates the culpability of the humour; the great frequency of the humour makes up for the rare incidence of murder.

Meanwhile, in a complementary construction of a slippery slope: sexual images are alleged to devalue women as sexual objects, in turn shaping and reinforcing attitudes that devalue women's lives and worth generally, which, in turn, are organized into systems of belief that confer privilege and authority upon males and teach females to be subordinate, which in turn support practices that discriminate against women in employment, housing, goods and services, and other arenas of life, and in turn expose women to constant harassment and violence. The slope is a relentless slide from heterosexuality to "heterosexism," from sex and sexual representation to "sexism," then discrimination on the basis of sex, and then violence against women. I showed in chapter VII just how the Supreme Court of Canada has come to adopt exactly this kind of slippery slope thinking in defining the "inference of a risk of harm" against women, on the basis of biofeminist legal advocacy in the paranoid tradition of American "wacko" feminism (as A. Dworkin and MacKinnon have been described: see O'Connell).

To defeat the slippery slope fallacy, we have to deny the slipperiness of the slope, and/or the need to take the first step down. That is, we have to contest the inevitability of original sin and the fall. We do not have to accept either that sex produces "sexism," or that "violence is sexism's hideous off-spring" (Federation of Women Teachers' Associations of Ontario, "Newsletter 8, cited in CAUT, Educational Handbook" 6: 2-3). In fact, we may be better able to resist the emotional tyranny of the biofeminist approach if we can spot the fallacies on which it is based.

The slippery slope conceals a complicated series of fallacious steps. Take the example of marijuana. For decades, police chiefs have held back the decriminalization of soft drugs by telling us that they lead to hard-drug use. Heroin is marijuana's offspring, so to speak. The slippery slope here shares a feature with the clinical fallacy. Heroin addicts report, when asked, that indeed, their heroin use was preceded by marijuana use. They report this in fairly large numbers. The numbers are given only as percentages, and soon we forget that the number of heroin users is very small. All we have here is a correlation between marijuana use and heroin use in a small clinical sample. It soon turns into a causal chain: if most heroin users started on marijuana, it must be that marijuana use causes heroin use.

This is a very common argument, but utterly fallacious. No matter how many times it is employed, it is always employed to mislead. We might as well ask the heroin addicts whether they "started" on some form of milk (breast milk or bottled milk), and we would get 100% correlation between heroin users and their earlier use of milk. Or oxygen. Or polluted air, if we prefer. We could say, if we shy away from saying that milk leads to heroin use (because, after all, we don't like to derive something bad from something apparently good), that breathing polluted air leads to heroin use. We have then satisfied our need to have a correlation between two bad things. But the assumption of causality is still ridiculous, as we know, because we know that we all (pretty much) breathe polluted air, just as we all started on milk, and yet we are not all heroin addicts. Similarly, of the large general population of marijuana users, only an insignificant number turned to heroin.

What happens here? First, you find something acknowledged to be bad: heroin use. If it is acknowledged to be bad, it is usually in limited supply. Then you establish a correlation between *it* and something much more wide-spread and controversial, which you want to make out to be bad: marijuana use. You permit the bad, clinical source to contaminate your target: heroin users started on marijuana. This is the *contaminating correlation*. It flows from the limited, clinical population of bad things to the much larger and more general target population.

Next, the correlation is inverted and, what is more, upgraded to a cause-effect relationship. So far, heroin use has cast doubt on marijuana use (guilt by association); now marijuana use is made the *cause* of heroin use. This is a false cause by correlation; a one-way contaminating correlation has been turned into a cause-effect relationship, going the other way. Moreover, the false cause is a *cancerous cause*, proliferating like cancer cells throughout the large population domain, indicting all marijuana use. The fallacy of cancerous cause by contaminating correlation and inversion has scapegoated a whole population which, whatever may be the merits or demerits of marijuana use (a separate issue that the fallacy does not touch), bears no responsibility for the ostensible object of concern: heroin addiction.

Of course, if we started from a random sample of the general population of marijuana users, we would discover no significant correlation with heroin use, much less any causal relationship or slippery slope. The cancerous cause fallacy is a hasty generalization with a peculiarly deceptive structure that is false at every step. In this particular example, marijuana use becomes a biopolitical health issue, all mixed up with moral panic and generational conflicts. Arguably, the continuing criminalization of marijuana and soft drugs has made manifest the vengeance of an older generation against the younger generation.

Sex and Sex Crime

But the slippery slope and the cancerous cause work the same way in the case of the violence-against-women argument, where the vengeance of an older generation of women against the active sexuality of the young has promoted relentless hostility against men and unyielding panic among women. Psychotic mass murder in the form of Marc Lépine is correlated with (and used to contaminate) anti-feminist or "sexist" beliefs. The correlation is then inverted, and upgraded to the status of cause: sexism or anti-feminism come to be seen as the cause of the murder of women. "Violence is sexism's offspring." Indeed, the cause is cancerous; the whole population of "sexist" men is implicated in the production of violence against women. All women are at risk from all men.

Regressing one step back, as did the Supreme Court, we have the same logic. Sexism (the degrading of women) is now accepted as a causal factor in violence against women. Going further back, sexist beliefs are correlated with sex videos to contaminate their representations, now described as degrading. The kinds of examples the Court cites as degrading and dehumanizing involve portraying women as "waiting for a huge male penis to come along, on the person of a so-called sex therapist or window washer, supposedly to transport them into complete sexual ecstasy" (24). These are ordinary sexual fantasies, narratives that appear degrading only by virtue of a puritanical narrowness derived from the theory of "sexism," which is permitted to contaminate sexual expression. Then the inversion, and the cause by correlation, and the judgment in which the legal suppression of the videos, an acknowledged violation of fundamental guarantees of freedom of expression, is considered to be justified in order to prevent the inferred slide down the slope of harm to women.

What is astonishing is that the slide down the slippery slope, from sex to violence, is so firmly pre-scripted as an attack on the general target (sex) that even major distinctions between one step and another—for example, consensual and non-consensual sex—are smoothed out and disappear. The learned judges insist, for example, that consent makes no difference: "Consent cannot save materials that otherwise contain degrading or dehumanizing scenes. Sometimes the very appearance of consent makes the depicted acts even more degrading or dehumanizing" (25). In just the same way, the judges also held in 1989 (*Janzen v. Platy*) that intention has nothing to do with harassment; it is not a relevant factor in connection with inappropriate behaviour that is discrimination on the basis of sex. Neither consent nor intent can halt the slide down the slope from sex to harm. In so ruling, the Canadian judiciary contributes to the subordination of both free expression and substantive due process to the biopolitical agenda.

No examination of any random sample of sex-video consumers, male and female, has given rise to a conclusion that they pose a significant risk of harm to women, much less to society. Instead, going the other way, the fact of some violence against some women is correlated with some negative attitudes toward women, which are generalized to a large population and then blamed for the violence. In turn, these attitudes, which allegedly favour discrimination on the basis of sex, are blamed on sexual representations and sexual fantasies. Violence has been allowed to contaminate sex, and then sex is blamed as the cause of violence. Not only are we dealing with panic about violence, but also a sex panic fed by a born-again puritanism masked as biofeminist concern for women's safety.

By the cancerous cause version of the slippery slope fallacy, sex causes violence, passing through sexism and sexual harassment on the way. As the cancer proliferates, any and all sexual exchange, in symbols or conduct, is infected and implicated. By the time that the Ontario Ministry of Education puts jokes and graffiti in the same category as physical and sexual assault ("Framework"), the contaminating correlation has achieved a nearly pure form: contamination by mere contiguity. Mere contiguity is a formula for total contagion, for an epidemic of infection, for panic without end.

To reclaim sexuality, we are required and entitled to insist on a different experience: refusal of the first step (sex is degradation) by assertion of the alternative bold proposition that sex is good, that the pleasure of women is good, as is the pleasure of men, and their pleasure for and with one another, and that sexual representation is also good (Christensen). Also, refusal of the slide down the slope (sex leads to degradation and violence), by asserting the alternative bold proposition that sex does not produce sex crime (Kutchynski), the law does. Sex crime that is part of the criminal sample should not be permitted to indict all sex by the fallacy of cancerous cause.

First, biofeminists took the sex out of rape (Brownmiller 1975), by insisting that rape was a type of sexual assault that was no sex, all assault. Pure exercise of power and violence. Then they took the consent out of consent (Pateman 150), by arguing that women are subordinates and therefore cannot effectively refuse or withdraw consent, with the result that "we can no longer speak of 'consent' in any genuine sense." Then, they said, in survey after survey (Russell 1983; Koss 1987), that rape was a runaway problem, though most of their respondents did not consider themselves raped. Biofeminists began to speak, not just *for* women, but *instead of* and over the voices of the women who spoke for themselves. They inflated the incidence and prevalence of rape to levels that made rape the norm instead of the exception, and therefore implicated all men as rapists: among the young, "boys rape and girls get raped as *a normal course of events*" (Wolf, *Beauty Myth* 167).

Then they took the sex out of sex (MacKinnon, *Toward* 146): rape and sex look a lot alike when you compare victims' reports of rape and women's reports of sex. Then they moved in on the sexual manners of high-school teens, and announced that "sexual harassment is verbal rape"

(Susan Strauss, cited in Baurac). Finally, they moved to attack the children, and kill sexual interest at the source, where the slippery slope starts. The Minnesota Department of Education has a Hostile Environment Sexual Harassment Program to police the schools, kindergartens, and playgrounds, to make sure kids do not make sexual gestures, tease each other about body development, or brag about their own. During the 1991-92 school year, more than 1,000 children in Minneapolis alone were suspended or expelled on charges relating to sexual harassment.

California's law expels children for sexual harassment only from the fourth grade up. Minnesota hardliners like Sue Sattel, sex-equity specialist for the Department of Education, condemn this kind of "leniency." "California is sending a message that it's okay for very little kids to sexually harass each other," she says. In the communicative universe of biopolitics, everyone is always sending a message, and the message is always unambiguous and sure to have clear and predictable consequences. If you're not 100% party line, you are considered 100% enemy. It's the Stalinist mentality: if you are not with us, you are against us. No gradations, no middle ground.

In fact, in the time-honoured Stalinist fashion, in order to be with us, everyone has to be *proactive*. It is not enough to pursue and prosecute misdeeds when they occur. That leaves too much freedom, too much latitude for misdeed. There must be prevention. Stop the deed before it occurs, stop the attitude before it shapes the deed, stop the expression before its message prepares an attitude, stop the thought before it becomes expressed. Prevention is the policy program of totalitarianism. It is our tragedy that it appeals so much to ill-educated common sense. In the frame of the sex panic, all our institutions are climbing aboard the "prevention" bandwagon.

Why is this so important to do? Says Ms. Sattel, quoting *continuum*, but meaning *cancerous cause/slippery slope*: "Serial killers tell interviewers they started sexually harassing at age 10, and got away with it" (Shalil, "Child's Play"). This is no better than using heroin addicts to indict marijuana, or rapists to indict sex magazines. It draws on the same faulty reasoning, and carries the same faulty emotional appeal. If you want to stigmatize something, contaminate it by arbitrary association with a small, bad, clinical sample, the worst you can find, then invert the correlation and upgrade it to a cause. All kids who flirt with sex obviously do not become serial killers; but biowarriors are getting away with transferring the stigma of serial killers to kiddie sex, and blaming child sexuality for adult violence, up to and including serial killing.

As usual, Canadians should have no illusions that Canadian governments will forgo the pleasures of benign state terror. Ontario Attorney General Marion Boyd has recently announced that Ontario is embarking on a costly program to eliminate sexual harassment by school children.

Structural Causality and Partial Attention

What is noteworthy is that the vertical scale of slippery slope (from sex to sex crime; from some violent men to all men as potential rapists) and the horizontal scale of corrupt continuum (rape culture) converge and support one another. Both go from consensual sex to violent rape, from consensual friction to savage physical cruelty, and so on. Researchers themselves disagree, as do Carleton professors Kelly and DeKeseredy (see chapter II), whether to classify certain acts, such as psychological "abuse," as steps on a slippery slope that descends to physical abuse (insults lead to blows) or as part of a continuum of abuse (i.e., themselves acts of abuse, where insults *are* verbal blows).

In fact, corrupt continuum and cancerous cause reinforce each other through the concept of *structural causality*. The items on a continuum are linked, as are the steps on a sliding scale, by the force of an underlying structure, increasingly called a system. The slide down the slope can be seen then as systematic; and the corruption of the

331

continuum as systemic. The principle that holds together so many acts and so many relationships, and gives them all the same negative character, is revealed as a system, a principle of organization, a model, a theory, a fiction. The fact that this theory is a grand theory and tells a big story (the theory and narrative of "patriarchy") does not make it any less a simulacrum, a figment of the imagination, a virtual account of virtual data.

As a virtual explanatory framework, patriarchy, the biopolitical fantasy of female subjugation, compounds hasty generalization (in the form of corrupt continuum and cancerous cause) with *partial attention.* All perception is shaped to fit the virtual models by filtering information in such a way that men are always only perpetrators, and women are always only victims and survivors. This makes for supple (if somewhat tediously repetitive) scenarios, but neither its women nor its men are capable of exercising anything like a full range of human powers. Perhaps the only thing worse than the demonization of the human (males) is its other side, the angelicization of the human (females). Both are a crime against humanity. Their gamble is that the acute polarization can sustain a current of double standards, myths, and stereotypes that lend support to and take advantage of the panic mindset organized around the virtual figurations: continuum, slippery slope, partial attention, systemic causality.

Biofeminism rests on the worst stereotypes, which will be sources of terrible embarrassment before long. Women are oppressed; women alone are oppressed. Two centuries worth of documented industrial alienation is irrelevant to women. Sex demeans women. Women are always getting screwed. Violence is a symptom of a war against women. Women are nurturers. Men are abusers. Men have to get hard consent before sex. Women do not have to get hard consent before pregnancy. Conception is a woman's choice. Why don't men take responsibility for contraception? Assisted reproduction is a male plot against women's

NOTICE TO PASSENGERS

✳ PASSENGER RECEIPT ✳

GST 89164665RT0001

ORIGIN:

TORONTO ON

DESTINATION:

OTTAWA ON

OW STUDENT

$49.67

	$47.30 FARE
	$2.37 GST
	$49.67 VISA

DEPART: 06/03/10
CHANGE OF DATE FEE: $15.00

TORONTO ON	OW
OTTAWA ON	GCT

EX040/20% REFUND FEE

201-05 BAY ST TERMINAL
WICKET 15 AGENT 41
06/03/10 1:43 PM
TRANS 398146
TICKET606 872782

GREYHOUND CDA TRANS
877 GREYHOUND WAY SOUTH WEST CALGARY ,ALBERTA T3C 3V8
NOT GOOD FOR TRANSPORTATION

FORM 337 REV 11/14/05

bodies. Men should not get custody of children; women should not be at risk of losing children.

Women are entitled to be free of discomfort and unwanted sexual approaches. But women are also entitled to sexual experimentation [which, in male experience, has always meant that you get a lot of what you don't finally want, before you find, if you're lucky, what you do want]. And women are entitled to sexual experimentation without ever being hurt by mismatch or rejection! The economy of sex [in which women control the supply and men beg and pay], should not be altered; except that women may create demand and expect satisfaction. Rejection of women, after a consensual start [somewhat of a middle-class novelty], should be punishable through sexual-harassment procedures and rape trials for "humiliation" and "exploitation."

Men should be invisible: firemen, policemen, garbagemen, mailmen, seamen, lumberjacks, and all the other men [who do indispensable daily tasks and often selfless, heroic deeds, for women, for children, for other men], should disappear into gender-neutral employment categories. Men should only be identified as men when they can be accused by women. Men earn more money. Men assault women. Men just don't get it. Men should be forgotten when they are men enjoyed, loved, admired, or appreciated by women, as lovers, husbands, dates, sons, brothers, fathers, friends or colleagues. Women should be identified as women at all times, lest they be marginalized and silenced. Women should be constantly noticed, appreciated, celebrated, and rewarded. Men are disposable. Women need protection.

This last pair is paradoxical, and it is resolved in the most authoritarian manner: individual men are disposable, mostly abusers; the state (though mostly men) must protect women. Warren Farrell's *Myth of Male Power* is compelling reading on the new role of the state as substitute husband. Of course, it is only in a chivalrous culture, where women are the protected sex, that the image of rape and violence against women would produce such a rich and immediate yield in guilt, shame, and self-flagellation. (In a true "rape culture," the image would have little effect; it would be a mirror of nature, rather than a construction of identity.)

Fundamentalism and Construction

Biofeminism is epistemologically schizophrenic. It is prepared to take at face value all the mythologies that support its essential group interests and to consider everything that supports its standpoint as objective truth, from patriarchy theory to lesbian utopia. Its basic outlook in this respect is fundamentalist, especially insofar as it rests on the postulate that a biologically defined grouping is the key to the deepest levels of identity, i.e., that the most useful and illuminating way of dividing up the world is by sex. This fundamentalism about *identity* is parallel to those other fundamentalisms of our century that insist on dividing up people on the basis of race, or class, or some scriptural revelation.

At the same time, biofeminism is not objectivist but constructivist about its *prospects*. Everything it wants to see different is conceived by definition as mutable and volatile—socially constructed, and therefore in principle alterable: deconstructable and reconstructable. Biofeminism talks about symbolic life as constructed and artificial too: male philosophy, male technology, male music.

What is so remarkable, apart from the mind-boggling simple-mindedness of reducing culture to sex-differentiated genotype, is that biofeminism fails to recognize its own models as also constructions. It fails to see its own mental productions as players on the symbolic stage. As a result, it fails to see either its achievements or its disasters in the light of their epistemological activism. "Better dead than raped" is no more likely to outlast the contemporary sex economy, partly defined by the image of "war against women," than "better dead than red" outlasted the Cold War. To give credit, it may be that the promotion of rape pathos and rape taboo is a lasting contribution to the list of (mostly) widely respected taboos, such as the taboos on incest, cannibalism, and murder—raised to this level, perhaps ironically, just at the time when these others are somewhat loosening up. On the other side, biofeminism's investment in the promotion of fear is *creative* of panic, not descriptive of its conditions, and exacts its costs in both the diminished autonomy of affected women, and in the poisoned culture that bears its traces.

Consciousness raising, and the biopolitical "education" programs that governments and institutions seem to favour, produce heightened consciousness of *simulations*, not reality. These are manufactured patterns, processed phenomena in virtual form. Raised consciousness sees life with a trained perception or, in its own image, a perception retrained to counteract the prejudices promoted in the "oppressor" culture dominated by the biopolitical adversary. Such retraining leaves room for a great deal of retroactive revisionism. This makes for a dynamic and unsettling principle in historical scholarship, but it makes for a devastating instability and one-sidedness in interpersonal and political relationships. And it makes for profound injustice when it becomes a principle of discipline and conflict management.

We create the culture inside which we live. A panic culture of group antagonisms is worse than one dedicated to individually based liberties, equalities, and communities. It is better to seek strength than protection, equality than equity, personal responsibility than scapegoating, and complexity than simplicity. We have to cope with each other as real people, and we cannot rely on regulations to govern all our interactions, much less what we say to each other. We approach each other on the basis of our differences and have to negotiate shared transactions, not take offence at differences. Adults have to be encouraged and expected to act like adults, and acquaintances and strangers have to be allowed to enact themselves in public space, rather than be made to conform to the desires of designated groups for pacification of their surroundings. Women have to be invited and enabled to ally with men in public political life, for or against other women, and/or men. Individuals have to be able to escape from groups. Intellectuals have to be able and willing to be rude to movements.[2]

Why is this so hard? Why does biopanic have so much latitude and force in our culture? One can only speculate about some of the trend lines of our culture, as we navigate through this whirlpool period of history. One can see, first, that the intervention of biopolitics impinges on debates over the prospects of liberal democracy. It calls for an assessment of the manifold, and somewhat contradictory, legacies of the 1960s, and of the biopolitical backlash against the 1960s—its free love and free spirits, its sexual and (counter)cultural innovations, its politics and economics, and its deinstitutionalizing complexity. It is set against the collapse of communism and the subsequent convergence between Left and Right. It is a harbinger of changing relationships between domestic and public domains and in the division of labour and it is a factor in the potential clash between social revolution and political counterrevolution.

Power politics, special interests, emergencies of the social formation, and the dictates of virtue aside, biopolitics can be seen also in a second way: as a response to future shock, with bio-identity framed in the rear-view mirror of 21st century technology, especially biotechnology.[3] The tempation to regress to some kind of biological fundamentalism, then, may be intelligible as a panic defence against the technicism of the postmodern cultural and scientific moment.[4]

Marshall McLuhan said that we now live mythically and in depth. We also live theatrically, as all our experience becomes a put-on: a prosthetic addition of processed data that we try on for look and feel. Everything is scrutinized for the information it delivers, and all information is increasingly interchangeable, substitutable, promiscuous, circulating at, what McLuhan delightfully called, angelic speed. A kind of vertigo of seduction, of information overload, of losing ourselves in acceleration, like a ride forever speeding up at the fairground, produces panic as a normal rather than exceptional state of mind. The French cultural sociologist, Jean Baudrillard, would call this the semiurgical panic of postmodern culture. Many people, of course, would like to get off the ride. Thirdly, then, informational panic (underpinning sex-pol panic and future-shock techno-panic) may also engender and accelerate biopolitical fundamentalism, as the flip side of the pleasures of surfing on simulations.

Endnotes

Notes to Chapter One

1. Kai Erikson has written a classic study of the three crime waves motivated by panic hysteria in 17th-century Massachusetts: the persecution by the orthodox Puritan community of the antinomian heretics, the Quakers, and the alleged witches of Salem Village. He argues that "the styles of deviation a people experiences have something to do with the way it visualizes the boundaries of its cultural universe" (1966, ix). Mary Buckley also describes a wave of moral panic in the Soviet Union in 1987 over new revelations. "Regular media coverage of increases in crime, for instance, sometimes with lurid details of brutality, made women anxious, afraid, and appalled. They felt vulnerable to mugging, theft and gang rape" (2).

2. Canada ranks No. 1 in the United Nation's June 1, 1994 "Human Development Report." Canada remains in the top ten even when the figures are adjusted for gender and income differences ("Quality of life best in Canada"). General-satisfaction polls always show very high rates of satisfaction among Canadians.

3. The characteristic presentation in the early 1990s was one of pathos, captured in the concept of a war *against* women, some of it organized around annual mourning after the Lépine "Montreal massacre." In November 1991, the *Toronto Star*, introduced a new four-part feature: "THE WAR AGAINST WOMEN: BEGINS TODAY IN THE LIFE SECTION." The first part, "The Killing Goes On" (Scotton), printed pictures, with story captions, of every woman killed in Ontario during the year, without the slightest hint that several times as many men lost their lives with equally dramatic and involuntary poignancy. Pat Marshall lowered the level a few notches further, when she told a journalist that it is the women "who are forced to eat dog meat by their spouses and who have to dance to rifle shots."

4. Warren Farrell, who rescued this story from the archives, observes caustically: "Not a single headline or article summary in the index to the Chicago *Tribune* pointed out that every person killed or wounded by the Chicago woman was a boy. No government spent millions reeducating women on their attitudes toward men." He goes on to point out that when men are victims, their *maleness* tends to be invisible to the public eye.

5. All these numbers and more appear in the fact sheet called "Sexual Assault: Dispelling the Myths," issued in 1994 by the Ontario Women's Directorate of the provincial government of Ontario.

6. Nara Schoenberg and Sam Roe's article, "The numbers are alarming, but why don't they add up?" prepared for the Special Report of the Toledo *Blade* on "Rape: The Making of an Epidemic" (Oct. 1993) contains the Kilpatrick story as part of a general analysis. This article and the work of Cathy Young, Katherine Dunn, and Katie Roiphe, among others, are beginning to make a dent in the previously unsceptical journalistic treatment of the violence-against-women theme in the U.S. The academic critiques by Camille Paglia, Neil Gilbert, and Christina Hoff Sommers are also pioneering in this domain, and are soon to be followed by others. Warren Farrell's work, of course, looms very large in its dimensions and influence. In Canada, the critical culture is much less determined or consistent, but *Toronto Star* columnists Rosie DiManno, Susan Kastner, and Donna Laframboise often stand out as voices of sanity, as does *Globe and Mail* columnist Robert Fulford. There is also a strong potential in a group of male journalists who are very good on censorship issues, especially with respect to the arts.

7. Pat Stevens, a radio talk show host, in an interview on CNN's "Crossfire" in June 1994, estimated that, corrected for underreporting, the true number of battered women in the U.S. is 60 million. This happens to be more than 100% of all the women in the U.S. currently in a relationship with a man (see Brott). This kind of advocacy is designed to spread panic and justify panic policies.

Notes to Chapter Two

1. Ninety-six percent of charges are made at sexual assault level 1 (*Juristat*, 14.7, 9), and no one can tell if they refer to touching by uncle, neighbour, or friend, or to a forceful rape without bodily harm other than the sexual assault itself.

2. Mary Ritter, my very capable research assistant for the materials in chapters II-VI, was indispensable in finding leads, contacting people, interviewing, and following up on outstanding matters.

3. Russell's 1-in-4 rape figure, if it were to be used at all, should have been adjusted for a difference in American and Canadian crime cultures, for a difference in moving from high-crime San Francisco to much lower-crime Peterborough, and corrected for the biases of the population sample, which would differ sharply from the local situation here. Nobody can say without research what the over-all adjustment might be. Just to make a fair extrapolation from Russell's data, 1 in 4

might become 1 in 8 or 1 in 20. The leaflet does harm to the public in reporting a phantom figure like 1 in 2.

4. Farrell, who corresponded with McDowell to confirm this story in 1992, also cites additional corroboration of figures around this level from police files and from investigative work by the *Washington Post*. He notes, too, that there are all kinds of reasons to lie, and cites (329, 421) one of the most famous cases from a *New York Times* story by Kenneth B. Noble: "In order to get an abortion, Norma McCorvey, the 'Jane Roe' of *Roe* v. *Wade*, claimed she was raped. Fourteen years later, she acknowledged she had lied."

5. According to "Beauty Pageant Official Drops Tyson Lawsuit" (*Los Angeles Times*), when eleven women from the 1991 Miss Black America Beauty Pageant all claimed that Mike Tyson had touched their rears, the founder of the pageant filed a $607 million lawsuit against Mike Tyson. "Several of the contestants eventually admitted they had lied in the hope of getting publicity and cashing in on the award money" (Farrell 328, 421).

Notes to Chapter Three

1. According to the 1985 National Family Violence Survey, no effective gender difference was discernible with respect to severe assaults, that is, the frequency of assaults that carry a greater risk of causing physical injury, such as punching, kicking, and attacks with weapons. Thirty-five percent of the severe assaults were situations of husband-only attack, 30% were wife-only attack, and 35% were cases where both were violent (Straus, "Physical Assaults" 74). This is not to deny that women report more injuries.

2. Research into who initiates the violence has found approximately equal rates for both men and women. Straus's National Family Violence Survey in 1985 found that women hit first in 53.1% of the cases. In a quarter of the cases, the wife alone was violent over the previous 12 months; in a quarter of the cases, the husband alone was violent; and both were violent in half the cases over the year (Straus, "Physical Assaults" 74). Similar results have been obtained by several other studies (Bland and Orne 1986, Saunders 1989, Henton, Cate, Koval, Lloyd, and Christopher 1983). Another such study, according to Straus in "Physical Assaults," is an unpublished large-scale Canadian study. Straus suggests that it is not published, "perhaps because [the findings] are not 'politically correct'" (75). I suspect he is referring to Eugen Lupri's "Hidden in the Home," published only in Germany.

3. About as many women as men, roughly a quarter of violent couples in each case, seem to attack spouses who have *not* hit them

during a one-year period (Straus, "Physical Assaults" 74). One of the main criticisms of the CTS is that it cannot measure context; if it could, many critics argue, it would perceive that most women act violently in self-defence. This seems to have become a conformist truism among many social scientists in this field. But most of the research which has been done to support this thesis has been qualitative, not quantitative. That is, it has looked at detailed case reports and focussed on specific violent events (e.g. Browne 1987, Campbell 1992, Dobash and Dobash 1979, 1984, Jones 1980, Jurik and Gregware 1989, Pagelow 1984, Polk and Ranson 1991, Saunders 1986). Usually these studies have not concentrated on a large number of examples or cases. For example, Jurik and Gregware's study looks at 24 cases in which women killed husbands or lovers.

One of the researchers most frequently cited with approval by feminists is Saunders. Sometimes, his is the only study cited when a researcher is making the self-defence argument (Lupri). Saunders's "Wife Abuse, Husband Abuse, or Mutual Combat?: A Feminist Perspective on the Empirical Findings," to an extent replicates "When Battered Women Use Violence: Husband Abuse or Self-Defense?" Saunders admits that "very little is known about the extent to which the violence of battered women is motivated by self-defense" (98). Saunders examines 52 battered women, all of whom were asked by a counselling agency to participate in the study. Forty-five of the women had used a shelter. Twenty-three percent were married, 56% separated or divorced, and 19% single. The average number of years of education was 12.2; 8% of these women held college degrees. The sample is self-selected, and moreover diverges from the general population in marital status and education. It is neither random nor representative, and, in any event, its numbers are too small to be generalized to a large population.

4. The studies Straus himself highlights as corroborating his own findings are respected scholars like Scanzoni (1978) and Tyree and Malone (1991), and large-scale studies such as the Los Angeles Epidemiology Catchment Area study (Sorenson and Telles 1991), the National Survey of Households and Families (Brush 1990), and the survey conducted for the Kentucky Commission on Women (Schulman 1979). In addition, in their literature review in "The Myth of Sexual Symmetry in Marital Violence," Dobash, Dobash, Wilson and Daly report that the following studies are among those that suggest that "assaults upon men by their wives constitute a social problem comparable in nature and magnitude to that of wifebeating" (71-72): Farrell 1986; McNeely and Mann 1990; McNeely and Robinson-Simpson 1987; Shupe, Stacey, and Hazelwood 1987; Steinmetz 1977/78; Steinmetz and Lucca 1988; Straus and Gelles 1979, 1986, 1990 (which contains a further bibliography, 95-105); and Straus, Gelles, and Steinmetz 1980.

They also cite the following as examples of "other surveys using the CTS in the United States and in other countries [which] have replicated the finding that wives are about as violent as husbands" (73): Brinkerhoff and Lupri 1988; Browning and Dutton 1986; Brutz and Ingoldsby 1984; Jouriles and O'Leary 1985; Kennedy and Dutton 1989; Mason and Blankenship 1987; Meredith, Abbott, and Adams 1986; Nisonoff and Bitman 1979; Rouse, Breen, and Howell 1988; Steinmetz 1981; Stets 1990; and Szinovacz 1983 (73). Further, they acknowledge that many studies of violence in dating relationships have produced the same results, for example: Arias and Johnson 1989; Arias, Samios, and O'Leary 1987; Cate et al. 1982; DeMaris 1987; Lane and Gwartney-Gibbs 1985; Laner and Thompson 1982; Makepeace 1986; Marshall and Rose 1990; Rouse et al. 1988; and Sigelman, Berry, and Wiles 1984. Straus (1993, 70-71) offers additional and more recent studies on dating: Sugarman and Hotaling's 1989 study of 21 studies; Pirog-Good and Stets (1989), Stets and Straus (1990).

In some, and perhaps many, of the studies cited above, the rates of female-perpetrated violence are slightly higher than those of male-perpetrated violence. McNeely and Mann 1990, Lupri 1990, Sommer 1992, Sommer 1994, Brinkerhoff, Grandin, and Lupri 1992, Straus 1977/78, and Straus and Gelles 1986, for example, all find this to be the case.

Straus states in "Physical Assaults" that some researchers (Dutton 1988, Edleson and Brygger 1986, Jouriles and O'Leary 1985, Stets and Straus 1990, Szinovacz 1983) have suggested that the seeming equality in rates of assault for husbands and wives "may occur because of a tendency by husbands to underreport their own assaults" (68). But when Straus, for example, recomputes the assault rates on the basis of information provided by the 2,994 women in the 1985 National Family Violence Survey, to avoid the problem of male underreporting, "the resulting overall rate for assaults by wives is 124 per 1,000 couples, compared with 122 per 1,000 for assaults by husbands *as reported by wives*" (69; Straus's emphasis).

5. The last thing the clinical population wants to hear about, of course, is female perpetrators. As a result, Statistics Canada chose to accommodate some basic scientific considerations in the design of the survey to the biopolitics of statistical abuse and the *Reactions and Concerns of Women's Groups to the Proposed National Survey on Violence Against Women* (Linda MacLeod, April 1992), which is singled out for mention. Linda MacLeod is one of Canada's leading advocates on wife battering, and responsible for some of the most alarmist statistical battering: nearly a million Canadian women (1 in 8) battered *each* year, deduced from unreliable generalization on the basis of information about transition houses (1987). Statistics Canada has made a fundamental error by permitting biopolitics to carry the day: it has utterly

confused the general population with the clinical population. It has not only permitted an unwarranted generalization. It has sacrificed the general population methodologically to the insatiable need of the clinical population.

6. The *Violence Against Women Survey* indicates that 18% of the violent *incidents* reported in their survey (20,543,000) resulted in injury (*Daily* 6). This may be about the same as Sommer's finding that 21% of males' partners required medical attention. It is difficult to know, since they do not say how many *women* were injured in the incidents, and it may be that the incidents are not evenly distributed over all the women who complained of some violence. However, according to StatsCan, fewer than 5% of the total violent incidents reported in their study were serious enough to *receive* medical attention (6). They do not show how many women are involved, or what proportion of married women or all Canadian women suffer these injuries. Their numbers in these tables always refer to the subsample of those who allegedly are abused. In just over 4% of the total incidents was someone arrested and charged.

It is to be remembered that Sommer's figures, like the others over which the self-defence controversy remains heated, refer to marital or dating conflict. The StatsCan tables refer to all victimization by spouses, strangers, dates, boyfriends, and other known men, and of course, list only female injuries. They also list physical assaults alongside sexual assaults, nearly half of which latter (45%) were apparently unwanted touching.

Notes to Chapter Four

1. The panelists: co-chair Pat Marshall, executive director of Metro [Toronto] Action Committee on Public Violence Against Women and Children; co-chair Marthe Asselin Vaillancourt, director general of a centre offering assistance to female victims; Judy Hughes, executive director of Tearmann House for battered women and children in Nova Scotia; Peter Jaffe, executive director of the London Family Court Clinic; Mobina Jaffer, East Indian lawyer, chair of the B.C. task force on family violence (and vice-president of the National Organization of Immigrant and Visible Minority Women of Canada); Ginette Larouche, Montreal social worker, director of programs at the Centre des services sociaux du Montréal métropolitain; Diane Lemieux, provincial co-ordinator for the Quebec Coalition of Sexual Assault Centres; Donna Lovelace, project co-ordinator of Iris Kirby House for battered women and children in Newfoundland; and Eva McKay, a native elder and lecturer on family violence (Murray 1991).

2. The co-chairs were paid at the deputy-minister level ($100,000 to 150,000 per year), and the panelists around $60,000 per year, at the rate of $500 per day, 10 days planned per month (according to Linda Blackwell, the panel's executive director—see Fine, "Panel takes aim" A4).

3. We got in touch with Status of Women Canada to ask whether the program of the CanPan would be carried forward under the new government, and were advised by Cathy McRae of the Communications Directorate that Chaviva Hosek (former president of the National Action Committee on the Status of Women, and now the very influential research director in the Prime Minister's Office) was fully familiar with the CanPan's final report, that the CanPan had contributed to a body of research that was now being drafted into policy, and that reference to this was incorporated into the electoral platform in the famous "Red Book" that Hosek is credited with drafting: *Creating Opportunity: the Liberal Party Plan for Canada.* (August 18, 1994, telephone interview with Cathy McRae, conducted by Mary Ritter, my research assistant).

4. In fact, some men appear to have less control than women over their quality of life (greater stress, shorter life expectancy), their socio-economic position (slaves to family obligation and women's dependency, alienated labour, hazardous work, risks to life and limb in military service), or their sex roles (chauvinist, instrumental, sexually and emotionally dependent, technophilic, "disposable"). See Warren Farrell, *The Myth of Male Power,* and Camille Paglia, *Sexual Personae,* who remind us, in original and pathbreaking ways, of things we used to know and talk about collectively as a culture and a civilization, before two decades of biofeminism succeeded in infecting our thoughts and feelings with the viral cancer of half truths and the emotional tyranny of false appeals.

5. This scenario, like the famous Super Bowl hoax, is a favourite fiction of biofeminists. Journalist Ken Ringle and author Christina Hoff Sommers have demonstrated, however, that it is utterly without foundation (Sommer, 189ff.).

6. This is Karen Jean Braun's letter. She is not identified in either the *Scrapbook* or the Report, but she uses her name in the "Without Fear" video and in her public activism.

7. Nara Schoenberg and Sam Roe point out that: "Researchers say they can just as easily design a study that finds 1 in 4 women have been raped as 1 in 50. A slight change in the definition of rape or the way questions are worded can yield drastically different results." ("Rape: The Making of an Epidemic").

The Canadian police figures put the rate of sexual assault in Canadian society at just a little over 1 per 1,000 population. This is the annual incidence of crime; if you discount half of this as sexual touching, you get 0.5 in 1,000, or 0.05%, for more serious assault, though not necessarily rape. And all of that is without bodily harm. If one assumes that an annual incidence rate of 0.05% might translate into a lifetime prevalence rate of 0.5%, half of one percent, using a 10 to 1 ratio between prevalence and incidence (which is even more than Statistics Canada found in its *Violence Against Women* survey: between 6 to 1 and 8 to 1), then the lifetime risk for women, half of the population, would be 1%, with much of that risk falling into the age groups of youth. These figures are too high to be regarded casually, and teen violence generally is a problem that merits special attention. The women's movement's desire to make rape one of the great taboos in our time is entirely admirable—provided the definition is not stretched to include a range of other behaviour. At the same time, a risk of 1 in 100 lifetime, or 1 in 1,000 annual, of forced sex without bodily harm is not in the same category of panic as 1 in 2 women raped. In other words, when the CanPan accepts at face value the Women's Safety Project and its alarming claim that one in two women have been raped or attempted raped, it is irresponsibly padding the numbers and falsely alarming women and falsely scapegoating men.

Notes to Chapter Five

1. My assistant, Mary Ritter, talked with Professor Sobsey at the Research Centre for the Developmentally Disabled at the University of Alberta on August 18, 1994. That there are no pure, reliable numbers based on a random-sample survey, he underlined "with absolute certainty." He himself has never studied any nonabused sample, nor conducted any incidence study. The most that one can conclude from the prevalence research is that people with disabilities are at greater risk of sexual offences than others—perhaps a ratio of 1.5. No one has done a controlled study, with controls for severity or repetition. Moreover, the available studies suggest that the problem of sexual offences against people with disabilities is not a feminist problem: among children, for example, a large number of boys are at risk, as well as girls.

2. The women who said they were physically abused as children reported that the aggressors in more than two thirds of the cases (68%) were women—mothers (42%) and female caregivers (26%). Only a third (32%) were fathers. Of the women who disclosed childhood sexual abuse, 1 in 7 were assaulted by women (relatives); of the women who reported physical abuse in adulthood, 30% were attacked by women.

The numbers here are very small. Nineteen women disclosed childhood physical abuse. The perpetrators: 8 mothers, 6 fathers, 5 female caregivers. Fourteen women disclosed childhood sexual abuse. Ten women disclosed physical abuse in adulthood. The Doucette study, partly funded by the Ontario Ministry of Community and Social Services, is much too small and biased to be the basis for national generalization. This is the study, however, which came out with the prevalence figure that half of all disabled women have been sexually assaulted at some point in their lives. Fifteen activist women, attending an activist conference, are not demonstrably representative to the extent that one can project nearly one million of the nearly two million women with disabilities have been sexually assaulted! And yet, in the curious calculus of victimization, this has become a very popular statistic (Lees 98). Unfortunately, people are attracted to big numbers, the bigger the better, because they imagine that a big number will show that there is a big problem. But this is true only if the number is credible. In any case, apart from incredulity, very big numbers can foster panic and hopelessness more readily than a drive for remedial policy. What is hard to defeat is the emotional fantasy that the very vulnerability of disabled women is irresistibly attractive sexually and also lures physically violent sadists like bees to honey. Jillian Ridington of the DisAbled Women's Network says: "Pornography explicitly encourages men to go after women with disabilities because they're more helpless."

3. According to Statistics Canada's report *Disabled Persons in Canada* (1990), there are 12,714,830 women in Canada. The panel accepts McPherson's estimate of 18% women with disabilities: that means 2,288,669 women. The 83% figure means that, according to the CanPan, 1,899,855 Canadian women with disabilities *will be sexually assaulted*. However, as I mentioned in connection with the McPherson study above, according to Statistics Canada, 13.8% of the Canadian female population are disabled, that is, 1,748,455. In short, the CanPan proposes that 151,140 *more* disabled Canadian women will be sexually assaulted than the sum total of existing persons who fit that description (according to Statistics Canada's count): the Canadian panel tells women that 109% of Canadian women with disabilities will be sexually assaulted in their lifetimes!

This kind of insatiable inflation of numbers is beginning to produce a rash of over-100% estimates. Lori Haskell and Melanie Randall, authors of the Women's Safety Project which produced the "finding" for the Canadian Panel that 98% of women suffer sexual violation, consider that the implications of "underreporting" plus the 1992 changes in Canadian sexual assault laws regarding consent mean that "future research could yield even higher prevalence rates" (CL A17, notes 16 and 17). Although the note is specifically about rape and attempted rape, one can see the writing on the wall, especially considering their interest in the "entire range" of sexual experiences.

Note to Chapter Six

1. Randall has been consistent over the years, and the WSP results simply confirm the advocacy parameters that were built into its design. Years earlier, she received financial support from the Ontario Women's Directorate for a discussion paper that she wrote for Education Wife Assault, "The Politics of Woman Abuse." There, Randall insisted that there was a "national epidemic" of physical assault against women in their relationships with men (1), affecting up to 6.25 million Canadian women; that abused women lived in a "state of psychological and physical terrorism" akin to the Stockholm Syndrome induced in hostages (3); that virtually every woman's life is touched by "men's sexual intrusion and aggression," from date rape to images of sexual violence in entertainment media and pornography (4); and that there is "a general problem with men, masculinity and male behaviour in our society" (4). Given her extreme views, and also her modest credentials in an academic or scientific community, it is noteworthy that the panel would have been satisfied to feature Randall's findings so prominently. The panel, apparently, was engaged in the same kind of advocacy.

Notes to Chapter Seven

1. This logic is immensely powerful, and currently forces us to revisit the whole tradition of free-speech arguments, with a view to beefing up the instrumental force of the argument (service to society), as well as the constitutive forms of the argument (moral autonomy, human right) (see R. Dworkin, "Coming Battles").

2. MacKinnon and colleague Andrea Dworkin have worked for a decade for anti-pornography legislation in the U.S., on the argument that sexually explicit materials violate the civil rights of women and undermine equality. Their limited success at the municipal level—as in the notorious Minneapolis ordinance—has been matched by their failure to sustain their gains against challenge at higher levels. The U.S. Supreme Court struck down the Minneapolis ordinance, and MacKinnon's efforts, in Indiana, in Massachusetts, and through Congress, have failed to dent the strong American First Amendment protections of free speech. It is important to note that the MacKinnon attack on symbolic sex (in words, texts, images, film, and video) is the front line of a new type of anti-sex argument. Its principle is the allegation of *harm* to equality rights, not the allegation of a risk of "corrupting" the reader or spectator, nor allegation of a moral danger to society from

arousing or servicing "prurient" interests. The point is to knock out the traditional defences (consenting adults, socially redeeming features, the supervening value of free expression) by regarding free speech as a merely instrumental value, a means to something else (democratic politics, check on abuse of authority, etc.) and arguing that, by comparison, the prevention of harm to women has a higher utility. Against MacKinnon, it is worth remembering that neither is the allegation of harm to women from sexually explicit materials demonstrated (indeed, there is much evidence and argument to doubt it—see, for example, Kutchynski, 1992, and Christensen, 1990), nor is the value of free speech merely instrumental, but also constitutive (R. Dworkin, 1992) of our very notion of moral considerability (which also underpins the question of who has sufficient moral standing to be protected from harm—i.e., women, but not mosquitos or bacteria).

3. Donald Butler, a Vancouver video-store owner, appealed to the Supreme Court against a Crown appeal that had overturned his acquittal on obscenity charges. On February 27, 1992, the Supreme Court held that the obscenity law does indeed violate the Canadian Charter of Rights and Freedoms section 2 protection of the "fundamental" freedom of expression. It also held, however, that this infringement is nevertheless justified under the overriding test in section 1 of the Charter which authorizes limits even on fundamental rights: i.e. that the infringement falls into the category of "such reasonable limits prescribed by law as can be justified in a free and democratic society." The two-stage test, first testing whether a right or freedom has been infringed, and then testing whether the infringement is justified, seems to be unique to Canadian jurisprudence. Certainly, nothing like this kind of balancing act pertains to the First Amendment in the U.S.

4. Biopolitical law-reform feminists, such as LEAF (Legal Education and Action Fund), were very active and very influential in the Butler decision. LEAF counsel Kathleen Mahoney has been reported as saying that LEAF won over the judges by describing gay male porn: "We made the point that the abused men in these films were being treated like women—and the judges got it." Christie Jefferson, LEAF executive director at the time, recently denounced the Canadian Civil Liberties Association (CCLA), which opposed the Butler decision for its negative impact on freedom of expression, as "diametrically opposed to our rights and liberties as women." Michelle Landsberg, one of Canada's most prominent biofeminists and a regular columnist in the *Globe and Mail*, hailed the Butler decision in May 1992 in *Ms.* magazine as a "landmark case" which was supported by most women's groups in Canada, "where the freespeech tradition is not as dominant as it is in the U.S." Chris Bearchell's 1993 article for the Toronto *Star* contains all the quotations above and more, in a discussion (from an anti-cen-

sorship point of view concerned with gay porn) of the Butler case and its fallout for freedom of expression and sexual publications.

5. Canadian law is flirting with double standards, but not yet consistently. The changes to the sexual-assault legislation in 1993 provide a legal definition of "consent" in such a way that the onus is placed on men to show that they obtained consent, even while the concept of "incapacitation," through drinking, for example, exempts women from being held to the consent that they may have actually given while "incapacitated."

On September 30, 1994, however, a 6-3 decision of the Supreme Court of Canada produced an ironic twist. The Court chose to interpret incapacitation and diminished responsibility in a universalistic way, rather than as a special privilege for women. If you cannot consent to sex when drunk, they said in effect, it is possible that you also cannot form the criminal intent to assault sexually and may not know what you are doing. Extreme drunkenness can be a defence against rape in some circumstances. The drunkenness defence, producing a state of temporary insanity, is already available as a mitigating factor to reduce murder charges to manslaughter, but has not previously been used in assault cases. Henri Daviault, a 72-year-old man accused of sexually assaulting a 65-year-old woman in a wheelchair, will now get a new trial.

Feminist lawyers have denounced the decision (Vienneau, "Drink can beat a rape charge"). This was to be expected. So were the street demonstrations. Less easy to anticipate, although it follows from my argument that biopolitics has been taking command of the highest levels of Canadian policy-making institutions, was the response of the Canadian government, and also the immediacy of that response. Within days, the Justice Department announced that it would look at ways to reduce the impact of the previous week's Court decision, and might go so far as to amend the Criminal Code. Russell MacLellan, Parliamentary Secretary to Minister Allan Rock, told the House of Commons on October 3rd: "The Minister of Justice is deeply troubled" (Abbate).

The issue here, of course, is not drunkenness or women's rights, but legal responsibility, and equal responsibility. Most of us would agree to further scrutiny of the possibility of closing the doors on *voluntary* intoxication as an argument for diminished responsibility, if it were not only men who were to be held legally responsible for their actions. In an era where the courts and legislators are constantly inventing diminished responsibility for women, the principle has taken on the status of a double standard which offends the sense of justice and the project of equality. If the Justice Department re-examines the drunkenness defence, it should also re-examine the consent definition. What is sauce for the goose is sauce for the gander.

6. I have detailed the course of this campaign in "Disabling Interpretive Authorities: Offense and the University" (forthcoming in a volume of essays edited by Len Findlay in 1994 for the University of Toronto Press). One particularly intriguing aspect of it was the comparison of the Trent initiative to the archetypal protestant act by *Globe and Mail* columnist Robert Fulford ("Defending the right to be offensive"): "This may not be quite as earthshaking as the critique of Catholicism that Martin Luther pinned to a church door in 1517, but in education today it's equally heretical. The Trent professors have attacked the reigning belief that a university should provide a harmonious, friction-free environment."

Notes to Chapter Eight

1. Katie Roiphe's book, *The Morning After*, and Christina Hoff Sommers's *Who Stole Feminism*, both provide chillingly accurate pictures of the pattern and scope of biofeminist organizing in the United States. Hoff Sommers's description of "gender-feminists" (roughly the group I would call biofeminists) demonstrates their ubiquity in education, in particular. Their impact on universities and schools has to be reckoned with in Canada as well, and urgently. I should add that her term for an alternative feminism, "equity feminism," does not work well in Canada, where "equity" is precisely the code word around which gender-obsessed biofeminists organize.

2. Governments are trying to circumvent the protections usually accorded to the expression of ideas by subordinating ideas to their manner of expression. The pretense is that interference with the manner of presentation does not touch the ideas presented. In defending the repressive "Framework Regarding Prevention of Harassment and Discrimination in Ontario Universities," the minister of education and training, Dave Cooke, announced to universities and the media (February 9, 1994) that free speech and academic freedom were not endangered by the policy directives because "the real issue is not so much what ideas are discussed and explored, but rather how these ideas are presented ..." (letter).

3. For a review of the sequence of the Vandervort case, and some of its procedural implications, see Keith Johnstone's account in "Defence of Tenure" (*CAUT Bulletin*, September 1994).

4. Bora Laskin, a professor of law at the University of Toronto, eventually president of the CAUT, and Chief Justice of the Supreme Court of Canada, showed in *A Place of Liberty* that the courts were not friendly to the protection of academic freedom. Throughout the 19th and 20th centuries—until Canadian faculty, with Laskin's inspiration,

and the CAUT as a dedicated instrument, shifted the norms—the courts have endorsed the arbitrary dismissal of faculty from their university posts.

The dismissal of Professor Crowe (a popular, if abrasive, social democratic historian) from United College (Winnipeg) in 1958 signalled to the Canadian academic community that academic freedom would have to be defended by academics, in the university, or else it would not be defended at all. The CAUT strategy was contractual, and very successful for 30 years.

5. Arguments to the effect that expressive freedoms belong to inegalitarian traditions that are useless for women or racial minorities are biting the hand that feeds them. Marginal and oppositional groups have in fact benefited immensely from the liberal university's secular opennness to all points of view, and have found there a strong platform. Canadian studies and feminist studies, to name only two curricular innovations, have both had major impact in universities in the past twenty years, through the normal channels of debate and reform (Schrank 10). Those whose political programs depend, however, not on expanding the range of freedoms, but on monopolizing them for designated groups, and who define their biopolitically viewed adversaries as too corrupt or offensive to retain their fundamental entitlements to speech, must be treated with great suspicion by everyone, including the constituencies whose interests they thus misrepresent.

Diversity of mind is as crucial to diversity as equality of expressive freedoms is to equality. If we concede that some people's speech must be shut down in order that others may speak, or imagine that all speech is entitled to the same guarantees of sympathetic and competent understanding, or that taking offence at ideas and their expressions can be a valid reason to censor them, then we begin to make equality "something to be feared rather than celebrated, a mocking, 'correct' euphemism for tyranny" (R. Dworkin, "Women" 42).

6. The Supreme Court of Canada, in *McKinney* v. *Board of Governors of the University of Guelph*, recognized that tenure and security of employment are fundamental to the preservation of academic freedom, and endorsed the comment by the Ontario Court of Appeal: "Faculty members can take unpopular decisions without fear of loss of employment."

Notes to Chapter Nine

1. *Readers' Digest* carries a brief report on Surovell's case in an article by Parker Donham in January 1995. Other media will likely get interested, too.

2. On December 17, members of the department held a meeting about Westhues. Out of this meeting came two letters to the Chair, demanding that Westhues be punished. One was dated December 20, signed by four professors, and was copied to Westhues, Nelson, three deans, the associate provost, the president of the university, and the president of the faculty association. The other was dated January 5, 1994, and was signed by seven other professors. Westhues had had conflict with nine of the eleven signatories in connection with the failed student's program, and other kinds of conflict with several of them. He did not learn about the extent of his department's animosity to him (these eleven, plus Lambert and Nelson, make up all but two of the regular members) until January, when the petitions arrived in his mailbox, delayed for unknown reasons. By that time, the Faculty Association president, Professor Jim Brox, had already replied to the first four signatories, rejecting their actions and demands for sanctions as being "without due process" (December 22, 1993). These four, signing themselves as "academic citizens of the University of Waterloo," alleged reprehensible cruelty on Westhues' part toward Nelson, vicious verbal attacks amounting to intimidation and harassment, even a general pattern of such behaviour in the department, intolerable because it subverts the graduate program. They demanded that Westhues be removed from the graduate program for at least five years, until he can show that he is trying to "become a good departmental citizen." Indeed, they cast him out immediately. "So far as the undersigned are concerned, Ken Westhues is no longer a member of the graduate faculty, effective immediately."

The letter from the seven others alleges "serious misconduct," and insists that "steps must be taken to try to ensure that such offenses are not again practised in the department by Westhues or anyone else who might emulate this behaviour." They want immediate action from the chair, immediate because something must be done immediately to stop Westhues from continuing to abuse Nelson. Indeed, the sanctions should be substantial, because Nelson has suffered particularly "offensive and hurtful" abuse. He should be officially reprimanded, and his role in the graduate program cut back. They fear trouble from him if he "has contact with those of us who believe in following the regulations developed by the department."

3. There is no coherent relationship or hierarchy defined at Waterloo between Policy 63, under which faculty have their grievances

reviewed, and Policy 33, under which complaints of ethical violation are examined. In June of 1993, the Faculty Association declared that the procedures under Policy 33 and Policy 63 were not working, and demanded immediate action to rewrite them. They advised members to be cautious in bringing cases to these committees, and indicated that, unless there are improvements in six months, they will ask the Administration to suspend the Ethics and Grievance Committees ("Faculty demand grievance changes"). Meanwhile, the Provost has established an ad-hoc grievance committee, under the chairship of Dr. Greg Bennett, current chair of the Grievance Panel, to review a long list of overlapping existing committees, including ethics and grievance, but also equal rights, sexual harassment, human rights, human resources, staff grievances, and student appeals ("Unethical behaviour").

4. Magnusson's attention to celebration actually touches on deep roots in contemporary feminism, and points to an argument that deserves critical scrutiny: the promotion of celebration, in the place of liberal criticism, as an academic style. Leading feminists insist that the modernist conception of pedagogy—developing an appreciation of the monuments of civilization combined with a critical mind that is trained to independence through defamiliarization, through unsettling of the cliches and commonplace assumptions of ordinary life—is harmful to women and has to be replaced by its opposite: hostility to the great achievements and celebration of familiar feelings. This is called "sensitivity," and it is said that liberal scepticism, romantic-Brechtian estrangement, scientific doubt may be ok for white men, but women and minorities need a learning process that strokes them and builds their "self-assurance" through celebration of their "identities" (Drakich, Taylor, and Bankier 2-3). The crucial question here is, of course, not only whether one or another pedagogy is contextually, much less absolutely, superior, but rather how such disputes are to be developed and provisionally resolved, monolithically or pluralistically, through the educational process itself, or by means of regulative or disciplinary intervention.

Notes to Chapter Ten

1. In the summer of 1992, when Richard Allen, then minister of universities and colleges, and Marion Boyd, attorney general, greeted the report of the Ontario Council of Regents' Task Force on Harassment, these are the terms in which they chose to express their commitments. I had never previously heard an Ontario government use this kind of language of "rooting out" to attack the universities.

2. This idea about the role of the public intellectual was the last public statement I heard Ferenc Fehér, the noted Hungarian philosopher, make, during a heated exchange with Ernesto Leclau at a workshop on biopolitics in Vienna, May 1994. Fehér died shortly afterwards, in June—an untimely death. His own brushes with biopolitics, and his integrity in responding to it as both a densely articulated human personality and a public intellectual, remain a complex source of inspiration.

3. Much of the best contemporary cultural theory (especially theory inspired by the French, German, and Canadian reflections on the *metaphysics* of postmodern technological culture: Barthes, Baudrillard, Deleuze, Heidegger, Nietzsche, Grant, McLuhan, Kroker) speaks of the triumph of the unrestricted technical will: *techne* is finally wedded to *logos*. But also, at the level of the *biophysics* of technological culture, if the modernist promise to reintegrate spirit and body is on the agenda at all (Fehér and Heller), it may be in the form of the technological body, the virtual body, the body which is no natural body at all. The liberal body, the body as a biomorph, may be about to give way to the technomorph.

4. In this respect it hardly matters whether one evokes the euphoric perspectives of wired science with its digital revolution and designer culture, including the designer body, genetically, prosthetically, and cybernetically refashioned, or conjures up the entropies of dystopian postmodernism. Biopolitical fundamentalism may be one form of anxiety-ridden and panicked Luddite resistance assumed in the face of exactly this process of etherealization and subordination of the body "meat" to the data flow. On this argument, it needs to be considered, not only in relationship to sexual politics, but also in the context of the current transition to what is increasingly described by scientists, science fiction writers, and cultural theorists in terms of cyborgs and cyberspace—i.e., a novel meeting of organicism, machinery, and textuality.

A selection of recent thinking on these lines will be found in the following: Verena Andermatt Conley, ed. *Rethinking Technologies*. Minneapolis: U of Minnesota P, 1993; esp. N. Katherine Hayles. "The Seductions of Cyberspace." 173-90. Mark Dery, ed. *Flame Wars: the Discourse of Cyberculture*. Special issue, *The South Atlantic Quarterly* 92.4 (Fall 1993). Durham: Duke UP, 1993. Donna Haraway. *Simians, Cyborgs, and Women: the Reinvention of Nature*. New York: Routledge, 1991. N. Katherine Hayles. "The Life Cycle of Cyborgs: Writing the Posthuman." *A Question of Identity: Women, Science, and Literature*. New Brunswick, N.J.: Rutgers UP, 1993. Hans Moravec. *Mind Children: The Future of Robot and Human Intelligence*. Cambridge: Harvard UP, 1989. See also *Whole Earth Review*, 57 (Winter 1987) and 63 (Summer 1989).

Works Cited

"46% abuse patients, nurses tell survey." *Toronto Star* 25 Sept. 1993: A6.

"8 in 10 native girls sexually abused, study finds." *Toronto Star* 28 Jan. 1994.

"Architecture prof. has UM suspension reduced from one year to six months ." *Bulletin* 24 Jun. 1993: 3.

"Bobbitt acquitted of sex assault." *Peterborough Examiner* 11 Nov. 1993: A3.

"Bobbitt can't remember severing penis, court told." *Toronto Star* 15 Jan. 1994: A3.

"Bodyguard admits role in attack on skater." *Toronto Star* 15 Jan. 1994: A3.

"Child sex-abuse article based on misread data." *Edmonton Journal* 18 Feb. 1989.

"Churches admit failings on violence." *Toronto Star* 30 Mar. 1992: C3.

"Couple reconciles." *Peterborough Examiner* 20 Nov. 1993.

"Court quashes Board's decision on dismissal." *McMaster Courier* 4 May 1993: 1-2.

The Daily. See Statistics Canada. *Violence Against Women Survey:* 18 Nov. 1993.

"Faculty demand grievance changes." *UW Gazette* 29 Jun. 1994.

"Feuding in the family." *Toronto Star* 8 Aug. 1992, Editorial.

"Fifth group turns back on panel: REAL Women seek to join fold." *Globe and Mail* 13 Aug. 1992.

"Girls aggressors in high-pressure teen-sex scene." *Peterborough Examiner* 29 Jan. 1992: C3.

Harassment Police. 30 minute interview segment with Profs. H.-J. Klatt and Marjorie Ratcliffe. W5 with Eric Malling. CTV, 11 Oct. 1994.

"Hell hath no fury." *Peterborough Examiner* 14 Nov. 1993: B5.

"Homolka blackouts contravene regulations, CRTC says." *Toronto Star* 4 Dec. 1994.

"Judge OKs holiday for castrated man, wife." *Peterborough Examiner* 19 Nov. 1993.

Juristat. See Statistics Canada. Ottawa: Canadian Centre for Justice Statistics, 1994.

"Marked for failure." *Ottawa Citizen* 2 Feb. 1994 .

"Media reports on child abuse were incorrect." *Native Press* 24 Feb. 1989.

"Men must take responsibility for violence, panel told." *Toronto Star* 24 Jan. 1992: F1.

"Mom to be charged with killing sons." *Peterborough Examiner* 23 Aug. 1994: A2.

"National shame: violence to women." *Toronto Star* 7 Aug. 1993: B2.

"Penis attack." *Peterborough Examiner* 12 Jan. 1994: A2.

A Plan for Positive Action: The Report of the Presidential Advisory Committee on Sexual Harassment. Halifax: Dalhousie University, Jan. 1984.

"Quality of life best in Canada: UN report." *Peterborough Examiner* 1 Jun. 1994.

Re Belbeck and Board of Governors of McMaster University. Unreported. Divisional Court: Ontario Court of Justice, 10 May 1993.

Report of the Hearing Panel (Re Bradley v. Surovell). Halifax: Dalhousie University, 24 Jan. 1994.

"Safety fears cancel march." *Peterborough Examiner* 18 Sept. 1991: 7.

"Service work." *Peterborough Examiner* 22 Nov. 1993.

"Snipped penis." *Peterborough Examiner* 31 Jul. 1994: A6.

"Sociology professor at centre of dispute." *UW Gazette* 4 May 1994.

"Swastika 'probably' self-inflicted lawyer says." *Toronto Star* 15 Jan. 1993: A3.

"TV killing." *Peterborough Examiner* 8 Mar. 1994: A3.

"Unethical behaviour: Ad hoc committee looks at all the policies and committees." *UW Gazette* 29 Jun. 1994: 5.

"University loses appeal motion." *McMaster Courier* 14 Sept. 1993.

"Video threat." *Peterborough Examiner* 18 Nov. 1993: B1.

"Viewpoints: Responses to the recommendations of the Berger Bilson Report." *The Ring* 28 Jan. 1994: 6.

"Woman with bat charged for threats." *Peterborough Examiner* 22 Aug. 1994.

"Women threaten to boycott violence hearings." *Toronto Star* 8 Jun. 1992: A1.

"words from committee on academic freedom ..." *UW Gazette* 22 Jun. 1994, Letters.

"Written apology in Westhues case." *UW Gazette* 8 Jun. 1994.

"Zero marks for a new policy: a plan for zero tolerance against violence in high schools disturbs those it was meant to serve." *Globe and Mail* 6 Jan. 1994: A13.

Adam, G. Stuart. "Truth, the State, and Democracy: The Scope of the Legal Right of Free Expression." *Canadian Journal of Communication* 17 (1992): 343-60.

A.R.A. Consultants. *Wife Battering Among Rural, Native and Immigrant Women.* Ottawa: Ministry of Community and Social Services, 1985.

Arendt, Hannah. *The Origins of Totalitarianism.* 2nd enl. ed. London: George Allen & Unwin, 1958.

Arias, Ileana, and P. Johnson. "Evaluations of Physical Aggression Among Intimate Dyads." *Journal of Interpersonal Violence* 4 (1989): 298-307.

Arias, Ileana, Mary Samios, and Daniel K. O'Leary. "Prevalence and Correlates of Physical Aggression During Courtship." *Journal of Interpersonal Violence* 2 (1987): 82-90.

Arthurs, H. W., Chair., Roger A. Blais, and Jon Thompson, the Independent Committee of Inquiry into Academic and Scientific Integrity. *Integrity in Scholarship: A Report to Concordia University.* Apr. 1994.

Badgley, Robin F. *Sexual Offences Against Children.* Ottawa: Minister of Supply and Services Canada, 1984. Vols. 1 & 2.

Barclay, Linwood. "Tolerance for zero tolerance." *Toronto Star,* 21 Oct. 1994: D6.

Barthelme, Donald. *Snow White.* New York: Bantam, 1967.

Baudrillard, Jean. *The Evil Demon of Images.* Trans. Paul Patton, and Paul Foss. Sydney: The Power Institute of Fine Arts, U of Sydney, NSW, 1987.

—. *The Transparency of Evil: Essays on Extreme Phenomena* [La transparence du mal: essai sur les phénomènes extrêmes]. Trans. James Benedict. Paris: Éditions Galilée, 1990. London; New York: Verso, 1993.

Baurac, Deborah Rissing. "Sexually harassed at school: teen girls suffer in silence" [From the Chicago Tribune]. *Peterborough Examiner* 28 Nov. 1992: B10.

Bergman, Brian, and Kim Honey. "Conflict on campus." *Maclean's* 29 Nov. 1993: 16, 18.

BSFA. "Formal Charge of Harassment and Sexual Harassment Against Dr. Warren Magnusson." Unpub. complaint, University of Victoria, 3 Jun 1993.

Bilson, Beth, and Thomas R. Berger. *Report of the Review Committee Into the Political Science Department.* Victoria: University of Victoria, 21 Jan. 1994. 70 pp.

Blackwell, Tom. "Canadians fear rising tide of violent crime." *Peterborough Examiner* 7 Oct. 1994: A1, A8.

Bland, R., and H. Orne. "Family Violence and Psychiatric Disorder." *Canadian Journal of Psychiatry* 31 (1986): 129-37.

Bled, Cynthia. *Submission to the Ontario Royal Commission on Learning.* Ottawa: Nov. 1993.

Bolan, Kim. "UVic governors give president their support over alleged harassment issue." *Vancouver Sun* 20 Dec. 1993: B3.

Borges, Jorge Luis. *Labyrinths: Selected Stories and Other Writings.* Ed. and trans. Donald A. Yates and James E. Irby. New York: New Directions, 1962.

Borovoy, Alan A. "Campus thought police give substance to phantom." *Toronto Star* 1 Feb. 1993: A18.

Bowker, L.H. *Beating Wife-Beating.* Lexington, MA.: Lexington, 1983.

Bowman, David E. Arbitrator. *The University of Manitoba and the University of Manitoba Faculty Association (Grievance of Jacques Collin).* 16 Dec. 1993.

Boyce, Jim. "Male victims ignored: report on violence against women reveals sexism against men." *Kitchener-Waterloo Record* 25 Aug. 1993: A9.

Boyle, Theresa. "Report on Violence: 98% of Metro women suffer sexual violation, panel says." *Toronto Star* 30 Jul. 1993: A23.

Bradley, Lynn. *Complaint of Sexual Harassment.* Halifax: Dalhousie University, 28 Jun. 1993.

Brickman, Julie, and John Briere. "Incidence of Rape and Sexual Assault in an Urban Canadian Population." *International Journal of Women's Studies* 7.3 (1984): 195-206.

Brinkerhoff, Merlin B., and Eugen Lupri. "Interspousal Violence." *Canadian Journal of Sociology* 13.4 (1988): 407-31.

—. "Power and Authority in Families." *Family and Marriage: Cross-Cultural Perspectives.* Ed. K. Ishwaran. Toronto: Wall and Thompson, 1992. 213-36.

Brinkerhoff, Merlin B., Elaine Grandin, and Eugen Lupri. "Religious Involvement and Spousal Abuse: The Canadian Case." *Journal for the Scientific Study of Religion* 31.1 (1992): 15-31.

Brodribb, Somer. "Apolitical Correctness in a Period of Reaction." *CAUT Bulletin: Status of Women Supplement* 1994: 5.

—. *Nothing Mat(t)ers: A Feminist Critique of Postmodernism.* North Melbourne: Spinifex P, 1992.

—. "Submission to Academic Freedom and Tenure Committee CAUT," University of Victoria. *The Ring,* 30 Sept. 1994, Letters.

Bromwich, David. *Politics By Other Means.* New Haven: Yale UP, 1992.

Brott, Armin A. "Battered-Truth Syndrome: Hyped Stats on Wife Abuse Only Worsen the Problem." *The Washington Post (Outlook)* 31 Jul. 1994.

Brown, Glen. "Response Expected Soon on Recommendation for Provincial Standards on Harassment." *OCUFA Forum* Jan-Feb. 1993, Special Supplement on Faculty Associations and Sexual Harassment: 1-4.

Browne, Angela. *When Battered Women Kill.* New York: Free Press, 1987.

Browne, A., and K.R. Williams. "Exploring the Effect of Resource Availability and the Likelihood of Female-Perpetrated Homicides." *Law and Society Review* 23.1 (1989): 75-94.

Browne, Malcolm W. "What Is Intelligence, and Who Has It?" *New York Times* 16 Oct. 1994, Book Review: 3, 41, 45.

Browning, James, and Donald G. Dutton. "Assessment of Wife Assault With the Conflict Tactics Scale: Using Couple Data to Quantify the Differential Reporting Effect." *Journal of Marriage and the Family* 48 (1986): 375-79.

Brownmiller, Susan. *Against Our Will: Men, Women and Rape.* New York: Bantam, 1975.

Brush, Lisa D. "Violent Acts and Injurious Outcomes in Married Couples: Methodological Issues in the National Survey of Families and Households." *Gender and Society* 4 (1990): 56-67.

Brutz, Judith L., and Bron B. Ingoldsby. "Conflict Resolution in Quaker Families." *Journal of Marriage and the Family* 46 (1984): 21-84.

Buckley, Mary. "Introduction: Women and Perestroika." *Perestroika and Soviet Women.* Ed. Mary Buckley. Cambridge UP, 1992.

Bula, Frances. "Gender war in UVic department created cruel climate, report says." *Vancouver Sun* 26 Jan. 1994: A2.

Burt, Sandra. "Issue was resolved, and in Nelson's favour." *UW Gazette* 29 Jun. 1994, Letters.

Burtt, Sandra. "Nielsen should open his eyes to violence against women." *Telegraph Journal* 21 Apr. 1994: A9.

Byfield, Ted. "$10M violence report plans an Orwellian utopia." *Financial Post* 4 Sept. 1993: S3.

Callahan, Marilyn, and Andrew Pirie. *Findings of the Review of the Situation in the Department of Political Science At the University of Victoria.* Victoria: University of Victoria, 11 May 1993. 10 pp.

Campbell, Jacqueline C. "If I Can't Have You, No One Can: Issues of Power and Control in Homicide of Female Partners." *Femicide: The Politics of Woman Killing.* Ed. Jill Radford, and Diana E.H. Russell. New York: Twayne, 1992.

Canadian Association of University Teachers (CAUT). *Educational Handbook on Violence and Harassment on Campus: Draft Outline.* Ottawa: Feb. 1994.

——. *Reply to the Ontario Government: Academic Staff and the Ontario Government's Framework Document.* Ottawa: Apr. 1994.

Canadian Civil Liberties Association (CCLA). *Submission to the Honourable Dave Cooke, Minister of Education and Training for Ontario. Re: Framework Regarding Prevention of Harassment and Discrimination in Ontario Universities.* Toronto: 15 Mar. 1994.

The Canadian Panel on Violence Against Women. *Changing the Landscape: Ending Violence — Achieving Equality.* Ottawa: Minister of Supply and Services Canada, 1993.

——. *Collecting the Voices: A Scrapbook.* Ottawa: 1992.

——. *A Facilitator's Guide: "Without Fear." Ottawa: 1993.*

——.Without Fear. Video. Canadian Panel on Violence Against Women. Dir. Aerlyn Weissman. Minister of Supplies and Services, 1993.

Carroll, Lewis. *The Lewis Carroll Book.* Ed. Richard Herrick, and ill. John Tenniel. New York: Tudor, 1944.

Cate, Rodney M., et al. "Premarital Abuse. A Social Psychological Perspective." *Journal of Family Issues* 3 (1982): 79-90.

Charnas, Suzy McKee. *Motherlines.* New York: Berkley, 1978.

Chernomas, Robert. "UMFA objects to coverage on Collin arbitration: says other viewpoints needed." *Bulletin* 10 Feb. 1994, Campus comment: 4.

Christensen, F. M. *Pornography: The Other Side.* New York: Praeger, 1990.

Christie, Innis, Q.C., Chair. *The University of Saskatchewan Faculty Association and the University of Saskatchewan (Re: Professor L. Vandervort and the College of Law).* 25 Apr. 1994.

Coleman, D.H., and Murray A. Straus. "Marital Power, Conflict and Violence." *Violence and Victims* 1 (1986): 141-57.

Collins, Mary. *Minister's Opening Statement. News Conference for the Release of the Report of the Canadian Panel on Violence Against Women.* Ottawa: Status of Women Canada, 29 Jul. 1993.

Conley, Verena Andermatt, ed. *Rethinking Technologies.* Minneapolis: U. of Minnesota P., 1993.

Cooke, Dave. Minister of Education and Training. *Letter to Universities and the Media.* Toronto: 9 Feb. 1994.

Coté, Andrée. *La rage au coeur: Rapport de recherche sur le traitement judiciaire de l'homicide conjugal au Québec.* Baie Comeau, Qc.: Regroupement de femmes de la Côte-Nord, 1991.

Cowan, John Scott. "Lessons from the Fabrikant File: A Report to the Board of Governors of Concordia University." 42 pp. Unpub. ms., May 1994.

Crawford, Maria, and Rosemary Gartner. *Woman Killing: Intimate Femicide in Ontario 1974-1990.* Toronto: Women We Honour Action Committeee, 1992.

Crook, Farrell. "Woman gets 7 years for strangling lover." *Toronto Star* 30 Jan. 1993: A5.

Cuff, John Haslett. "Stories of abuse deeply affecting." *Globe and Mail* 29 Jul. 1993: C3.

Dafoe, Chris. "Ushers as censors: a funny business." *Globe and Mail* 28 Nov. 1992: C1, C16.

Darroch, Wendy. "Woman guilty of enslaving roommate." *Toronto Star* 12 Mar. 1994: A17.

Davis-Barron, Sherri. "Violence against women report ignored." *Ottawa Citizen* 3 Oct. 1993: D10.

DeKeseredy, Walter S. "Addressing the Complexities of Woman Abuse in Dating: A Response to Gartner and Fox." *Canadian Journal of Sociology* 19.1 (1994): 75-80.

——. "In Defence of Self-Defence: Demystifying Female Violence Against Male Intimates." *Crosscurrents: Debates in Canadian Society.* Ed. Ronald Hinch. Toronto: Nelson, 1992.

——. "Male Peer Support and Woman Abuse in University Dating Relationships: An Exploratory Study." *Atlantis* 14.2 (1989): 55-62.

——. "Woman Abuse in Dating Relationships: An Exploratory Study." *Atlantis* 14 (1989): 55-62.

DeKeseredy, Walter S., and Ronald Hinch. *Woman Abuse: Sociological Perspectives.* Toronto: Thompson Educational Publishing, 1991.

DeKeseredy, Walter S., and Katharine Kelly. "Woman Abuse in University and College Dating Relationships: The Contribution of the Ideology of Familial Patriarchy." *Journal of Human Justice* 4.2 (1993): 25-52.

DeKeseredy, Walter S., and Katharine D. Kelly. "The Incidence and Prevalence of Woman Abuse in Canadian University and College Dating Relationships." *Canadian Journal of Sociology* 18.2 (1993): 137-59.

DeMaris, Alfred. "The Efficacy of a Spouse Abuse Model in Accounting for Courtship Violence." *Journal of Family Issues* 8 (1987): 291-305.

Demelo, Lucrecia. "Letter: To Whom It May Concern." 28 Jun. 1991.

Depradine, Lincoln. "Women's groups want conviction appealed." *Share* 12 Sept. 1991: 1-2.

Dery, Mark, ed. *Flame Wars: The Discourse of Cyberculture.* Durham: Duke UP, 1993.

Devine, Sheila M. *Report on an Allegation of Harassment under the University of Victoria's Harassment Policy and Procedures.* Victoria: Office of Equity Issues, University of Victoria, 28 Jul. 1994.

Devlin, Richard. "A counter attack in defence of political correctness." *Toronto Star* 8 Mar. 1993: A15.

DiManno, Rosie. "Issue of violence hijacked by those with wider aims." *Toronto Star* 18 Mar. 1992: A7.

—. "Let's get real on sex-assault." *Toronto Star* 4 Aug. 1993: A7.

Dobash, R. Emerson, and Russell P. Dobash. "The Nature and Antecedents of Violent Events." *British Journal of Criminology* 24 (1984): 269-88.

—. "Social Science and Social Action: The Case of Wife Beating." *Journal of Family Issues* 2.4 (1981): 439-70.

—. *Violence Against Wives: A Case Against the Patriarchy.* New York: Free Press, 1979.

Dobash, Russell P., et al. "The Myth of Sexual Symmetry in Marital Violence." *Social Problems* 39 (1992): 71-91.

Doucette, Joanne. *Violent Acts Against Disabled Women.* Toronto: Dis-Abled Women's Network - Toronto, 1987.

Drakich, Janice, Marilyn Taylor, and Jennifer Bankier. "Academic Freedom is the Inclusive University." *CAUT Bulletin: Status of Women Supplement* 1994: 2-4.

D'Souza, Dinesh. *Illiberal Education: The Politics of Race and Sex on Campus.* Vintage Books ed. New York: Random House, 1992.

Dumont-Smith, Claudette, and Pauline Sioui-Labelle. *National Family Violence Survey.* Ottawa: Indian and Inuit Nurses of Canada, 1991.

Dunn, Katherine. "The Politics of Fear." *This World* 12 Jun. 1994: 5-10.

Dutton, D.G. *The Domestic Assault of Women: Psychological and Criminal Justice Perspectives.* Boston: Allyn and Bacon, 1988.

Dworkin, Andrea. "Terror, Torture and Resistance." *Canadian Woman Studies/les cahiers de la femme* 12.1 (1991): 37-42.

Dworkin, Ronald. "The Coming Battles Over Free Speech." *The New York Review of Books* 11 Jun. 1992: 55-58, 61-64.

—. "Pornography: An Exchange [Letter to the Editors]." *The New York Review of Books* 3 Mar. 1994: 48-49.

—. "Women and Pornography." *The New York Review of Books* 21 Oct. 1993: 36, 38, 40-42.

Eagly, A.H., and V.J. Steffen. "Gender and Aggressive Behaviour: A Meta-Analytic Review of the Social Psychological Literature." *Psychological Bulletin* 100 (1986): 309-30.

Edleson, J.L., and M.P. Brygger. "Gender Difference in Reporting of Battering Incidents." *Family Relations* 35 (1986): 377-82.

Emberley, Peter C., and Waller R. Newell. *Bankrupt Education: The Decline of Liberal Education in Canada.* Toronto: U of Toronto P, 1994.

Erikson, Kai T. *Wayward Puritans: A Study in the Sociology of Deviance.* New York: John Wiley & Sons, 1966.

F.A.C.T. (Feminist Anti-Censorship Task Force) Book Committee. *Caught Looking: Feminism, Pornography & Censorship.* 3rd ed. 1986. East Haven, CT: LongRiver Books, 1992.

Faludi, Susan. *Backlash: The Undeclared War Against American Women.* Anchor Books ed. New York: Doubleday, 1992.

Farrell, Warren. *The Myth of Male Power: Why Men Are the Disposable Sex.* New York: Simon & Schuster, 1993.

Federal Bureau of Investigation. *Crime in the United States.* Washington, DC: U.S. Department of Justice, 1989.

Fehér Ferenc, and Agnes Heller. *Biopolitics.* Aldershot: Avebury, 1994.

Fekete, John, et al. *On Free Inquiry and Expression.* Peterborough: Dec. 1993-Jan. 1994.

Fekete, John. "Arthur Kroker's Possessed Individual." *University of Toronto Quarterly* 63.1 (1993): 148 50.

— *The Critical Twilight: Explorations in the Ideology of Anglo American Literary Theory from Eliot to McLuhan.* London: Routledge & Kegan Paul, 1978.

—, ed. and intro. *Life After Postmodernism: Essays on Value and Culture.* New York: St. Martin's P, 1987.

—, ed. and intro. *The Structural Allegory: Reconstructive Encounters With the New French Thought.* Minneapolis: U of Minnesota P, 1984.

Feld, S.L., and Murray A. Straus. "Escalation and Desistance of Wife Assault in Marriage." *Criminology* 27 (1989): 141-61.

Fennell, Tom, et al. "The Silencers." *Maclean's* 27 May 1991: 40-45, 48-50.

Fine, Sean. "Panel takes aim at abuse of women." *Globe and Mail* 17 Jan. 1992: A4.

Firsten, Temi. *An Exploration of the Role of Physical and Sexual Abuse for Psychiatrically Institutionalized Women.* Toronto: Ontario Women's Directorate, Nov. 1990.

Fischer, Doug. "Violence Against Women: By asking for everything, women may gain little." *Kingston Whig-Standard* 31 Jul. 1993: 7.

Fox, Bonnie J. "On Violent Men and Female Victims: A Comment on DeKeseredy and Kelly." *Canadian Journal of Sociology* 18.3 (1993): 321-24.

Fraser, Duncan. "Canadians still face, and must resist, threats to freedom." *Halifax Chronicle Herald* 18 Sept. 1993: D2.

Freedman, Martin H., Q.C. Arbitrator. *The University of Manitoba and the University of Manitoba Faculty Association (Grievance of Jacques Collin).* 13 May 1993.

French, Marilyn. *The War Against Women.* Summit Books, 1992.

Fulford, Robert. "Defending the right to be offensive." *Globe and Mail* 2 Feb. 1994: C1.

——. "George Orwell, call your office." *Globe and Mail* 30 Mar. 1994: C1.

Gaquin, D.A. "Spouse Abuse: Data from the National Crime Survey." *Victimology* 2 (1989): 632-42.

Gartner, Rosemary. "Studying Woman Abuse: A Comment on DeKeseredy and Kelly." *Canadian Journal of Sociology* 18.3 (1993): 313-20.

Gelles, Richard J. "Violence and Pregnancy: Are Pregnant Women At Greater Risk of Abuse?" *Physical Violence in American Families.* Ed. Murray A. Straus and Richard J. Gelles. New Brunswick, NJ.: Transaction, 1990. 279-85.

Gilbert, Neil. "Examining the Facts: Advocacy Research Overstates the Incidence of Date and Acquaintance Rape." *Current Controversies on Family Violence.* Ed. Richard J. Gelles and Donileen R. Loseke. Newbury Park, CA.: Sage Publications, 1993. 120-32.

——. "Miscounting Social Ills." *Society* (Mar-Apr. 1994): 18-26.

——. "The Phantom Epidemic of Sexual Assault." *Public Interest* 103 (1991): 54-65.

——. "Realities and Mythologies of Rape." *Society* 29.4 (May-Jun 1992): 4-10.

Gildiner, Catherine. "Banning Books at the Library." *Globe and Mail* 6 May 1993, Facts & Arguments.

Gilman, Charlotte Perkins. *Herland.* Ser. in the *Forerunner,* 1915. New York: Pantheon, 1979.

Goar, Carol. "Infighting mars task force on violence." *Toronto Star* 4 Aug. 1992: A17.

——. "Panel on Violence Against Women lost numbers game." *Toronto Star* 17 Aug. 1994: A15.

Goetting, Ann. "When Females Kill One Another." *Criminal Justice and Behavior* 15.2 (1988): 179-89.

Grandmaison, Aline. *Protection des personnes agées: Étude exploratoire de la violence à l'égard de la clientèle des personnes agées du CSSMM.* Montréal: Centre de services sociaux du Montréal métropolitain, Direction des services professionnels, 1988.

Granatstein, J. L. "Academic Freefall: Whatever Happened to Free Speech? Address to Annual Meeting, May 7, 1994" [Society for Academic Freedom & Scholarship]. *Newsletter* (Jun. 1994): 1, 3 8.

Griffiths, Dorothy. *Lecture.* Conference at Northern College. Timmins, Ont.: unpub., 21 Jun. 1991.

Gross, Barry. "The Case of Philippe Rushton." *Academic Questions* 3.4 (Fall 1990): 35-46.

Gunz, Sally. Chair. *Report of the Ethics Hearing Committee (94-3): Re Nelson/Westhues, Department of Sociology.* University of Waterloo, 9 May 1994. 9pp.

Hallinan, Joe. "Twisted 'Facts' of Domestic Violence Fizzle Under Scrutiny." *The Oregonian* 7 Jul. 1994.

Hammond, N. "Lesbian Victims of Relationship Violence." *Women and Therapy* 8: 89-105.

Haraway, Donna. *Simians, Cyborgs, and Women: The Reinvention of Nature.* New York: Routledge, 1991.

Hard, S. *Sexual Abuse of the Developmentally Disabled: A Case Study.* Paper presented at the National Conference of Executives of Associations for Retarded Citizens. Omaha, Nebr.: unpub., 22 Oct. 1986.

Hart, B. "Lesbian Battering: An Examination." *Naming the Violence.* Ed. K. Lobel. Seattle: Seal, n.d. 173-89.

Haskell, Lori, and Melanie Randall. "The extent of sexual violence in women's lives." *Globe and Mail* 9 Sept. 1993: A23.

——. *The Women's Safety Project: A Community-Based Study of Sexual Violence in Women's Lives.* Toronto: Unpub., 1993.

Hayles, N. Katherine. "The Life Cycle of Cyborgs: Writing the Posthuman." *A Question of Identity: Women, Science, and Literature.* New Brunswick, N.J.: Rutgers UP, 1993.

——. "The Seductions of Cyberspace." *Rethinking Technologies.* Ed. Verena Andermatt Conley. Minneapolis: U. of Minnesota P., 1993. 173 90.

Heller, Agnes. *Beyond Justice.* Oxford and New York: Basil Blackwell, 1987.

——. "Has Biopolitics Changed the Concept of the Political? (Some Further Thoughts About Biopolitics)." Unpub. lecture. Workshop on Biopolitics. Organized by the European Centre for Social Welfare Research and Policy. Vienna, 25 May 1994.

Helm, Denise. "UVic hails hike in complaints of harassment." *Victoria Times-Colonist* 22 Feb. 1994.

Hill, Alice. *Press Release.* Yellowknife: Native Women's Association of the N.W.T., Feb. 1989.

Hippensteele, Susan K., Meda Chesney-Lind, and Rosemary C. Veniegas. "Some Comments on the National Survey on Woman Abuse in Canadian University and College Dating Relationships." *Journal of Human Justice* 4.2 (1993): 67-71.

Hoffman, Donella. "Key incident in U of S case." *Saskatoon Star Phoenix* 21 Jun. 1994: A2.

Hornung, C. A., B. C. McCullough, and T. Sugimoto. "Status Relationships in Marriage: Risk Factors in Spouse Abuse." *Journal of Marriage and the Family* 43 (1981): 675-92.

Howard, Ross. "NAC delegates issue ultimatum: Radical changes to federal inquiry on violence demanded." *Globe and Mail* 8 Jun 1992: A4.

Hughes, Margaret E. *Confidential Report to President D.F. Strong Re: Allegation of Harassment and Sexual Harassment By the BFSA Against Dr. Warren Magnusson.* Victoria: University of Victoria, 31 Oct. 1993. 18 pp. plus Appendix.

Hummell, Richard. "Fairness and Justice at the U of T: Honi soit qui mal y pense." Newsletter, self-pub. , 1991.

Hunter, Justine. "UVic convulsed by sexist politics." *Vancouver Sun* 22 May 1993: B10.

Hurst, Lynda. "'Politically correct'? Think before you speak." *Toronto Star* 2 Jun. 1991: A1, A12.

Irving, John. *The World Accoding to Garp.* Pocket Books ed. New York: Simon & Schuster, 1976.

Johnstone, Keith. "Defence of Tenure At the University of Saskatchewan." *CAUT Bulletin* Sept. 1994: 1, 5-6.

Jones, Ann. "Still Going on Out There: Women Beaten Senseless By Men." *Cosmopolitan* (Sept. 1994): 228-31.

——. *Women Who Kill.* New York: Holt, Rinehart and Winston, 1980.

Jouriles, Ernest N., and K. Daniel O'Leary. "Interspousal Reliability of Reports of Marital Violence." *Journal of Consulting and Clinical Psychology* 53 (1985): 419-21.

Kafka, Franz. *The Metamorphosis, the Penal Colony, and Other Stories.* Trans. Willa and Edwin Muir. New York: Schocken, 1948.

——. *The Trial.* Trans. Willa and Edwin Muir. Knopf, 1956. New York: Schocken, 1968.

Kanin, Eugene. "False Rape Alleghations." *Archives of Sexual Behavior* (Feb. 1994): 81-92.

Kelly, Katharine D. "The Politics of Data." *Canadian Journal of Sociology* 19.1 (1994): 81-85.

Kennedy, Leslie W., and Donald G. Dutton. "The Incidence of Wife Assault in Alberta." *Canadian Journal of Behavioral Science* 21 (1989): 40-54.

Kimura, Doreen. "Fear of Offending Stifles Intellectual Debate" [Society for Academic Freedom and Scholarship]. *Newsletter* Oct. 1993: 3 5.

Klatt, H.-J. "Censorship At King's College—the Index of Forbidden Nouns and Adjectives." Letter (4 pp.), unpub., 25 Nov. 1992.

——. "Kowtowing to politics." *London Free Press* 27 Apr. 1993, Letters.

——. "A Sexual Harassment Policy As a Tool of Power and a Weapon to Censor, Harass, and Control." Report (4 pp.), unpub., Jan. 1993.

Klein, Andrew. *Spousal/Partner Assault: A Protocol for the Sentencing and Supervision of Offenders.* Quincy, MA: Quincy Court, 1993.

Klein, Naomi. "Why universities feel harassed by zero tolerance." *Globe and Mail* 6 Jan. 1994: A13.

Koss, M. P., and C. A. Gidycz. "Sexual Experiences Survey: Reliability and Validity." *Journal of Consulting and Clinical Psychology* 53 (1985): 422-23.

Koss, M. P., C. A. Gidycz, and N. Wisniewski. "The Scope of Rape: Incidence and Prevalence of Sexual Aggression and Victimization in a National Sample of Higher Education Students." *Journal of Consulting and Clinical Psychology* 55 (1987): 162-70.

Koss, M. P., and C. Oros. "The Sexual Experiences Survey: A Research Instrument Investigating Sexual Aggression and Victimization." *Journal of Consulting and Clinical Psychology* 50 (1982): 455-57.

Koss, Mary P., and Sarah L. Cook. "Facing the Facts: Date and Acquaintance Rape Are Significant Problems for Women." *Current Controversies on Family Violence.* Ed. Richard J. Gelles, and Donileen R. Loseke. Newbury Park, CA: Sage Publications, 1993. 104-19.

Krauthammer, Charles. "The Indictment of Ozzie and Harriet." *Globe and Mail* 27 Nov. 1993: D5.

Kroker, Arthur. *The Possessed Individual: Technology and the French Postmodern.* Montreal: New World Perspectives, 1992.

Kroker, Arthur, Marilouise Kroker, and David Cook. *Panic Encyclopedia: the definitive guide to the postmodern scene.* New York: St. Martin's P, 1989.

Kubara, Michael. Rev. of *Catholic Higher Education, Theology and Academic Freedom,* by Charles E. Curran. *CAUT Bulletin* (Apr. 1994): 19.

Kundera, Milan. *The Book of Laughter and Forgetting.* Trans. Michael Henry Heim. Paris: Éditions Gallimard, 1979. New York: Penguin Books, 1981.

Kutchinsky, Berl. "The Politics of Pornography Research." *Law and Society Review* 1992: 447-54.

Laframboise, Donna. "Men also get stuck in a rut." *Toronto Star* 23 Aug. 1993: A13.

Lamy, Paul. "Offenders, Victims and Academic Freedom." *Society* (May 1994): 9-11.

Lane, Katherine E., and Patricia A. Gwartney-Gibbs. "Violence in the Context of Dating and Sex." *Journal of Family Issues* 6 (1985): 45-59.

Laner, Mary R., and Jeanine Thompson. "Abuse and Aggression in Courting Couples." *Deviant Behavior* 3 (1982): 229-44.

Laskin, Bora. *A Place of Liberty.* Toronto: U of Toronto P, 1964.

Lees, David. "The War Against Men." Dec. 1992: 45-49, 98-100, 102, 104.

Leishman, Rory. "Professors shackled by language." *London Free Press* 1 Apr. 1993.

Leonard, John. "Report 'an improvement' but 'problems' remain." *Western News* 23 Sept. 1993.

Levan, Mary Beth. *Report on Child Sexual Abuse Needs Assessment.* Proceedings of the Conference on "Communities' Voice on Child Sexual Abuse." Yellowknife, N.W.T.: Native Women's Association of the N.W.T., 24 Jan-26 Jan. 1989. 28-32.

Lie, Gwat-Yong, et al. "Lesbians in Currently Agressive Relationships: How Frequently Do They Report Aggressive Past Relationships?" *Violence and Victims* 6.2 (1991): 121-35.

Levan, Mary Beth, and Marja van Nieuwenhuyzen. *Needs Assessment Study for Victims and Perpetrators of Sexual Abuse in the Inuvik Region.* N.W.T.: unpub., Oct. 1988. 18 pp., plus questionnaire and terms of reference.

Lupri, Eugen. "Harmonie und Aggression: Über die Dialektik ehlicher Gewalt" [Hidden in the Home: The Dialectics of Conjugal Violence—the Case Canada]. *Kölner Zeitschrift für Soziologie und Sozial-psychologie* 42.3 (1990): 479-501.

—. "Male Violence in the Home." *Canadian Social Trends* 14 (1989): 19-31.

—. "Spousal Violence: Wife Abuse Across the Life Course." *Zeitschrift fur Sozialisationsforschung und Erziehungssoziologie* 13.3 (1993): 232-57.

Lupri, Eugen, Elaine Grandin, and Merlin B. Brinkerhoff. "Socioeconomic Status and Male Violence in the Canadian Home: A Reexamination." *Canadian Journal of Sociology* 19.1 (1994): 47-72.

MacInnis, Craig. "Don McKellar's baby Blue movie puts 'X' back in sex." *Toronto Star* 11 Sept. 1992: C1, C3.

MacKinnon, Catharine A. *Feminism Unmodified: Discourses on Life and Law.* Cambridge: Harvard UP, 1987.

—. *Only Words.* Cambridge: Harvard UP, 1993.

—. *Toward a Feminist Theory of the State.* Cambridge: Harvard UP, 1989.

—. "Pornography: An Exchange [Letter to the Editors]." *The New York Review of Books* 3 Mar. 1994: 47-48.

MacLeod, Linda. *Battered But Not Beaten: Preventing Wife Battering in Canada.* Ottawa: Canadian Advisory Council on the Status of Women, 1987.

—. *Wife Battering in Canada: The Vicious Circle.* Ottawa: Canadian Advisory Council on the Status of Women, 1980.

Magnusson, Warren. "[BFSA] v. Magnusson." Unpub. response to the Devine "Report," University of Victoria, 10 Aug. 1993.

—. "Feminism, McCarthyism, and Sexist Fundamentalism: Reflections on Recent Events at the University of Victoria." Unpub. ms., 13 May 1993.

Makepeace, James M. "Gender Differences in Courtship Violence Victimization." *Family Relations* 35 (1986): 383-88.

Marchand, Philip. "Threat of censorship never more worrisome." *Toronto Star* 2 Mar. 1994: D3.

Marshall, Linda L., and Patricia Rose. "Premarital Violence: The Impact of Family of Origin Violence, Stress, and Reciprocity." *Violence and Victims* 5 (1990): 51-64.

Mascoll, Philip. "Woman's nails slash open scrotum." *Toronto Star* 26 Mar. 1994: A12.

Mason, Avonne, and Virginia Blankenship. "Power and Affiliation Motivation, Stress, and Abuse in Intimate Relationships." *Journal of Personality and Social Psychology* 52 (1987): 203-10.

McBride, Catherine, and Ellen Bobet. *Health of Indian Women.* Ottawa: Minister of Supply and Services Canada, 1992.

McInnes, Craig. "Beasts in Suits and Ties." *Globe and Mail* 23 Jan. 1993: A6.

McMaster University. *A chronology of decisions and developments leading up to the reinstatement of Dr. Larry W. Belbeck.* "A matter of public record—

to be distributed for background following the March 24 Board meeting." Hamilton: McMaster University, 24 Mar. 1994.

——. *News: University Dismisses Faculty Member for Sexual Harassment.* Hamilton: Office of Public Relations, 11 Feb. 1992.

——. *Revised Policy and Regulations with Respect to Academic Appointment, Tenure and Promotion.* Section VI: "Dismissal and Dismissal Procedures." Hamilton: 1977.

McNeely, R.L., and CoraMae Richey Mann. "Domestic Violence Is a Human Issue." *Journal of Interpersonal Violence* 5 (1990): 129-32.

McNeely, R.L., and Gloria Robinson-Simpson. "The Truth About Domestic Violence: A Falsely Framed Issue." *Social Work* 32 (1987): 485-90.

McPherson, Cathy. "Out of Sight, Out of Mind: Violence Against Women With Disabilities." *Canadian Women's Studies Journal* 11.4 (1991).

Mercer, Shirley Litch. *Not a Pretty Picture: An Exploratory Study of Violence Against Women in High School Dating Relationships.* Toronto: Education Wife Assault, 1988.

Meredith, William H., Douglas A. Abbott, and Scot L. Adams. "Family Violence: Its Relation to Marital and Parental Satisfaction and Family Strengths." *Journal of Family Violence* 1 (1986): 299-305.

Moravec, Hans. Mind Children: *The Future of Robot and Human Intelligence.* Cambridge: Harvard UP, 1989.

Morin, Hélène and Josée Boisvert. *Submission to the Canadian Panel on Violence Against Women.* Ottawa: L'Association de Montréal pour la déficience intellectuelle, 1992.

Morley, Terry. "Political science prof speaks out." *The Ring* 15 Apr. 1994: 9.

Muehlenhard, Charlene L., and Stephen W. Cook. "Men's Self Reports of Unwanted Sexual Activity." *Journal of Sex Research* 24 (1988): 58-72.

Murray, Don. "Londoner on panel is expecting results from abuse probe." *London Free Press* 16 Aug. 1991.

Murray, Kathleen. "A Backlash on Harassment Cases." *New York Times* 18 Sept. 1994.

Nelson, Adie. "Complaint Against Professor Ken Westhues in Accordance with Policy 33." Waterloo, 25 Mar. 1994. 6pp unpub.

Ney, Philip. "Report on violence to women just worsens problem." *Victoria Times-Colonist* 7 Sept. 1993: A5.

Nisonoff, Linda, and Irving Bitman. "Spouse Abuse: Incidence and Relationship to Selected Demographic Variables." *Victimology* 4 (1979): 133-40.

O'Connell, Loraine. "The Fight Over Feminism." *[Orig. Orlando Sentinel] Montreal Gazette* 11 Jul. 1994.

O'Farrell, Elaine. "Conspiracy of Silence: Child Abuse and Incest Often a Family Secret." *Windspeaker* 1989: 12.

Ontario. Ministry of Citizenship. *An Act to provide for Employment Equity for Aboriginal People, People with Disabilities, Members of Racial Minorities and Women.* Bill 79. Toronto: Legislative Assembly of Ontario, 1993.

Ontario. Ministry of Education and Training. *Antiracism and Ethnocultural Equity in School Boards: Guidelines for Policy Development and Implementation.* Toronto: Queen's Printer for Ontario, 1993.

——. *Framework Regarding Prevention of Harassment and Discrimination in Ontario Universities.* Toronto: Oct. 1993.

——. *Policy/Program Memorandum No. 119: Development and Implementation of School Board Policies on Antiracism and Ethnocultural Equity.* Toronto: 13 Jul. 1993.

Ontario Confederation of University Faculty Associations (OCUFA). *Brief to the Employment Equity Commissioner on Educational Equity.* Toronto: 18 Feb. 1992.

——. "Restructuring Committee Submits Draft Agenda to Allen." *OCUFA Forum* Nov-Dec. 1992: 3.

Ontario Council on University Affairs (OCUA). *Sustaining Quality in Changing Times: Funding Ontario Universities.* Toronto: Aug. 1993.

Ontario Native Women's Association. *Breaking Free: A Proposal for Change to Aboriginal Family Violence.* Thunder Bay, Ont.: Ontario Native Women's Association, 1989.

Ontario Women's Directorate. *Sexual Assault: Dispelling the Myths; Dating and Acquaintance Relationships; Reporting Issues; The Impact on Health.* 1994.

Pagelow, Mildred D. *Family Violence.* New York: Praeger, 1984.

Paglia, Camille. *Sexual Personae: Art and Decadence from Nefertiti to Emily Dickinson.* New Haven: Yale UP, 1990.

——. *Sex, Art, and American Culture: Essays.* Vintage Books ed. New York: Random House, 1992.

Parkes, Debbie. "Report on violence makes sense out of jigsaw puzzle." *Gazette* 10 Apr. 1994: C3.

Pateman, Carole. "Women and Consent." *Political Theory* 8.2 (May 1980): 149-68.

Peters, Ken. "McMaster reinstates fired professor." *Hamilton Spectator* 8 Apr. 1994, Metro.

Pillemer, Karl A., and David Finkelhor. "The Prevalence of Elder Abuse: A Random Sample Survey." *The Gerontologist* 28.1 (1988): 51-57.

Pirog-Good, M. A., and J. Stets, eds. *Violence in Dating Relationships: Emerging Social Issues.* New York: Praeger, 1989.

Pleck, E., et al. "The Battered Data Syndrome: A Comment on Steinmetz's Article." *Victimology* 2 (1978): 680-84.

Polk, Kenneth, and David Ranson. "The Role of Gender in Intimate Violence." *Australia and New Zealand Journal of Criminology* 24 (1991): 15-24.

Pritchard, Anne. "Sex abuse widespread." *Native Press* 10 Feb. 1989: 1, 3.

Pynchon, Thomas. *The Crying of Lot 49.* New York: Bantam, 1967.

Rabinowitz, Dorothy. "Child abuse: a sex case built on air." *Globe & Mail* 1 May 1993.

Rae, Stephen. "Who's Afraid of the Big Bad Phobia?" *Cosmopolitan* Sept. 1994: 219-21.

Rauch, Jonathan. Kindly Inquisitors: *The New Attacks on Free Thought.* Chicago: U of Chicago P, 1993.

Renzetti, Claire M. *Violent Betrayal: Partner Abuse in Lesbian Relationships.* Newbury Park, CA: Sage, 1992.

Ridington, Jillian. *Beating the "Odds": Violence and Women with Disabilities.* Toronto: DisAbled Women's Network - Canada, 1989.

—. *Different Therefore Unequal: Employment and Women with Disabilites.* Toronto: DisAbled Women's Network - Canada, 1989.

Riley, Susan. "Numbers don't lie, and neither do victims." *Ottawa Citizen* 19 Nov. 1993: B1.

Roiphe, Katie. *The Morning After: Sex, Fear and Feminism on Campus.* New York: Little, Brown and Company, 1993.

Rouse, Linda P., Richard Breen, and Marilyn Howell. "Abuse in Intimate Relationships. A Comparison of Married and Dating College Students." *Journal of Interpersonal Violence* 3 (1988): 414-29.

Rushton, Philippe. *Race, Evolution, and Behavior: A Life History Perspective.* New Brunswick, N.J.: Transaction, 1994.

Russ, Joanna. *The Female Man.* New York: Bantam, 1975.

Russell, Diana E. H. *Rape in Marriage.* New York: Macmillan, 1982.

—. *The Secret Trauma: Incest in the Lives of Girls and Women.* New York: Basic Books, 1986.

—. *Sexual Exploitation.* Beverly Hills: Sage, 1984.

Russell, Diana E. H., and Nancy Howell. "The Prevalence of Rape in the United States Revisited." *Signs* 8.4 (1983): 688-95.

Santin, Aldo. "Prof fights suspension for vulgarity." *Winnipeg Free Press* 1 Sept. 1992: 1.

Sarick, Lila. "Women urge panel to seek changes to the legal system." *Globe and Mail* 24 Mar. 1992: A4.

Sarrel, Philip M., and William H. Masters. "Sexual Molestation of Men by Women." *Archives of Sexual Behaviour* 11.2 (1982): 117-31.

Saunders, Daniel G. "When Battered Women Use Violence: Husband-Abuse Or Self-Defense?" *Violence and Victims* 1 (1986): 47-60.

—. "Wife Abuse, Husband Abuse, Or Mutual Combat? A Feminist Perspective on the Empirical Findings." *Feminist Perspectives on Wife Abuse.* Ed. Kersti Yllo, and Michele Bograd. Newbury Park, CA: Sage Publications, 1988. 90-113.

Savage, Donald. "Fraud and Misconduct in Academic Research and Scholarship." Draft, Canadian Association of University Teachers, Feb. 1994.

Scanzoni, J. *Sex Roles, Women's Work, and Marital Conflict.* Lexington, MA: Lexington, 1978.

Schilit, Rebecca, et al. "Intergenerational Transmission of Violence in Lesbian Relationships." *Affilia* 6.1(1991): 72-87.

Schoenberg, Nara and Sam Roe. "The numbers are alarming, but why don't they add up?" Special Report on "Rape: The Making of an Epidemic." *Toledo Blade* (Oct. 1993).

Schrank, Bernice. "Academic Freedom and the Inclusive University." *CAUT Bulletin* (May 1994): 9-11.

Schulman, M. *A Survey of Spousal Violence Against Women in Kentucky.* Washington: Kentucky Commission on Women, Jul. 1979. Study no. 792701.

Schulman, Perry W. Q.C. *University of Manitoba Faculty Association and University of Manitoba (Dr. Vedanand Grievance).* Winnipeg: 11 Feb. 1991.

Scotton, Lindsay. "The Killing Goes On: The War Against Women." *Toronto Star* 30 Nov. 1991, Life.

Senn, Charlene Y. *Vulnerable: Sexual Abuse and People With an Intellectual Handicap.* 3rd ed. Downsview, ON: G. Allan Roeher Institute, 1989.

Shalil, Ruth. "Child's play: sexual harassment hits the sandbox." [From the New Republic]. *Globe and Mail* 10 Apr. 1993: D1.

Shell, Donna. *Protection of the Elderly: A Study of Elder Abuse.* Winnipeg: Senior Women Against Abuse, 1982.

Shupe, Anson, William A. Stacey, and Lonnie R. Hazelwood. *Violent Men, Violent Couples: The Dynamics of Domestic Violence.* Lexington, MA.: Lexington Books, 1987.

Sigelman, Carol K., Carol J. Berry, and Katharine A. Wiles. "Violence in College Students' Dating Relationships." *Journal of Applied Social Psychology* 14 (1984): 530-48.

Smith, Vivian, and Alanna Mitchell. "Barbie's problem with math causes deluge of complaints." *Globe and Mail* 10 Oct. 1992: A1-A2.

Sobsey, Dick. "Sexual Offenses and Disabled Victims: Research and Practical Implications." *Vis-à-Vis* 6.4 (1988): 1-2.

Sommer, Reena. "Male and Female Perpetrated Partner Abuse: Testing a Diathesis-Stress Model." U. of Manitoba Ph.D. Diss., unpub., 1994.

Sommer, Reena, Gordon E. Barnes, and Robert P. Murray. "Alcohol Consumption, Alcohol Abuse, Personality and Female Perpetrated Spouse Abuse." *Personality and Individual Differences* 13.12 (1992): 1315-23.

Sommers, Christina Hoff. *Who Stole Feminism? How Women Have Betrayed Women.* New York: Simon and Schuster, 1994.

Sorenson, S. B., and C. A. Telles. "Self-Reports of Spousal Violence in a Mexican-American and Non-Hispanic White Population." *Violence and Victims* 6 (1991): 3-15.

Stanko, Elizabeth. *Everyday Violence: How Women and Men Experience Sexual and Physical Danger.* London: Pandora, 1990.

Statistics Canada. *The Violence Against Women Survey. The Daily.* Ottawa: 18 Nov. 1993.

——. *Violence Against Women Survey: Planning Document.* Ottawa: Jul. 1994.

——. *Violence Against Women Survey: Questionnaire Package.* 1993.

——. *Violence Against Women Survey: Survey Highlights 1993.* 1993.

Statistics Canada. Canadian Centre for Justice Statistics. Juristat. Roberts, Julian V. *Criminal Justice Processing of Sexual Assault Cases.* Vol. 14, No. 7. Ottawa: Mar. 1994.

——. Juristat. Wilson, Margo and Martin Daly. *Spousal Homicide.* Vol. 14, No. 8. Ottawa: Mar. 1994.

——. Juristat. Rodgers, Karen. *Wife Assault: The Findings of a National Survey.* Vol. 14, No. 9. Ottawa: Mar. 1994.

Status of Women Canada. *Minister Collins Calls Panel's Report "Historic.".* News Release. Ottawa: 29 Jul. 1993.

Steinmetz, Suzanne K. "The Battered Husband Syndrome." *Victimology* 2 (1977): 499-509.

——. "A Cross-Cultural Comparison of Marital Abuse." *Journal of Sociology and Social Welfare* 8 (1981): 404-14.

——. "Family Violence. Past, Present, and Future." *Handbook of Marriage and the Family.* Ed. Marvin B. Sussman, and Suzanne K. Steinmetz. New York: Plenum Press, 1986. 725-65.

Steinmetz, Suzanne K., and Joseph S. Lucca. "Husband Battering." *Handbook of Family Violence.* Ed. Vincent B. Van Hasselt, et al. New York: Plenum Press, 1988. 233-46.

Stets, Jan E. "Verbal and Physical Aggression in Marriage." *Journal of Marriage and the Family* 52 (1990): 501-14.

Stets, Jan E., and Murray A. Straus. "Gender Differences in Reporting Marital Violence and Its Medical and Psychological Consequences." *Physical Violence in American Families.* Ed. Murray A. Straus, and Richard J. Gelles. New Brunswick, N.J.: Transaction, 1990. 151-65.

Stimpson, Liz, and Margaret C. Best. *Courage Above All: Sexual Assault Against Women With Disabilities.* Toronto: DisAbled Women's Network-Toronto, 1991.

Straus, Murray A. "The Conflict Tactics Scales and Its Critics: An Evaluation and New Data on Validity and Reliability." *Physical Violence in American Families.* Ed. Murray A. Straus, and Richard J. Gelles. New Brunswick, NJ: Transaction, 1990. 49-71.

——. "Measuring Intrafamily Conflict and Violence: The Conflict Tactics (CT) Scales." *Journal of Marriage and the Family* 41 (1979): 75-88.

——. "Physical Assaults By Wives: A Major Social Problem." *Current Controversies on Family Violence.* Ed. Richard J. Gelles and Donileen R. Loseke. Newbury Park, Calif.: Sage Publications, 1993. 67-87.

——. "Wife-Beating: How Common, and Why?" *Victimology* 2 (1978): 443-58.

Straus, Murray A., and Richard J. Gelles, eds. *Physical Violence in American Families.* New Brunswick, NJ: Transaction, 1990.

——. "Societal Change and Change in Family Violence from 1975 to 1985 As Revealed By Two National Surveys." *Journal of Marriage and the Family* 48 (1986): 465-80.

Straus, Murray A., Richard J. Gelles, and Suzanne K. Steinmetz. *Behind Closed Doors: Violence in the American Family.* New York: Doubleday/Anchor, 1980.

Strauss, Stephen. "Bah to Michael Coren and the panel on violence against women." *Globe and Mail* 25 Sept. 1993: D8.

Strauss, Susan. *Sexual Harassment and Teens.* Chaska, MN: Free Spirit, 1992.

Sugarman, D. B., and G. T. Hotaling. "Dating Violence: Prevalence, Context, and Risk Markers." *Violence in Dating Relationships: Emerging Social Issues.* Ed. M. A Pirog-Good, and J. E. Stets. New York: Praeger, 1989.

Sullivan, Paul, and David Munoz. "The Klatt Case: Some of the Facts." *Western News* 22 Apr. 1993.

Sullivan, Philip. "Too Much Heat." *University of Toronto Bulletin* 22 Nov. 1993: 9.

Supreme Court of Canada. *Donald Victor Butler v. Her Majesty the Queen.* File no. 22191. Ottawa: Supreme Court of Canada, 27 Feb. 1992.

—. *Janzen et al. v. Platy Enterprises Ltd.* 59 D.L.R. (4th) 352, 1989.

—. *Re McKinney and Board of Governors of the University of Guelph et al.* (1986), 63 O.R. (2d) 1 (CA); (1990), 2 O.R. (3rd), 319n (S.C.C.).

Surovell, Alan. *Hearing Summation.* Halifax: Dalhousie University, 29 Nov. 1993.

Szinovacz, Maximiliane E. "Using Couple Data As a Methodological Tool: The Case of Marital Violence." *Journal of Marriage and the Family* 45 (1983): 633-44.

Tepper, Sheri S. *The Gate to Women's Country.* New York: Bantam, 1989.

Thompson, Mark. "Left joins right to censor schoolbooks." *Toronto Star* 2 Mar. 1993: A15.

Tyler, Tracey. "Woman who knifed lover to be used in sexism ads." *Toronto Star* 27 Jul. 1991.

Tyree, A., and J. Malone. "How Can It Be that Wives Hit Husbands as Much as Husbands Hit Wives and None of Us Knew It?" Paper presented at the annual meeting of the American Sociological Association, 1991.

Viemeister, Peter E. *The Lightning Book.* Cambridge, MA: MIT Press, 1961.

Vienneau, David. "Abuse of women at crisis level, panel says." *Toronto Star* 30 Jul. 1993: A22.

—. "Drink Can Beat a Rape Charge." *Toronto Star* 1 Oct. 1994: A1, A16.

—. "Map charts landscape of horror." *Toronto Star* 19 Aug. 1992: A12.

Walker, Lenore E. The Battered Woman Syndrome. New York: Springer, 1984.

Walkom, Thomas. "How an NDP faction tried to sink *Show Boat*" [Exrpt. From *Rae Days, The Rise and Follies of the NDP*]. *Toronto Star* 1 Oct. 1994: B1, B4.

Watson, Stuart. "BoG rejects harassment policy." *Dalhousie News* 30 Mar. 1994.

Wente, Margaret. "Porn law overhaul results surprising." *Peterborough Examiner* [from the *Globe and Mail*] 29 Oct. 1994: B6

Westhues, Ken. "Dear Gail." Circular Letter to Gail Grant. 15 March 1994. 6pp. unpub.

—. "Summary Statement to UW Ethics Hearing Committee (94-3)." Waterloo: 26 April, 1994. 3pp. unpub.

Whitaker, Reg. "The cutting edge of Ontario's bad law." *Globe and Mail* 6 Jan. 1994.

Wilson, Deborah. "Sexual politics battle rages in university." *Globe and Mail* 19 Apr. 1993: A1, A2.

—. "Students join fray on B.C. campus: Report alleging sexual harassment not representative, open letter says." *Globe and Mail* 12 May 1993: A4.

Wolf, Naomi. *The Beauty Myth.* Toronto: Vintage Books, 1991.

Wolfe, Alan. "The Gender Question: Women and Men in the Mirror of Feminist Theory." *The New Republic* 6 Jun. 1994: 27-34.

Woolf, Virginia. *A Room of One's Own.* 1929. London: Grafton Books, 1977.

Wright, Lisa. "Women's prison teaches violence, federal panel told." *Toronto Star* 28 May 1993: A6.

—. "Sex offenders want help inmates tell violence panel." *Toronto Star* 27 May 1992: A9.

York, Geoffrey. "Poll shows many Canadians believe recession fuels sexual violence." *Globe and Mail* 29 Jul. 1993: A1.

Young, Cathy. "Abused Statistics." *The National Review* 1 Aug. 1994.

—. "Victimhood Is Powerful: Both Feminists and Antifeminists See Advantages in Keeping Women Down." *Reason* (Oct. 1992).

INDEX

PRINTED IN CANADA